Cognitive Science Series, 7

Eric Wanner, General Editor

Cognitive Science Series

Language Learnability and Language Development

Steven Pinker

Harvard University Press
Cambridge, Massachusetts
and London, England
1984

P
118
.P55
1984

Library of Congress Cataloging in Publication Data

Pinker, Steven, 1954–
  Language learnability and language development.

  (Cognitive science series ; 7)
  Bibliography: p.
  Includes index.
  1. Language acquisition. I. Title. II. Series.
P118.P55 1984   401′.9   84-659
ISBN 0-674-51054-2 (alk. paper)

To Nancy

Preface

The research reported in this book grew out of the disillusionment that accompanies a graduate student's transition from consumer to producer of ideas. Like many undergraduates, I was intrigued by the debate over the innateness of language and excited about the prospect that the study of language acquisition could shed light on that issue. But when I began to attend seminars and read the literature on language acquisition as a first-year graduate student in cognitive psychology at Harvard in 1976, I discovered that that prospect was more remote than the textbooks had promised. First, the field appeared to be afflicted with the syndrome endemic to psychology whereby empirical phenomena originally examined in order to learn about an important theoretical issue take on a life of their own and become the subject of intensive study with little regard for their relevance to the original issue. Second, although there was no shortage of controversy over issues such as species-specificity or the respective role of the environment versus the learner, it was clear that few of the debaters possessed the means of settling or even clarifying the debate. Most of the arguments were of the form "you can/can't learn a language without X," but it was clear that no one had the vaguest notion about what sorts of mental mechanisms or input information were or were not necessary for language acquisition to proceed. There were virtually no explicit theories about the process by which the child succeeds at learning the rules of his or her community's language, and hence no basis for claims about what would or would not work in language acquisition. This was in stark contrast to other areas of cognitive science, where explicit or formal models had often allowed debates to focus on the relative merits of specific mechanisms.

That year I began to examine existing formal models of language acquisition from automata theory, artificial intelligence, and theoretical linguistics; this work culminated in a literature review that appeared in 1979. When I moved to MIT as a post-doctoral fellow in 1979–80, discussions in an informal research seminar organized by Joan Bresnan and Jane Grimshaw led me to conceive of how a psychologically and linguistically plausible acquisition theory might work. I wrote up a preliminary description of those ideas in a 1980 technical report, later to appear in a volume edited by Bresnan. I was not so deluded as to think that that effort solved any of the problems I had perceived, but I was encouraged that small steps in the right direction could be made.

Thanks to the feedback I received from many readers of that paper and the experience of teaching courses on language development at Harvard in 1980–81, I was able to develop and revise those early ideas, and in the spring of 1981 I accepted an invitation to write up a more complete set of proposals for inclusion in an edited volume on children's language. David Lebeaux, then a graduate student at Harvard, was a co-author on that paper, which we entitled "A Learnability-Theoretic Approach to Children's Language." The manuscript grew to a length at which it was no longer appropriate for the intended volume, but, with the encouragement of Eric Wanner, we decided to expand it into a book-length treatment. By then I had taken a position at Stanford and the long-distance collaboration had become increasingly difficult, so I took full responsibility for the book-length version while Lebeaux, now in the Department of Linguistics at the University of Massachusetts at Amherst, has continued to develop his proposals in a number of papers. Many of the ideas in this book originated in Lebeaux's work or in our collaboration; in particular, much of the material on inflection and paradigm learning in Chapter 5 and on lexical entries and lexical rules in Chapter 8 is based to varying extents on his work on these topics (Lebeaux, 1982, 1983, in preparation). I would like to express my appreciation to him for these contributions and for his helpful critical comments on other sections of later drafts. But there are many claims in this version that Lebeaux would not agree with, and all mistakes and deficiencies must be attributed solely to me.

In the summer of 1982 I wrote new drafts of Chapters 1–6 shortly before moving back to MIT. The remaining three chapters and several rounds of revisions of the whole manuscript were completed there in 1983.

It is a great pleasure to acknowledge the many generous people who offered encouragement during the writing of this book and improved its quality by their constructive criticism. Perhaps my biggest debt is to Dan Slobin, who wrote a detailed commentary on the earlier draft, pointing out many empirical and conceptual problems. He also provided me with a gold mine of invaluable data in the form of his summaries of developmental patterns in the acquisition of a variety of languages, and a draft of the conclusion to his forthcoming book. Roger Brown has been a source of encouragement and wisdom since my first days as a graduate student; I am especially grateful to him for making transcripts, grammars, and categorized corpora available to me. Tom Wasow and Eve Clark offered many incisive comments on the first draft and called my attention to a number of pertinent facts and arguments from the linguistics and psycholinguistics literatures, respectively. Ron Kaplan arranged a consultantship for me at Xerox PARC, and our conversations there did much to improve the formal precision of this book and my understanding of many computational and theoretical issues. Joan Bresnan has been a continuing source of insight, helpful criticism, and specific suggestions for as long as I have thought about the issues raised in the book. Jane Grimshaw was an invaluable colleague in the early phases of this project, and conceived of many of the arguments in Chapter 2 that served as the foundations for the proposed theory. She also suggested many improvements to the earlier draft that eventually found their way into Chapters 1 and 4. Jay Keyser helped me to think through a number of issues, most notably in Chapter 6. Kenneth Wexler provided me in 1980 with a detailed critique of the theory as originally proposed, and much of the work outlined in this book has been done in an attempt to remedy the problems he pointed out. Stephen Kosslyn has been a close friend and colleague for many years; although language acquisition is not among his interests, many parts of this book bear the stamp of his teaching and advice. I have also benefited from the wise suggestions of Eric Wanner at every stage of work on the manuscript and from the superb editing of Katarina Rice at Harvard University Press. My gratitude to these people extends far beyond an appreciation of their effects on this book; their warmth, encouragement, and advice did much to lighten the burden of this undertaking.

The only thing to be said for writing a book at three universities in three successive years is that it gives one the opportunity to exchange ideas with a large number of colleagues. I would like to thank in particular the friends and colleagues with whom I discussed the issues that preoccupied me during the writing of this book, especially Bob Berwick, Gordon Bower, Susan Carey, Noam Chomsky, Herb Clark, Bill Cooper, John Flavell, Jerry Fodor, Merrill Garrett, Ellen Markman, Julius Moravscik, Dan Osherson, Molly Potter, Ewart Thomas, and Ivan Sag. In addition, I have benefited from correspondence and comments from Elizabeth Bates, Derek Bickerton, Jill de Villiers, Lila Gleitman, Helen Goodluck, Peter Gordon, Kenji Hakuta, Ray Jackendoff, Kyle Johnson, John Macnamara, Brian MacWhinney, Joan Maling, Michael Maratsos, Robert Matthews, Robert May, Jacques Mehler, Elissa Newport, Tom Roeper, Marilyn Shatz, Larry Solan, Helen Tager Flusberg, and Annie Zaenen. I also thank the students and participants in the graduate seminars on language acquisition I have led at Harvard, Stanford, and MIT for their many helpful comments and suggestions.

A number of students and research assistants helped in the collection and analysis of data, including Loren Ann Frost, Mary Herlihy, Judith Hochberg, Janet Huang, Jeanne Niedzelski, Karin Stromswold, and Ronald Wilson. Many typists spent countless hours in front of video terminals entering and editing the manuscript, and I am especially grateful to Christina Branger, Peter Gardner, Susan Nelson, and Susan Sahatjian for their efforts. Loren Ann Frost, Karin Stromswold, and Laura Vanderpool also pitched in at various points, and Karin performed heroic feats in chasing down references. Kathy Murphy provided skilled and conscientious secretarial help and expedited the completion of the book in many ways. Scott Bradner, Cathryn Downing, Alan Doyle, Jim Hodgson, Peter Smith, and Ronald Wilson offered much-appreciated assistance and advice in manipulating the text files at various computer installations. Jess Gropen compiled the index.

Finally, I thank my parents, Harry and Roslyn Pinker, my grandparents, Carl and Clara Wiesenfeld and Poli Pinker, my siblings, Susan and Robert, and the rest of my extended family for their continuing interest and support. And most of all I thank my wife, Nancy Etcoff, for her love, insight, sound advice, encouragement, and patience with an oft-times distracted spouse during an extended period that coincided exactly with her own demanding dissertation work.

The research reported in this book, and preparation of the manuscript, were supported by NSF grants BNS 80-24337, BNS 81-14916, and BNS 82-16546 ("The Mental Representation of 3-D Space"), NSF grant BNS 82-19450 ("Language Learnability and Language Development"), and NIH grant 1 R01 HD 18381-01 ("Language Learnability and Language Development"), under the administration of Joseph Young, Paul Chapin, and Phyllis Berman, respectively. In addition, I have received support from Biomedical Research Support Grants to Stanford and MIT, MIT's Undergraduate Research Opportunities Program, and Harvard's Milton Fund and Graduate Society Fund. The computer facilities at which the manuscript was edited were supported by NSF multi-user equipment grants to Harvard, Stanford, and MIT and by grants from the Sloan Foundation to the Centers for Cognitive Science at Stanford and MIT. Part of this work was done while I was a consultant at the Cognitive and Instructional Sciences Group at the Xerox Corporation Palo Alto Research Centers.

Contents

Language Learnability and
Language Development

1 | Introduction

THE MODERN STUDY of language acquisition began about twenty-five years ago, and it is no coincidence that its birthday followed fairly closely upon the birth of what we now call cognitive science.[1] One of the first human abilities that was shown to be "cognitive," in the sense of best being explained in terms of mental computations or rules acting on representations, was the child's acquisition of the syntax of his or her first language (Chomsky, 1959; Brown, 1958; Berko, 1958; Braine, 1963). It became clear early on that to understand why children say what they say, and how they learn to speak as adults, one must know what is in the child's mind, and that what is in the child's mind is best described in terms of "rules," "categories," "operations," and the like. The versions of functionalism, information-processing psychology, and cognitivism developed by Chomsky (1957), Newell and Simon (1961), Miller, Galanter, and Pribram (1960), Broadbent (1958), and Putnam (1960) sanctioned the mentalistic approach to language acquisition that was being forced upon developmental psycholinguists by their own empirical investigations.

At the same time, language acquisition appeared to be an ideal testing ground for rival theories about the precise nature of human computational mechanisms. Linguistic knowledge was recognized to be extremely intricate, yet children acquired it uniformly and effortlessly. It became clear that specific approaches to cognition would succeed or fail according to how well they could account for this feat. Thus in the early 1960s language acquisition came to occupy a central place in debates within psychology, linguistics, philosophy of mind, and—later—computer science.

For two reasons, however, the field of language acquisition has disappointed early hopes that a cognitivist theory of acquisition would emerge from a detailed study of children's language. First, as the connection between children's language and linguistic theory became more obscure (see Fodor, Bever, and Garrett, 1974; Pinker, 1982; Wexler and Culicover, 1980), developmental psycholinguists' attention turned away from using child language data to illuminate the process of language acquisition and turned toward characterizing children's language in its own terms, without regard to how the child ever attains adult linguistic proficiency (witness the popular use of the term "child language" for the field that used to be called "language acquisition"). The most exciting promise of the early field of developmental psycholinguistics was that it would provide an account of the mental processes by which a child interprets ambient speech and thereby induces the rules of the language of the adult community. Now that this goal has largely been abandoned, debates about the nature of children's word combinations assume less cross-disciplinary theoretical interest.

The second disappointment of developmental psycholinguistics has been its inability to arrive at a consensus as to how to solve its less ambitious goal, that of characterizing children's language. The catalog of computational machinery from which psycholinguistic theories could draw has proved to be an embarrassment of riches. The problem was no longer one of finding a single coherent model to account for the child's abilities but of deciding among alternative accounts, any one of which could handle the data as well as the others. It turned out to be nearly impossible to determine which grammar best fit a corpus of child speech (Brown, Fraser, and Bellugi, 1964; Brown, 1973), especially since the rules in the grammars proposed often contained arbitrary mixtures of adult syntactic categories, ad hoc syntactic categories, semantic features, phonological features, and specific words (see Atkinson, 1982, for discussion). Furthermore, as the field of developmental psycholinguistics matured, more and more classes of cognitive mechanisms, with far greater flexibility than grammatical formalisms alone, became available to the theorist. Comprehension strategies (Bever, 1970), for example, can be stated in terms of any information that the child's mind can entertain, from linear order and syntactic category membership to knowledge about the probabilities of physical events. Since the advent of the "method of rich interpretation," whereby the investigator uses the context of an utterance to posit linguistic structures that are not revealed in the utterance itself, models of the mental representations underlying children's abilities have also included symbols for general thematic relations such as "agent" and "location" (e.g., Brown, 1973); specific semantic relations such as "eater" and "eaten entity" (Bowerman, 1973); and speech acts and pragmatic intentions (e.g., Halliday, 1975; Bruner, 1975). Fine-grained analyses of corpora of early speech have led others to suggest that the child uses rote patterns (R. Clark, 1971; MacWhinney, 1982) or utterance templates containing variables and constants (e.g., Braine, 1976), with the constant terms allowed to consist of specific words, semantic classes of various degrees of inclusivity (as in "custody for the purpose of oral ingestion"), or classes defined by features (MacWhinney, 1982). The child is also given credit for a variety of formal devices acting in concert with his or her rule systems, such as deletion operators (Bloom, 1970), output order biases (MacWhinney, 1982), elementary transformational operations (Erreich, Valian, and Winzemer, 1980), attentional filters (Slobin, 1973; Newport, Gleitman, and Gleitman, 1977), and rules of interpretation and construal (Lust, 1981). Indeed, some investigators, (e.g., MacWhinney, 1982) have come to the conclusion that to understand child language, one must posit a large set of relatively heterogeneous mechanisms.

This proliferation of representational symbol structures and computational mechanisms is a natural consequence of the complexity of child language and the increasing sophistication of cognitivist theories. It makes it increasingly difficult, however, to offer *explanations* of why children say what they say. The mechanisms proposed in the literature are powerful enough to account not only for the observed data but also for many patterns of data that do not occur. (See Atkinson, 1982, for detailed arguments to this effect concerning theories of language development proposed in the last two decades.) To take a simple example, a child who is credited with powers of rote memory for adult sentence fragments could, in principle, spend his or her future linguistic life producing only memorized sentences. That this does not occur but could occur, given the mechanisms attributed to the child, is a fact in want of an explanation. Furthermore, it has become almost an article of faith among psycholinguists that child language data can be accounted for in many ways (de Villiers and de Villiers, 1977; see also MacWhinney, 1982, where the same data are used to exemplify completely different sorts of mechanisms). Since the substantive claims of any cognitivist theory are embodied in the class of internal computational mechanisms they posit (Pylyshyn, 1980), mechanisms that are too powerful and flexible do not allow one to explain why the data come out the way they do, rather than in countless conceivable alternative ways. Furthermore, there is the danger, as Roger Brown (1977) has put it, of the mass of theories and data becoming "cognitively ugly and so repellent as to be swiftly deserted, its issues unresolved."

The problem of the increasing descriptive power of available cognitive mechanisms, and the consequent decrease in distinguishability and explanatory power, is not unique to developmental psycholinguistics. (For discussions of indistinguishability relating to short-term recognition memory, visual imagery, and concept representation, see Townsend, 1974; Anderson, 1978; and Palmer, 1978.) This state of affairs has led cognitive theorists to considerable soul-searching and to a growing realization that theories of cognitive abilities should be stated in two parts: the basic computational processes, types of data structures, and information pathways made available by the neurophysiology of the brain; and the particular tokens, combinations, and sequences of those operations that specify how the basic mechanisms are actually used in a particular type of task. Pylyshyn (1980) refers to this distinction as the "architecture of the cognitive virtual machine" versus particular "programs" that run on that architecture; Kosslyn (1980) and Pinker and Kosslyn (1983) distinguish between "general theories" and "specific theories"; in the domain of syntax, Chomsky (1965) distinguishes between principles of universal grammar and grammars for particular languages. The hope is that the basic, universal cognitive mechanisms will explain intelligent behavior in a strong sense: we behave as we do because of properties of the "mental program" we execute, which (crucially) can be nothing more or less than combinations of the computational mechanisms stated to be part of the "cognitive virtual machine."

But how, in practice, can we specify the architecture of the cognitive virtual machine, given that it is underdetermined by behavior? Naturally, there is no simple, universally applicable method. The standard solution to indeterminacy problems in science is to seek external constraints on the explanatory mechanisms of a theory, from outside the immediate domain of data that the theory addresses. For cognitive theories, these external constraints can take several forms. For example, one can constrain computational theories of early visual processing by taking into account the cellular physiology of the retina and visual cortex, the ways that physical objects in an ecologically typical environment structure the ambient light array, and the abstract nature of the computational problem that the visual system solves (Marr and Nishihara, 1978). Or one can constrain theories of visual imagery by exploring its commonalities with visual perception, and thereby inducing which of its structures and processes must be identical to those posited separately by a successful theory of vision (Finke, 1980; Pinker and Kosslyn, 1983).

What sort of external constraint could assist developmental psycholinguists in characterizing child language? One place to look is to a field with an analogous problem: generative grammar. Just as in the case of child language, it is all too easy to formulate multiple mechanisms (grammars, in this case), any of which can account for all the data at hand (adults' syntactic judgments). It was Chomsky who first pointed out the existence of a very strong external constraint on theories of grammar: they must account for the fact that a correctly formulated grammar for an individual language is acquired by children on the basis of sentences they hear in their first few years. A theory of a grammar for particular languages must be embedded in a theory of Universal Grammar that allows only one grammar (specifically, the grammar proposed as correct by the theorist) to be compatible with the sorts of sentences children hear. A grammar that is motivated by a theory of universal grammar explaining the possibility of language acquisition is said to be *explanatorily adequate* (Chomsky, 1965). Although only recently has the explanatory adequacy criterion as it pertains to language acquisition been explicitly invoked to settle disputes among competing theories of grammar (e.g., in Wexler and Culicover, 1980; Baker, 1979; and Baker and McCarthy, 1981), it has already become the focus of many debates within linguistics and has at least temporarily banished the worry that the mechanisms motivated by linguistic research might be powerful enough to generate any recursively enumerable language (see Chomsky, 1980, 1981; Wexler and Culicover, 1980; Pinker, 1982).

Developmental psycholinguistics can avail itself of an external constraint on its theories of children's language that is similar to the explanatory adequacy criterion in linguistics. Just as the adult's linguistic knowledge must be the final product of an acquisition mechanism, the child's linguistic knowledge must be an intermediate product of that mechanism. That is, we may view the child's abilities at any stage of development as a waystation in a process that takes the child from a state at which he or she knows nothing about the target language to a state at which he or she has acquired the language completely. This puts a severe constraint on descriptions of the rule systems underlying child language at a given stage of development. First, a rule system at a particular stage must have been constructed by an acquisition mechanism that began with no knowledge about the particular target language and that arrived at the current state on the basis of the parental input it received in the interim. Second, the rule system must be convertible by the acquisition mechanism into a rule system adequate to represent adult abilities, also on the basis of parental input. In other words, for us to take a characterization of a developmental state seriously, there must be a way into the developmental state and also a way out of it. This is a simple consequence of the fact that all children learn to speak the language of their community, that the process is not instantaneous, and that children are presumably engaged in the process at the ages when we most often try to tap their abilities (1 to 5 years).

Because the external constraint I am suggesting is inspired by children's ultimate success at learning the language, this constraint can be called the *learnability condition* (see Pinker, 1979).[2] Note that by invoking it we can kill two birds with one stone: not only do we have constraints on how children's language at a given stage may be accounted for, but we are also forced to attempt to solve the core theoretical problem in language acquisition, the one most neglected in developmental psycholinguistics—how the child succeeds.

At first glance, this approach might seem either hopelessly naive or doomed to failure. The approach, by encouraging one to treat the child's abilities at each stage as simply an intermediate state of knowledge in an acquisition process, ignores all the other differences between children and adults, such as attention, memory, cognitive sophistication, and perceptual acuity. If these differences were acknowledged, however, there would be so many degrees of freedom available in specifying properties of the child's memory, attention, and so on, that one would be left in the same unconstrained, unexplanatory state as before.

The solution to this dilemma lies in applying Occam's Razor in a way that is somewhat unorthodox for developmental psychology. Recall that the substantive portion of a cognitivist theory is the set of computational mechanisms composing the cognitive virtual machine. Since all of a theory's accounts of data must refer to combinations of these mechanisms, the fewer the mechanisms, the more parsimonious the theory and the more explanatory its accounts. That implies that the most explanatory theory will posit the fewest developmental changes in the mechanisms of the virtual machine, attributing developmental changes, where necessary, to increases in the child's knowledge base, increasing access of computational procedures to the knowledge base, and quantitative changes in parameters like the size of working memory. As Macnamara (1982) has put it, the null hypothesis in developmental psychology is that the cognitive mechanisms of children and adults are identical; hence it is a hypothesis that should not be rejected until the data leave us no other choice. It is also an additional source of external constraints on models of children's language: in the ideal case, one would only attribute to the child extralinguistic cognitive mechanisms that have independent motivation from the study of adult cognition (possibly with the quantitative modifications mentioned above). Let us call this assumption the *continuity assumption* (see, for related arguments, Atkinson, 1982; Carey, in press; Keil, 1981; Kosslyn, 1978; and Macnamara, 1982).

A similar constraint can be invoked to eliminate two other degrees of freedom that otherwise would weaken this strategy. First, there is nothing in the learnability requirement, or in the assumption of unchanging cognitive mechanisms, that would prevent a theorist from attributing grammars with arbitrary formal properties to the child, as long as the theorist posits a (possibly equally arbitrary) mechanism that transforms the child grammar into the adult grammar at a certain point in development. That is, there could be an ad hoc child grammar, with no resemblance in form to the adult grammar, plus a mechanism that simply expunges the entire child grammar at a given stage and inserts the full-blown adult grammar in its place (to be interpreted, perhaps, as a consequence of neural maturation). Again, no constraints on accounts of children's language would follow. Thus the continuity assumption should apply not only to the child's cognitive mechanisms but to his or her grammatical mechanisms as well: in the absence of compelling evidence to the contrary, the child's grammatical rules should be drawn from the same basic rule types, and be composed of primitive symbols from the same class, as the grammatical rules attributed to adults in standard linguistic investigations. This, of course, is not a dogmatic denial that maturation affects language development, just a reminder that there is a burden of proof on proponents of maturational change.

A remaining loophole in this strategy is how the grammatical rule system attributed to the child will be realized in concrete instances of a child's comprehension and production. Again, a theorist could provide ad hoc accounts of children's behavior, while respecting the learnability condition and the continuity assumption as it relates to cognitive mechanisms and grammatical formalisms, by positing that the grammar is realized in different ways in on-line performance at different stages of development. For example, the parsing mechanisms that interpret the grammatical rules during comprehension could use different types of scheduling rules, or recruit different types of short-term memory structures, at different points in development, or the rules themselves could be translated into a parser-usable form in different ways at different stages. Again, I suggest that the continuity assumption be applied: until evidence shows otherwise, one should assume that the child's grammar is realized in his or her linguistic performance in the same qualitative way as for adults. In sum, I propose that the continuity assumption be applied to accounts of children's language in three ways: in the qualitative nature of the child's abilities, in the formal nature of the child's grammatical rules, and in the way that those rules are realized in comprehension and production.

There are two principal alternatives to the continuity assumption. One is the Piagetian view that the child simultaneously learns about the world and builds the mind whereby he knows the world (as Macnamara, 1982, has put it). But this view is both unparsimonious (according to the view outlined here) and incomplete as to how the progression from one cognitive stage to a qualitatively different one can be accomplished solely by the cognitive mechanisms existing at the earlier stage (see Fodor, 1975; Macnamara, 1976; and the contributions of Chomsky and Fodor in Piatelli-Palmarini, 1980, for extensive discussion). The other alternative is the possibility that neural maturation may alter qualitatively the mechanisms of the cognitive virtual machine (a hypothesis that Chomsky, 1980, entertains for the case of language and which Gleitman, 1981, has dubbed the "tadpole hypothesis"). Though this is certainly possible, and logically coherent, it too is unparsimonious: in one's postulates of what constitutes the primitive computational machinery of the human mind, one must independently postulate the linguistic mechanisms of the immature state, and the maturational process that replaces the immature mechanisms by the mature ones (see Fodor, 1981, for an argument as to why a maturational process is not reducible to other mechanisms of the initial state). Under the continuity hypothesis, in contrast, one need postulate only the initial state, which includes the induction mechanisms that add rules to the grammar in response to input data. Subsequent stages are deducible as the products of the induction mechanisms operating on the inputs. Furthermore, the tadpole hypothesis is flexible enough to impede the development of explanatory accounts of children's abilities, since any model of a child's abilities can be transformed into the adult state by arbitrary maturational processes. The best approach, according to the logic I have sketched out, is to assume that there are no qualitative maturational changes until the theory positing constant computational mechanisms cannot account for the data. This view is more parsimonious and falsifiable (and hence potentially explanatory) and does not entail a serious risk of overlooking maturational changes that do exist, since these will be discovered if and when the theory with constant mechanisms fails.

I have been writing as if there were a one-way street between the theory of language learnability and the study of language development, with learnability theory acting as a source of constraints on descriptions of child language. In fact the constraints can be applied in both directions. Though there is certainly less freedom in devising accounts of language induction than there is in devising accounts of a child's two-word utterances, usually there are theoretical options, free parameters, and sets of alternative variants within learnability theories as well. Since such alternatives often make different predictions about the intermediate stages of the learning mechanism, empirical facts about children's language should be sufficient to rule out some of the alternatives. That is, at the same time that the learnability theory constrains the possible descriptions of the child's abilities, the developmental data can help decide among possible options within the learnability theory.

This might strike the reader as a recipe for circularity—after all, how can a theory in one domain constrain accounts of data in another if the theory itself has free parameters that are to be fixed by the very same data that the theory is trying to provide constrained accounts of? The answer is that there is no circularity as long as not *all* the options within a learnability theory are consistent with *all* the possible descriptions of the data. If some, but not all of the theoretical options are consistent with descriptions of the data, and furthermore the members of that subset are consistent with only some of those descriptions, progress can be made. This argument is illustrated in Figure 1.1, where the mutually compatible data description and theoretical variant are circled.

In sum, I argue that for accounts of child language to be restrictive and explanatory, they should be couched in terms of a fixed set of computational mechanisms with independent mo-

Figure I.I

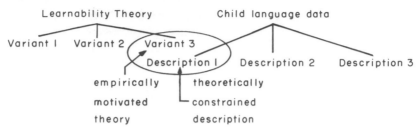

tivation. The two most promising sources of independent motivation are the fact that children are engaged in a process of acquiring the language of adults, and the null-hypothesis assumption that the nongrammatical cognitive mechanisms, grammatical primitives, and manner of grammatical realization for children are qualitatively (though not necessarily quantitatively) the same as those for adults. Any rule system posited as a description of child language, then, should be the intermediate product of an acquisition mechanism that eventually converts that rule system into the adult system on the basis of parental input. Additional nongrammatical mechanisms should be independently motivated by the study of adults' and children's cognitive abilities. At the same time, data on children's language will allow us to decide among theoretical options that the learnability theory leaves open.

The purpose of this book is to demonstrate that this research strategy is viable, that progress can be made in accounting for language learnability and language development within a single framework. I think such a demonstration is necessary because nothing like this strategy has ever been used in the study of language acquisition. As mentioned, research in developmental psycholinguistics has largely ignored the logical problem of language acquisition (see Atkinson, 1982; Pinker, 1979; Gleitman and Wanner, 1982a; Wexler and Culicover, 1980). On the other hand, Kenneth Wexler and Peter Culicover, in presenting their landmark "Degree-2 Theory" of language learnability (1980), argue for the potential importance of developmental data in constraining their acquisition theory but end on a pessimistic note when discussing the usefulness of such data in practice.

To illustrate the strategy, I will use a theory of language acquisition first outlined in Pinker (1982;[3] see also Pinker, 1981a, and in press, a). That theory was designed principally to account for the acquisition of certain types of adult grammatical rules, while being consistent with certain gross properties of child language development such as the gradual development of language, the rapid and error-free acquisition of word order and constituency, the semantic properties of early word combinations, the order of acquisition of grammatical morphemes, and the absence of errors of control in early speech. It was also conjectured in that paper that with some simple extensions, the theory would provide satisfactory accounts of many other aspects of language development. A second goal of this book, then, is to evaluate that conjecture. I will examine a number of salient empirical patterns in the language development literature, and attempt to account for those patterns within the confines of the acquisition theory, modifying and extending that theory as necessary. I will always try to motivate such modifications not only by their ability to account for some set of developmental phenomena, but also by their salubrious effect on accounting for learnability. That is, at the same time that a proposed modification provides more accurate accounts for some pattern of child language data, it should provide more general or more economical accounts of the acquisition of other rules in the language or rules in other languages, or of universal regularities in language. The theory is then to be evaluated in terms of its joint success in both domains: accounting for the acquisition of linguistic rules per se, and accounting for the developmental course of acquisition.

I wish to stress that elaborating and defending the theory in Pinker (1982) is only one of the goals of the book. Even if many of the specific proposals I make turn out to be incorrect (which I cheerfully expect), I hope to have demonstrated that bringing learnability theories to bear on developmental issues, and vice versa, is a profitable avenue of inquiry in the study of language acquisition.

In Chapter 2 I sketch out the theoretical foundations and overall structure of the acquisition theory and defend each of its postulates. In each of the following six chapters I choose a particular class of syntactic rules, describe the theory's acquisition mechanisms for those rules, summarize the principal developmental data relevant to the acquisition of the rules, attempt to account for those data using the acquisition mechanisms, modify the acquisition mechanisms if necessary, point out the principal empirical and theoretical claims implicit in the final mechanisms, and discuss the issues left open. I will follow this strategy for five classes of rules: (1) the phrase structure rules that define the linear order and hierarchical composition of sentences; (2) inflectional rules, defining a language's system of case and agreement markers, determiners, and other closed-class morphemes;

(3) rules of complementation and control, which determine the form of complements to predicates and the reference of missing subjects in those complements; (4) rules governing the form and placement of auxiliaries and the coordination of auxiliaries with sentence modality and main verb morphology; and (5) rules that specify the expression of predicate-argument relations for verb forms in the lexicon, and lexical rules such as passivization, dativization, and causativization that allow for productivity in the use of verb forms.

2 | The Acquisition Theory: Assumptions and Postulates

IN THE MATHEMATICAL study of language learnability, a learning model is said to have four parts: a characterization of the class of languages within the scope of the learner's acquisition powers, one of which is the "target language" spoken by the adult community; an input sample containing the information that the learner uses to learn; a learning strategy, describing what computations the learner performs on the input data; and a success criterion that the learner has to meet in order for us to conclude that his or her learning strategy works. In this chapter I describe a modified version of the acquisition theory originally presented in Pinker (1982) by discussing the assumptions and postulates of each of the first three parts separately, along with brief justifications for each such choice. The fourth part, the success criterion, will not be discussed in this chapter. It is primarily relevant to mathematical models of learning, where one must formally define "success" in order to prove that some learning model can or cannot attain it. In the present case, I am proposing a nonformal theory of the child's learning strategies, and will argue for the success of various strategies at learning the relevant rules on a case-by-case basis. Given the complexity and heterogeneity of the linguistic knowledge whose acquisition I will be trying to account for, and the specificity of the learning strategies to detailed properties of linguistic rules, it will be impossible to prove or even argue in one place that the theory is capable of acquiring any human language. Instead, the "success criterion" for the proposed learning strategy will be embedded in the success criteria for the theory as a whole, and these will be the usual criteria for scientific theories in general: data coverage, parsimony, elegance, consistency with theories in other domains, and so forth. The success of the theory at meeting these criteria is the subject of Chapters 3 through 8.

What Is Acquired

I will assume that the child is equipped to learn a rule system conforming to Bresnan and Kaplan's theory of Lexical Functional Grammar ("LFG"; also known in earlier incarnations as "lexical interpretive grammar" or "extended lexical grammar"—see Bresnan, 1978, 1982a,b,c; Kaplan and Bresnan, 1982). Lexical Functional Grammar is a theory of generative grammar with no transformational component, an extensive use of grammatical relations or grammatical functions such as "subject," "object," and "complement," and a powerful lexical component.

Lexical Functional Grammar: An Overview

Constituent Structures and Constituent Structure Rules

An LFG generates two structures for every well-formed sentence in the language: a constituent structure, or c-structure, and a functional structure, or f-structure. A c-structure is similar to a surface structure or phrase marker tree, as in the "Standard Theory" of transformational grammar (Chomsky, 1965), with two important differences: First, all c-structures are generated directly by phrase structure rewrite rules, rather than being derived by the application of transformations to a deep structure tree. That means that every type of phrase (e.g., active, passive, dative, dative passive) will be generated directly by phrase structure rules, with no phrase structure serving as an "underlying" form for another phrase structure.[1] Second, major constituents in the phrase structure tree are annotated with functional equations that specify the grammatical relations (also called grammatical functions) that the constituent bears to the larger constituent it is a part of. These equations also serve to ensure that local dependencies among constituents (e.g., agreement) are satisfied. Figure 2.1 shows a c-structure for the sentence *John told Mary to leave Bill*, in which the NP dominating *John* is annotated as the subject (SUBJ) of the sentence, the NPs dominating *Mary* and *Bill* are annotated as the object (OBJ) of their respective VPs, and the VP dominating *to leave Bill* is annotated as the verb phrase complement (V-COMP) of the main verb phrase.[2]

The c-structure was generated by the annotated phrase structure rules listed in (1), which are similar to base rewrite rules in

Figure 2.1

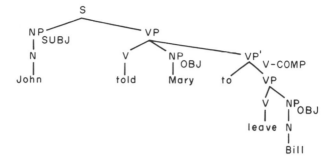

the Standard Theory with the addition of functional annotations (e.g., that for the subject).

(1) S → NP$_{SUBJ}$ VP
    NP → (det) N
    VP → V (NP$_{OBJ}$) (VP'$_{V\text{-}COMP}$)
    VP' → (to) VP

Functional Structures and Lexical Entries

The f-structure underlying a sentence is an explicit compilation of all the grammatical information relevant to the semantic interpretation of the sentence (see Halvorsen, 1983, for a description of the mapping between f-structures and semantic structures). It is generated by the annotated phrase structure rules and the lexical entries for the morphemes in the sentence acting in concert. The f-structure corresponding to Figure 2.1 is presented in Figure 2.2. The lexical entries that participated in the generation of Figure 2.2 are listed in simplified form in (2).

Figure 2.2

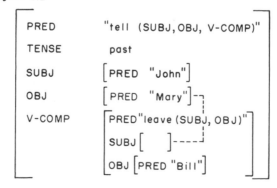

(2) John: N: PRED = "John"
    Mary: N: PRED = "Mary"

Bill: N: PRED = "Bill"
told: V: PRED = "tell (SUBJ, OBJ, V-COMP)"
          TENSE = past
          OBJ = V-COMP's SUBJ
leave: V: PRED = "leave (SUBJ, OBJ)"

The heart of the f-structure is its PRED or predicate entry, which specifies how to compute the predicate-argument relations (the "who did what to whom" information) expressed by the sentence. The predicate statement is taken from the lexical entry of the main verb. In the notation used in LFG, the particular semantic relation signified by the verb (e.g., eating versus hitting) is symbolized simply as the name of the word, printed in lower case within quotes (e.g., *"tell"*). This is simply a surrogate for a semantic representation, to be specified by a theory of word meaning. The arguments of the predicate are individuated by places separated by commas within the parentheses; for *"tell (, ,)"* the first place corresponds to the teller, the second to the hearer, and the third to the tale told. In the PRED statement in the lexical entry for the verb, each place is filled with the name of the grammatical function that labels the particular argument in the c-structure tree. In the case of *"tell* (SUBJ, OBJ, V-COMP)," the first slot within parentheses, corresponding to the teller, is filled by the function SUBJ, indicating that the constituent labeled SUBJ in the tree (in this case, the NP dominating *John*) stands for the first argument, the teller, of the relation *tell*. The other functions similarly indicate where to look in the c-structure tree to find the second and third arguments of *tell*. Grammatical functions, then, act as links between surface structure positions and the logical arguments of a predicate by virtue of being mentioned in two locations within the grammar: in the appropriate slot of the lexical entry for a multiargument predicate, and as an annotation to a constituent in a phrase structure rule. In languages that express grammatical relations using case and agreement markers, the functions would serve as links between morphological markers and arguments and would be mentioned in the rules specifying the distribution of affixes as well as in lexical entries and phrase structure rules.

Within the f-structure, the functions label the various arguments of the verb, each one enclosed in its own set of square brackets. The f-structure also contains the grammatically encoded semantic and formal features of the words of the sentence such as the tense and aspect of verbs, and the gender, number, person, and so on, of the noun phrases. These too are taken from the lexical entries for the various words and entered in the appropriate places within the f-structure (see Kaplan and Bresnan, 1982, for a more complete account of the mechanics of the grammar).

Control

The f-structure, with the help of lexically encoded information, also lists the arguments and predicate-argument relations that are not encoded explicitly in the c-structure. In this case, the argument *Mary* is both the object argument of the verb *tell* and the subject argument of the verb *leave*. It is a property of the verb *tell* that its object can also serve as a subject of an embedded complement (as opposed to, say, **John informed Mary to leave Bill*, which is ungrammatical, or *John promised Mary to leave Bill*, in which the subject, not the object, of the matrix verb corefers with the complement subject). This property is encoded in the functional equation OBJ = V-COMP's SUBJ, annotated to the lexical entry for *tell*. In the f-structure, this coreference is expressed by the presence of a SUBJ f-substructure within the V-COMP f-structure and by the dashed line linking it to the OBJ f-substructure one level up.

Defining and Constraining Equations

Equations like those described above for control declare that some fact is true about the sentence. In addition, LFG has a formal mechanism used by some rules to ensure that some *other* rule declares some fact to be true. Such constraints are expressed in the form of *constraining equations* using the relation $=_c$ (roughly paraphrased as "must be defined somewhere as"). For example, the lexical entry for *help* requires that its complement be infinitival (**John helped Mary left Bill*). This can be enforced by an equation appended to the lexical entry of *help*: V-COMP's MORPHOLOGY $=_c$ *infinitival* ("the verb in the complement must have infinitival morphology"); if the verb in fact contains the equation MORPHOLOGY = *infinitival*, the constraint is satisfied; if it either lacks such an equation or has an equation defining some other value for the morphology feature, the constraint is not satisfied and the sentence is deemed ungrammatical.

Multiple Subcategorizations and Lexical Rules

Since there are no transformations within an LFG, every verb that can appear in two or more surface structures with different sets of grammatical functions must have more than one lexical entry, one for each structure. Thus the passive version of Figure

2.1 will have the surface structure shown in Figure 2.3 and the f-structure shown in Figure 2.4, constructed from the passive lexical entry for *tell* shown in (3). (I ignore the auxiliary in the f-structure for brevity's sake; the treatment of auxiliaries within LFG will be described in a later section.)

Figure 2.3

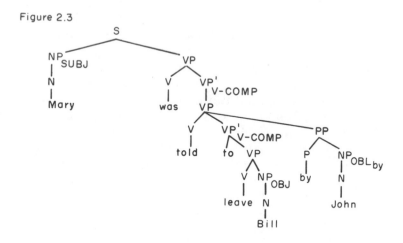

Figure 2.4

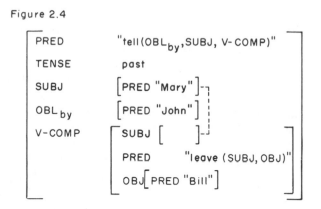

(3) PRED = "tell (OBL$_{by}$, SUBJ, V-COMP)"
    MORPH = passivepart
    SUBJ = V-COMP's SUBJ

As can be seen, the number of places within the argument structure of the passive predicate of *tell* in (3) is the same as the number in the active predicate in (2). Likewise, the semantic roles of the arguments corresponding to each of the places are identical in the two entries. What differentiates the passive entry from the active entry is the set of grammatical functions that encode the arguments: SUBJ and OBJ encoding the teller and hearer, respectively, in the active version; versus OBL (oblique object) and SUBJ in the passive version. The fact that most active verbs have passive counterparts is captured by a lexical rule, which, applied to the active lexical entry, generates a passive entry corresponding to it. Once the passive entry is created, it alone is invoked in its passive sentence; the active entry plays no role. The passive lexical rule, shown in (4), replaces each mention of OBJ in a lexical entry by SUBJ, and replaces each mention of SUBJ by OBL. Another part of the rule indicates the change in morphology by adding the equation specifying that the verb is a passive participle.[3]

(4) OBJ $\mapsto$ SUBJ
  SUBJ $\mapsto$ OBL$_{by}$
  $\mapsto$ MORPH $=$ passivepart

Long-Distance Binding

The theory has mechanisms for the "long-distance" binding of traces to their antecedents found in relative clauses, *wh*-questions, and *tough*-movement sentences. I describe these mechanisms here only in bare outline, and must refer the reader to Kaplan and Bresnan (1982) for details. In these constructions, a constituent is absent from its usual place in the string, and the argument defined by that "gap" corefers with another element an arbitrary distance away in the tree, usually a focused, quantified, or topicalized element, such as the questioned element in a *wh*-question. To allow for the possibility of gaps, an LFG grammar for English includes a rewrite rule generating them directly, for example, NP $\rightarrow t$ (t being a trace element) for noun phrase gaps (note that in standard theories of transformational grammar, traces are seen as indicating the former position of an element displaced by a movement transformation). In addition, there must be variables that indicate the binding of the trace by the higher element (say, the questioned element); in LFG the "subjacency metavariables" $\Uparrow$ and $\Downarrow$ are the symbols linking pairs of elements separated by arbitrary distances. $\Uparrow$ would be annotated to the rule generating gaps, and $\Downarrow$ would be annotated to the rule generating the questioned element; the process that builds f-structures would link the elements with corresponding $\Uparrow$ and $\Downarrow$ subjacency metavariables, thereby indicating that the matrix element with $\Downarrow$ also has the particular function associated with the gap in the embedded phrase. Figure 2.5

Figure 2.5

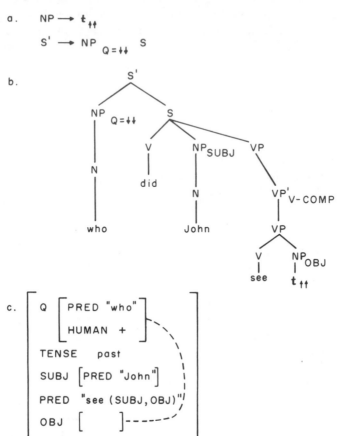

shows in outline how this is accomplished; the phrase structure rules are in part (a), the c-structure in part (b), and the f-structure in part (c). (Q is the function symbolizing the questioned element.) As in Figure 2.4, I ignore several facts about the auxiliary when showing the f-structure.

Formal Conditions

I conclude this summary of LFG by mentioning two more sets of principles. First, there are several sets of conditions that must be true of f-structures for their corresponding sentences to be well formed. In particular, every function name must have a single value at a given hierarchical level in an f-structure (e.g., there can be a single PRED statement at any level, and features like TENSE cannot be given contradictory values like *past* and *present*). This is called the *consistency* requirement. All functions listed in an argument-taking predicate must be instantiated somewhere in the f-structure (e.g., if the predicate statement for a verb indicates that it takes an OBJ, there must be an OBJ defined in the f-structure). This is called the *completeness* requirement. Conversely, every "governable" function (SUBJ, OBJ, OBL, OBJ2 or second object, and COMP) labeling an f-substructure must be listed somewhere in a predicate statement; this is called the *coherence* requirement. And the subjacency metavariables must occur in matched pairs and obey an additional set of complex conditions; this is called the *proper instantiation* requirement (see Kaplan and Bresnan, 1982).

Substantive Conditions

The formal theory defining the mechanics of LFG must be augmented by a substantive theory stating the set of symbols and functions natural languages may use, constraints on which types of equations may recruit which symbols, constraints on the composition of equations, and statements of universal rules or conditions on rules. These conditions constitute LFG's substantive theory of universal grammar; the empirical claim implicit in Kaplan and Bresnan's use of the LFG formal machinery is that the universal constraints on language can be stated in the vocabulary of the LFG formalisms. I will mention these substantive constraints throughout the book as I discuss specific types of rules and their acquisition; many of them are embedded in the language acquisition procedures I propose. Some examples of these constraints are: only SUBJs and TOPICs of embedded complements may be controlled by arguments of matrix verbs; only the OBJs, OBJ2s, and SUBJs of matrix verbs may be controlling arguments (Bresnan, 1982c); there exists a universal rule of passivization that replaces an OBJ by a SUBJ and a SUBJ by either an OBL or a null function (Bresnan, 1982b); the symbols S, S', and NP may function as "bounding nodes" in particular rule expansions, limiting the possible linking of subjacency metavariables when these intervene between binder and trace (Kaplan and Bresnan, 1982); and many others (see Bresnan, 1982a, c).

JUSTIFYING THE ASSUMPTIONS ABOUT WHAT IS LEARNED

Acquiring a Grammar

In proposing that a lexical functional grammar is what the child acquires, I am making a set of commitments that require some justification. First, why should one take a grammar of any sort as the structure whose acquisition one is trying to account for, as opposed to specific procedures that are used in production and comprehension (e.g., Anderson, 1983; Langley, 1982; Selfridge, 1980)? I do so for several reasons. First, given that by and large adults can produce, comprehend, and judge the well-formedness of the same set of sentences, it is the simplest assumption. Rather than accounting for three systems, which are used to control the abilities to comprehend, produce, and judge sentences, and which redundantly specify the same information about sentence structure, one can account for a single system that defines the possible sentence structures in a language. This system would interface with comprehension, production, and judgment routines that control the temporal flow of information in those processes (see Bresnan and Kaplan, 1982, for further detailed arguments). The case for simplicity is strengthened when one considers that the grammar/parser distinction also partitions linguistic abilities into those that *need not* be acquired (the control procedures for information flow and storage during on-line performance, which need not vary drastically from language to language), and those that *must* be acquired (information about the set of grammatical sentences in the particular language, though there presumably are universal unlearned aspects of that knowledge as well). Thus in setting oneself the goal of accounting for the ability to acquire grammars, one can be more confident that one is accounting for the induction of just that knowledge that must be induced on logical grounds, and that one will not be sidetracked by trying to account for the acquisition of knowledge that need not, hence might not, be induced from the input at all (such as stack operations in parsing). Finally, the input available to the child (adult sentences plus other information; see the next section) gives the learner information that is equally useful in acquiring the ability to comprehend, produce, and judge sentences of that type, while providing little or no information about the control operations involved in the comprehension or production process per se. For these reasons, grammatical rules themselves seem to be the natural domain for an acquisition theory.

Developmental psycholinguists might find this assumption preposterous, given the many cases in which children have been shown to be able to produce a structure without comprehending it, or show other dissociations (e.g., Fraser, Bellugi, and Brown, 1963; de Villiers and de Villiers, 1974). First, it should be stressed that the hypothesis that grammatical rules are acquired in a neutral format makes predictions about the acquisition of grammatical structures, not sentences. Thus if a child produces a sentence by rote but cannot comprehend it, or if the child can act out a sentence using some nonsyntactic strategy but cannot utter it spontaneously, this would not count against the hypothesis. What *would* count against it is a demonstration that children have knowledge structures sufficient to compose sentences from the correct grammatical units but that this knowledge may only be used in production, not in comprehension or judgment. Second, even when special cases such as rote or nonlinguistic comprehension strategies are ruled out, a simple demonstration that a sentence structure can be produced but not comprehended, or produced and comprehended but not judged, may simply indicate that the judgment process itself is not yet developed or is severely limited in processing capacity, rather than that the linguistic knowledge is tailor-made for production or comprehension. That is, such demonstrations may only indicate that the difficulty inherent in the complexity of a grammatical rule and the difficulty contributed by the resource limitations of a process that accesses it might be additive. To refute the hypothesis that rules are acquired in a neutral format, at the very least one must show an interaction between performance mode and grammatical structure, with the relative difficulties of different structures or the performance patterns or type of productivity for an individual structure being qualitatively different in comprehension, production, and judgment. And even in such cases one must be sure that the particular interaction observed is not attributable to the different behavior of two routines in processing different types of rules, such as the interaction of right- versus left-branching rules, top-down versus bottom-up parsing schedules, and production versus comprehension (Yngve, 1960). That is because in such cases the rules themselves could be the same in other processes despite the presence of an interaction. In sum, I have not seen in the developmental literature the sorts of arguments that would refute the simplest hypothesis, that grammatical rules are acquired in a neutral format.

Acquiring a Grammar Motivated by Linguistic Research

The acquisition theory I will propose is designed to acquire grammatical formalisms of some complexity, formalisms that have been motivated by linguistic investigations. In many cases the formalisms are more complex than they have to be to characterize the set of grammatical phenomena that I will be referring to. Therefore it is natural to wonder why I do not simply devise a fragment of a grammar that is sufficient to handle the set of grammatical facts that it is feasible to consider, and show how that fragment is acquired (this is the strategy usually followed in computer simulations of language acquisition; see Pinker, 1979).

There are two reasons why I believe that the best strategy for an acquisition theorist is to focus on a theory of grammar that is independently motivated by linguistic arguments. First, it is a guard against the ad hoc accounts that could result when both the acquisition mechanisms and the rules acquired are degrees of freedom for the theorist. Second, it ensures that the acquisition theory will be naturally extendible beyond the domain of rules addressed when the theory was first devised. Linguistic theories are designed to posit the smallest set of primitives and rule types that can generate the widest possible range of structures empirically observed in the world's languages. As a result, even if an acquisition theory only accounts for the acquisition of a limited class of rules (as must be the case, given resource limitations of individual theorists), as long as the rules are acquired in the format proposed by an adequate linguistic theory, the acquisition of hitherto ignored rules that interact with the ones considered, or rules for other languages, can be explained by simple additions to the original theory. On the other hand, if the rules acquired are in a format that is ad hoc to the range of linguistic phenomena originally considered, the entire acquisition theory might have to be revamped when broader linguistic domains are addressed. This division of labor between linguists and acquisition-minded psychologists ensures that acquisition theories will be "upward compatible" and that the development of acquisition theories will be cumulative. In Pinker (1979), I found that many language acquisition theories that acquire ad hoc grammars, especially those formulated in the past as computer simulations, fail dramatically as soon as one considers classes of grammatical rules other than the ones that the theorist originally had in mind. It is to avoid this problem that I will often attribute more structure to the child's grammar, and thus to his or her acquisition mechanisms, than the examples I discuss strictly require.[4]

Acquiring a Lexical Functional Grammar

It is no surprise that linguistics has never reached a consensus as to the correct theory of grammar. Thus what sort of commitments to particular theories psychologists should make is one of the thorniest issues in psycholinguistics. On one hand, it is impossible to provide precise accounts of the acquisition (or processing) of a given structure without committing oneself to a theory of what that structure is. On the other hand, the psycholinguistic landscape is littered with the remains of psychological efforts that may have been made largely obsolete when the linguistic analysis they presupposed was found to be wanting on linguistic grounds (see Fodor, Bever, and Garrett, 1974); hence George Miller's (1981) admonition to developmental psycholinguists: "Hang loose!" In this section I briefly justify the choice of LFG as a characterization of what is acquired.

I would like to stress at the outset that the purpose of the research to be reported here is not to use language acquisition as a battleground for the debate among contemporary linguistic theories. Rather, it is to try to attain the best possible theory of language acquisition. There are several reasons why these two goals are not identical. In certain respects, the logical problem of language acquisition is similar to classical problems in perception—the task is to specify how the learner/perceiver uses certain types of evidence in the sensory input to draw certain conclusions about the state of the environment (which language is spoken, in the case of language acquisition). Linguistic theories differ as to the sorts of conclusions they assume the child is allowed to draw, but most are mute as to the perceptual premises the child uses to draw the conclusions. It is this mapping between premises and conclusions that defines the domain of an acquisition theory, and that domain overlaps, but does not coincide with, the domain of linguistic theory. Furthermore, despite the disagreements among various contemporary theories, there is currently a fair degree of consensus as to what general sorts of mechanisms and constraints are required in grammars for natural languages. In most theories one finds the same small sets of grammatical categories and relations, phrase structure rules, inflectional paradigms, lexical entries, lexical rules, grammatical features, and so on (or their equivalents). Thus there is a large domain of rule types whose acquisition one can try to account for with relatively little risk of parochialism or impending obsolescence. Much of the work I will report is intended to be of this character.

At the same time it is important to commit oneself to *some* motivated linguistic theory as a characterization of what is acquired, so that one's acquisition theory is forced to be explicit, formally adequate given the full complexity of natural language, and internally consistent. Any such theory should provide a detailed and descriptively adequate account of English syntax, so that the wealth of data on the acquisition of English can be interpreted teleologically. Of course, it must be capable of characterizing the syntax of other natural languages, especially those with radically different properties from English. More important, it should embed those accounts in a universal grammar that spells out the inventory of formal devices that a child will need to acquire any language, plus the parameters of variation in the use of those devices across languages. To help constrain child language accounts in accordance with the third version of the continuity assumption (that grammars are realized in the same way throughout development), the theory should specify how the grammar is realized in adult comprehension and production, in a way motivated by empirical studies of those processes. For the same reason there should be a specification of how the theory interfaces with an adequate theory of semantics for adults.

In many respects LFG is an ideal choice, given these criteria. Bresnan and Kaplan have provided explicit accounts of many syntactic phenomena in English, and in many cases have been able to argue that their accounts are descriptively superior to alternative theories.[5] LFG accounts have also been provided for a wide range of grammatical phenomena that are absent or degenerate in English, such as cliticization (e.g., Grimshaw, 1982a), case marking (Andrews, 1982; Neidle, 1982), context-sensitive cross-serial dependencies (Bresnan, Kaplan, Peters, and Zaenen, 1982), and constituent-order freedom (Mohanan, 1982; Simpson, 1982). Many of these accounts are embedded in theories of universal linguistic constraints that can be directly put to work in various acquisition mechanisms (Bresnan, 1982b, c). The theory is committed to the claim that the grammar serves directly as the knowledge component in a model of language use (see Bresnan and Kaplan, 1982), and so questions about the way the grammar is realized in linguistic performance cannot become another degree of freedom in accounting for developmental data. Better yet, LFG is accompanied by explicit theories of parsing (Ford, Bresnan, and Kaplan, 1982), production (Ford, 1982), and semantic interpretation (Halvorsen, 1983); and its computation-theoretic properties have been explored in some detail (Kaplan and Bresnan, 1982; Bresnan et al., 1982; Berwick, 1981). Finally, LFG to some extent represents a central tendency among contemporary linguistic theories, in that many of its mechanisms have close counterparts in other theories. For example, phrase structure rules obeying the "X-bar" conventions play a role in the "Extended Standard Theory" of Chomsky (1981) and in the theory of "Generalized Phrase Structure Grammar" proposed by Gazdar, Pullum, and Sag (Gazdar, 1982; Gazdar, Pullum, and Sag, 1982). Base generation of surface structures is a feature of the theories of Gazdar et al. and of Brame, 1978; grammatical relations are employed in Chomsky's theory and in Perlmutter and Postal's "Relational Grammar" (Perlmutter, 1980; Perlmutter and Postal, 1977); lexically encoded constraints on complement features are exploited by Gazdar et al. and by Lapointe (1980, 1981a, 1981c); trace binding mechanisms and lexical entries and lexical rules may be found in many theories; and so on. Few of the mechanisms are so exotic that they would be entirely unfamiliar to grammarians working in alternative frameworks. There are important differences in the ways in which these theories employ and constrain the mechanisms, of course, but they tend to implicate similar acquisition problems, and so an acquisition theory using LFG should have a good degree of cross-grammar generality.

Strategic convenience aside, I believe that there is a fact of the matter as to whether a given linguistic theory characterizes human linguistic abilities. Therefore it is appropriate to ask what the status of a given acquisition theory will be if it appears to be successful but if the theory of grammar upon which it is based turns out to be deficient. In the present case, the acquisition theory I will propose here consists of several independent subtheories, and each subtheory could suffer a different fate depending on the long-term empirical status of LFG. Different subtheories of acquisition could be transported whole to an alternative theory, could be translated with minor substantive alterations, or could be irretrievably inconsistent with it, depending on the relation between the two and the overall sort of acquisition theory that is found to work harmoniously with the alternative grammatical theory.

It is beyond the scope of this book to examine in detail how compatible the proposed acquisition mechanisms are with every current theory of grammar. Nonetheless, when feasible I will attempt to point out the dependencies of the acquisition mechanisms on specific claims of LFG and the degree of compatibility of these mechanisms with alternative theories. Furthermore, until acquisition theories of comparable scope are constructed for other current grammatical theories, it will be premature to compare the general merits of different grammatical theories in helping to account for language development. However, to whatever degree my accounts of learnability and children's language are successful, LFG receives tentative indirect support, and the burden of proof is shifted to the proponents of rival linguistic frameworks to show that explicit and motivated acquisition theories are compatible with those frameworks.

Input

There can be no doubt that children learn a language at least in part by hearing sentences of that language from their parents or peers. I model this sort of input as a string of words, on the tentative assumption that the process of segmenting the continuous sound stream into words and morphemes interacts in only limited ways with the rule acquisition processes proposed herein (an exception is Chapter 5, where I present a theory of how the child segments affixes from stems). Perhaps segmentation, for example, can be accomplished in part by a combination of stochastic methods that tabulate syllable transition probabilities (e.g., see Anderson, 1983; Olivier, 1968; Wolff, 1977). Alternatively (or perhaps in addition), the child could store auditory templates of words or short phrases heard in isolation, then match these templates against the input stream, recursively defining as new words those series of segments found in between the recognized portions of the stream.[6] (See Peters, 1983, for further discussion of the segmentation problem.)

I also assume that not all sentences heard by the child, nor all the parts of a sentence, will be used as input to his or her acquisition mechanisms. Presumably children encode most reliably the parts of sentences whose words they understand individually, and the whole sentences most of whose words they understand. This is a plausible variant of the assumption that children know the meaning of every word in the input sentences before syntax acquisition begins (e.g., Anderson, 1974, 1975, 1977; Pinker, 1979, 1982; Wexler and Culicover, 1980). In addition, children seem more likely to encode the stressed syllables of a sentence (Gleitman and Wanner, 1982a) and the words near the beginnings (Newport, Gleitman and Gleitman, 1977) and ends (Slobin, 1973) of sentences. These biases may also be observed in adults (see Rudnicky, 1980, concerning effects of word knowledge; Cole and Jakimik, 1980, concerning effects of stress; and countless short-term memory studies concerning effects of serial position; see Crowder, 1976).

Another possible source of input to the child's language induction mechanisms might consist of parental corrections or subtle feedback when the child speaks ungrammatically. However, available evidence suggests that parents do not correct children in a way contingent on the syntactic well-formedness of the child's prior utterance; nor is comprehension failure by the parent diagnostic of whether the child's prior utterance was grammatical (Brown and Hanlon, 1970). Brown and Hanlon's studies were not directly addressed to the question of "negative evidence," and there are inherent difficulties in investigating certain questions about it. As Brown and Hanlon point out, for example, to observe whether parental comprehension failure is a possible source of information to the child, the investigator must be prepared to consider himself or herself a better judge of the child's intentions than the child's parents. Nonetheless, I think the assumption that negative evidence is not available to the child's learning mechanisms is warranted. There are, no doubt, cases in which parents correct their children (e.g., over-regularized affixing). However, there is anecdotal evidence that even in such cases, children are oblivious to such corrections (Braine, 1971a; McNeill, 1966). Furthermore, even if the child's environment did contain information about the well-formedness of his or her sentences, and even if the child was able to exploit such evidence, it still seems unlikely that negative evidence would be *necessary* for language acquisition to take place. In general, language acquisition is a stubbornly robust process; from what we can tell there is virtually no way to prevent it from happening short of raising a child in a barrel. And even in the case of the acquisition of specific constructions within a language, unless one is prepared to predict that a person who happens never to have been corrected for some error will continue to make it throughout adulthood, it seems wisest to design acquisition mechanisms that do not depend on negatve evidence.[7]

A third possible source of input that I *will* exploit (in agreement with Macnamara, 1972; Schlesinger, 1971; Anderson, 1977; and Wexler and Culicover, 1980) depends on the assumption that the child can infer the meaning of adults' utterances from their physical and discourse contexts and from the meanings of the individual words in the sentence. (The contexts need not, of course, be perceived by the visual sense alone—see Gleitman, 1981, 1983). Thus the input to the acquisition mechanisms might be a pair consisting of a sentence and its meaning. (See Macnamara, 1972; Slobin, 1977; Hoff-Ginsberg and Shatz, 1981; Newport, Gleitman, and Gleitman, 1977; Wexler, 1981; and Pinker, 1979, 1981b, for discussions of the plausibility of this assumption.) In support of this assumption, it has been noted that parental speech tends to refer to the here and now (Snow, 1977), that it tends to encode a limited number of propositions and a limited number of types of semantic relations (Snow, 1977), and, most important, that its meaning tends to be predictable from an understanding of the individual meanings of content words independent of their order or affixation (Slobin, 1977).

If the child deduces the meanings of as yet uncomprehended input sentences from their contexts and from the meanings of their individual words, he or she would have to have learned those word meanings beforehand. This could be accomplished by attending to single words used in isolation, to emphatically stressed single words, or to the single uncomprehended word in a sentence (when there is only one such word), and pairing it with a predicate corresponding to an entity or relation that is singled out ostensively, one that is salient in the discourse context, or one that appears to be expressed in the speech act but for which there is no known word in the sentence expressing it (Pinker, 1982). Evidence that children learn words by hearing isolated usages comes from MacWhinney (1978), who shows that in case-marking languages children usually use the citation form of a noun as the most basic form in their speech.

The particular assumption about semantic input that I will need is that the child can extract the meanings of predicates and their arguments, the relations of arguments to their predicates, the potentially grammatically relevant semantic features of the sentence participants (their number, person, sex, etc.) and of the proposition as a whole (tense, aspect, modality, etc.), and the discourse features of the speech act (e.g., whether it is declarative, interrogative, exclamative, negative, or emphatic; whether some other proposition is presupposed). Most of this information can be encoded in what I call an "uncommitted" f-structure, uncommitted in the sense that it does not contain information specific to any given language. For example, its features will include some that the target language does not in fact use (e.g., animacy for English), and the learning procedure will have to select from among them. What are grammatical functions like SUBJ in an f-structure will be named in the input representation by neutral labels such as ARG1, ARG2, and so on. Note that, as in the case of the assumption that word learning is complete before syntax acquisition begins, the assumption that sentence meanings are available contextually may be weakened by turning the assumption into an input filter. The assumption could be that the child only processes for the purposes of rule induction those sentences whose meanings are available contextually, ignoring the rest. Presumably, the child could recognize whether or not a putative contextually induced meaning was appropriate for the sentence in part by confirming that the meaning of every word was integrated into the proposition representing the sentence meaning as a whole.

The Learning Mechanisms: General Principles

The learning theory consists of a set of subtheories, each proposing a set of procedures designed to acquire a particular class of LFG rules. In each of the chapters to follow, I describe a subtheory or set of subtheories in detail, together with the relevant developmental evidence. In the rest of this chapter, I discuss the general form of these procedures and justify the theoretical commitments behind them.

Several general properties of the learning mechanisms either are noncontroversial or have already been motivated by the arguments in Chapter 1. First, I assume that the child has no memory for the input other than the current sentence-plus-inferred-meaning and whatever information about past inputs is encoded into the grammar at that point, that is, that the strategy is *one-memory limited* (see Osherson and Weinstein, in press; Osherson, Stob, and Weinstein, 1982). Second, I assume that the learning mechanisms themselves do not change over time, that is, that they are *stationary* (see Pinker, 1981b). Third, I assume that each mechanism is designed to acquire an adult rule efficiently with respect to some criterion such as generality, speed, or accuracy. That is, no acquisition procedure will be introduced if its sole purpose is to generate some developmental pattern such as errors or delayed acquisition. (This property can be called *directness*.) In the rest of this chapter, I discuss two other general properties of the learning mechanisms that are far more controversial.

THE TASK-SPECIFICITY AND INNATENESS OF THE LEARNING MECHANISMS

In the acquisition theory I will propose, the child is assumed to know, prior to acquiring a language, the overall structure of the grammar, the formal nature of the different sorts of rules it contains, and the primitives from which those rules may be composed. Furthermore, many of these acquisition procedures freely exploit constraints inspired by linguistic universals; I have felt no compunction about proposing mechanisms that are tailor-made to the acquisition of language. I will not defend the task-specificity of the theory at length here; it is not a background assumption to be defended a priori so much as it is a substantive claim embedded in the theory that will stand or fall together with it (and other such theories). But I have found that some readers think that this property loses points for a theory, however otherwise successful that theory may be, and so I will say a few words about the property in this section.

First, the assumption of task-specificity is justified largely by its track record. There has been notably little success so far in accounting for the acquisition of linguistic rules in a psychologically plausible way. In my review of formal language learning models (Pinker, 1979), I concluded that the only theories that even approached this goal were ones designed to exploit specific linguistic regularities.[8] Likewise, models of learning in other domains (e.g., sports, block figures, physics) were found to owe their success largely to their exploiting constraints that were specific to those domains. Furthermore, my experience in the present project has confirmed this earlier assessment, in my opinion. As the reader shall see, in many instances the most plausible way of solving a learnability problem, given the facts about linguistic diversity and children's language, was to posit a learning procedure that performed some inductive generalization that may have been "eccentric." That is, the linguistic generalization implicit in the procedure worked well for the learning task at hand but did not seem to be a candidate for instantiation in any multipurpose learning strategy. See Chomsky (1975, 1980, 1981), Baker (1979), and Wexler and Culicover (1980) for extensive arguments that the facts of linguistic diversity and linguistic universals call for "eccentric" inductive leaps. Note that these arguments all attempt to explain highly specific facts about language structure. Any counterargument must provide alternative accounts of those facts. I have found that most do not even try.

It will probably seem suspect to some readers that I am attempting to justify an assumption on which a theory is based by pointing to the putative success of that very theory. I believe, however, that this is the only proper way to resolve the question about whether the assumption of task-specificity is true. Indeed, I am puzzled that people resist task-specific theories on account of their task-specificity, as opposed to their empirical or conceptual difficulties. It seems to me that we should simply aim for the best theory; if it posits task-specific mechanisms (as I suspect it will), so be it. Certainly there are no sound a priori arguments against task-specificity. Unlike many task-specific theories in information-processing psychology (e.g., models of paired-associate learning or of chess performance), language acquisition is a species-wide and universally solved task, and so mechanisms devoted to it could easily be a part of the human cognitive architecture without violating ecological or evolutionary considerations. Our knowledge of the biology of language, though modest, is certainly consistent with the supposition that there is a special cognitive faculty for learning and using language (see, e.g., Gleitman, 1981, 1983; Lenneberg, 1967; Caplan, 1979; Curtiss, Yamada, and Fromkin, 1979; Walker, 1978). Furthermore, many of the a priori arguments raised against task-specificity do not hold water. For example, the notion that a special language acquisition mechanism is intrinsically unparsimonious is unwarranted, since we have no right to trust our intuitions about how many faculties the brain divides into before we examine the empirical problems facing us and determine how few mechanisms we can get away with. In other words, parsimony criteria can only be applied when deciding among several theories that are equivalent in their explanatory and empirical strengths. Another oftentimes spurious argument against task-specific learning theories is based on the existence of some non-task-specific model that can acquire some fragment of a language. Unless a model is capable of acquiring the complex and elegant linguistic systems of the sort characterized by linguists and addressed in part in this book, it is irrelevant to the debate over task-specificity. Finally, it is not uncommon for skeptics to say, "Well, maybe there is an equally powerful nonspecific theory of language acquisition that no one has thought of yet." But this is simply handwaving of a sort that is not likely to shed much light on the issue one way or another.

I take it to be noncontroversial that a theory that can explain facts in some domain has a prima facie claim to being considered true. To refute such a claim, one would be better off proposing an alternative theory than reiterating one's skepticism or appealing to aprioristic arguments. And so far, task-general learning theories adequate to account for the acquisition of complex linguistic patterns are nowhere to be found (though see Anderson, 1983, for a recent partial attempt).

Not surprisingly, task-specificity is controversial because it is associated with nativism. Strictly speaking, the two issues are independent: it is possible that the child learns a set of procedures that then can be used to learn language and nothing but language. I will argue, however, that a conclusion of task-specificity of the learning mechanisms quickly leads one to a tentative conclusion of nativism because of certain parsimony considerations (above and beyond the various biological arguments for the innateness of language). At the same time, I will suggest a way in which the issue of nativism might be resolved short of biological arguments (see also Osherson and Wasow, 1976, for related arguments).

Task-specific theories try to equip the child with a maximally simple set of universal rule schemata containing parameters whose values vary from language to language, together with procedures for setting those parameters. This is schematized in Figure 2.6, where the set of schemata is referred to as "the acquisition procedure for language" or AP(L). The alternative to positing that a task-specific acquisition procedure is innate is to posit that it itself is learned, by another acquisition procedure one can call AP(AP(L)), schematized in Figure 2.7. However, because the original acquisition procedure AP(L) is, by hypothesis, universal, there is no logical necessity that it be learned (unlike rules for particular languages, which necessarily must be learned), and so the AP(AP(L)) is superfluous to the induction task facing the child. Furthermore, because the acquisition procedure is, also by hypothesis, maximally simple—that is, none of the schemata can be deduced from the rest, and the entire set cannot be deduced from any smaller set of principles (if they could, the smaller set would be the acquisition procedure)—then the acquisition procedure for the acquisition procedure would have to be at least as complex as the acquisition procedure itself. It would have to consist of a mechanism that awaited some piece of input information and then put the AP(L) into place. Because there is a (logically superfluous) contingency between the input and the AP(L) built into AP(AP(L)), the former is more parsimonious (it only needs a statement of the acquisition procedures themselves), and so the hypothesis depicted in Figure 2.6 is to be preferred to that in Figure 2.7.[9]

Of course, the parsimony calculations could change when domains other than language are taken into account once again. Let's say there was a mechanism that acquired not only a task-specific acquisition procedure for language, but also an acquisition procedure for some other cognitive domain, such as logical reasoning, spatial abilities, social cognition, or motor skills, shown as part (a) of Figure 2.8. Alternatively, imagine mechanisms that

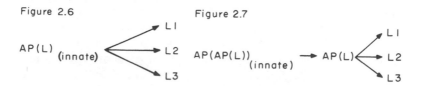

Figure 2.6

AP(L) (innate) → L1
              → L2
              → L3

Figure 2.7

AP(AP(L)) (innate) → AP(L) → L1
                            → L2
                            → L3

Figure 2.8

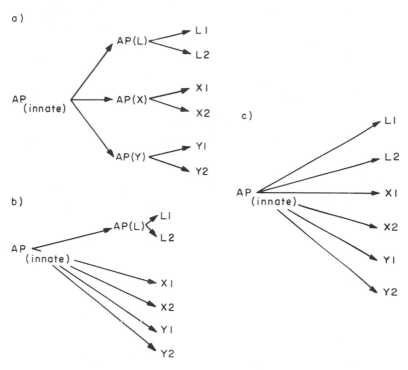

a)

b)

c)

acquire a task-specific language acquisition procedure plus those other nonlinguistic skills directly, part (b) of Figure 2.8. (For ease of comparison, I have also diagrammed, in part (c) of the figure, an acquisition procedure that eschews linguistic task-specificity altogether and that acquires individual languages and individual nonlinguistic cognitive skills directly.) Then the alternative hypotheses shown in Figure 2.8 (a) and (b), namely that there is a "super-acquisition procedure," would be preferred on parsimony grounds to the hypothesis that there is an innate language-specific acquisition procedure. That is because with the super-acquisition procedure one specifies a single mechanism rather than n separate mechanisms for n cognitive faculties. Of course, all this presupposes that the super-acquisition procedure exploits some general principles from which the faculty-specific acquisition procedures can be deduced. If the super-acquisition procedure merely listed a disjunction of the faculty-specific acquisition procedures plus some arbitrary set of input triggers for putting them into place, there would be no parsimony gain in positing the super-acquisition procedures, just as there is no advantage in positing the AP(AP(L)) in Figure 2.7.

According to this argument, then, if the task-specific learning theory I propose in this book is viable, the conclusion that there are innate language acquisition mechanisms is strengthened. The assumption that such a mechanism is innate is more parsimonious than the alternative in Figure 2.7 that would posit a superfluous acquisition procedure for the acquisition procedure. Although it is less parsimonious than the possibilities depicted in Figure 2.8 (a) and (b), at present I see even less cause for optimism that a psychologically plausible super-acquisition procedure can be developed than that a task-general acquisition procedure can be developed. Of course, the question is still very much open, and the conclusions about innateness could be falsified by the discovery of a super-acquisition procedure.[10] In other words, I am proposing that the innateness debate in the study of language acquisition be recast as a parsimony debate concerning rival acquisition theories for language and other cognitive domains. This debate then becomes an empirical one— inasmuch as any empirical debate ultimately hinges on parsimony and elegance, it being commonly accepted that data always underdetermine the theories explaining them.

I expect that the foregoing argument will be seen as obvious by some, as outlandish by others. The conclusion that language acquisition mechanisms are innate, some argue, is so repugnant that any line of reasoning leading to that conclusion must be flawed. There is little to say in response to that argument, since it carries no logical force, other than to note (paraphrasing Jerry Fodor) that stranger things have happened in science. A second argument I have heard is that it is illegitimate to posit innate mechanisms on such indirect argumentation, that what is needed is a more direct empirical demonstration such as neonate studies (see Eimas, Siqueland, Jusczyk and Vigorito, 1971) or genetic, embryological, or neurophysiological evidence. Here one should note that it is commonplace in science for an entity's participation in the best explanation of a phenomenon to be sufficient grounds for proposing that such an entity exists (as with quarks in subatomic physics). In particular, it has long been recognized that a reasonable goal for cognitive science is to use behavioral evidence to discover the innate "elementary information processing mechanisms" (Newell and Simon, 1961, 1972) or "architecture of the cognitive virtual machine" (Pylyshyn, 1980).

A third argument against the proposals is that innateness theories are to be rejected if possible because calling a phenomenon innate leaves the phenomenon unexplained, or postpones an explanation for it. I argue the opposite: that the only way a cognitive phenomenon is explained according to the doctrine of cognitivism is by showing how the phenomenon arises as a result of the operation of some set of innate information-processing mechanisms. All cognitivist theories must presuppose the existence of innate mechanisms (on pain of regress), and those theories that make commitments as to what the minimally necessary set of such mechanisms are have fewer degrees of freedom, hence are more explanatory, than those that ignore the entire question and introduce arbitrary mechanisms as they are needed (see Pylyshyn, 1980, in press, for amplification). A related criticism is that positing innate mechanisms makes the problem "too easy": if all that scientists can say about a skill is that it is innate, that would be a rather trivial contribution to our understanding of the psychology of that skill. I find it hard to believe that anyone can raise this concern in the case of language acquisition. Any language acquisition theory, no matter how nativist, must posit learning mechanisms sufficiently powerful to acquire some five thousand languages differing in hundreds of ways. This puts an extremely high lower bound on the sophistication of the learning component in a nativist theory (ironically, far higher than for many other cognitive skills). Ending up with a trivial learning component is the least of our worries; indeed, given linguistic diversity it is a striking discovery of modern linguistics and psycholinguistics that it is possible to make remotely tenable nativist claims at all. Finally, some argue that calling a phenomenon innate prematurely cuts off an avenue of investigation, namely, the possible precursors, underlying cognitive basis, or deeper nonlinguistic principles that explain the putatively "innate" mechanisms. Again, I see little merit in this argument. Either there exists an underlying nonlinguistic basis for language acquisition mechanisms or there does not. If there does, any theorist is free to propose a theory of what those general mechanisms are, and if such a theory really does account for language acquisition and other phenomena in a simpler manner than a language-specific innateness theory, the latter theory can be rejected as unparsimonious. If no such theory exists, then the innateness theory will win out over all competitors.[11]

THE BOOTSTRAPPING PROBLEM

The Problem

There is another criticism against nativist proposals of language acquisition that I think has greater force. The universal properties of linguistic rules and their parameters of variation concern highly abstract symbols such as noun and verb, subject and object, constituent structure branching geometry, and so on. The child must be sensitive to the behavior of just those symbols in the parental input in order to fix the parameters of variation in his or her universal rule schemas. However, such linguistic entities are not marked in the linguistic input to the prelinguistic child in any way. Nouns, for example, do not appear in any single serial position in the world's languages, do not have a universal pitch or stress level, and do not contain a universal identifying affix. In any particular language, to be sure, nouns have a characteristic distribution: they appear in particular phrase structure positions and are marked with particular affixes, or both. However, this cannot be much help to the child, since the particular phrase structure rules and affixes that signal the presence of nouns in a language are part of what the child has to learn in the first place. What the child does have access to is the linear order of words in the input string, their prosodic properties, and (by hypothesis) the meaning of the sentence. But, as mentioned, linguistic entities such as noun cannot be defined in terms of these properties. As Fodor (1966) has noted, it is not sufficient for a child to know "there exist nouns"; the child must have some way of *finding* nouns in the input (see also Grimshaw 1981; Chomsky, 1981; Macnamara, 1982). And so it is for verbs, subjects, objects, phrase structure, syntactic features, and other symbols included in the rule schemata that theories of universal grammar attribute to the prelinguistic child.

The problem, and the solution to it that I will adopt, can best be illustrated by an example inspired by Grimshaw (1981). Let us simplify the problem drastically by assuming that the only parameter of variation among languages is the order of constituents in phrase structure rules. A schema-plus-parameter theory would have the child know the composition of all constituents in languages but not the linear order of subconstituents within a constituent. This is symbolized by (5), where $X \rightarrow \{Y_1, Y_2, \ldots, Y_n\}$ represents the knowledge that the constituent X consists of the constituents $Y_1 \ldots Y_n$ with no commitments as to which of the $n!$ orders are permissible in particular languages.

(5) $S \rightarrow \{NP_{SUBJ}, VP\}$
   $NP \rightarrow \{(det), N\}$
   $VP \rightarrow \{NP_{OBJ}, V\}$

Let's say the child now hears the sentence *the boy threw rocks*. Intuitively, one would guess that this sentence contains enough

Figure 2.9

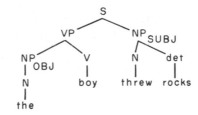

information to fix the order parameter left open by the rule schemata in (5). However, there is nothing to prevent the child from analyzing the sentence as shown in Figure 2.9, from which he or she could deduce the incorrect set of phrase structure rules and lexical entries for English shown in (6).

(6) $S \rightarrow VP\ NP_{SUBJ}$
     $NP \rightarrow N\ (det)$
     $VP \rightarrow NP_{OBJ}\ V$

     the: N
     boy: V
     threw: N
     rocks: det

These rules would cause severe problems when they interacted with other rules or with innate rule acquisition procedures that referred to these symbols (more on this later).

A Solution: The Semantic Bootstrapping Hypothesis

Grimshaw, as well as Macnamara (1982), proposes a solution to the bootstrapping problem. Although grammatical entities do not have semantic definitions in adult grammars, it is possible that such entities refer to identifiable semantic classes in parent-child discourse. That is, it is plausible that, when speaking to infants, parents refer to people and physical objects using nouns, that they refer to physical actions and changes of state using verbs, that they communicate definiteness using determiners, and so on. In addition, propositions with action predicates involving the semantic relations agent-of-action and patient-of-action may be expressed using the grammatical relations SUBJ and OBJ. Presumably, such notions as physical object, physical action, agent-of-action, and so on, unlike nounhood, verbhood, and subjecthood, are available to the child perceptually and are elements of the semantic representation that I proposed as part of the input to the language acquisition mechanisms. If the child tentatively assumes these syntax-semantics correspondences to hold, and if they do hold, he or she can make the correct inferences in the example. The categorization of words can be inferred from their semantic properties, and their grammatical relations can be inferred from the semantic relations in the event witnessed. Together with the schemata in (5) this uniquely determines the correct phrase structure tree shown in Figure 2.10 and the rules and lexical entries of (7).

Figure 2.10

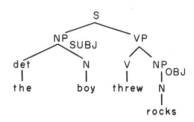

(7) $S \rightarrow NP_{SUBJ} VP$
$NP \rightarrow det N$
$VP \rightarrow V NP_{OBJ}$

the: det
boy: N
threw: V
rocks: N

The hypothesis that the child initially uses semantic notions as evidence for the presence of grammatical entities in the input was called the "semantic bootstrapping hypothesis" in Pinker (1982), and was based on Grimshaw's (1981) proposal that syntactic entities are "canonical structural realizations" of semantic entities and Macnamara's (1982) similar proposal that object, action, and attribute are the "inductive bases" for noun, verb, and adjective. According to the version of the hypothesis I am advancing, the child assumes that the correspondences shown in Table 2.1 hold in the linguistic input.

Structure-Dependent Distributional Learning

Of course, the child can only get so far with semantic bootstrapping, since many nouns do not refer to objects (e.g., *the flight of the bird*), many subjects do not denote agents of actions (e.g., *John sustained an injury; John received a parcel*), and so on. Grimshaw and Macnamara propose that once a basic scaffolding of semantically induced rules and lexical items is in place, the

Table 2.1*

Grammatical element	Semantic inductive basis[12]
SYNTACTIC CATEGORIES	
Noun	Name of person or thing
Verb	Action or change of state
Adjective	Attribute
Preposition	Spatial relation, path, or direction
Sentence	Main proposition
GRAMMATICAL FUNCTIONS[13]	
Subject	Agent of action; cause of causal event; subject of an attribution of location, state, or circumstance; argument with "autonomous reference"
Object and Object2	Patient or theme
Oblique	Source, goal, location, instrument
Complement	Proposition serving as an argument within another proposition
Topic	Discourse topic distinct from the arguments of the main predicate[14]
Focus	Discourse focus
CASES[15]	
Nominative or Ergative	Agent of transitive action
Accusative or Absolutive	Patient of transitive action
Nominative or Absolutive	Actor of intransitive action
Dative	Goal or beneficiary
Instrumental	Instrument
Etc.	
GRAMMATICAL FEATURES	
Tense	Relative times of event, speech act, and reference point
Aspect	Durativity
Number	Number
Human	Humanness
Animate	Animacy
Etc.	
TREE CONFIGURATIONS	
Sister of X	Argument of X
Sister of X' (Aunt of X)	Restrictive modifier of X
Sister of X" (Great-aunt of X)	Nonrestrictive modifier of X

(to be discussed further in Chapter 3)

*Footnotes to this table can be found with the other notes to this chapter.

semantically neutral items and rules can be learned by observing their distribution within the known structures. For example, for the sentence *the situation justified extreme measures*, the child could inspect the grammatical rules in (7) induced from the sentence shown in Figure 2.10. Those rules state that *the* is a determiner, that determiners are only introduced by the phrase structure rule NP → det N, that sentences begin with an NP, and that therefore *situation*, the word following *the* within the NP, must be a noun. Similarly, the phrase *the situation* could be recognized as the subject of the sentence and *justified* as its verb, thanks to the rule S → NP$_{SUBJ}$ VP in the grammar, in turn leading the child to conclude that *justified* uses the function SUBJ to express one of its arguments. Affixes, once they are learned, can also be used to identify syntactic categories—for example, if the past tense marker *-ed* had been identified from semantically transparent cases similar to that shown in Figure 2.10, it too could be used to identify the verbhood of the word *justified*. This process may be called *structure-dependent distributional learning*, "structure-dependent" because it is the distribution of words within constituent or inflectional structures already acquired that triggers learning. This is in contrast to learning procedures based on the distribution of entities in particular serial positions or in particular adjacency or co-occurrence relations with other words (see Pinker, 1979, for discussion).

The hypothesis that the child's learning strategies use a combination of semantic bootstrapping and distributional learning is subtle and controversial, and hence deserves further amplification. In particular, I will address these questions: What exactly is being claimed, anyway? Is the claim viable? What are the alternatives? What is the relevant evidence?

The Logical Status of the Semantic Bootstrapping Hypothesis

Let me begin by pointing out what the semantic bootstrapping hypothesis does not claim. It does not claim that the young child lacks formal categories, or that his or her initial categories are organized around or defined by semantic criteria. Rather, the hypothesis presupposes that the child uses formal categories at all stages, and is intended to explain how the child knows *which* formal categories to posit in response to particular input sequences. Second, it does not claim that children fail to perform distributional analyses or that they allow semantically based analyses to override distributionally based analyses. Rather, it claims that children always give priority to distributionally based analyses, and is intended to explain how the child knows *which* distributional contexts are the relevant ones to examine. In the rest of the chapter, I will spell out these points in detail.

First of all, what does it mean to say that the child has a procedure to recognize antecedently specified formal categories and relations like "nouns" and "subjects"? "Noun" is, after all, just the name for a symbol, and according to the computational theory of cognition the only significance of the name of a symbol in a cognitive account is that the process that manipulates such symbols treats all the symbols with a given name alike but differently from symbols with different names. Thus, if one replaced the symbols *noun, verb, noun phrase,* and *verb phrase* by *Ethel, Fred, Ethel phrase,* and *Fred phrase* everywhere in the adult grammar and processor, the Ethel-Fred grammar would be indistinguishable from the noun-verb grammar. Why worry, then, about how the child learns "nouns" when all he or she really needs to do is learn discriminable symbols?

The answer is that in using a single name to refer to symbols in grammars for different languages, one is committing oneself to the hypothesis that there exist symbols with universal properties across languages. On pain of circularity, this hypothesis must be translated into the hypothesis that certain phenomena tend to be correlated with one another across languages, the names themselves merely denoting the symbols that enter into the correlated set of phenomena. The correlations need not be perfect, and it is not strictly necessary for there to be some subset of phenomena that invariably accompany the symbol; a family resemblance structure will suffice to give meaning to the concept of a universal grammatical symbol.

The concept of "subject" can illustrate this point. In LFG, SUBJ is a symbol referring to (a) the agentive argument of active action predicates; (b) the noun phrase position that is usually the leftmost NP daughter of S; (c) the argument of an embedded complement that may be unexpressed and controlled by an argument of the matrix predicate; (d) the matrix argument that controls an unexpressed complement subject when there is no matrix object present; (e) the argument in active clauses receiving either nominative or ergative case marking in two-place predicates and nominative or absolutive case marking in one-place predicates; (f) the function that objects assume during passivization; (g) the function that becomes oblique during passivization; (h) the function not permitted in the phrase structure rules expanding VP, AP, and nonpredicative NP and PP; (i) the function that can be unexpressed and controlled in an adjunct (this is distinct from (c), which refers to complements as opposed to adjuncts—see Bresnan, 1982c); (j) one of the functions that may be controlled anaphorically (this is distinct from (c) and (i), which refer to functional as opposed to anaphoric control); (k) the specific function whose binding is determined by principles of "obviation" in anaphoric control; (l) the label for one of the set of constituent positions whose grammatical features may be encoded in agreement affixes on verbs. This list could be extended by including several other phenomena such as those involving bounding nodes, reflexives and reciprocals, ellipsis, and other lexical rules. (Many of these conditions are imperfectly stated, and many are probable but not necessary in a given language. See Bresnan, 1982a, c, for further details about these conditions, and Keenan, 1976, for a similar list that is less formal but more firmly grounded in research on linguistic diversity.)

When a linguist examining a particular language uses the term SUBJ, then, to refer to an element in a rule accounting for one of the phenomena in a family resemblance structure such as (a)–(l), he or she is making the empirical prediction that the element so labeled should enter into the remaining phenomena in (a)–(l) (some necessarily, others probabilistically). The use of the term SUBJ in rules for different languages is identical to the hypothesis that (a)–(l) are universally correlated. Such a correlation is unlikely to arise again and again in historically unrelated languages unless there was some property of the minds of speakers of those languages that caused one of the correlated properties to trigger the rest. Thus, the universal correlations in (a)–(l) suggest that the symbols labeled SUBJ which one attributes to the minds of speakers of different languages are in some sense of the same psychological kind.[16] How the child identifies exemplars of that kind in the linguistic input then becomes a meaningful psychological question.

The semantic bootstrapping hypothesis, as it applies to subjects, amounts to the claim that (1) the child uses phenomenon (a) to label certain entities as SUBJs in the first rules he or she coins; (2) thereafter he or she expects the entities labeled SUBJ in those rules to enter into phenomena (b)–(l) as well; and thus (3) those entities are subject, without further learning, to any of the conditions in (b)–(l) that are universally true; and (4) the child fixes the parameters of those phenomena in (b)–(l) that admit of cross-linguistic variation by checking the input for a restricted set of properties of the SUBJ-labeled entities, and a restricted set of co-occurrence relations between the SUBJ-labeled entities and certain other entities. In other words, the child is spared from having to record all perceptible properties and correlations involving the input elements; thanks to having identified certain universal symbols, he or she can exploit formal and substantive linguistic universals to focus the learning process upon those properties and correlations that define differences among languages. Another way of putting it is that the child exploits the "rich deductive structure" (Chomsky, 1981) inherent in the family resemblance correlations defining substantive universals, and at the very start he or she uses the semantically transparent members of the family as the first "premises" of the deductions.

To extend this argument to some other grammatical symbol, it is necessary to show that (1) the symbol enters into a set of phenomena that are universally correlated, analogous to (a)–(l) above (if this is not true, then linguists' use of that same symbol in rules for different languages would be theoretically meaningless, if not downright misleading, see Steele, 1981); (2) one of those phenomena must include some notion that is perceptually available to the child in the semantic portion of his or her input (analogous to (a) above); and (3) when parents express that notion in their speech to the child, they must use the symbol in question (though this need not be true of adult-to-adult discourse). If these conditions are true, then the semantic bootstrapping hypothesis can be applied to the problem of how rules incorporating that symbol are first acquired: the child can use the phenomenon that includes the perceptually available notion as the inductive basis for the symbol in question, expecting the rest of the phenomena involving that symbol to follow (as before, subject to parametric variation).

Do the necessary correlations exist? Of course, if there are no true substantive universals—that is, no family resemblance structures involving collections of semantic and formal phenomena— then the semantic bootstrapping hypothesis cannot be true. Jane Grimshaw (personal communication) points out that there is a great deal of indirect and informal evidence for such substantive universals implicit in the practice of comparative linguists. Grimshaw points out that linguists often do not apply formal tests involving the universally valid earmarks of a category when assigning words to syntactic categories in a newly studied language. For example, even if it is true that the best diagnostic of nounhood is strictly formal, such as that complex phrases headed by nouns cannot be extracted from, comparative linguists do not generally test for extractability from various constituents before deciding whether to call the head of such a constituent a noun.

Rather, they use semantic notions as their first hypothesis about the category membership of an unknown word: for example, if a word is a proper name, they call it a noun. All this is unexceptional. But what is interesting is that such a strategy rarely leads to trouble. Linguists seldom have to recategorize large sets of words after examining other phenomena in the language; for example, there do not seem to be languages in which the extraction phenomena associated with noun phrases in English pertain to action words but not names. To the extent that semantically inspired categorization of common word types (e.g., those likely to be used in parent-child discourse) does not lead to descriptive crises for the linguist, it is not unreasonable to assume that the child, too, can safely begin by categorizing words in this way.

There are also more systematic studies of substantive universals. Names for individual things and people are almost always nouns (Gleason, 1961; Greenberg, 1963; Macnamara, 1982).[17] Auxiliaries have the semantic property of designating sentence modality, tense, aspect, epistemic status, and modal concepts such as necessity, possibility, impossibility, and the like; this semantic property correlates universally with the syntactic and morphological privileges of auxiliaries, such as appearing in designated phrase structure positions, lacking productive morphology, being contractible, constituting a closed class, and signaling sentence modality by virtue of the positions they appear in (Steele, 1981). And subjects, as mentioned, have the semantic properties of designating agents of actions, causes of causal sequences, subjects of an attribution, autonomous reference, and definiteness, together with their formal properties of occurring to the left of the object, being unexpressed in complements, easily taking zero case marking, and so on (Keenan, 1976).[18]

One must place an important proviso, however, on the use of semantic information to infer the presence of syntactic symbols, especially grammatical relations. Keenan argues that the semantic properties of subjecthood hold only in what he calls "basic sentences": roughly, those that are simple, active, affirmative, declarative, pragmatically neutral, and minimally presuppositional. In nonbasic sentences, these properties may not hold. In English passives, for example, agents can be oblique objects and patients subjects, and in stylistically varied or contextually dependent sentences the agent can be found in nonsubject positions (e.g., *eats a lot of pizza, that guy*). Thus one must have the child not draw conclusions about grammatical relations from nonbasic sentences. This could be done in two ways: the parents or caretakers might filter out nonbasic sentences from their speech when they talk to infants, or the child might filter out nonbasic sentences from the input using various contextual or phonological diagnostics of nonbasicness such as special intonation, extra marking on the verb, presuppositions set up by the preceding discourse or the context, nonlinguistic signals of the interrogative or negative illocutionary force of an utterance, and so on. (Sentences perceived to be nonbasic need not be filtered out altogether, of course; the child can use them to learn aspects of grammar that are not sensitive to basicness such as the internal structure of noun phrases, while denying those inputs access to the mechanisms that learn about grammatical relations). Later in the chapter I will discuss some evidence pertaining to the speech of adults to children; I know of no research directly addressed to the question of whether children can reliably perceive the nonlinguistic correlates of basicness in Keenan's sense (though see Hoff-Ginsberg and Shatz, 1982). My guess is that both types of filtering are at work; but in any case it is important to point out that a viable version of the semantic bootstrapping hypothesis requires that the semantically driven inferences occur only on the inputs that pass through such filters, given what we know about the nature of the linguistic universals pertaining to subjects.

ALTERNATIVES TO THE SEMANTIC BOOTSTRAPPING HYPOTHESIS

There are two sorts of alternatives to semantic bootstrapping. One is the possibility that the child discovers entire patterns of correlations among grammatical phenomena rather than identifying one phenomenon in a correlated set and using it to predict the rest. The second is the possibility that some phenomenon in the correlated set other than a semantic phenomenon is used to identify the set. I discuss each set of alternatives separately.

Discovering the Pattern of Correlation

According to this hypothesis, a version of which is outlined by Maratsos and Chalkley (1981), the child constructs a contingency table—say a lower triangular matrix—whose rows, and therefore columns, correspond to various sentence positions, arguments, and inflections (including the semantic notions they encode), and whose cells are filled with the words that are found to participate in the conjunction of phenomena indicated by the row and column. The equivalent of a grammatical category arises when the child notices that certain cells in the matrix are filled with large numbers of words, or when various cells contain the same set of words.[19] To take a simplified example, the same set of words (what we would call nouns) occurs in all six cells representing the pairings of preverbal position, postverbal position, inflection with -s encoding plurality, and inflection with -s encoding possession. According to this model, the larger the set of words occurring in the same set of cells, the more likely the child is to generalize that a new word found in one cell may be placed in the rest. This model differs from the one I have proposed in that here the child discovers the pattern of correlation among grammatical phenomena, rather than identifying an item as having a critical, semantically defined property and then innately predicting that it is likely to have the rest of the correlated properties. I have two arguments against various forms of the contingency-table hypothesis, which I will call the *learnability argument* and the *efficiency argument*.

The learnability argument, conceived by Jane Grimshaw (personal communication), is that some of the properties that the child must come to know about grammatical entities are unlearnable in the absence of negative evidence (which is the situation human children are faced with). If so, having versus not having such a property cannot be one of the things that the child learns is correlated with other properties. Since children do come to know (as adults) that that property is correlated with the others, it cannot be that they discovered the correlation; they must have deduced it instead. An example of such a property is being the head of a complex phrase from which nothing can be extracted, which is true of nouns (e.g., *who did he believe the claim that John saw?*) but not of other categories (e.g., *who did he say that John saw?*) This is Ross's (1967) "Complex Noun Phrase Constraint," which I use for convenience; the argument also works when we consider more sophisticated theories of the extractability phenomena addressed by the CNPC. Since the child is not corrected for speaking ungrammatically, he or she cannot learn that certain elements have this property by uttering complex phrases of various sorts with extracted constituents and waiting for feedback as to their admissibility. The only possible clue in the input that nouns have such a property is that adults never use sentences involving extraction from complex noun phrases. But the child cannot use this absence as evidence, since as far as he or she is concerned the very next sentence in the input could have extraction from a complex noun phrase, and their absence until then could have arisen from sampling error or a paucity of opportunities for the adult to utter such sentences.

Thus the child must antecedently know that an element is a noun to predict that it obeys the Complex Noun Phrase Constraint; he or she cannot use conformity with the Complex Noun Phrase Constraint as part of the discovery procedure for nounhood.

The second argument concerns properties of elements that *are* detectable from positive evidence. The problem here is the selection of the rows and columns of the contingency table, that is, the properties of elements whose intercorrelations the child will attend to. As I argued in Pinker (1979), in most distributional learning procedures there are vast numbers of properties that a learner could record, and since the child is looking for correlations among these properties, he or she faces a combinatorial explosion of possibilities. For example, he or she could record of a given word that it occurs in the first (or second, or third, or *n*th) position in a sentence, that it is to the left (or right) of word X or word Y or . . . , or that it is to the left of the word sequence $WXYZ$, or that it occurs in the same sentence with word X (or words X, Y, Z, or some subset of them), and so on. Adding semantic and inflectional information to the space of possibilities only makes the explosion more explosive. To be sure, the inappropriate properties will correlate with no others and hence will eventually be ignored, leaving only the appropriate grammatical properties, but only after astronomical amounts of memory space, computation, or both.

In any case, most of these properties should be eliminated by an astute learner as being inappropriate to learning a human language in the first place. For example, there is no linguistic phenomenon in any language that is contingent upon a word's occupying the third serial position in a sentence, so why bother testing for one? Testing for correlations among irrelevant properties is not only wasteful but potentially dangerous, since many spurious correlations will arise in local samples of the input. For example, the child could hear the sentences *John eats meat, John eats slowly*, and *the meat is good* and then conclude that *the slowly is good* is a possible English sentence (see Pinker, 1979, for further discussion).

Perhaps, then, one can constrain the child to test for correlations only among linguistically relevant properties. There are two problems with this move. First of all, most linguistically relevant properties are abstract, pertaining to phrase structure configurations, syntactic categories, grammatical relations, and so on. (For instance, there are grammatically relevant consequences of a word's appearing in the subject noun phrase of a sentence, not of its being in the first serial position of a sentence.) But these abstract properties are just the ones that the child cannot detect in the input prior to learning, for the reasons I outlined when proposing semantic bootstrapping. (The argument in the previous paragraph owes its force to the fact that the contrapositive (roughly) is true: the properties that the child can detect in the input—such as the serial positions and adjacency and co-occurrence relations among words—are in general linguistically irrelevant.) Furthermore, even looking for correlations among linguistically relevant properties is unnecessarily wasteful, for not only do languages use only certain properties and not others, they sanction only certain types of correlations among those properties. For example, being positioned between a determiner and a noun is noteworthy in general, for such a property is true of all words that can be inflected for comparative degree of intensity, that are heads of phrases that cannot contain objects, that can be interrogated in *wh*-questions, that can be modified by adverbs, and so on (namely adjectives). However, it is not the kind of property that is true of all words whose phrasal constituents could undergo passivization (e.g., *John became senile/*Senile was become by John*), nor all words whose phrasal nodes block extraction (e.g., *which race are you happy that John won?*), nor all words that can be inverted to form questions (e.g., **happy the man went?*). In these cases, the necessary property is having the grammatical relation OBJ, being a bounding node, or bearing the feature AUX, respectively. Similarly, being inflected for tense and aspect is linguistically relevant in general, since it may be true of verbs and auxiliaries, but it is not the kind of property that is ever correlated with the properties of nouns. The child will learn fastest, and make the fewest errors, if he constrains his search for correlations to those correlations that are possible in language. Furthermore, if the child's learning mechanisms are designed to do so, one has an explanation as to why the entire pattern of correlations should exist across languages to begin with. Under the contingency table hypothesis, this would be a mystery.

Nonsemantic Bootstrapping

The second alternative to the bootstrapping hypothesis would differ from the contingency table hypothesis in that, like my proposal, it would have the child look for the presence of universal syntactic symbols from which a variety of properties could then be deduced. However, it would differ from the bootstrapping hypothesis in not designating any semantic property as the inductive basis for the symbol. Instead, some other property of that symbol chosen from the correlated set would serve as the inductive basis. The problem with almost every nonsemantic property that I have heard proposed as inductive bases is that the property is itself defined over configurations of abstract symbols that are not part of the child's input, that themselves have to be learned. For example, some informal proposals I have heard start from the assumption that the child knows the geometry of the phrase structure tree of a sentence, or the fact that two words in the sentence belong to the same category, or, even worse, the syntactic categories and grammatical relations of phrases. But how the child comes to know such things, which are not marked explicitly in the input stream, is precisely what the semantic bootstrapping hypothesis is designed to explain.

However, there is one nonsemantic property I have not discussed that is available in the child's input: the prosodic properties of the word string (primarily intonation, pausing, and lengthening). Morgan and Newport (1981), having demonstrated that college students learn artificial languages rapidly when they are provided with information about constituent structure, speculate that prosodic cues might provide the child with similar information, and thereby allow the child to coin rules containing the right sorts of units (i.e., phrase types; see also Gleitman and Wanner, 1982b). For example, Cooper and Paccia-Cooper (1980) have found that timing, lengthening, and pausing in spoken English are systematically related to the geometry of the phrase structure tree. If the child can invert the function mapping syntactic structure onto the prosodic contour, he or she could recover the syntactic analysis of input sentences without depending on any correspondence between syntax and semantics, and would then be in a position to coin correct rules for the language.

In the absence of a proposal on how such a scheme would work in practice, it is too early to evaluate the hypothesis, although I feel it is an avenue of research well worth pursuing. I am pessimistic, however, about the possibility that some "prosodic bootstrapping" model could do without the assumptions about semantics that I have made altogether. First of all, it is not clear whether Cooper and Paccia-Cooper's correlations between syntax and prosody are universal, as opposed to being rules of English phonology, and they would have to be universal for the child to be able to exploit them in learning an arbitrary natural language. Furthermore, Cooper and Paccia-Cooper's effects were demonstrated by having college students read aloud carefully designed sets of minimally contrasting sentences. This was necessary because the effects they sought are quite small in comparison with the effects of intrinsic word length, syllable structure, phonetic composition, sentence length, word frequency, word-finding difficulties, and other confounding factors. Thus the child must have some way of mentally subtracting the effects of all these factors in natural discourse before he or she can invert the syntax-to-speech encoding function and recover the syntactic analyses of sentences. I think it is fairly unlikely that a universally valid subtraction-and-inversion procedure of this sort exists, let alone that it is available to a child who has not yet learned anything about his or her language. Finally, Cooper and Paccia-Cooper note that they failed to find any prosodic reflexes of syntactic categories, only of tree geometry. Thus the child would need some other sort of information to know whether a phrase is a noun phrase or a verb phrase. Thus some use of prosodic information can perhaps be made in language acquisition, but I doubt that it can replace the use of semantic information entirely.

EVIDENCE PERTAINING TO THE SEMANTIC BOOTSTRAPPING HYPOTHESIS

Can the semantic bootstrapping hypothesis be submitted to an empirical test? In this section I try to answer that question. First, of course, inasmuch as the hypothesis plays a role in successful accounts of the empirical fact that languages are successfully learned, the hypothesis receives indirect empirical support. Furthermore, the hypothesis also accounts for the fact that universally certain semantic notions (e.g., names for physical objects) are canonically encoded by syntactic primitives that have certain formal properties not predictable from the semantic notions (e.g., the property of being the head of a complex phrase from which nothing can be extracted). However, given that these two facts motivated the hypothesis in the first place, they cannot be taken as strong evidence for it. Here I discuss potential evidence pertaining to the hypothesis from the domains of children's language and parental speech to children.

What Would Not Be Evidence

Before I begin the discussion, I must stress that the predictions of the semantic bootstrapping hypothesis pertain to the mentally represented rules of the child, not to his or her behavior directly. Thus children's communicative interests, their use of rote patterns, their arbitrary word combinations when no rule ordering words has yet been learned, and their processing limitations must be factored out of any corpus of their speech before it can be used to test hypotheses about the nature of the rules learned from the input.

It might be thought that the semantic bootstrapping hypothesis predicts that children's speech should at first be governed by rules referring to semantic categories such as agent and action and that the hypothesis would be supported if the regularities in children's early speech were all semantic, weakened if they were syntactic. Unfortunately, matters are not so simple. First of all, the version of the hypothesis that I am arguing for predicts that children use semantic notions as evidence that a particular grammatical category or relation is being used in the input. The conclusions they draw about the language are purely syntactic. That is, when the child hears *snails eat leaves*, he or she uses the actionhood of *eat* to infer that it is a verb, the agenthood of *snails* to infer that it plays the role of subject, and so on. However, the rules induced as a result are those in (8), not (9).

(8) (a) $S \rightarrow NP_{SUBJ} \, VP$
    (b) $VP \rightarrow V \, NP_{OBJ}$

(9) (a) $S \rightarrow PHYS\text{-}OBJ\text{-}PHRASE_{AGENT}$ ACTION-PHRASE
    (b) ACTION-PHRASE $\rightarrow$ ACTION-WORD PHYS-OBJ-PHRASE$_{PATIENT}$

At this stage, all the child's nouns are object words, all his or her verbs are action words, and so on; thus the child's grammar (8) mimics grammar (9). However, as soon as the child's distributional learning procedures begin to operate, non-action verbs are learned (e.g., *resemble* can be learned at that point from the sentence *snails resemble leaves*). At that point the outputs of the two grammars can begin to diverge. And there is nothing in the theory as I have presented it so far that specifies when in development the distributional procedures could begin to operate, other than that there must be enough semantically induced rules in the child's grammar to specify the phrase structure position of the unknown word. Distributional learning could even proceed on the second input sentence, and the child could, in principle, learn abstract words at that point. Thus while the semantic bootstrapping hypothesis predicts that the set of rules and lexical entries learned from the *first* sentence should generate a semantically restricted set of sentences (and this is because of the range of lexical entries learned, not because of the phrase structure rules, which are strictly syntactic), the hypothesis by itself does not predict what the semantic properties of the *second* set of rules learned must be.

Another way of stating this limitation is that the hypothesis makes predictions about which rules the child will induce in response to particular sequences of inputs, not simply about which rules the child should possess at any given stage. It is, after all, a hypothesis about language acquisition, not about children's linguistic abilities per se. If the child hears semantically arbitrary constructions as his or her first inputs, he or she will not induce any rules; if the child hears semantically arbitrary constructions close enough in form (a notion I will define later) to semantically transparent sentences heard earlier in the input, he or she can learn syntactic rules generating such sentences; if the semantically arbitrary sentences the child hears are not close enough in form to previously heard sentences to be analyzed distributionally, his or her grammar will continue to generate only semantically restricted sentences.

What Would Be Evidence

Since the bootstrapping hypothesis is a hypothesis about learning—the relation of the child's rule system to prior inputs—it can be tested empirically only by manipulating the inputs to the child and by ascertaining the nature of the rule system induced. Naturally, the former is impossible to do for ethical reasons, and the latter must be done by highly indirect methods, but the point is that, at least in principle, many experiments testing the semantic bootstrapping hypothesis are possible. For example, let's say an infant subject was exposed to the same range of syntactic constructions, and in the same order, as real-life children, but the sentences never referred to actions, objects, and the like. According to the hypothesis, no syntactic learning should take place. Unfortunately, an alternative explanation for such a result might be that the child did not find enough of interest in that abstract input sequence even to pay attention (though if a child could be created, perhaps through genetic engineering, with more abstract interests but with intact language acquisition mechanisms, he or she should still not learn in that experiment, according to the hypothesis).

Still, one can conceive of experiments that circumvent that problem. Imagine exposing a child to an input sequence beginning with passive sentences only. According to the hypothesis, the child would mistakenly conclude that English is an OVS language, since he uses patienthood as evidence for OBJ, agenthood as evidence for SUBJ (the *by* in the agent phrase could be conceived of as an optional nominative case marker, the various forms of *be* as obligatory tense-carrying auxiliaries). Then active sentences could be introduced, which the child would interpret as OVS sentences containing an alternative, "passive" lexical entry for the main verb (the reason the child does this will become apparent in the next chapter). Thus, in this scenario, the child would have the means to encode a full range of semantic notions in the same way that a real-life child does (unlike the previous thought experiment), and he or she would be exposed to the full range of syntactic constructions in the adult language, satisfying a theorist believing only in distributional analysis as a learning mechanism. According to the bootstrapping hypothesis, however, that child's rules should differ crucially from those of real-life children in having the SUBJ and OBJ functions appearing in the wrong places in the phrase structure rules. Though to a casual observer the child might appear to be doing fine at that point, any subsequent learning that uses mechanisms that invoke SUBJ and OBJ should go awry. For example, when the child hears *John told Bill to kiss Mary*, he or she would use a procedure that allows a missing complement subject to be equated with the matrix object if there is one, the matrix subject otherwise. Our experimental child would be unable to analyze this sentence, since as far as he or she is concerned, it is not the subject that is missing from the complement but the object. If somehow the child did manage to analyze the complement phrase, he or she would interpret it incorrectly (or have trouble learning the correct interpretation if it was pointed out to him or her): the child would interpret *John*, the object according to his or her grammar, as the intended kisser, rather than *Bill*, the object for a real-life child. And if the child somehow overcame that problem, unlike real-life learners, he or she should accept as grammatical the sentence *John was promised by Bill to leave*, since *by Bill*, analyzed as the subject by this child, is then allowed to be a controller, whereas its real-life analysis as an oblique object precludes it from having that role (see Chapter 6 for further details).

An analogous experiment, pertaining to syntactic categories this time, might give an experimental child an artificial input sequence in which physical objects were encoded by categories having the same distribution as verbs in real English, and actions were encoded by categories having the same characteristics as English nouns (thus *snails eat leaves* would be expressed perhaps as *eat snails to leaves*; *snails like to slither* might be expressed as *like snails slither*). According to the bootstrapping hypothesis, such a child would be unable to extract from what are, distributionally, and for ordinary English speakers, complex verb phrases (since the child has mistakenly analyzed them as noun phrases because they refer to objects), and would extract freely from what are, to us, complex noun phrases.

Of course, if ethical considerations did not prevent us from doing these experiments, we would still have to design them carefully to rule out various alternative explanations. My rough description of possible experiments is intended only to make the logical point that the semantic bootstrapping hypothesis is indeed testable in principle, albeit not as easily in practice.

Early Speech as Evidence

It still is possible, however, to use children's speech as indirect evidence pertaining to the bootstrapping hypothesis. I have stressed that the hypothesis, strictly speaking, makes only the prediction that the *first* classified words in each category respect the syntax-semantics correlations, leaving it open what the properties of the *second* classified words in each category should be. In the preceding section, I downplayed the use of evidence from spontaneous speech on this matter because of limitations on investigators' abilities to record the exact antecedent parental inputs, to be sure that the combinations recorded were indeed the child's first exemplars of given categories, and to be sure that the order of appearance of rule exemplars in a corpus actually reflected the order of acquisition of the rules themselves. (For example, the child could first learn rule *A* but not use it right away in uttering a sentence in the presence of an investigator, then learn rule *B* and use it immediately.)

Despite all these worries, in practice it would certainly be reasonable to expect that *in general* children's very early speech will reflect the syntax-semantics correspondences. In general, the first combinations recorded will be the first combinations uttered (especially in diary studies by parent-investigators); in general, the first rules learned will manifest themselves in the child's speech (since nothing would lead us to expect that rules would be latent or dormant, and opportunities for using the rules should be frequent); in general, one expects that parents do not relax the syntax-semantics correlations in their speech the instant that the child learns a single exemplar of each relevant category; and in general, one expects the accretion of rules (and possibly, the strengthening of rules) to be slow enough that large amounts of structure-dependent distributional learning do not follow the very first acquisitions. The effect of all these reasonable assumptions is that the bootstrapping hypothesis predicts that (more or less) children's earliest combinations will respect the syntax-semantics correlations outlined earlier. Detailed discussion of the nature of children's early word combinations will be reserved for Chapter 4, but I would like to mention here the noteworthy fact that children's first nouns appear universally to refer to physical objects, their first verbs to actions, adjectives to attributes, grammatical subjects to actors, experiencers, or subjects of a predication (e.g., location, attribute, or class), their grammatical objects to patients, and so on (e.g., Brown, 1973; Bowerman, 1973; Macnamara, 1982; Nelson, 1973; Slobin, 1973). In saying this I am admittedly opening several cans of worms (to mention two: How do we know that what are nouns and verbs for us are also nouns and verbs for the child? Are the supposed semantic categories as broad for the child as I have construed them?). I will try to round up those worms in the next chapter. However, I mention this general observation, which has been widely noted informally even if its precise statement is controversial, because if it were not observed (e.g., if children first used what are, to us, nouns that did not refer to physical objects), the bootstrapping hypothesis would be in deep trouble.

Other bits and pieces of indirect developmental evidence for semantic bootstrapping can be found. It has been noted that children occasionally use a grammatical device at first to refer only to a semantically restricted set of entities (e.g., the accusative case marker to refer to patients of physical actions: Slobin, 1973; the ergative case marker to refer only to agents of physical actions: Slobin, 1984a; consistent verb-object order only when the objects are not potential actors: Braine, 1976). Furthermore, children also occasionally assign verbhood to sounds that could be taken to denote actions, with agents appearing preverbally and patients postverbally, such as *Mommy oops* (Bowerman, 1973); *Betty hhh* [a blowing sound] *Stevie*; *Odi hello* (= talks on the telephone); or *doggie wuf-wuf* (Braine, 1971a). Other cases where the child invents verbs for actions, always with agent-patient order, are discussed in detail in Chapter 8, including cases in which the relationship between the novel form created by the child and the input word that the child based his or her creation on are not exemplified in the adult language. Slobin (1984a) reports an observation from Clancy that Japanese children mistakenly apply markers for true adjectives to a class of words that refer to attributes but have the syntactic privileges of nouns ("nominal adjectives"), even though the adjectives in the nominal adjective class are more frequent in the children's speech.

Marantz (1982) presented 3-, 4-, and 5-year-olds with a made-up verb in a sentence together with a novel action illustrating the sentence. The verb either corresponded in form to what the child would hypothesize under the bootstrapping hypothesis, with SUBJ encoding the agent argument and OBJ the patient argument (*John is moaking the table* would mean he is pounding it with his elbow), or the verb used SUBJ to encode the patient argument and OBJ for the agent argument (*the table is moaking John* would be the way to use *moak* to express the fact that he is pounding it with his elbow). Marantz found that the 3- and 4-year-old children had little trouble learning the canonical verbs but considerable difficulty learning the noncanonical ones.[20]

All of these phenomena are to be expected if children's first rules containing particular grammatical symbols are learned from input sentences using these symbols in semantically restricted ways. For many reasons, these phenomena are controversial and must be interpreted with care. To take just one problem, the children who created the novel agent-action-patient sequences had been contaminated by hearing many such sequences in the input (in Chapters 4 and 8, I examine these data in more detail). However, the "semantic look" of children's first words and rules has been widely (albeit informally) documented, and it is consistent with the semantic bootstrapping hypothesis under the set of assumptions listed above.

Evidence Pertaining to Structure-Dependent Distributional Learning

Even more so than for semantic bootstrapping, the proper empirical tests of structure-dependent distributional learning will be from experiments controlling the input to the child and testing his or her resulting learning rather than from spontaneous speech analyses. Unfortunately, few such studies have been done, and those that have been done have necessarily focused on the acquisition of lexical entries and of syntactic features such as *count* versus *mass* rather than fundamental phrase structure rules and grammatical relations (necessarily, because it is unlikely that a few minutes of exposure to a new syntactic construction in a laboratory would be sufficient to establish a basic rule conflicting with those acquired on the basis of years of exposure). A further problem is that children will generally submit to the appropriate experimental procedures only at a relatively advanced age.

Still, there are some informative studies that have manipulated the syntactic form of a novel word independently of its semantic referent. In Marantz's study, for noncanonical verbs like *moak* in the sentence *the table is moaking John,* children could learn the grammatical relations encoding the verb arguments only from their distribution within the sentence. He found that 5-year-olds had relatively little difficulty in acquiring the anomalous verbs, though 4-year-olds and 3-year-olds had more difficulty. In a similar vein, Lebeaux and Pinker (1981) found that 4-year-olds had no trouble acquiring novel verbs modeled in the passive voice. Since passive lexical entries always violate the syntax-semantics correspondence presupposed by the bootstrapping hypothesis, they must have been acquired distributionally.[21] (These and other examples are discussed in more detail in Chapter 8.) Brown (1957) showed that when a single picture contains an action, a countable object, and a substance (e.g., hands kneading a substance in a container) and the picture is paired with a description containing a novel word with the syntactic distribution of a verb (e.g., *sibbing*), children interpret the word as referring to the action. The same word presented in conjunction with the same picture but used with the syntactic distribution of a count noun (*the sib*) was understood as referring to the object; with the distribution of a mass noun (*some sib*) it was understood as referring to the substance. Gordon (1982) obtained similar results. Since the semantics of the situation were ambiguous, the children must have been attending to the syntactic distribution of the words (and, incidentally, using the syntactic categories or features thereby induced to predict the semantic properties of the words). The experiment showing the youngest use of distributional information to learn semantically indeterminate words was done by Katz, Baker, and Macnamara (1974), recently replicated by Gelman and Taylor (1983). They showed that girls as young as 17 months tended to treat a novel name for a doll as a common noun if it was preceded by an article in the experimenters' speech, and as a proper noun otherwise (though this distinction was not made by boys of the same age, nor by girls of that age when the name referred to a block rather than a doll).

In sum, there is good reason to believe that children from 1½ to 6 years can use the syntactic distribution of a newly heard word to induce its linguistic properties, even when the semantics of the accompanying situation are ambiguous or are contrary to the syntax. At the same time, it should be pointed out that this distributional learning seems to sum or interact with semantically driven inductions. In the Marantz study, young children learned canonical verbs more easily than the noncanonical ones; in the Lebeaux and Pinker study, children learned actives more easily than passives; and in the Katz et al. study, the girls attended to the syntactic markers of the common-proper distinction only when the referent had a semantic property—personhood—that was compatible with its being able to receive a proper name at all. (Quite possibly, the boys failed to attend to the syntactic distinction because they were less willing to bestow personhood on dolls.) For the present purposes, though, it is sufficient to show that children do engage in distributional learning during most of their language acquisition years.

Evidence on Parental Speech

As I have mentioned, for semantic bootstrapping to work for grammatical relations, either the child must filter out nonbasic sentences using contextual information concerning illocutionary force, presupposition, intonation, and so on, or else the parent or caretaker must filter out such sentences from his or her own speech. These two filtering processes can trade off against each other, so long as the child can always identify unambiguously basic sentences. Thus if the child cannot filter out certain classes of nonbasic sentences, there is a corresponding burden on the parent not to say them. Similarly, if there are sentences violating the canonical syntax-semantics correspondences assumed by the bootstrapping mechanism that cannot be ruled out by any analogue of Keenan's "basicness," parental filtering is the only thing standing in the way of incorrect learning. Thus the degree to which such correspondences are respected in parental speech is an important issue for semantic bootstrapping theories; specifically, its importance is inversely proportional to the power of the syntactically relevant input filters one can plausibly attribute to the child.

We know that adult-to-adult speech contains many violations of these correspondences. In sentences like *bellicose foreign policies divert attention from domestic economic failures*, the word meanings and semantic relations are abstract. However, if parental speech merely contains abstract relations, no harm is done to the child. Even if the child understands such sentences, they contain no semantic triggers for syntactic entities, and so the child will simply not change his or her rule system. Problems arise only when adults use some semantic trigger in a syntactic construction other than the one that canonically corresponds to it. Examples include verbal passives (for reasons mentioned); nominalizations (*I'm going to give you a spanking*); verbs whose subjects could be construed as patients or other semantic relations having their own canonical grammatical function (*Tiny sus-*

tained an injury; trees surrounded the house; John received a parcel); nouns that could be construed as referring to spatial relations (*the underside of the table*), or actions (*the fight between the men*), or attributes (*the redness of the sun*); adjectives that could be construed as referring to actions (*John is rambunctious*) or spatial relations (*close to the barn*); and so on. If parents used such constructions as the first exemplars of a given syntactic form when speaking to their children, the child could make serious errors not only in categorizing a given item but in postulating the phrase structure rules, inflectional paradigms, and syntactic parameters of the language. For example, if a child heard *you will get a spanking from me* in his or her first inputs, the child might conclude that English is an OVS language, with *from* as a nominative case marker and *a* as a verb phrase complementizer or modifier. The plausibility of the hypothesis, then, depends on constructions with noncanonical syntax-semantics pairings being rare in early parental speech to children. Note that the regularities are unidirectional—physical objects must be expressed as nouns, but nouns need not express only physical objects; the same is true for agents of action predicates and subjects.

Many people have studied semantic properties of parental speech in the last decade (see Snow and Ferguson, 1977), but most of these studies have not examined the way in which the semantic notions were expressed syntactically and so are not relevant to the hypothesis under consideration. However, Pinker and Hochberg (in preparation) have examined the syntax-semantics correspondences in the transcribed speech of the parents of Brown's (1973) Adam, Eve, and Sarah when the children were in Brown's "Stage I." We sorted the verbs, nouns, adjectives, and prepositions in that speech into semantic categories such as object, person, spatial relation, physical attribute, possession, epistemic relation, path, psychological state, abstract, and several others. Similarly, we classified instances of the grammatical relations subject, object, indirect object, and various prepositional objects into classes of thematic or semantic relations such as agent, patient, recipient, experiencer, beneficiary, instrument, actor, subject of a predication, and so on. Care was taken to sort each syntactic element into a semantic category on the basis of its semantics alone, ignoring the syntax. In addition, frequencies of various complex syntactic constructions were tabulated. Although the data from this study have not yet been completely analyzed, several preliminary findings have emerged, and they are consistent with the semantic bootstrapping hypothesis. All the agents of actions were expressed as subjects of verbs (there were no full passives in the entire sample examined); 88 percent of the actions were expressed as verbs (there were few nominalizations); all the mentions of physical objects used nouns or pronouns (as would be the case for adult-to-adult speech as well); all the physical attributes were expressed as adjectives (there was nothing like a de-adjectival noun); and all the spatial relations were expressed as prepositions or pro-prepositions like *there* and *downstairs*.

The converses of these statements did not always hold; for example, only 37 percent of verbs referred to actions and only 51 percent of nouns referred to things. As mentioned, however, this does not lead the child astray unless the noncanonical semantic notion expressed by a syntactic unit happens to be a trigger for some other syntactic unit, in which case it would then have entered into the percentages reported in the paragraph above. I tentatively assume, therefore, that parental speech to children, at least for English-speaking children, respects canonical syntax-semantics correspondences closely enough that a semantic bootstrapping strategy will lead to few serious errors even in the absence of sophisticated input filtering by the child.

Incidentally, I do not conclude from these analyses that parents are modifying their speech so as to facilitate their children's language learning. Rather, I would conjecture that the various semantic entities and relations that serve as inductive bases are simply the most salient elements in infants' cognitive repertoires, and that adults talk about things and actions because that's what infants are preoccupied with. Languages evolved with canonical grammaticizations of just these elements so that infants could learn them.

3 | Phrase Structure Rules

PHRASE STRUCTURE RULES are at the heart of a Lexical Functional Grammar and are also among the child's first acquisitions—hence they are an appropriate starting point for my investigations. In this chapter I present a set of procedures that take a string of words plus a semantic representation as input, and yield phrase structure rules as output. In the next chapter I examine the facts of children's acquisition of those rules and attempt to account for the facts in terms of the intermediate outputs of the acquisition mechanisms, sometimes modifying the mechanisms as a result if that can be done in a motivated way.

The X-bar Theory of Phrase Structure Rules

Before presenting the procedures that acquire phrase structure rules, it is necessary to outline the theory of phrase structure rules that defines what the procedures acquire. I will adopt a version of Chomsky's (1970) and Jackendoff's (1977) "X-bar" theory of phrase structure rules—in particular, the following provisions:

1. Major lexical categories (N, V, A, P) are introduced as constituents (specifically, the "head" constituent) of phrasal categories specific to them (NP, VP, AP, PP, or, in the notation of the theory, N', V', A', P'; I will use a notation whereby primes rather than bars designate phrasal categories). These phrasal categories are in turn introduced as head constituents of superordinate phrasal categories (N", V", A", P"). (In some versions of the theory—e.g., Jackendoff, 1977—there must be a third "level of projection," and this is what I assumed in Pinker, 1982. In this section I will assume, with Bresnan, 1977, 1982c, a two-level theory.)

2. All constituents other than the head are either specifiers (minor lexical categories like determiners and complementizers, with no superordinate projections) or complements (the maximal projections of the major categories N, V, A, and P). Specifiers are attached at a level of projection that varies from one type of specifier to another in a manner related to their relative scopes (see, e.g., Baker, 1979, and Wexler and Culicover, 1980, who suggest that determiners are universally attached at a higher level than numbers, which in turn are attached at a higher level than adjectives). In the canonical or unmarkéd case, complements are attached at a level that depends on the semantic relation between the complement and the head. Specifically, a complement that is a logical argument of the predicate symbolized by the head (e.g., *John* in *Mary hit John, a picture of John, proud of John,* or *near John*) is attached as a sister of the head, that is, as a daughter of X'. Modifiers of the head, on the other hand (e.g., *in the park* in *John hit Mary in the park*), are attached as the sister of the category dominating the head, that is, as a daughter of X''. Thus, the verb phrase structure permitted by X-bar theory in the sentence just cited is shown in Figure 3.1. Subjects are exceptions to the "argument = sister" rule, and are attached as daughters of the node dominating the maximal projection of the predicate of which it is an argument.

3. There are three permissible exceptions to the constraint in (1) that major syntactic phrasal categories must have a unique head that is of the same category but with one fewer bar:

(a) For any major category X at any level of projection n, there can be a rule introducing conjoined instances of that category: $X^n \rightarrow X^n$ (*conj* X^n)* (Jackendoff, 1977).

Figure 3.1

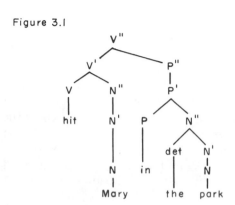

(b) For any major category X at a level of projection n, there can be a rule that introduces V^n as its head, rather than X^{n-1}, if the V is inflected (these are examples of "exocentric" phrases such as English gerunds; see Jackendoff, 1977; Bresnan, 1982c).

(c) The S-node has as its head V^{max} if that is one of its daughters, or the maximal projection of another major category encoding the main predicate of the sentence if not (this is similar to proposals by Bresnan 1982c, and Hornstein, 1977a, and differs from Jackendoff, 1977, and Pinker, 1982, who assumed that S is identical to V^{max}).

4. Categories are annotated by functional equations in the following way: only heads of phrases and specifiers may be annotated with the equation $\uparrow = \downarrow$ which collapses grammatical information associated with different tree-structure levels into a single level in the functional structure. Complements (i.e., maximal projections other than the head) must be annotated with equations of the form $\uparrow \text{FUNCTION} = \downarrow$, which define a new level of embedding in the functional structure (see Kaplan and Bresnan, 1982; Bresnan, 1982c).

Naturally, there will be no point in trying to show how the child learns the different levels of projection of phrasal categories unless having different levels of projection makes some difference in how the grammar functions. Jackendoff (1977) argues that several grammatical phenomena are best explained by positing rules that are sensitive to differences between levels of projection of a single category. For example, the phrase *do so* can substitute for a V' (i.e., a verb plus its arguments without its modifiers) but not for a V (compare *John pitched for the Red Sox on Wednesday, and Fred did so on Thursday* with **Bill put the plant on the table, and Stan did so on the ledge*). Likewise, the pronoun *one* can be followed by an *of*-complement only if it substitutes for an N' (i.e., a noun plus its arguments without its modifiers), not an N (compare *John met the governor from Vermont, and Bill met the one from New Hampshire* with **John met the governor of Vermont, and Bill met the one of New Hampshire*). Furthermore, since complements of X' cannot be closer to X than complements of X itself without crossing branches, generally arguments will be closer to the head of a phrase than modifiers (compare *the governor of Vermont from Connecticut* with **the governor from Connecticut of Vermont*; later in the chapter I will show how the child can learn exceptions to this generalization). Jackendoff also argues that the scope of quantifiers like *few* is determined by the level of projection of the phrase in which the quantifier is found.

Since LFG has the means to distinguish tokens of a given phrasal category at a single level of projection thanks to functional annotations, it is not clear whether it needs more than one level of projection in order to capture the facts that Jackendoff cites. I will assume that two levels of projection *are* necessary and will propose mechanisms capable of acquiring phrase structure rules that define two levels. If it turns out that only a single level is necessary, the acquisition mechanisms can be simplified accordingly.

Categorial Features and Cross-Category Generalizations

There is one other feature of X-bar theory that I will appeal to in the discussion to follow, though it will play a relatively minor role. Chomsky and Jackendoff, citing Greenberg (1963), note that the linear order of a head and its complement within a phrase at a given level of projection tends to be constant across different categories within a language. For example, if verbs precede their objects in a given language, then prepositions will tend to precede their objects, nouns will precede their complements, and so on, whereas if verbs follow their objects, there will be postpositions following their objects, nouns following their complements, and so on. These regularities can be captured by proposing that syntactic categories are defined by conjunctions of features (e.g., $[+S, +O]$ defines verbs and $[+S, -O]$ defines nouns, where "S" and "O" are mnemonic labels reflecting whether the category may contain subjects or objects, respectively). Languages would contain a small number of schemata defining the relative order of head and complement for all categories bearing a given feature, rather than a separate phrase structure rule for each category.

As it turned out, this notation was discovered to be quite cumbersome when the full complexity of the phrase structure of English was considered (see Jackendoff, 1977; Williams, 1981a). Instead, it has been argued that one should account for cross-category generalizations by listing each phrase structure rule separately, and by defining an evaluation metric for grammars that would "favor" grammars with consistent head-complement orders across categories. Translated into learning-theoretic terms, that would mean that the child would be more likely to learn a phrase structure rule (that is, learn it to a given degree of strength or confidence with less input evidence) if the constituent order it defined corresponded to those of already learned rules for different categories. One of the learning procedures I will present incorporates this heuristic, but since, as we shall see, constituent order is not hard to learn as long as the constituents can be reliably identified, exploiting cross-category generalizations simply makes the acquisition of phrase struc- ure a bit more robust rather than making it possible to begin with.

Acquisition Mechanisms for Phrase Structure Rules

I will begin by listing the procedures themselves, modified slightly from Pinker (1982). Procedures that are crucial to the learning of phrase structure rules are given numbers beginning wth "P"; there is also a procedure for learning lexical categori- zations and subcategorizations that I will call "L1" (in Chapter 8 I will discuss procedures for the acquisition of lexical entries in more detail). The procedures are applied in the order listed; their use will be illustrated in a concrete example in the para- graph immediately following the list.

P1. Build as complete a tree for the string as possible by parsing it with existing phrase structure rules and existing lexical entries, if there are any.

P2. For the parts of the sentence that do not yet subtend branches of the tree, label the words with the lexical categories that are the canonical grammaticizations of the semantic properties of the word meaning (e.g., noun for thing, verb for action). Build a branch extending each lexical category upward to its maximal projection (i.e., X'' according to the version of X-bar theory adopted here). S is the maximal projection of the head of the sentence. The head of the sentence is the V'' encoding tense, aspect, and modality if there is one among the major constituents in the string; otherwise it is X'', where X is the major predicate of the proposition encoded in the sentence.

P3. Annotate the maximally projected node subtended by each ar- gument word with the equation $\uparrow$ FUNCTION $= \downarrow$, using the grammatical function specified for that argument by the semantics of its relation to its predicate (e.g. SUBJ for agent of action). Add the equation $\uparrow = \downarrow$ to all nodes representing heads and specifiers. If the lexical head of a constituent is marked for case (Chapter 5 describes a procedure for the acquisition of case markers), append the equation CASE $= n$ to the phrase, where n is the case signified by the inflected head according to the inflectional paradigm for case in the language. If a sentence-initial constituent refers to the discourse topic and all the arguments of the main predicate are expressed by other constituents, append the equation $\uparrow$ TOPIC $= \downarrow$ to that constituent.

P4. (a) Connect the SUBJ noun phrase as the daughter of the root
S-node.[1] (b) Connect the remaining branches according to the information in the uncommitted f-structure and the X-bar principles
(e.g., functional argument = sister of X, modifier = sister of X'),
and the analogous conditions for specifiers. (c) If the connections
mandated by (a) and (b) are impossible without crossing branches,
connect the complement one node higher than the specified node.
Apply this procedure recursively if necessary.

P5. Create annotated phrase structure rules corresponding to the tree
fit onto the sentence by P1–P4, according to the conventions relating trees to rewrite rules. If one of the rules thus created already
exists, increase its strength. If an existing rule for a different category defines the same head-complement order as the rule just
coined or strengthened, increment the strength of both rules.

L1. Add entries to the lexicon corresponding to the categorizations of
input words defined by the tree, or strengthen any existing lexical
categorizations that are identical to the ones defined by the tree.
Add subcategorization information to the lexical entries of argument-taking predicates by examining the functions encoding its
arguments in the tree and listing those functions in the PRED
equation for that entry. If an argument is not encoded by any
phrase in the tree, assign it the symbol "∅" in the PRED equation.

P6. If a newly created rule expands the same symbol as an existing
rule, collapse the two as follows (in (a–d), two annotated categories
are to be considered the same if both the categories and the equations appended to them are identical, distinct if the categories or
any of the equations are different): (a) Append the "Kleene-star"
operator * to any annotated category that appears twice in succession in an expansion in one rule. (b) If a sequence of annotated
categories in one expansion is properly contained within another
expansion, combine the two expansions, putting parentheses around
the annotated categories not contained in the smaller expansion.
(c) If two expansions are identical except for one position that
contains one annotated category in one rule, another annotated
category in the other, collapse expressions by placing the noncom-
mon ones within braces. Do the same if the two rules are identical
except for having two nonidentical positions if the two rules contain exactly the same set of annotated categories. (d) If two annotated categories appear in braces in one rule, and successively
in the other (with the rest of the expansions identical), discard the
braces and retain the annotated categories in the indicated sequence, each within a pair of parentheses.

An English Active Concrete Sentence

The first rules and lexical entries are acquired by building a
tree for the sentence with the help of syntax-semantics corre-

spondences, then reading the appropriate rules off the tree (see Anderson, 1977). Let us consider as a first illustration of the phrase structure acquisition mechanisms the simple example shown in Figure 3.2, where part (a) is the string of words the child hears, and part (b) is the f-structure he or she creates on the basis of the inferred meaning of the sentence. In this example, I will assume that the entire word string was encoded intact and that the meaning of each word is already known. (See Chapter 5 and Pinker, 1982, for an account of how the meaning of words like *the* can be acquired. In effect, I have the child treat *the dog* at first as if it were a single inflected word; then the child learns the properties encoded by *the*, and then he or she learns that *the* can be separated from the noun. In Chapter 5 I discuss the details of the mechanisms that accomplish this. Thus the example shown in Figure 3.2 telescopes two phases of learning

Figure 3.2

(a) Sentence: "the dog bit the cat"

(b) f-structure:

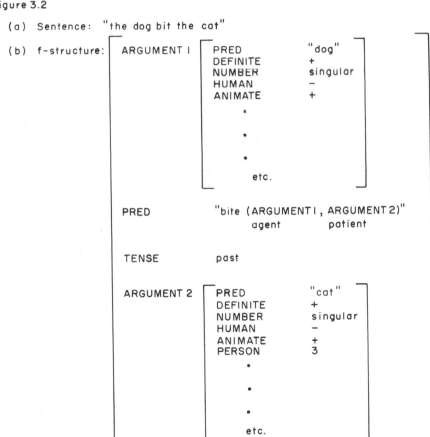

into one: the acquisition of the phrase structure of the sentence and of major categories, which can proceed from the start, and the acquisition of the phrase structure positions of determiners, which of course must await the segmentation of the determiner from the noun and so on. For expository purposes I assume that *the* has been acquired at this point.)

The first thing the child does is create lexical category nodes for each word in the sentence, using the correspondences between semantic categories and syntactic categories assumed earlier (here I also assume that the canonical category for a word that refers to definiteness in discourse is *det*). The result is shown in Figure 3.3.

Figure 3.3

The next task is to deduce how that sequence of lexical categories is grouped into phrases. In principle, this could be done in an infinite number of ways (e.g., a word could be introduced by an arbitrarily long chain of application of phrase structure rules, and hence could be found at the bottom of an arbitrarily long branch of the tree). However, the constraints implicit in X-bar theory provide a unique geometry for the tree to be fit onto the string of words. First, X-bar theory leaves the child no choice but to posit the maximal projections of each of the major lexical categories. Second, V dominates the main predicate of the sentence (which also is a verb encoding tense and aspect), and so it is designated the head of the sentence. As a result, it is provided with S as its mother. Thus we have Figure 3.4.

Each constituent is linked to its appropriate f-structure, so the child can see that *the dog* is the agent argument of the predicate

Figure 3.4

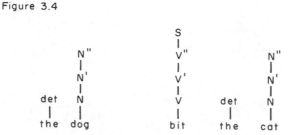

bit—hence, by semantic bootstrapping, the SUBJ argument. Subjects, as mentioned, are assumed to be daughters of the node that dominates the maximal projection of their predicates (S here), so the child makes the corresponding attachment, shown in Figure 3.5 (though see also n. 1). Using f-structure information and syntax-semantics correspondences, the child annotates the remaining maximal projections of words with the grammatical functions that relate them to predicates (OBJ in this example), yielding Figure 3.6.

Figure 3.5

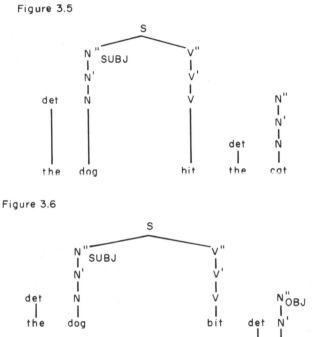

Figure 3.6

The child's f-structure and lexical entries similarly indicate that the two determiners *the* express the definiteness of the first and last noun phrases, respectively, and that the phrase *the cat* is an argument (the object argument, by hypothesis) of the predicate expressed by *bit*. Using the provisions of X-bar theory that state that arguments are attached as sisters of X and specifiers as sisters of X', the child completes the tree and ends up with Figure 3.7.[2]

One usually derives trees using phrase structure rules, but given a tree, as is the case for our child at this moment, one can

Figure 3.7

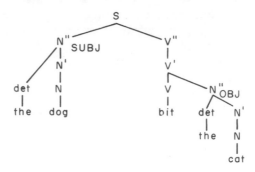

just as easily derive the phrase structure rules and lexical entries that generated it:

(1) S → N"$_{SUBJ}$ V" (analogous to S → NP$_{SUBJ}$ VP)
     N" → det N'
     N' → N   (analogous to NP → det N)
     V" → V'
     V' → V N"$_{OBJ}$ (analogous to VP → V NP$_{OBJ}$)

     the: det: DEFINITE = +
     dog: N: PRED = "dog"
     cat: N: PRED = "cat"
     bit: V: PRED = "bite (SUBJ, OBJ)"

(All categories lacking annotations in the right-hand sides of rules may be assumed to have the annotation ↑ = ↓.)

The child has, with a single [string: f-structure] pair, induced five phrase structure rules complete with functional annotations, and lexical entries for each word.

An Abstract Sentence

The child owes much of his or her success in the last example to the canonical semantics-syntax correlations that, luckily, held in that sentence. What about cases where these correlations do not hold? As mentioned, these will generally come later than more canonical sentences (Pinker and Hochberg, in preparation), so the child can use the rules acquired from the canonical cases to analyze the noncanonical cases. This is done by attempting as far as possible to parse the sentence using existing rules (just as adults do in normal comprehension). If there is some portion of the sentence that cannot be parsed (e.g., if there are no lexical entries for the words), then the parse is completed by building the tree top-down and labeling the as-yet-unknown elements in a way that makes this possible. This is the "structure-dependent distributional learning" that I referred to earlier; it can be accomplished by procedure D1:

D1. If a sentence contains either a word W or a phrase X^m that cannot be attached to the tree by existing rules, and if the constituents of X^m cannot be parsed into any phrases other than X^m, and if existing rules specify that some symbol Y^n, and only that symbol, may occur in that position, then (1) add word W to the lexicon with categorization Y; or (2) add the rule $Y^n \rightarrow \ldots X^m \ldots$ to the grammar, respectively, if doing so would result in a complete tree for the sentence.

Consider, as an example, the sentence *the situation justified the measures.* Since the content words are abstract, the procedure used in the last example will not be triggered. However, the child will know the categorization of the word *the,* and thus can begin to parse the sentence with his or her existing rules, as shown in Figure 3.8. The only rule in the child's current grammar introducing determiners is $N'' \rightarrow$ det N', so the child can confidently build the part of the tree subtended by *the* (see Figure 3.9). N' expands only to N in the current grammar, justifying the next stage of the parse, shown in Figure 3.10.

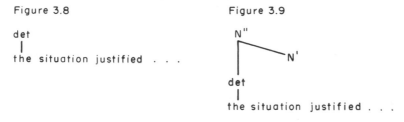

Figure 3.8

```
det
 |
the situation justified . . .
```

Figure 3.9

```
     N''
    /   \
   |      N'
  det     |
   |
  the situation justified . . .
```

Figure 3.10

```
        N''
       /   \
     det    N'
      |      |
     the     N

     situation   justified . . .
```

Normally the parse would grind to a halt at this point, since *situation* has no category label in the lexicon. But because the grammar allows only one possible category in this position, N, procedure D1 declares that the categorization of the unknown word is just that category, and makes the corresponding entry to the lexicon:

(2) situation: N: PRED = "situation"

Now that there is a complete noun phrase at the beginning of the sentence, the learner can continue the parsing process, using the previously learned rules introducing N" (S → N"$_{SUBJ}$ V") and V (V" → V' and V' → V' N"$_{OBJ}$) to build an additional portion of the tree (Figure 3.11). To continue the partial parse using D1, the learner hypothesizes that *justified* is a verb. Then using pro-

Figure 3.11

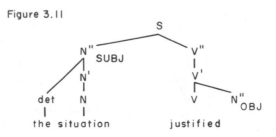

cedure L1, the child notices that the two abstract arguments of *justify* (the justification and the deed, respectively) are expressed syntactically by the functions SUBJ and OBJ, since these functions are annotated to the NPs that dominate its arguments in the tree. This results in the lexical entry shown in (3):

(3) justify: V: PRED = "justify (SUBJ, OBJ)"

Continuing with these procedures, the learner can parse the rest of the sentence and make the corresponding additions to the grammar and lexicon. Inflections and morphology, once learned from canonical cases, can presumably also be used to identify the category membership of inscrutable words.

The same procedure will be used when the child acquires rules for exocentric phrases (i.e., a category Y^n headed by a category with a label other than Y) when a complete phrase X is observed in a position where Y^n is the only superordinate category allowed by the grammar, given the rest of the sentence. One example might be the English gerund: when a child hears *John's eating the rabbit shocked the bystanders*, he or she parses *eating the rabbit* as a currently unattached V' and parses the subject of the sentence as an N" which currently lacks an N. D1 would then mandate the rule N' → V' to complete the parse, possibly abetted by the provision of X-bar theory that allows inflected verbs to be exocentric heads of any category. A similar procedure perhaps could acquire rules generating sentential NPs.

The example in Figures 3.8–3.11 showed several instances of

procedure D1 being applied in the same sentence. In fact, procedure D1 is stated so as to apply only in cases in which the entire sentence can be parsed with existing rules except for the single item in question, and that item appears in a position whose category label is uniquely determined by the existing rules. This stringency was introduced to prevent spurious distributional analyses—e.g., interpreting *situation* as an adjective if the rule NP → (det) (A) N was already in the grammar. (A more plausible-sounding example recently appeared in a comic strip called "The Family Circus": a grandmother seated at the dinner table exclaims, "Mmm! This is scrumptious!"—to which her grandchild replies, "Can I have some scrumptious, Mommy?") One might worry, however, that once the grammar had grown to a certain degree of complexity, such a stringent requirement would rule out *all* the instances that could teach a particular rule, and that in no case would there be a *unique* prediction as to the category membership of an unknown word or phrase. One solution was outlined in Pinker (1982), where I proposed that the "unique-prediction-within-complete-parse" requirement of D1 be weakened so as to apply when there was a parse that was very much "stronger"—in the sense of Ford, Bresnan, and Kaplan (1982)—than alternative parses. Alternatively, one could allow D1 to operate when a complete major phrase could be parsed, rather than a complete sentence, or one could add various "conflict resolution rules" that would give one type of parse priority over another regardless of their relative "strengths" when both were compatible with the sentence (e.g., choose the analysis creating fewer nodes in the tree). Quite possibly such principles could be taken from the study of sentence parsing in adults (e.g., Frazier and Fodor, 1978), since syntactically ambiguous words pose the same computational problem for the adult comprehender that syntactically unknown words pose for the child learner.

A Sentence in a VSO Language

The X-bar principles governing attachment relations in trees are actually too stringent for many constructions in the world's languages. There must be a procedure by which the child discovers this. In the next three sections I show how a single subprocedure, P4(c), allows the child to circumvent the default attachment relations provided by X-bar theory in three types of constructions: VSO clause structure, English oblique objects, and sentences in nonconfigurational languages.

Consider first a VSO language like Irish. An input sentence analogous to Figure 3.2a would be (4).

(4) Bit the dog the cat.

Figure 3.12

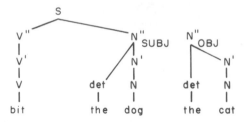

The child would apply P1 through P3 and arrive at the analysis shown in Figure 3.12. Now the attachment of the object noun phrase poses a problem. The "argument = sister" provision of X-bar theory would dictate that it be attached as a daughter of V'. But this is impossible without tangling the branches of the tree. Here, procedure P4(c) springs into action: unable to attach the NP at its designated point, it tries to attach it as a daughter of V", the node immediately dominating V'. Stymied again, it applies recursively and tries to attach the NP to the node dominating V", S. Here it succeeds, and the rule $S \rightarrow V\ N''_{\text{SUBJ}}\ N''_{\text{OBJ}}$ is added to the grammar. The nonbranching categories V" and V' are, of course, superfluous, but no harm is done by including rules generating them. In Chapter 4 I present an alternative mechanism that does not postulate superfluous nonbranching structure.

A Passive Sentence

This section is divided into two subsections, one dealing with the acquisition of the phrase structure of a passive sentence, the other dealing with the acquisition of the predicate-argument relations in a passive sentence.

Acquiring Passive Phrase Structure

The Spatial-Oblique Parallelism Hypothesis

In accounting for the acquisition of the passive in English, the first problem we must face is how the child analyzes the structure of the passive *by*-phrase, as in (5).

(5) The cat was bitten by the dog.

Since *by* has no semantic correlate indicating its category membership, the child has little to go on in figuring out how to parse that phrase. To solve this problem, in Pinker (1982) I proposed that the similarity across the world's languages between case-marking prepositions, like *by* in the passive *by*-phrase in (5), and spatial prepositions, like *by* in the locative in (6), is no coincidence.

(6) The cat was sitting by the fence.

I suggested that when the child hears a sentence with spatial *by*—e.g., (6)—he or she categorizes *by* as a preposition because of its spatial meaning. As a result, the rules PP → P NP$_{OBJ}$ and VP → V PP can be induced via X-bar principles. Then when a passive like (5) is encountered, the distributional procedures can use these rules to analyze it, just as in the section "An Abstract Sentence" above, and the passive sentence would have a tree structure identical to the tree structure of (6). From there other procedures would attend to the modifications necessary to account for the proper predicate-argument relations.

Complicating the Hypothesis

In that simplified presentation, I ignored both the proper X-bar analysis of passive phrase structure and the functional equations annotated to the phrase structure rules. Unfortunately, when one introduces this additional formal precision, the account must become somewhat more complex. Consider the exact LFG phrase structure rules and lexical entries for passive (oblique) and locative (adjunct) PPs, listed in (7)–(9):

(7) Lexical entries:
ADJUNCT: (a) by: P: PRED = "by (OBJ)"
OBLIQUE: (b) by: P: PCASE = OBL$_{agent}$

(8) Internal structures:[3]
ADJUNCT: (a) P' → P N"$_{OBJ}$
OBLIQUE: (b) P' → P N"

(9) External distribution:[4]
ADJUNCT: (a) V" → V' P"$_{ADJ}$
OBLIQUE: (b) V" → V' P"$_{OBL_{agent}}$

With these rules spelled out, we can see that the child could exploit the similarity between adjunct and oblique PPs in three separate ways, listed in (10).

(10) (i) *Homonymity*. The child notices that the word *by* in the passive is similar to the word *by* in the locative adjunct (7a) acquired earlier, and so infers that its categorization (7b) is the same as in (7a), and that its internal structure (8b) will be the same as (8a) (mutatis mutandis).[5]

(ii) *Parallel External Distribution*. The child notices that the external distribution or position of the PP within the VP is the same for the passive sentence as it was in the locative adjunct acquired earlier (9a) and so infers that its external distribution (9b) is the same as (9a), and that its internal structure (8b) will be the same as (8a) (mutatis mutandis).

(iii) *Parallel Internal Structure*. The child has inferred from either (i) or (ii) that the internal structure of the passive PP in (8b) is the same as the internal structure of the adjunct PP in (8a) acquired earlier, and so infers that the external distribution of the passive PP (9b) will be the same as (9a), or that the lexical categorization of the passive *by* (7b) is the same as that for the locative *by* (7a) (mutatis mutandis), depending respectively on whether (i) or (ii) had already been applied.

Procedures (ii) and (iii) could also be applied to oblique spatial arguments of verbs of motion or transfer, or to spatial complements of verbs of predication or change of state (more on this later).

Using Homonymity to Acquire Passive Phrase Structure

Let us consider procedure (10i) first. To apply the procedure, the child must have encountered a sentence like (6) with the specific locative *by* before being able to analyze the passive *by*-phrase. If this has happened, the child can analyze the subject, verb phrase, and agent NP in (5) using P1 and existing rules, and can categorize *by* as a preposition, yielding Figure 3.13. Then (10i) applies, using rule (8a) to infer the structure in Figure 3.14 and then the corresponding rule (8b).

Recall that according to the hypothesis being considered here, the child is not using the external distribution of adjunct PPs to

Figure 3.13

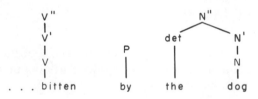

Figure 3.14

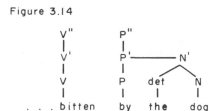

Figure 3.15

a.

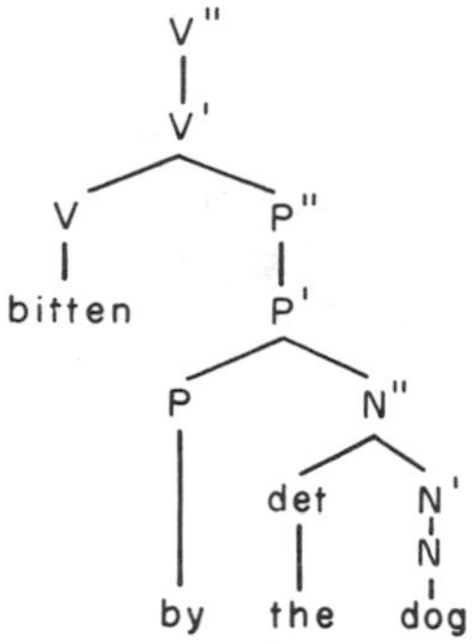

b. V' ⟶ V P"

infer the external distribution of oblique PPs. That has to be learned separately. Thus the child would then have to use the fact that *the dog* is an argument of *bitten* and the "argument = sister" rule to attach the P" as a daughter of V', yielding the analysis in part (a) of Figure 3.15 and the rule governing the external distribution of the passive PP in part (b).

This is bad news and good news. The bad news is that the child has gotten the rule wrong: in English, passive PPs are better analyzed as daughters of V" than as daughters of V', Jackendoff's "argument = sister" rule notwithstanding. That is because locative adjuncts can intervene between the passive PP and the verb, as in (11).

(11) John was bitten last Tuesday in the park by a dog.[6]

Since I assume, with Jackendoff, that adjuncts or modifiers are attached as daughters of V", passive PPs must also be daughters of V"; otherwise branches would cross. The good news is that the child can use the temptation to cross branches in that way to conclude that the "argument = sister" rule cannot apply here, via the same procedure, P4(c), that acquired the VSO rule. When

Figure 3.16

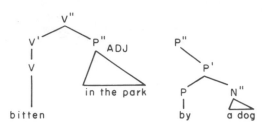

the child hears a sentence like the one shown in Figure 3.16, he
or she would create the structure in Figure 3.16, and would be
unable to attach the oblique P'' as a daughter of V' without
crossing branches. But, as in the VSO section above, procedure
P4(c) tries to attach it one level higher as a daughter of V'', which
it can do successfully, yielding the correct rule (12).

(12) $V'' \rightarrow V' \ P''_{ADJ} \ P''_{OBL}$

Procedure P6, collapsing this rule with those acquired from past
or future inputs, would eventually yield the final rule (13).

(13) $V'' \rightarrow V' \ (P''_{\{^{ADJ}_{OBL}\}})^*$

*Empirical problems for the homonymity version of the spatial-oblique
parallelism hypothesis.* Though I have shown how the full X-bar
structure of passive *by*-phrases can be learned according to the
homonymity hypothesis outlined in Pinker (1982), there are good
reasons to doubt that this scenario represents the process whereby
children acquire the phrase structure of the English passive. First
of all, the locative use of *by* is vanishingly rare in parental speech
to children (Pinker and Hochberg, in preparation), so it is unlikely that hearing locative *by* is a prerequisite to analyzing passive sentences. Second, once children do acquire passives, they
seem for a time to be indifferent to the exact preposition marking
the oblique agent. In production they will often substitute the
preposition *from* or *with* (Maratsos, 1978; Maratsos and Abramovitch, 1975; Bowerman, 1982a); and in comprehension they
successfully act out passive sentences with a variety of prepositions other than *by*. At the same time, the children balk when
a nonsense word like *po* is used instead (Maratsos, 1978; Maratsos and Abramovitch, 1975); this suggests that children have
successfully analyzed passives as requiring a prepositional phrase
but have not firmly acquired the knowledge that it is the preposition *by* that must head the phrase. Thus it is unlikely that the

analysis of the passve PP hinges on acquisition of the word *by*.

It *is* possible that homonymity is used in the many languages whose passive agents are marked by the instrumental case, since instrumental PPs are not uncommon in speech to children (Pinker and Hochberg, in preparation). Furthermore, children learning English learn *with* easily, and sometimes confuse it with the agentive preposition. If these patterns are general, then in conjunction with the learning mechanism I have been considering they would help to explain why more languages use the instrumental preposition or case marker to mark the passive agent than use the equivalent of *by*.

Using External and Internal Parallelism to Acquire Passive Phrase Structure

Given the developmental facts, I now need to show how children learn agentive markers that do not have accessible adjunctive homonyms, such as the English *by*. Mechanisms (ii) and (iii) of (10), which exploit the parallelisms between the internal structures, and between the external distributions, of spatial and oblique phrases, seem more plausible, at least for English. Here the child could use procedure P1 to create the partial parse in Figure 3.17. Procedure (10ii), recognizing an unattached potentially oblique argument NP in the position of an adjunct PP, can then substitute the OBL function for the ADJ function and make a guess about the internal structure of the oblique PP, resulting in Figure 3.18(a). Procedure (10iii) or D1 then completes the tree by concluding that *by* must be a preposition, adding the new entry for *by* to the lexicon.

The advantage of this account is that the child need only hear adjunct PPs in general, not adjunct PPs with *by*. For this reason the child could also apply (10iii) to prepositional phrases that are arguments of verbs of physical motion or transfer (e.g., *I gave the pillow to Marcy* or *I placed the roses underneath the table*) or

Figure 3.17

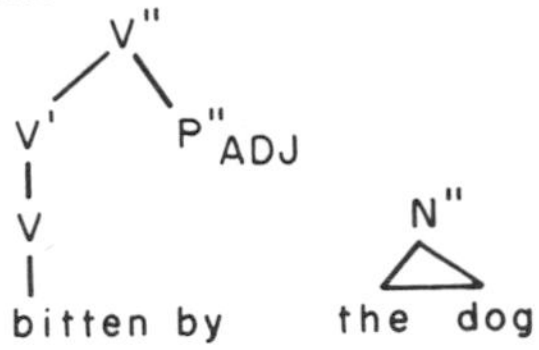

Figure 3.18

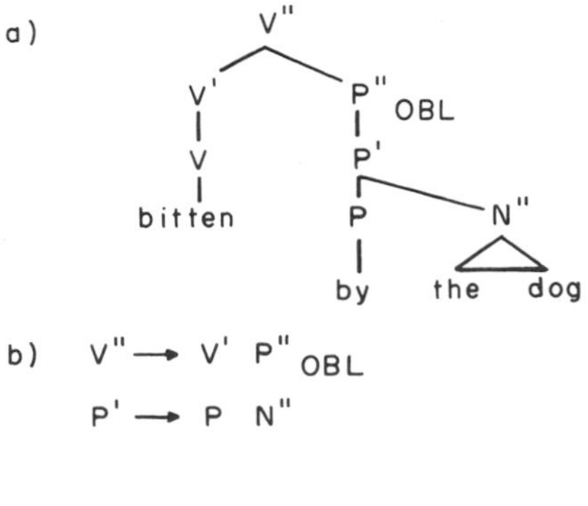

to prepositional phrases that are complements (e.g., *John stayed in the room*). In other words, the child is freed from having to base his or her generalization upon the homonymity of spatial *by* and agentive *by*. Empirically, this is more plausible than the hypothesis that the child learns passive phrase structure by exploiting the ambiguity of *by*. Adjunct PPs, spatial argument PPs, and complement PPs are plentiful in parental speech (Pinker and Hochberg, in press), and locative prepositions other than *by* are among the earliest closed-class morphemes acquired correctly (Brown, 1973; de Villiers and de Villiers, 1973a; Pinker, 1981c). Note that this variant makes a prediction about a language universal: if a language has both nonspatial oblique PPs and spatial PPs (oblique arguments, complements, or adjuncts), their external distributions must overlap. The prediction arises because according to this account, it is only by noting the external distribution of the spatial PP that the child can acquire the internal structure and prepositionhood of the oblique PP. It also predicts that children learning other languages should occasionally confuse particular locative morphemes and case-marking morphemes with one another while respecting the phrase structure of the prepositional phrase or the morphological structure of an inflected noun. Indeed, Slobin (1984a) reports examples of children mistakenly using locative prepositions to express possession (in German), or simultaneously starting to use a single preposition to mark location and possession if the language conflates those forms (e.g., in French); he also cites examples of children confusing allative and dative case markers (in Hungarian). Presumably these facts about development and adult competence are not arbitrary but reflect some psychological similarity between spatial and nonspatial relations. See Jackendoff (1983) and Chapter 8 for further discussion.

Acquiring Passive Predicate-Argument Relations

Now that the child has parsed the passive sentence completely, yielding the tree shown in Figure 3.19, he or she faces another conflict. The lexical entry for *bite* learned previously states that the "biter" argument appears as a SUBJ and the "victim" argument appears as an OBJ. However, the tree created with the help of existing phrase structure rules lists the biter as an oblique object (OBL$_{agent}$) and the victim as a SUBJ. This is just the sort of situation that presumably would inspire a transformationally-based learner to hypothesize a second, "deep" phrase structure tree conforming to the lexical entry, plus a transformation that mapped one tree onto another. In the model I am

Figure 3.19

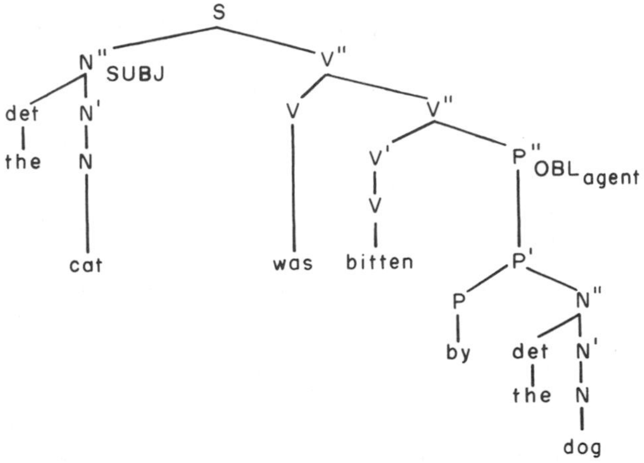

proposing, however, the learner resolves the conflict by creating a second lexical entry for the main predicate. The new entry preserves the predicate-argument structure of the old one, but uses new grammatical functions to map each argument onto phrase structures. L1 takes these new functions from the phrase structure tree created by P1 and (10i–iii). Thus the learner adds (14) to his or her lexicon (I assume morphological differences between active and passive versions of the verb are also listed in the new, passive entry; see Chapters 6, 7, and 8).

(14) bitten: V: PRED = "bite (OBL$_{agent}$, SUBJ)"

A Sentence from a Nonconfigurational Language

Two features differentiate the so-called "scrambling," "w-star," "nonconfigurational," or "free word order" languages, like Warlpiri or Malayalam, from "X-bar" or "configurational" languages, like English. First, nonconfigurational languages have a "flat" or nonbranching tree structure. That is, the elements of what would be a cohesive phrase in English may be scattered throughout the clause, each word attached as an immediate constituent of the S-node. Second, such languages often permit any of the $n!$ possible orders of n words or constituents in circumscribed portions of the sentence (e.g., after the auxiliary in Warlpiri, which occupies the second position in the sentence). I will treat the acquisition of each aspect separately.

NONBRANCHING PHRASE STRUCTURE

In his description of a computer simulation of the learning model in Pinker (1982), Richard Walsh (1981) points out that procedure P4(c) is adequate to acquire nonbranching phrase structure rules in languages like Warlpiri with no further modifications. This is the same procedure that acquired VSO phrase structure and V" attachment of passive oblique objects in previous sections.

Consider the Warlpiri-like sentence (15), in which the modifier *little* of the subject noun *boy* is separated from that noun by other constituents. (I will assign the modifier to the category A for convenience, even though modifiers in Warlpiri are really nominals; the same account can be applied if the modifier is a number, quantifier, determiner, or nominal.)

(15) boy Aux kangaroo ride little.

Procedures P2, P3, and P4(a) and (b) will create the partial tree shown in Figure 3.20. The adjective phrase A" should be attached under the subject N" by the "modifier = aunt" provision of X-bar theory. Since that attachment is impossible to make without tangling the tree, P4(c) will attach it higher, as a daughter of S. If the ergative and absolutive case markers on the nouns and adjectives have been acquired at this point (see Chapter 5), procedure P3 would append the equation CASE = *erg* and CASE = *abs* to the maximal projections of the NPs. Together these procedures would create the tree in part (a) of Figure 3.21 and the rule in part (b).[7]

Note that the grammar still contains an incorrect branching V' rule. The rule generating an object N" as a daughter of S rather than as a daughter of V' will be learned as soon as the child hears a sentence with a word from another phrase interposed between verb and object. In general, the child will have rules that permit the maximum amount of branching until evidence to the contrary comes in. Thus the learning mechanisms as stated automatically give the child the prerequisites he or she

Figure 3.20

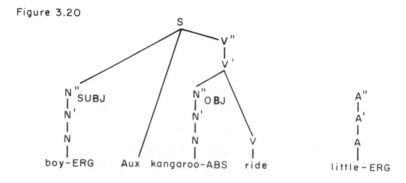

Figure 3.21

a)

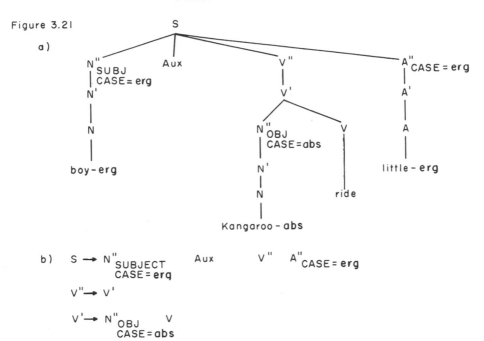

b) S ⟶ N″_{SUBJECT}   Aux   V″   A″_{CASE=erg}
         CASE=erg

V″⟶ V′

V′⟶ N″_{OBJ}   V
         CASE=abs

needs in order to learn the "structure-dependent" phenomena in the language, if any. Trace binding is one example; inverted auxiliaries are another, as in Chomsky's (1975) famous example in which the child must attend to phrase structure in order not to generalize from *the man is in the room/is the man in the room?* to *the man who is tall is in the room/*is the man who tall is in the room?* When evidence for nonconfigurationality in the form of tangled trees does come in, the child can learn the corresponding nonbranching structure, whatever it is.[8]

This mechanism is, I think, much more plausible than one working in the opposite direction—namely, by positing nonconfigurationality as the default. Since the input sentences from *any* language are consistent with the assumption of nonconfigurationality, it is not clear what would inform the child that his or her language *was* configurational, short of negative evidence.

Note that these mechanisms will leave the child with two rules generating the elements of a noun phrase, one with the elements contiguous under NP, the other with the elements generated as daughters of S, since so far there is nothing in the acquisition procedures that wipes out a branching rule once its nonbranching counterpart is hypothesized. It turns out that this feature has unanticipated desirable consequences. In Warlpiri, apparently, the elements of a noun phrase must be case-marked if they are noncontiguous, and are not casemarked (except for the final element) if they are contiguous (Nash, 1980; Simpson, 1982). This implies that contiguous NPs do have a separate status in Warlpiri grammar, that a Warlpiri speaker indeed has learned two rules for NP elements, as the procedure suggests. One rule would generate a branching N″ dictating casemarking only of its final element, another would generate its constituents as daughters of S, dictating casemarking of all those elements. Note that the presence or absence of a case-marking requirement on a constituent in a rule is decided upon by assessing whether the word at the bottom of its branch bears a case marker in an input sentence (which in turn can be assessed by examining the word's inflectional paradigm; see Chapter 5). The way in which the child generalizes from rules requiring particular case markers in particular positions to rules requiring that *any* case marker may occur in a particular position is discussed in the very next subsection.

PRODUCTIVITY AND CONSTITUENT ORDER FREEDOM

All the procedures discussed thus far coin a different phrase structure rule for each order of constituents found in the input. This constrains the child to uttering and comprehending only the constituent orders he or she has actually heard. In this section, I discuss the operation of mechanisms that allow the child to generalize to novel constituent orders.

Across-Constituent Order Freedom

Before discussing these processes, however, I wish to point out that although the child as characterized thus far cannot utter novel orders of constituents within their mother phrase, he or she certainly can utter and comprehend novel constituent orders within the sentence as a whole. If, for example, the child hears the two orders of subject and verb in input sentences (16a) and (b), he or she coins the two corresponding phrase structure rules in (16c) and (d).

(16) (a) Big dog runs.
    (b) Runs big dog.
    (c) S → NP VP
    (d) S → VP NP

When the child attends to the two orders of adjective and noun within the preverbal NPs in (17a) and (b), the two rules (17c) and (d) are coined as a result.

(17) (a) Big dog runs.
    (b) Dog big runs.
    (c) NP → AP N
    (d) NP → N AP

Note that the current grammar, consisting of rules (16c–d) and
(17c–d), automatically generates an order never heard: *runs dog
big*. This occurs despite the fact that each individual rule reflected
an order heard in the input. In a context-free grammar, the
internal structure of a phrase and its external distribution are
decoupled or stated separately, and not every possible internal
structure need be heard in every one of its external positions.
Thus the number of word orders the child can generate can grow
polynomially with a linear increase in the number of rules acquired. These facts will play an important role in the next chapter, in which I examine the evidence on whether young children
have acquired phrase structure rules.

A similar argument, incidentally, can show that a child who
only coins phrase structure rules attested in a finite number of
the inputs can still acquire the ability to generate an infinite
number of sentences. When the child hears a phrase like *the dog
in the park*, he or she coins the rules in (18).

(18) N″ → det N′ P″
     P″ → P′
     P′ → P N″

One can see in an instant that this grammar fragment is recursive: it can generate structures like *the dog in the park near the
church by the road to the city in the state by the bay* and so on. The
ability to acquire recursive structures falls out of two properties
of the model, without further stipulation: the assumption that
the child can encode recursive semantic or functional structures
from context (e.g., an object whose location object is encoded
as a subsidiary part of that object's description), and crucially,
the mechanism that assigns the same category symbol at the
same level of projection to the nodes introducing words for
physical objects wherever they may be found in the sentence.
This is another advantage for theories like the one discussed
in this book that attribute to the child acquisition procedures designed to acquire a small number of substantive syntactic categories. In contrast, acquisition theories that do not
draw on a small inventory of universal syntactic categories
but create arbitrary category labels as they are needed (e.g.,

Anderson, 1975, 1977, and other models discussed in Pinker, 1979) must introduce an extra procedure, or more complicated inputs, to recognize that a matrix phrase and an embedded phrase have the same label, which is what recursion requires.

Within-Constituent Order Freedom

Still, there is reason to believe that the productivity inherent in the notation of context-free grammars may not be sufficient and hence that the learning procedures, which acquire such rules one by one, must be supplemented. That is because context-free rules without abbreviatory conventions afford the child productivity and economy only in that they allow all possible internal orders of the constituents of a phrase to appear in any of the external positions that that phrase may assume. *Within* a given level of branching (i.e., within a constituent), each of the possible orderings of the daughters must be stipulated separately. There are two cases where this could lead to problems. First, in non-branching structures, such as Warlpiri, a large number of constituents must be generated as daughters of S, so each of their many potential orders would have to be stated, and acquired, separately. Second, there are potentially infinite sequences of constituents that have no syntactic or semantic embedding relations, such as English adjunct PPs (e.g., *I saw him in the park at 3 o'clock on Wednesday with my camera . . .*) or conjoined phrases. Without imposing an unmotivated right-branching structure on these sequences, it is impossible to state a rule generating an arbitrary number of them. Furthermore the child, perceiving no semantic embedding among them, could not give them the recursive right-branching structure that the procedures would require to coin rules generating infinite sequences.

The solution lies in procedure P6, which affords the child *within*-constituent productivity. It does so by collapsing a newly coined rule with an existing rule, resulting in new rules containing the Kleene-star (*) symbolizing iteration, parentheses symbolizing optionality, and braces symbolizing optional substitutability.[9]

Consider first procedure P6(a). If the child coins a rule with two successive identically annotated symbols of the same category, such as (19a)—which could be coined in response to a sentence like (20a), for example—P6(a) changes it to (19b), which can then generate sentence (20b), whose structure was never witnessed in the input.

(19) (a) $\text{VP} \rightarrow \text{V PP}_{\text{ADJ}} \text{PP}_{\text{ADJ}}$

    (b) $\text{VP} \rightarrow \text{V PP}^* \downarrow \epsilon \, (\uparrow \text{ADJs})$

(20) (a) I sang in the park last Tuesday.

    (b) I sang in the park at 3 pm last Tuesday without a micro-
phone.

(The equation $\downarrow \epsilon$ ($\uparrow$ADJs) is supplied as an automatic consequence of the Kleene-star and the ADJ function; see Kaplan
and Bresnan, 1982, and Bresnan, 1982c, for details.) Note that
the child is thus incapable of having a rule with two or more
successive identical elements, since he or she takes the presence
of a repeated annotated category as evidence that the annotated
category is infinitely repeatable. Note also, incidentally, that a
restriction on the learning procedure of this sort is necessary to
ensure that only a finite number of grammars is allowed by the
grammatical formalisms (see Pinker, 1981d, 1982, for discussion).

Procedure P6(b) uses the presence of a symbol in one rule and
its absence in an otherwise identical rule to infer that the constituent is optional in that expansion. Thus rules (21a–b), which
are learned from inputs (22a–b), respectively, are collapsed into
rule (21c), which in turn is collapsed with (21d), acquired from
sentence (22c), to form (21e), which generates as a result sentence (22d), whose structure has never been encountered in the
input.

(21) (a) $\text{VP} \rightarrow \text{V NP PP}$

    (b) $\text{VP} \rightarrow \text{V NP}$

    (c) $\text{VP} \rightarrow \text{V NP (PP)}$

    (d) $\text{VP} \rightarrow \text{V PP}$

    (e) $\text{VP} \rightarrow \text{V (NP) (PP)}$

(22) (a) He showed the snake to Sam.

    (b) Sam saw the snake.

    (c) Sam darted toward the car.

    (d) Sam left.

Procedure P6(c) uses the presence of two symbols in the same
position in two phrase structure rules to infer that they are optionally substitutable in that position. For example, rules (23a)
and (b), inspired by phrases (24a) and (b), are collapsed to form
(23c). That in turn is collapsed with rule (23d), acquired from
sentence (24c), to yield (23e), which generates sentence (24d),
the likes of which the child has never seen.

(23) (a) $NP \rightarrow NP_{POSS}$ N
     (b) $NP \rightarrow$ det N
     (c) $NP \rightarrow \begin{Bmatrix} NP_{POSS} \\ det \end{Bmatrix} N$
     (d) $NP \rightarrow$ det N PP
     (e) $NP \rightarrow \begin{Bmatrix} NP_{POSS} \\ det \end{Bmatrix} N$ (PP)

(24) (a) John's cat
     (b) the cat
     (c) the cat on the mat
     (d) John's cat on the mat

Procedure P6(d) ensures that if constituents are ordered with respect to one another, but both are optional, they will not be mistakenly stated as being in complementary distribution with one another by P6(c). This would otherwise happen, for example, if the child heard sentences (22b) and (c) before hearing (22a). (See Walsh, 1981, for a detailed discussion of the computational complexities of applying the P6 procedures correctly under various input orders, and for an improved statement of the procedures.)

How can the collapsing procedures give the child constituent order productivity in languages with freer word order than English? First note that procedure P6(c) can disjoin not only identically annotated categories having the same distribution but also sets of annotations on the same category. Consider a language resembling Japanese that permits any of the six possible orders of preverbal subject, object, and second object (OBJ2, in LFG notation; note that this is a grammatical function that is distinct from the quasi-semantic notion "indirect object").[10] The child will create rules (25a) and (b) upon hearing sentences (26a) and (b). The disjunction procedure P6(c) collapses them to form (25c), and the Kleene-star procedure P6(a) would in turn transform (25c) into (25d). (Note that Kaplan and Bresnan's Completeness and Consistency conditions will rule out the sequences with no subject, or five subjects, that this rule would otherwise generate.) When the second object, *bone*, is then encountered in sentences (26c) and (d), the rules (25e) and (f) will be coined. Procedure P6(c) applies once more to collapse them into (25g), which in turn is collapsed into (25h). Rule (25h) generates sentences (26e–h), exemplifying orders never before encountered. Note that Lapointe (1981b), Hale (1981), and Mohanan (1982) argue that X-bar rules with Kleene-stars, that is, the rules that P6 creates, may be sufficient to account for NP order freedom in non-configurational languages.

(25) (a) $S \rightarrow NP_{SUBJ} \ NP_{OBJ} \ V$

    (b) $S \rightarrow NP_{OBJ} \ NP_{SUBJ} \ V$

    (c) $S \rightarrow NP_{\{^{SUBJ}_{OBJ}\}} \ NP_{\{^{OBJ}_{SUBJ}\}} \ V$

    (d) $S \rightarrow NP^*_{\{^{SUBJ}_{OBJ}\}} \ V$

    (e) $S \rightarrow NP^*_{\{^{SUBJ}_{OBJ}\}} \ NP_{OBJ2} \ V$

    (f) $S \rightarrow NP_{OBJ2} \ NP^*_{\{^{SUBJ}_{OBJ}\}} \ V$

    (g) $S \rightarrow NP^*_{\{^{SUBJ}_{OBJ}_{OBJ2}\}} \ NP^*_{\{^{SUBJ}_{OBJ}_{OBJ2}\}} \ V$

    (h) $S \rightarrow NP^*_{\{^{SUBJ}_{OBJ}_{OBJ2}\}} \ V$

(26) (a) boy dog pat

    (b) dog boy pat

    (c) boy dog bone give

    (d) bone boy dog give

    (e) bone dog boy give

    (f) dog boy bone give

    (g) boy bone dog give

    (h) dog bone boy give

So far I have ignored the role of case markers in these non-configurational rules, but the existing procedures can acquire their distribution with no further modifications. Let us return to the Warlpiri example, where the child was left with rule (27a) (I ignore for now the other annotations on the AP).

(27) (a) $S \rightarrow NP_{SUBJ \atop CASE=ERG} \ \ Aux \ NP_{OBJ \atop CASE=ABS} \ \ VP \ AP_{CASE=ERG}$

    (b) $S \rightarrow NP_{OBJ \atop CASE=ABS} \ \ Aux \ NP_{SUBJ \atop CASE=ERG} \ \ VP \ AP_{CASE=ABS}$

    (c) $S \rightarrow NP_{\left\{^{SUBJ}_{CASE=ERG} \atop ^{OBJ}_{CASE=ABS}\right\}} \ \ Aux \ NP_{\left\{^{OBJ}_{CASE=ABS} \atop ^{SUBJ}_{CASE=ERG}\right\}} \ \ VP \ AP_{\left\{^{CASE=ERG}_{CASE=ABS}\right\}}$

As soon as the child hears a sentence in which subject and object are reversed, such as *kangaroo-ABS Aux boy-ERG ride bouncy-ABS*, he or she will coin rule (27b), which the disjunction procedure P6(c) collapses with (27a) to yield (27c). Mohanan (1982), Klavans (1982), and Bresnan (1982b) argue that disjoined pairs of functions and case equations, which is what the procedures acquire, are sufficient to account for case-marking constraints in non-configurational languages. The same procedure, incidentally, is what we needed to acquire the English V" rule in which adjunct and oblique PPs intermingle in any order.

Evidence that children in fact first coin phrase structure rules in which case markers are specified for particular positions comes from an elegant set of experiments on sentence comprehension and production in Japanese children by Hakuta (1982). In Japanese, the nominative case marker can appear in either the first or second noun phrase position, and can refer either to the agent or patient argument of an action verb in either position, depending on the voice of the verb. If children first acquire rules specifying only order, not case marking, they should invariably interpret the first noun phrase as the subject (since that is its more frequent position), regardless of case marking. If they first acquire rules for case marking, not order, they should invariably interpret the noun phrase marked as nominative as the subject, regardless of order. If they first acquire independent rules specifying order and specifying case, their comprehension rate should be an additive function of the comprehension rate for order and the comprehension rate for case. Instead, Hakuta found a strong interaction between order and case, such that his least advanced subjects (measured in terms of mean length of utterance; the children were approximately 2–3 years old) comprehended sentences reliably only when the nominative case marker was in the first position. This tendency diminished somewhat with age, such that his most advanced subjects were able to exploit both case and order at a rate above chance in any combination. Children's distortions in an imitation task and their productions in a production task confirm this pattern; the younger children had a strong tendency to associate particular case markers with particular positions. Hakuta's experiments are thus consistent with an account in which the child first acquires phrase structure rules conflating particular cases with particular phrase structure positions; the child can then master a greater range of structures when he or she acquires a larger set of rules or begins to collapse rules.

Free constituent order versus topic-prominence: some differences. The process described in connection with (25)–(27) above leaves the child with a rule that specifies that *some* grammatical function, together with its case, must appear with each noun phrase, though any function will do. Interestingly, the child must also have the means to learn when *no* case or grammatical function may be assigned to a constituent. In topic-prominent languages, the topic or focus constituent need not have any grammatical function, and in fact, often *must* not have any function or else the Coherence requirement would be violated. This creates some problems. When the child hears a sentence whose topic happens to be construable as playing the role of subject, the procedures will append SUBJ to that constituent. Likewise, when he or she hears a sentence whose topic happens to play some other role, the corresponding function will be disjoined to SUBJ in the annotations on that constituent. However, unlike the case of simple free constituent order rules, the child cannot simply survive with a disjunction of several grammatical functions annotated to the TOPIC constituent, since that would incorrectly rule out topics that have no grammatical function. There is, however, a simple solution. As mentioned in Chapter 2, a good diagnostic of topic-prominence is the presence of topics that are not arguments of the main predicate (e.g., in sentences analogous to *as for seafood, I like scrod*; see Li and Thompson, 1976). Say the child was equipped with a procedure that not only appended the TOPIC symbol to a nonargument constituent that served as the current discourse topic, but that also expunged any disjunctions of grammatical functions currently appended to such a constituent. That would allow the child in the future to generate any topic constituent in topic position, regardless of its semantic relation to the predicate, as required. Such a procedure would be an embodiment of the topic-prominent/subject-prominent degree of freedom in language variation. That is, by being equipped with this procedure, the child would be prepared to learn that various parts of a target language could be noncommittal about grammatical relations while being dedicated instead to the expression of notions related to topic and focus. (See also Chapter 5, where I touch briefly on the acquisition of the morphological encoding of topic and focus.)

Cross-Category Constituent Order Freedom

One degree of order freedom still must be learned. So far I have shown how constituent order freedom can be acquired for different instances of a single category within an expansion of a parent category. It is also necessary to show how the child learns order freedom among different categories within an expansion, such as the free intermingling of verbs and nouns after the auxiliary in Warlpiri. Again, P6(a) and (c) do just that. Consider the Warlpiri-like rules (28a) and (b), ignoring annotations. P6(c) collapses them to form (28c), which P6(a) boils down to (28d). That rule generates sequences of adjectives and nouns in any order.

(28) (a) S → NP Aux NP AP V
  (b) S → NP Aux AP NP V
  (c) S → NP Aux $\begin{Bmatrix} NP \\ AP \end{Bmatrix} \begin{Bmatrix} AP \\ NP \end{Bmatrix}$ V
  (d) S → NP Aux $\begin{Bmatrix} NP \\ AP \end{Bmatrix}$* VP

A more economical notation for such disjunctions can be obtained by replacing the categories disjoined within braces with the variable *XP* or *X″*, plus the syntactic feature the categories share, in the sense of Chomsky's (1970), Jackendoff's (1977), and Bresnan's (1977, 1982c) versions of X-bar theory. For example, (28d) disjoins an NP and an AP, which share the syntactic feature [− *transitive*] (or [− *obj*] or [− O]) according to Bresnan's (1982c) and Jackendoff's (1977) X-bar theories. Thus (28d) can be expressed as (29).

(29) S → NP Aux $XP^*_{[-\text{transitive}]}$ VP

If a rule is subsequently coined that has the VP preceding the noun and adjective phrases, the syntactic feature [− *transitive*] will no longer apply and will be eliminated, leaving (30a). If a variety of individual categories sharing no common feature alternate in the pre-auxiliary position, P6(c), using the simplified variable-plus-feature notation, would create (30b). (I propose that *Aux* categories are never collapsed with any other category, based on the fact that auxiliaries are given distinguished positions in languages; see Chapter 7, and Steele, 1981.)

(30) (a) S → NP Aux XP*
  (b) S → XP Aux XP*

As a final note about the linguistic adequacy of the rules the procedures create, it may be pointed out that Hale (1981), Lapointe (1981b), Mohanan (1982), Klavans (1982), and others have argued that X-bar rules with Kleene-star operators and variables like X representing classes of syntactic categories may be adequate to account for free constituent order rules in both configurational and nonconfigurational languages.

It must be stressed that the P6 procedures are tentative, and their potential interactions and exact conditions of application must be worked out carefully (as in Walsh, 1981) to ensure that they do not wildly create word order freedom where a language does not permit it. It should be noted as well that the procedures make very strong predictions about language universals and children's language development. Note that in each example I have given in this section, the child hears a set of sentence types T and then collapses rules in such a way that he or she can then generate a new set of sentence types T' properly including T. Thus I have no choice but to predict that languages containing the sentence types in T but not those in $T' - T$ do not exist, because they would be unlearnable according to the theory I am proposing. Furthermore, any child with sufficient exposure to T should be able, without further inputs, to produce and comprehend $T' - T$, all other things being equal. If any prediction from among these two sets fails, procedures P6 would have to be modified or abandoned.

That having been noted, I would like to point out that the success of the P procedures in acquiring approximations of phrase structure rules for widely divergent languages is a noteworthy accomplishment of the acquisition theory. This is especially true given that the procedures have been modified in only tiny ways from their original presentation in Pinker (1982), where only very simplified English phrase structure rules, plus VSO clause structure, were considered. For if my arguments are on the right track, these procedures might embody some of the inferences needed to acquire exocentric constructions and X-bar violations in English, and nonconfigurationality, free constituent order, case-marking constraints, and topic-prominent constructions in languages unlike English. All of these linguistic phenomena are of course many times more complex than the discussion in this chapter suggests, but I think that the theory proposed here represents a good first step in the direction of accounting for their acquisition.

4 | Phrase Structure Rules: Developmental Considerations

I
T HAS LONG been noticed that children's first word combinations show regularities of word order and compositionality while largely lacking inflections, closed-class morphemes, control relations, and other complex properties of mature grammars (e.g., Brown and Fraser, 1963; Braine, 1963). Since word order and compositionality (i.e., the way that a sentence meaning is determined by the arrangement of the sentence's parts) are dictated by phrase structure rules, it is natural to expect that children are learning and using something resembling phrase structure rules when they first string words together. Not only is this expectation intuitively natural, but it is what the acquisition theory presented in Chapter 3 predicts under the simplest set of assumptions. Since the theory is designed to acquire phrase structure rules, it predicts that phrase structure rules are what the child acquires. Furthermore, the procedures for acquiring phrase structure rules, unlike those for such competences as control relations, auxiliaries, long-distance binding, and lexical productivity, do not presuppose for the most part that any other sort of syntactic knowledge has been acquired beforehand. Thus not only should phrase structure rules be acquired, they should be among the first grammatical devices acquired. In this chapter I attempt to show that this prediction is indeed tenable in light of the developmental evidence.

Showing that the child uses phrase structure rules in his or her first word combinations (what Brown, 1973, calls "Stage I") is a very ambitious goal.[1] Stage I speech is the aspect of children's language that historically has received the closest scrutiny. There have appeared well over a dozen accounts of Stage I abilities, and, as Brown (1973) has noted, enough word sequences have been recorded to provide counterexamples to almost any hypothesis. Furthermore, there is a near-consensus among developmental psycholinguists that phrase structure rules are in fact inappropriate as descriptions of the young child's abilities. In this chapter I will argue against the consensus and propose an account that I fully expect will be met with some counterexamples. My defense is that an acquisition theory that faces occasional counterexamples is better than no acquisition theory at all.

One might argue on other grounds that children's first word combinations are not the sort of data that an acquisition theory need address. Children in general are poor linguistic informants (see de Villiers and de Villiers, 1974); Stage I children in particular, being in the "terrible twos" or younger, are notoriously uncooperative as experimental subjects. Thus we are left mainly with their spontaneous word combinations, which, being two words or so in length, are not very likely to help us discriminate among alternative theories of their internal structure. Furthermore, it is entirely possible that Stage I speech represents a prelinguistic system akin to a fledgling's first flutterings, without substantial continuity with the adult state (as Chomsky, 1975, has conjectured). For these two reasons, there seems to be a near-consensus among linguists that one should not even expect that an acquisition theory will account for Stage I speech. Again, I will fly in the face of this consensus, appealing to the argument in Chapter 1 that a hypothesis of continuity should not be rejected until the evidence makes it untenable.

Any work that argues against the well-entrenched consensuses of two mutually unsympathetic groups of scholars is bound to contain something to offend almost everyone. And in a domain where the data contain numerous counterexamples to simple hypotheses but where each datum is too impoverished to support complex hypotheses, no single account will convince a skeptic. But if one is to approach the goal of constraining an acquisition theory with both learnability and developmental considerations, these risks must be taken. If in this most difficult of domains I succeed at constructing an account that is at least plausible in light of developmental and learnability considerations, I hope the reader will agree that the goals for language acquisition research spelled out in Chapter 1 are feasible in the general case.

In this chapter I first present an approximation of a grammar for Stage I speech of the sort that would be acquired by the learning procedures described in Chapter 3. This grammar is not motivated by a detailed examination of children's early word combinations, only by a consideration of children's most frequent gross utterance types and by a desire to posit rules that are as similar to adult rules (hence, learnable and extendible by the procedures) as possible. Following that, I consider five issues, each concerning an aspect of the rule system that admits of alternative formulations, and examine the developmental evidence relevant to selecting from among them. The discussion will be unconventional for developmental psycholinguistics in discussing accounts of child language in tandem with the learning mechanism that would have produced the knowledge described by the accounts, and thus in placing a high priority on constructing accounts that are independently motivated by learnability considerations. In addition, I adopt the parsimony metric argued for in Chapter 1, which values accounts that minimize qualitative changes in the child's underlying representational machinery.

A Partial Grammar for Stage I Speech

Let us consider the descriptive taxonomy of utterances that Brown (1973, p. 203) constructed, based on his study of three English-speaking children and on comparisons with data from other children acquiring a variety of languages. I will restrict the discussion to within-sentence syntax, ignoring vocatives and sentences adjoined with *hi* or anaphoric *no*. I will also ignore interrogatives, as these appear to be marked either by intonation (for yes-no questions) or by routinelike juxtaposition of a *wh*-word to a constituent (for *wh*-questions). (I discuss these constructions in detail in Chapter 7.)

Brown divides the remaining sentence types into three categories. "Main-verb sentences" consist of two- or three-word subsets, in their proper relative order, drawn from the sequence *agent-action-dative-object-locative*, or from the sequence *person affected-state-stimulus* (e.g. for perception verbs). "Noun phrases" consist of *attribute-entity*, which includes *recurrence-entity* (e.g., *more juice*), and *possessor-possessed*. "Missing copula sentences" include *demonstrative-entity, entity-locative*, and *entity-attribute*. Bloom, Lightbown, and Hood (1975) provide a similar taxonomy for the speech of their four subjects.

In (1) I present a fragment of a grammar and lexicon that is constructed to be consistent with Brown's taxonomy and to resemble an adult LFG (ignoring the X-bar distinctions).

(1) (a) S → NP$_{SUBJ}$ VP

(b) VP → (NP$_{OBJ}$) $\left\{ \begin{array}{l} (NP \{ {}^{OBJ2}_{N\text{-}COMP} \}) \\ (PP \{ {}^{OBL}_{P\text{-}COMP} \}) \\ (AP_{A\text{-}COMP}) \end{array} \right\}$

(c) NP → $\left\{ \begin{array}{l} (NP_{POSS}) \\ (AP_{MOD}) \\ (QP_{QUANT}) \end{array} \right\}$ N

(d) AP → A

(e) PP → P (NP$_{OBJ}$)

(f) QP → Q

Verbs: fix (SUBJ, OBJ)
give (SUBJ, OBJ2, OBJ)
put (SUBJ, OBJ, OBL$_{loc}$)
go (SUBJ, OBL$_{goal}$)
see (SUBJ, OBJ)
come (SUBJ)

Nouns: doggie
ball
I
it
Mommy
that

Adjectives: dirty
cool
wet

Prepositions: here
there
in

Quantifiers: more
no
other

Examples of the use of these rules, taken from Brown (1973), are listed in (2).

(2) (a) Mommy fix (S → NP$_{SUBJ}$VP) (Eve I)

(b) I ride horsie (VP → NP$_{OBJ}$) (Sarah I)

(c) give doggie paper (VP → V NP$_{OBJ}$ NP$_{OBJ2}$) (Adam I)

(d) put truck window (VP → V NP$_{OBJ}$ PP$_{OBL}$) (Adam I)

(e) that Mommy soup (VP → V NP$_{N\text{-}COMP}$; NP → NP$_{POSS}$ N) (Eve I)

(f) more tree there (NP → QP$_{QUANT}$ N; VP → V PP$_{P\text{-}COMP}$) (Sarah I)

(g) pillow dirty (VP → V AP$_{A\text{-}COMP}$) (Adam I)

(h) pretty boat (NP → AP$_{MOD}$ N)

Let us examine this grammar in terms of the criteria for adequate accounts of children's language introduced in Chapter 1: consistency with children's language, extendibility to an adult grammar, and learnability. The grammar embodies all the constituent orderings common in Stage I speech and thus will generate all the sentence types in Brown's taxonomy with their correct word orders. Rarer constructions, such as conjunctions, instrumentals, benefactives, and adjuncts, can be accounted for with minor extensions of the phrase structure rules and lexicon.

Unfortunately, (1) also generates many word combinations that are systematically absent from children's speech. It generates constituents in their adult positions regardless of their semantic roles, whereas children, it has been claimed, place words in particular positions only if they play certain semantic roles, have certain semantic properties, or belong to lists whose members are learned one by one. The grammar generates expanded NPs in any matrix position, whereas children tend to expand NPs only in sentence-final positions. And it generates sequences that are arbitrarily long, whereas children in Stage I speak in two- or at most three-word combinations. In each of these cases, the overgeneration of the phrase structure grammar has been used to argue that some other type of rule system is superior, and in each of these cases, I will argue in later sections either that the degree of undergeneration has been exaggerated, that there are independent reasons to expect the undergeneration to occur, or that the alternative accounts do not themselves solve the problems attributed to the phrase structure account. Here it suffices to point out that the phrase structure grammar in (1) is capable of generating the common patterns of Stage I speech.

The second aspect of grammar (1) that must be examined is its extendibility to a full adult grammar. In particular, one must examine two aspects of the grammar: adult rules or rule components that are *absent*, and adult rules or rule components that are *different*. Absent constituents, such as determiners and the constituents in the full expansions of NP, VP, and S, will simply be acquired by the P procedures as the relevant input exemplars are processed (which will in turn be determined by availability in the input, segmentation and isolation of grammatical morphemes, and whatever learning or maturation is prerequisite to grasping the semantics underlying the syntactic constructions to be acquired). The only rules of grammar (1) that are *different* from those of an adult grammar are the disjoined VP-final constituents in (1b) and prenominal constituents in (1a). In the adult grammar, for example, the noun phrase OBJ2 precedes the

A-COMP, N-COMP, and P-COMP, and in the NP the possessor NP, prenominal AP, and quantifier phrase are ordered with respect to one another. In grammar (1) I simply disjoined such constituents because there was no evidence that the child ordered them in his or her rules, unlike the other orderings in (1), which were all found to be reliable in children's speech (more on order later). Fortunately, procedure P6(d) orders disjoined constituents when they are heard contiguously in a sentence, and so the child will learn the proper order of these constituents as soon as they appear in an adult sentence. Alternatively, it is possible that these constituents are indeed ordered in the child's rules, and that the failure to find them in order may have been caused by sampling error, vocabulary deficiencies, or the speech planning limitations discussed below. In that case, there would be no developmental change toward adulthood to account for.

The third aspect of grammar (1) that I examine is its learnability in the first place. Unfortunately, there are three problems for the grammar that become evident when we consider certain facts about the child's abilities. These problems, and solutions to them, are discussed in the next section.

Three Learnability Problems for the Stage I Grammar

CATEGORIZATION OF PHRASES

The first problem arises when we ask how certain of the rules in (1) could have been learned from parental input given that the proper categorization of some of the constituents in (1) cannot be determined by the semantics of their referents alone. For example, locative complements and oblique arguments are both categorized as constituents of PPs in English only because the locative or case-marking preposition is a free morpheme. In other languages, the locative or case-marking relation could be marked by an affix on the noun (e.g., the so-called "allative," "sublative," and "illative" cases) and the constituent is generated directly as an NP, not as a daughter of PP. Similarly, the N-COMP, A-COMP, and P-COMP constituents used in demonstrative-entity, entity-attribute, and entity-locative utterances are generated as daughters of VP in English only because of the presence of the copula *be*. In languages without a copula, such complements could be generated directly as daughters of S. The rub is that the child appears to have no mastery of any locative prepositions until at least Stage II and no mastery of the copula until Stage III-V (for uncontractible copulas) or late Stage V (for contractible copulas) (Brown, 1973). How, then, could he or she know that

English locatives are in PPs and that English predicate complements are in VPs?

It will not suffice simply to say that the child begins with
deficient rules generating bare locatives and complements, then
adds rules for PPs and predicational VPs when prepositions and
copulas are eventually processed. In that case nothing would
then prevent the child, once grown to adulthood, from uttering
ungrammatical sentences like *Reagan went Washington*, or *Reagan
conservative Republican* unless the child had also found some way
of expunging the earlier incorrect rule. And in the absence of
negative evidence, it is unclear what would motivate the child
to do so.

A Hypothesis: Latent Mastery of Closed-Class Morphemes

One solution to this problem would be to claim that the child's
rules for locatives and complements were indeed adultlike, and
that his or her failure to use the grammatical morphemes could
be attributed to articulatory difficulties or production limitations
akin to the one limiting utterances to two words in length. On
this account, the child might even be able to understand the
copula or prepositions that were missing from his or her speech,
since they would still be generated by the child's competence
grammar. In support of this account, one could appeal to Shipley, Smith, and Gleitman's (1969) finding that children whose
speech is telegraphic obey imperatives containing closed-class
morphemes more often than imperatives lacking them, even
though at that age closed-class morphemes are lacking in the
children's speech. Unfortunately, it is possible that these children did not really assign any grammatical or semantic structure
to the grammatical morphemes in the full commands, since the
criterion for success on the task simply required the children to
attend to the utterance-final noun. Thus we do not know whether
the form of the children's responses were contingent upon the
actual grammatical morphemes inserted. It is possible, for example, that the children in the Shipley et al. experiment were
more receptive to the full commands because they contained a
greater number of familiar words and conformed to English prosodic patterns.

Furthermore, it is not as easy to use explanations based on
output limitations in the case of missing prepositions and copulas as it is for missing nominal or verbal constituents. In the
case of major constituents one finds the child "sampling" all
possible ordered subsets of a multiword sequence (e.g., *agent-*

action, agent-object, action-object; Bloom, 1970; Brown, 1973), and so an account based on processing limitations becomes more parsimonious than one listing each subset separately (this issue is discussed at length in a later section). In addition, the full three-word sequence appears shortly after all the two-word sub-sequences are uttered, and its appearance is coincidental with the productive use of three-word utterances in general. In contrast, children do not generally sample ordered subsets from the sequence NP-P-NP (e.g., we do not find *doggie on*), or from the sequence NP-*be*-XP (e.g., we do not find *that is*).[2] Furthermore, prepositions and copulas do not suddenly appear once the child begins to utter three-word sequences; rather, their occurrence can be delayed by $1\frac{1}{2}$ years or more (e.g., in the case of contractible copulas—Brown, 1973). Even when copulas are first used, often it is not clear that they are being treated as separate morphemes (Brown, 1973; Maratsos and Kuczaj, 1978). In general, it appears to be very common for unstressed closed-class morphemes not to be present in the earliest stages in the acquisition of many languages (Brown, 1973; Slobin, 1973; Gleitman and Wanner, 1982a). Thus as much as it would suit my purposes to claim that Stage I children have latent control over the morphemes whose presence defines the categorization of certain constituents, it does not seem to be tenable given available evidence.

Solving the Learnability Problem

Here I present a modification to the learning procedure that can acquire knowledge sufficient to order a major constituent relative to other constituents, while remaining uncommitted as to precisely how to attach that constituent pending future analysis. The problem for a prepositionless or copulaless child is that there is no way to determine the mother of the object or complement constituent. Either of the configurations in Figure 4.1

Figure 4.1

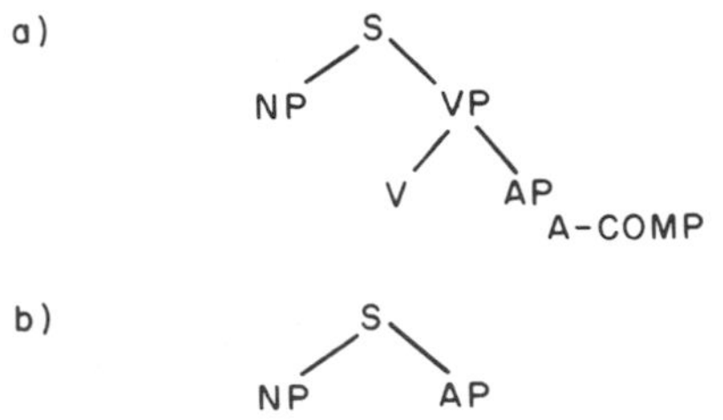

a)

b)

Figure 4.2

a)

b)

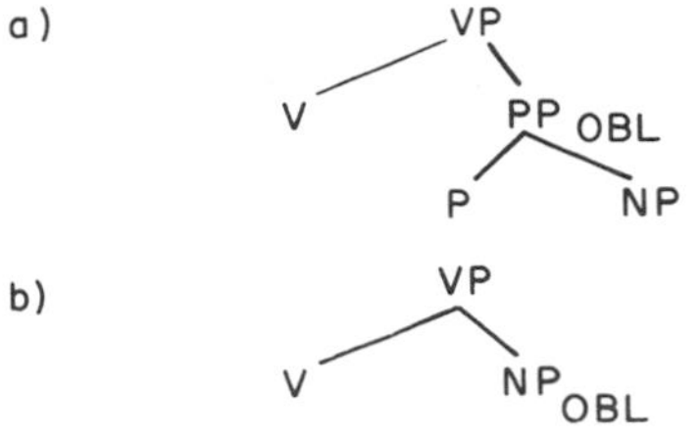

and Figure 4.2 might be possible in the language to be learned. In view of the fact that the mothers of these constituents are unknown, I will call them *orphans*. Note, though, that while the child does not know for certain what the mother node of the orphan is, he or she does know an *ancestor* node of the orphan: S in the case of the AP in Figure 4.1, VP in the case of the NP in Figure 4.2. Pursuing the metaphor, let us say that the child can give the ancestor *temporary custody* of the orphan. The rules in (3) embody this relationship, symbolized by the question marks surrounding the orphan constituent in temporary custody.

(3) S → NP$_{SUBJ}$?AP?
     VP → V ?NP?$_{OBL}$

Orphans are eventually assigned to their rightful parents, if the language requires them, according to principle (4):

(4) When an orphan constituent is encountered in the input as a daugh-
    ter of a phrase which in turn is a daughter of the ancestor phrase
    having temporary custody of the orphan, and the intervening phrase
    is in the same position within the ancestor phrase as that occupied
    by the orphan in the temporary rule: (a) replace the orphan symbol
    with the label for the intervening node in the expansion of the
    ancestor, and (b) add a rule generating the orphan as a daughter
    of the intervening phrase.

In other words, if a node is in temporary custody, it can be removed from its custodial parent if there is evidence that there should in fact be a node intervening between the two. Such evidence can arise when a preposition or copula is finally ana-lyzed and the phrase structure acquisition procedures P3 and P4 make it the head of a phrase immediately dominating the orphan. For example, if a Stage I child has the rules in (3), and then isolates prepositions and copulas and so can analyze var-ious inputs as in part (a) of Figure 4.1 and Figure 4.2, princi-ple (4) causes him or her to replace the rules in (3) with those in (5).

(5) S → NP$_{SUBJ}$ VP
     VP → V AP$_{A-COMP}$
     VP → V PP$_{OBL}$
     PP → P NP

(The addition of the A-COMP function to the AP is an automatic consequence of its now lacking an overt subject; see Bresnan,

1982c; and Chapter 6). Thanks to principle (4), the child has expunged rules that generate ungrammatical sentences, without requiring negative evidence. At the same time the child can utter or comprehend sentences containing the orphan constituent until the evidence indicating their proper parenthood is available.

Thus, a proper grammar for Stage I English-speaking children would look more like (6) than like (1).

(6) (a) $S \rightarrow NP_{SUBJ} \begin{Bmatrix} VP \\ ?AP? \\ ?PP? \\ ?NP? \end{Bmatrix}$

(b) $VP \rightarrow V\ (NP_{OBJ}) \begin{Bmatrix} (NP_{OBJ2}) \\ (?NP?_{N\text{-}COMP}) \\ (?NP?_{OBL}) \end{Bmatrix}$

(c) $NP \rightarrow \begin{Bmatrix} (NP_{POSS}) \\ (AP_{MOD}) \\ (QP_{QUANT}) \end{Bmatrix} N$

(d) $AP \rightarrow A$

(e) $PP \rightarrow P$ (for *in, here, there*)

(f) $QP \rightarrow Q$

Note that before all the head constituents in (6a) were collapsed within braces in a single rule, it would be possible for a child to know the order of subject and verb, without knowing the order of subject and locative complement. Braine (1976) argues that some English-speaking children in fact pass through such a stage; this argument will be examined in detail in a later section.

If the language to be learned is unlike English and does generate the "orphan" constituents within the custodial ancestor phrase, the child will never encounter configurations like part (a) of Figure 4.1 and Figure 4.2, and so will never apply principle (4) to alter the rules in (3). Temporary custody becomes de facto permanent custody, even if no procedure explicitly makes it so. Thus the term "temporary custody" does not really imply temporariness per se for the rule in question, only preemptability by other rules.

Unfortunately, if the language allows a phrase to be generated in both positions—that is, under its mother or grandmother (e.g., adverbial phrases in English, which can be generated as daughters of VP or S)—then procedure (4) as it stands would only allow the former rule to survive. Thus the effects of (4) should be modified by an additional proviso such as (7).

(7) If there exists a rule generating $[_z[_y \ldots A \ldots]]$, and then an exemplar of $[_z \ldots A \ldots]$ is encountered, do not expunge the rule generating $[_z \ldots A \ldots]$.

In other words, even though an expansion having temporary custody of a constituent will be preempted by later exemplars containing an intervening constituent, if the rule generating an intervening constituent has already been acquired and *then* an exemplar of the temporary custody relationship is processed, no preemption occurs. The assumption is that if a child has acquired rules like (5), he or she must have been able to isolate prepositions or copulas. Having that ability, the child may deduce that an input sentence that appears to lack prepositions or copulas must indeed lack them, and thus the input sentence as processed exemplifies a genuine rule of the target grammar. Thus languages that generate a constituent both as a daughter and as a granddaughter of another constituent are learnable, thanks to proviso (7).

One might wonder how a child decides whether a constituent should be entered as an orphan—after all, any constituent is a potential orphan. There are two possibilities. One is that a child might consider a phrase to be an orphan if he or she hears it adjacent to a potential closed-class morpheme (e.g., an unstressed segment lacking an argument-taking predicate), but is not yet sure whether that morpheme is serving as the head of an intervening phrase (e.g., the morpheme could simply be part of a different word, or be a case marker). This account would be consistent with the Shipley, Smith, and Gleitman (1969) experiment showing that the Stage I child is receptive at the very least to the presence of closed-class morphemes in adult speech, whether or not they are analyzed appropriately. A second possibility, which would not necessarily exclude the first, is that there is a universal class of potential orphans and that the child always treats them as such, pending evidence to the contrary. Each such potential orphan would be defined by two things: (1) A recognition procedure for the orphan. For the current examples, this might be the semantic function of the constituent, such as being one of the oblique arguments of a predicate (*goal, source, instrument*, etc.—this would signal potential PPs), or being a stative, locative, or nominal predicate (this would signal potential complements of a copula). (2) A pair of alternative phrase structure analyses, both of which are consistent with the semantic type, and one of which preempts the other when its appropriate morpheme is isolated. For oblique arguments, PP would preempt NP; for complements, X-COMP with VP would preempt sentential head. I have mentioned oblique arguments, locative adjuncts, and predicate complements as potential orphans; in general, any type of constituent that may occur in a phrase with a closed-class head in one language, but may also occur independently from such a phrase in another language, is a potential orphan.[3]

NONBRANCHING NODES AND THE LEARNABILITY OF SUBMAXIMAL CATEGORIES

In this section I present another case in which the mechanisms of orphanhood and preemption may be necessary to solve a learnability problem for the Stage I child. Rules (6d–f) contain a number of nonbranching rules, and because the grammars of (1) and (6) are written in traditional phrase structure notation rather than X-bar notation, they conceal still other nonbranching rules that a Stage I child would posit when applying the P procedures to the input. These would include $N' \rightarrow N$, $V'' \rightarrow V'$, $A'' \rightarrow A'$, $A' \rightarrow A$, $P'' \rightarrow P'$, $Q'' \rightarrow Q'$, and $Q' \rightarrow Q$. In a three-level X-bar theory like that assumed in Pinker (1982) there would be even more nonbranching rules. This strikes many people as attributing a lot of useless structure to the child's utterances, such as is shown in Figure 4.3.

The existence of the extra nonbranching nodes is somewhat unparsimonious, but there is an even better reason to be suspicious of the analysis: the type of generalization it represents the child as making presents us with an interesting learnability problem. The implicit generalization is that phrase structure rules can only define the positions of *maximal* projections of major nonhead categories (this aspect of the P procedures is taken directly from Jackendoff, 1977). For example, the child can learn that N" objects, say, follow the verb. This subsumes the case of

Figure 4.3

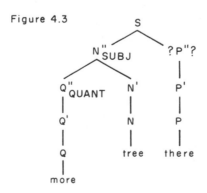

bare submaximal noun phrases occurring in that position, such as an N' or a bare noun, since they can be generated at the bottom of a nonbranching tree fragment (all nonheads are optional in X-bar theory). The child could *never* learn, however, that *only* a submaximal category of a given type can appear in a phrase. For example, no child could ever learn that bare nouns, but not modified nouns, may appear in a given position in a phrase because the P procedures in their current form cannot construct rules like $X'' \rightarrow X'$ N containing a submaximal complement.

Why should this be a problem? It is a problem because the child will in fact be faced with rules containing submaximal constituents, and the existing procedures will prevent him or her from learning them. English has at least two examples. First, I analyze fronted auxiliaries in English questions as verbs generated by a rule like $S \rightarrow V_{AUX=+} N''_{SUBJ} V''_{V\text{-}COMP}$ (see Chapter 7, and Kaplan and Bresnan, 1982). Currently, if the child successfully analyzes auxiliaries as verbs, he or she will generate them in the grammar as maximally projected verb phrases identical to predicate verb phrases, i.e., $S \rightarrow (V''_{AUX=+}) N''_{SUBJ} (V''_{V\text{-}COMP})$. But this generalization is invalid, leading to nonsentences such as (8).

(8) *Has been jogging John?[4]

Similarly, prenominal adjectives in English will be treated by the child as maximal adjective phrases identical to predicate APs, leading to (9).

(9) *The angry at Reagan man shouted.[5]

Other languages also require the specification of the positions of submaximal constituents, such as the rule generating verbs in second position in German root sentences, which Lapointe (1981b) proposes is $S \rightarrow X V Y'''^*$ (Lapointe proposes similar rules for other languages).

Simplifying the Child's Grammar and Solving the Learnability Problem

A simple modification of the learning procedures P2 and P4 will allow the child to posit no higher a projection than is warranted by the input data. Instead of building branches extending every lexical category node upward to its maximal projection, the procedure could build the branch just high enough to encompass the arguments, modifiers, and specifiers that appear contiguously with that category according to the X-bar principles of attachment. Thus the word sequences in (10) would be analyzed by the revised procedures as the structures shown in Figure 4.4.

(10) (a) I slept.
    (b) I saw pictures.
    (c) I saw pictures of her.
    (d) I saw the pictures of her.
    (e) I saw the pictures on Tuesday.
    (f) The children saw the pictures of her last Tuesday.

(Quite possibly the modified procedure whose behavior on the inputs in (10) is traced out in Figure 4.4 could itself be improved. For example, it could be constrained by positing only lexical categories X, or their maximal projections X'', never intermediate projections X', as Lapointe, 1981b, has argued. Or, it could make bolder generalizations in certain domains, such as generating the maximal projections of a specified subset of categories everywhere in the grammar if there was evidence for their maximal projection in any one position.)

This new procedure not only refrains from positing unnecessary structure in the language as a whole, but it also refrains from generalizing the amount of hierarchical structure in a phrase found in one position to other positions without direct evidence. Thus it will not mistakenly generate full verb phrases sentence-initially or full adjective phrases prenominally in English. Note, though, that the new procedure is not completely conservative either, since it generalizes the internal structure of a constituent at a given level of projection from one external position to any other external position. That is, all X^n are identical regardless of where they are generated, as long as n remains constant. Note also that the rest of the P procedures function identically to the way they did before.

Modifications to the Stage I Grammar

Now that we have altered the procedures for the acquisition of phrase structure so as to solve certain parsimony and learnability problems, is the tentative Stage I grammar still learnable and extendible according to the acquisition theory? No— one can show that the grammar contains information that the Stage I child could not reasonably have acquired given the revised procedures, the available input, and the child's lack of knowledge of closed-class morphemes. For example, a child who

Figure 4.4

a)

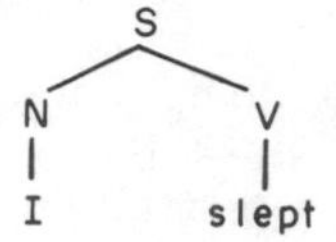

new rules: S ⟶ N V

b)

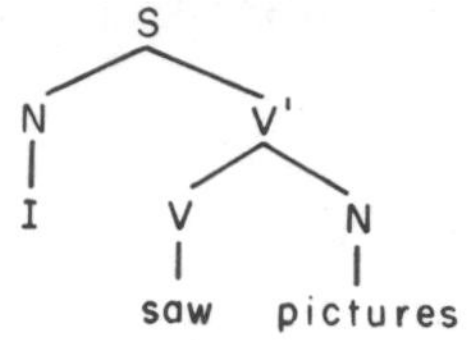

new rules: S ⟶ N V'
V' ⟶ V N

c)

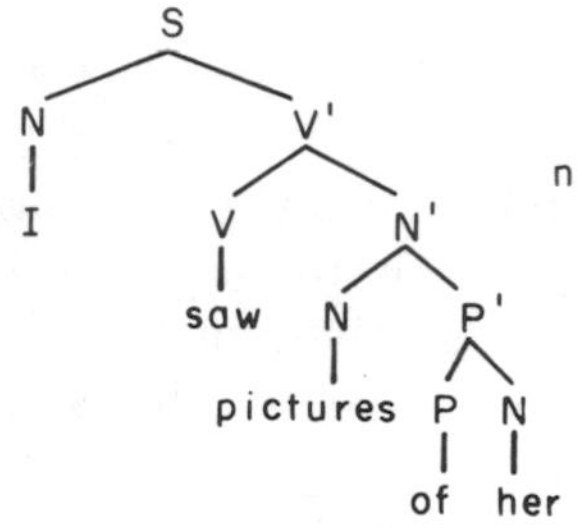

new rules: V' ⟶ V N'
N' ⟶ N P'
P' ⟶ P N

d)

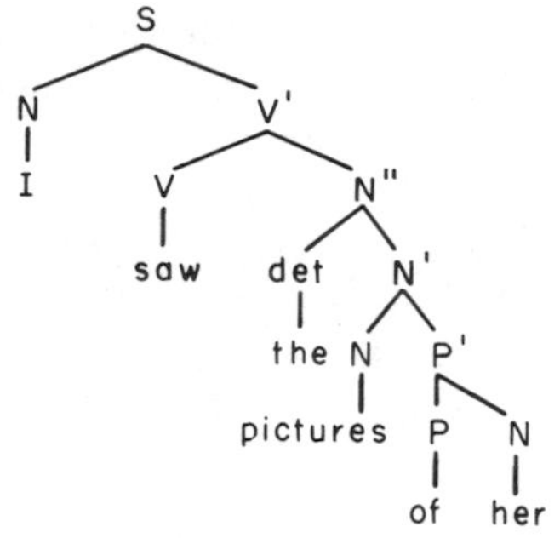

new rules: V' ⟶ V N"
N" ⟶ det N'

e)

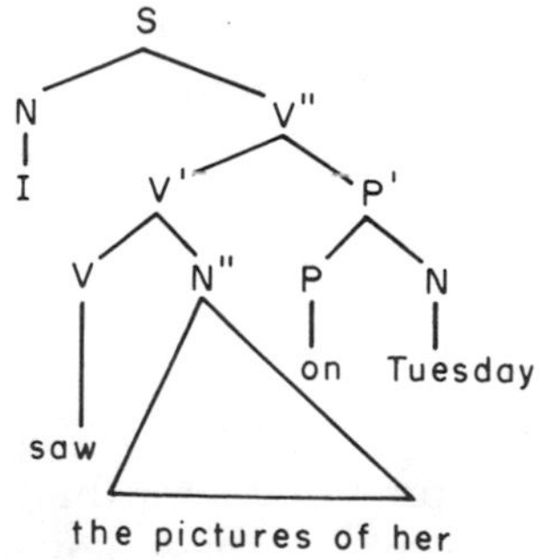

new rules: S ⟶ N V"
V" ⟶ V'P'

f)

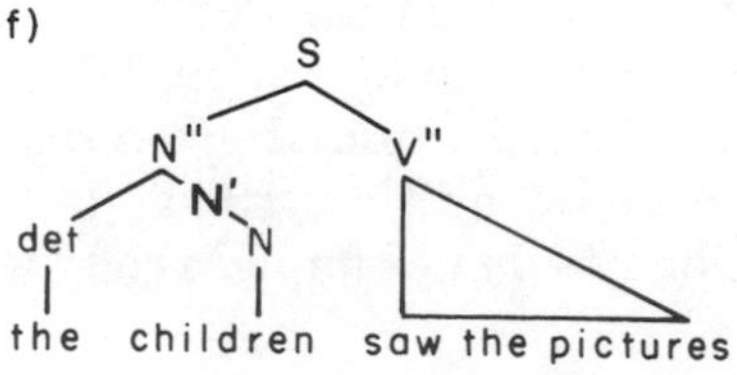

new rule: S ⟶ N" V"

knew only intransitive prepositions like *in, there,* or *downstairs* (see n. 2) would have no reason to posit a PP. Without having processed complement-taking adjectives like *fond of Mary* or preadjectival modifiers like *very,* there is no evidence for AP. For that matter, if the child has either not heard or not processed modifiers of subject NPs, he or she would have no evidence that there is more than a bare N in subject position (relevant developmental evidence is discussed later in the chapter). Thus grammar (6) would be more realistic if one eliminated the nonbranching structure that the revised P2 and P4 would probably not have posited, resulting in Figure 4.5. (It is uncertain which nominals should be bare Ns and which should be full NPs.)

Figure 4.5

$$S \rightarrow NP_{SUBJ} \left\{ \begin{array}{c} VP \\ P \\ A \\ NP \end{array} \right\}$$

$$NP \rightarrow \left\{ \begin{array}{c} N_{POSS} \\ A_{MOD} \\ Q_{QUANT} \end{array} \right\} N$$

$$VP \rightarrow V(NP_{OBJ}) \left\{ \begin{array}{c} P_{ADJ} \\ NP_{OBJ2} \\ N_{OBL} \\ N_{ADJ} \end{array} \right\}$$

An Extendibility Problem

Now that we have altered the child's grammar to contain only the amount of branching structure that the input would inspire him or her to posit, we are faced with the following question: what happens when the child obtains evidence that the maximal projection of a category can appear in a position that is currently filled with a submaximal category in the existing rule system? One possibility is that the child simply keeps the old rule and adds the new one—e.g., both $VP \rightarrow V P$ and $VP \rightarrow V PP$. Because all nonhead categories are optional in X-bar theory (Jackendoff, 1977), these two rules do not generate any more sentences than the latter rule would alone. Keeping both rules, however, would saddle the child's parsing mechanisms with computing a spurious ambiguity whenever such phrases are parsed—e.g., for the sentence *John went there* in Figure 4.6. The number of spurious parses would increase exponentially with the number of categories that were redundantly specified at more than one level of projection in the grammar (e.g., if the N denoting *John* could also be generated directly as a daughter of S, there would be four parses; if the V and P could be generalized as daughters both of V' and of V", there would be eight parses; and so on). Clearly this outcome is undesirable. There is a simple solution to this problem that uses existing mechanisms. Say the child considers all nonmaximal phrases other than the head to be orphans that are preemptable by maximal phrases in the same position. When the child encounters a VP consisting of a verb and a prolocative, he or she will posit VP → V ?P?. Thereafter, when the child encounters a full prepositional phrase within the VP, the rule VP → V PP will be added, and the original rule VP → V ?P? will be dropped. Thus submaximal phrases join locative adjuncts, oblique arguments, and predicate complements as potential orphans in the theory, and submaximal phrases can both be acquired to begin with and eliminated as the evidence warrants. Our Stage I grammar, then, would be as in Figure 4.5 but with the "?" flanking the submaximal nonhead phrases.[6]

Figure 4.6

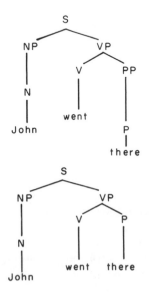

The Uniqueness Principle

Before I examine developmental data, I wish to point out that the notions of orphan phrases and preemption processes are examples of a general learnability principle that I appeal to many times in this book. The principle is that the need for negative evidence in language acquisition can be eliminated if the child knows that when he or she is faced with a set of alternative structures fulfilling the same function, only one of the structures is correct unless there is direct evidence that more than one is necessary. The phrases "set of alternative structures," "fulfilling the same function," and "direct evidence" are intentionally vague; they must be replaced with precise definitions every time I appeal to some version of the principle. Nonetheless, the principle, which allows the child to discard structures even when there is no negative feedback indicating that they are ungrammatical, can be recognized in a variety of guises. Wexler (1979) first proposed a version of this "Uniqueness Principle"; in his case the principle stated that a transformational component of a grammar must have the property that at most one surface structure can be derived from any deep structure, unless there is evidence in the input that more than one surface structure is derived from a given deep structure (see also Lasnik, 1981). In the absence of such positive evidence, the child is justified in changing his or her grammar to rule out all but one of the alternative surface structures. In the examples just discussed, I appealed to a similar principle stating that there are unique phrase structure rules introducing adjuncts, oblique arguments, predicate complements, and category types in a given phrase structure position, unless input evidence indicates otherwise. Roeper (1981) and Grimshaw (1981) conjecture that some version of the Uniqueness Principle may also be applicable to the acquisition of lexical entries, a suggestion I will explore in the next section and in Chapters 5, 6, and 8.

UNLEARNING MISCATEGORIZED WORDS

In this section I develop a version of the uniqueness principle consistent with Grimshaw's and Roeper's conjecture in order to solve a final problem with the phrase structure grammar for Stage I speech. If young children use semantics to induce syntactic categorizations they should occasionally make mistakes, and apparently they do: *ANOTHER ONE pencil* (Brown: Adam II, n.d.), *more SOME* (Menyuk, 1969), *Mommy TROUSERS me* (Clark, 1982), *PILLOW me!* (Clark, 1982), *make it BELL* (Clark,

1982), *give me the RUB* (= eraser, Maratsos and Chalkley, 1981), *where's the SHOOT* (= gun, Maratsos and Chalkley, 1981), *I see the HUNGRIES* (Menyuk, 1969), *his tail is FLAGGING* (Menyuk, 1969), *he's a BIGGER* (Menyuk, 1969), *I want the BLUE* (Menyuk, 1969), *ALLGONE stick* (Braine, 1976), *ALLGONE OUTSIDE* (Braine, 1976), *more CATCH* (Braine, 1976), and many others.[7] As it stands, these apprarently incorrect categorizations would remain in the child's grammar forever since negative evidence about their incorrectness cannot be depended upon. Thus a phrase structure grammar with incorrect categorizations would not be extendible to a correct adult grammar.

A lexical version of the Uniqueness Principle can solve this problem in the following way. Say the child considers all semantically induced categorizations (i.e., those created by the *thing* = N, *action* = V . . . procedures) as tentative, in the sense that further inputs can lead to the erasure of that categorization even in the absence of negative evidence. Imagine also that the "further evidence" that would expunge a categorization consists of distributional analyses showing that the same word has an alternative categorization—for example, hearing *bell* in the context of *the shiny bell*. Finally, let us assume that a categorization that is induced distributionally, unlike one that is induced semantically, is not expungeable by evidence for an alternative categorization. The effect of these procedures is as follows. If a child uses semantics to categorize a word correctly, and if the word has no other categorization in the adult language, that categorization will forever remain unchanged. If a child uses semantics to categorize a word *incorrectly*, then when the word is heard in a syntactic context that the child has correct rules for, the child will correctly recategorize the word on distributional grounds and expunge the incorrect entry. If the child correctly categorizes a word on semantic grounds, and if the language also permits a second categorization for the word, then when the child hears the second version of the word, he or she will mistakenly expunge the first. The first word, however, will eventually reappear in an analyzable context and will be recategorized correctly. Since distributionally induced categorizations are not preemptable (unlike semantically induced ones), both categorizations will survive. The learning procedure must thus be able to distinguish between categorizations that were initially made on semantic grounds and those initially made on distributional gounds. One can broaden the use of the "?" symbol from symbolizing preemptable orphans to symbolizing preemptability per se. Semantically induced categorizations in lexical entries will then look like (11a), distributionally induced ones like (11b).

(11) (a) red: ?A?: PRED = "red"
    (b) red: A: PRED = "red"

One might wonder whether this procedure nullifies the effect of the semantic bootstrapping hypothesis, since only stucture-dependent distributional analysis results in a permanent entry to the grammar. This is not the case. Even though an individual categorization is preemptable, it enters into the hypothesization of phrase structure rules and inflectional paradigms when the categorized word is analyzed as part of a phrase or as a stem of an inflected form, respectively. Thus a preemptable word could still have important effects upon the acquisition of other rules in the grammar, and the semantic bootstrapping hypothesis is not undermined.

This procedure raises some frightening possibilities, however. If a word's categorization was incorrect to begin with, the child will end up with an incorrect phrase structure rule (or inflection) as well. Worse, if the word is then heard a second time in that same phrase, the incorrect phrase structure rule will serve as a distributional context for it, and the incorrect rule will in turn make the incorrect categorization permanent. Other words subsequently found in that context will be given permanent incorrect categorizations as well. However, I would argue that this is unlikely to happen because it depends on an improbable conjunction of events: the child hears a word whose semantics violate the canonical syntax-semantics correlations, and the word is found inside a type of phrase that has never before been heard in the input (at least, not heard with a word that does conform to the syntax-semantics correlations). If the phrase has previously been heard in the input with a correctly categorized word in the position now occupied by the miscategorizable word, the correct phrase structure rule hypothesized then will preempt the incorrect categorization that the child would otherwise be tempted to make, and no harm will be done.

In general, the semantic bootstrapping hypothesis depends on the likelihood that phrases and inflections will first be exemplified, or at least will be far more frequently exemplified (if graded strength and threshold mechanisms are utilized), by words obeying the syntax-semantics correlations. The preemption mechanisms discussed here serve to correct the individual mistaken categorizations that result when the later and rarer exceptions to the correlation are encountered.

Is there evidence for such mechanisms? Macnamara (1982) argues that children have a strong bias to give words unique categorizations. He shows that Brown's (1973) subject Sarah tended to use individual words to refer either to an action alone or to an object alone even in cases where her parents used the same word as a verb and as a noun (e.g., *comb*). Furthermore, in an informal experiment and in careful naturalistic observations, Macnamara showed that his young son strove to avoid using the same word as a noun and as a verb, in one case to the extent of inventing a new word to avoid homonymity. Similarly, Slobin (1984a) summarizes several reports of children inventing novel word forms in order to avoid homonymity, for example, *du* and *da* as partitive prepositions and *de le* and *de la* as genitive prepositions in the French-speaking children studied by Karmiloff-Smith (1979). Furthermore, there is some evidence that when the child has mastered enough rules to support structure-dependent distributional analyses—that is, when multiword sequences with internal structure plus a few inflections have been acquired—overt miscategorizations are less common. It is difficult for an investigator to verify that miscategorizations have occurred in Stage I speech because of the lack of structure (e.g., *Melissa away*, from Bowerman, 1973, could be an example of *away* being used as a verb, or of the predicate *go* failing to be realized in the output string), but still some probable miscategorizations can be found, such as *allgone outside*. By Stages II and III, however, when children's parts of speech are differentiated enough for miscategorizations to be recognizable as such, one must search long and hard to find even one (Maratsos and Chalkley, 1981, make a similar point).[8] Thus when distributional analyses become possible they may eliminate earlier miscategorizations. Gordon (1982) shows that when distributional and semantic information are simultaneously available to children who are at an age at which they can use the former, they let the distributional evidence override the semantic evidence, at least in the case of assigning nouns to count and mass subcategories.

SUMMARY AND OPEN QUESTIONS

What have I claimed so far? I have endeavored to provide an LFG grammar for the major sentence types of the Stage I child. The only requirements placed on that grammar were that it correctly generate the child's utterances, that it be extendible into the adult grammar by the acquisition mechanisms described in Chapter 3, and that it be learnable by those acquisition mechanisms in the first place. The first requirement was met at the price of overgeneration, and in the next few sections I will argue that independent principles account for why the child does not utter all the sentence types permitted by his or her grammar. The second requirement was met by arguing that only the addition of new rules and the ordering of disjoined categories was necessary to convert the child's grammar into that of an adult. The third requirement was not met at first for three reasons. First, certain categories in the grammar could only have been posited on the basis of closed-class morphemes that the Stage I child probably did not control. Therefore, I revised the learning mechanisms to hypothesize preemptable "orphan" categories in rules in cases where the presence of a closed-class morpheme would decide between alternative attachments of a phrase. A second revision of the learning procedures, which allowed the child to posit submaximal categories when they were sufficient to handle the input data, also exploited the preemptability option in that all submaximal nonhead categories were designated as preemptable. This revision reduced the amount of nonbranching structure generated by the child's grammar, allowed the child to learn adult rules introducing submaximal categories, and prevented the child from positing maximal categories before the closed-class morphemes indicating their existence were mastered. As a result of these two revisions to the learning procedures, a slightly different set of phrase structure rules was proposed as a grammar for Stage I sentence types. Finally, I suggested a procedure that "unlearns" incorrect, semantically inspired categorizations of words. In all these cases I appealed to a version of the Uniqueness Principle, a principle that will play a large role elsewhere in the book.

Thus far what I have tried to accomplish is simply to show that there exists an LFG grammar that is learnable, extendible, and compatible with Stage I sentence types, keeping in mind the child's general processing capacities. I have not yet considered alternatives to these rules in light of a detailed examination of the developmental evidence; this examination will occupy the rest of the chapter. As I have mentioned, phrase structure treatments of Stage I speech are highly controversial. However, I think that most of the controversy has been misplaced; it has dealt with the coarse question of whether phrase structure rules are appropriate or inappropriate to describe children's speech. This has not led to much progress, because the use of conventional phrase structure rules represents an implicit commitment not to one but to a number of independent theoretical positions. It is the various theoretical positions that must be addressed in a discussion of phrase structure rules, not the wholesale applicability or nonapplicability of the rules per se. This consideration will guide my discussion of the developmental course of acquisition of phrase structure rules. In each of the sections to follow, I single out a particular aspect of phrase structure rules, entertain an alternative to that aspect including a learning procedure for that alternative, and use the developmental evidence to try to decide between the alternatives. The aspects I will discuss are the following:

(1) Phrase structure rules conflate information about the composition of phrases with information about the linear order of the constituents composing phrases. In an alternative model these types of information could be expressed and acquired separately.

(2) Phrase structure rules give identical labels to phrases found in different distributional positions. An alternative model might keep such labels distinct.

(3) Phrase structure rules specify the order and composition of syntactic categories. An alternative model could specify the order and composition of semantic categories or individual lexical items.

(4) Phrase structure rules specify certain categories as obligatory, requiring independent processing accounts to explain the omission of certain categories in children's speech. An alternative model could account for children's omissions in terms of properties of the grammar itself.

(5) Phrase structure rules use category labels that have cross-linguistic significance. An alternative model could use arbitrary, language-specific symbols.

Developmental Evidence on Five Properties of Phrase Structure Rules

Order and Composition in Phrase Structure Rules

The phrase structure rule VP → V NP specifies two things: that a verb phrase contains a verb and a noun phrase, and that the verb precedes the noun phrase in the linear order of the string. Logically, these two sorts of information need not be specified by the same rule. Pullum (1982), Higginbotham (1983), and Falk (1980a)—see also Chomsky (1965) for discussion of earlier proposals—have suggested that order and composition can be factored apart by stating phrase structure rules in two parts: the set of constituents composing the phrase, and the precedence relations among them. This can be called a "linear precedence/immediate dominance" or LP/ID notation (Falk, 1980a), and is exemplifed in (12) where (a) represents the fact that the verb phrase is composed of a verb and a noun phrase with order unspecified and (b) represents the fact that the verb precedes the noun phrase.

(12) (a) VP = {V, NP}
     (b) V > NP

One advantage of this notation is that it allows one to state partial orderings in an economical way when a language permits partial constituent order freedom. For example, if a language has a phrase X with the three constituents A, B, and C, and if A must always precede B while C can assume any position in the phrase, one would need three phrase structure rules to express that fact: $X \rightarrow ABC$, $X \rightarrow CAB$, and $X \rightarrow ACB$. In an LP/ID system, however, one need only state that A precedes B (i.e., $A > B$), and the three permissible orders are automatically specified.

A second possible advantage of an LP/ID system is that it provides a different conception of the default or unmarked case in word order typology. With conventional phrase structure rules, the simplest grammar would correspond to a fixed constituent order language. That is because the minimal rule for each phrase would necessarily specify an order for that phrase; multiple orders would have to be specified by multiple rules. This seems to make fixed constituent order languages like English most "natural" or easy to learn, with increasing "costs" for the learner as a language permits more constituent order freedom. Many people have the intuition that this conception is too Anglocentric—the widespread existence of constituent order freedom in the world's languages suggests to some that a notation that expresses such freedom uneconomically is missing a generalization. With LP/ID rules, on the other hand, the simplest grammar would correspond to a free constituent order language. That is because the minimal rule for each phrase could specify only the composition of that phrase; order constraints would have to be specified by increasing numbers of linear precedence rules akin to (12b). Thus LP/ID rules in some sense make free constituent order languages most natural or easy to learn, with increasing "costs" for the learner as a language constrains constituent order freedom. This is the aspect of LP/ID rules I wish to address in his section; the points I will make here do not bear on the arguments for LP/ID rules based on the economy of stating partial orderings.

Let us consider the possible developmental predictions made by the learning theory I have proposed and by one that acquires LP/ID rules. The learning mechanisms presented in Chapter 3 acquire individual phrase structure rules corresponding to each constituent order heard in the input. These individual rules are then subjected to the collapsing procedures of P6 that permit within-phrase orderings other than those attested in the input. That means that for fixed constituent order languages such as English, the child's grammar should not generate constituent orders not permitted by the adult grammar. The child's learning procedures record one by one the orders found in parental speech, and the child's utterances should reflect those orders and those generalizable from them by the collapsing procedures (to the extent that children's speech reflects their grammatical rule systems at all). Thus one would expect no overgeneration of constituent orders by children learning languages like English.[9]

However, for free constituent order languages, it is possible that a child using these procedures could pass through a stage in which he or she had recorded phrase structure rules corresponding to some subset of adult constituent orders that had been heard or attended to, but had not yet applied the collapsing procedures that generalized beyond those input orders. This could happen if, as seems warranted, the collapsing procedures require that their input rules reach some threshold of strength or permanence before they can apply. If so, one might expect that a child acquiring free constituent order languages would at first fail to exploit all the order possibilities permitted by the adult language—in other words, that he or she would undergenerate constituent orders. I say "might expect" rather than "expect" because it is also possible that the collapsing procedures, depending on their thresholds, would be called very quickly when faced with many input orders; if so, the undergeneration stage might be too brief to witness.

Turning now to the alternative, I must first insert a note of caution: I know of no learning theory that has been provided for LP/ID rules. In fact, I know of no learning theory that has been provided for any of the alternative grammars for Stage I speech that I will consider in this chapter. However, as I argued in Chapter 1, theories of children's linguistic abilities can only be compared with one another in the context of theories of the learning mechanisms that created those abilities and that would extend those abilities to full adult competence. Thus I cannot compare the proposed theory with the alternatives unless I posit what I think are reasonable learning theories to accompany the alternative accounts. In doing so, I may propose learning mechanisms different from those that the alternative theorists would have provided for their own accounts, and may thus reject an alternative account because of a faulty learning theory I provided for that account—proponents of the alternative could come back with a different learning theory that might rescue it. I recognize this risk but proceed wholeheartedly nonetheless. If these arguments inspire other theorists to propose learning mechanisms to accompany their accounts of children's language, and the resulting debates over children's language are elevated to considering rival learning theories as well as accounts of developmental data, I will have achieved the major goal of this book.

This caveat aside, let us consider a possible learning mechanism for LP/ID rules. If rule simplicity corresponds to the default, unmarked, or first acquisition, we would expect the child at first to record only the minimal information allowable in a rule, namely the sets of constituents composing phrases. This could be done by applying procedures similar to P1–P5 but retaining as permanent rules only the unordered sets of constituents found to compose each phrase, as opposed to the ordered phrase structure rules acquired by P5. At the same time, the child could tabulate the relative frequencies of all pairwise constituent orders within a phrase, and if a given order is eventually exemplified with overwhelmingly greater frequency than its opposite, a linear precedence relation would be appended to the corresponding rule. Pairwise precedence relations could then be collapsed into n-wise relations by exploiting the transitivity of linear precedence. This tabulation procedure would be called for to help the child learn which orders are ungrammatical in the target language. Given that the child has no access to negative evidence, only the absence of a given order in a sufficiently large sample would lead the child to the conclusion that that order is ungrammatical.

This model makes the following predictions. For instances of free constituent order, the child immediately learns the correct rules, namely the specification that a phrase is composed of certain constituents with their order left unspecified. Since many orders are exemplified in the input, no pair of candidate linear precedence relations would attain the frequency imbalance necessary for one of them to be made permanent. Thus we expect that children should not undergenerate constituent order in languages that permit the full range of possibilities, all else being equal. On the other hand, for fixed constituent orders, it is possible that a child could first pass through a stage in which the constituency of a phrase had been established but the linear precedence relations had not yet surpassed the thresholds necessary for any of them to be added to the grammar. In that case we might expect a child learning fixed constituent orders to overgenerate and utter orders that the target language does not permit. Again I say "might expect" rather than "expect" because if the thresholds for adding linear precedence relations were very low, a child might acquire them very quickly. The predictions of the two theories for the acquisition of free and fixed constituent orders are summarized in Table 4.1.

Adherence to Target Constituent Order

To decide between the theories, it is necessary to consider the developmental evidence corresponding to each column in Table 4.1. Let us start with fixed constituent order phrases, which predominate in English and which are found in most other languages as well. Brown (1973) notes, "In all the 17 samples of Stage I English listed in [Brown's] Table 9 the violations of normal order are triflingly few: *Nose blow* (Hildegard), *Slide go* (Gia I), *Apple more* (Christy), *Paper write* (Adam), *Horse . . . see it* (Kendall I), *See Kendall* (when Kendall sees, in Kendall II), and perhaps 100 or so others. Of utterances in normal order here are many thousands." Bloom, Lightbown, and Hood (1975) note in their monograph examining in detail the speech of four English-speaking children that "with few exceptions, word order was consistent within each category [of semantic-syntactic relations]." Bowerman (1973), in her study of the acquisition of several languages that allow some, but not all, word orders, notes that for Luo and Samoan as well as for English, "word

Table 4.1

	Type of phrase	
	Fixed constituent order	Free constituent order
Phrase structure rules, then collapsing	No overgeneration	Undergeneration possible
Immediate dominance, then linear precedence	Overgeneration possible	No undergeneration

order was quite stable and corresponded to the dominant or only adult pattern." Her Finnish-speaking children, she noted, virtually always used orders found in adult speech, which is also largely the case for children learning Korean, Hebrew, Russian, and Swedish (according to Brown's 1973 review, pp. 156–157). Slobin (1973) proposes as a universal of children's language that children adhere to the maxim "Pay attention to the order of words." The most detailed study of early Stage I speech is Braine's careful examination (1976) of a dozen exhaustive corpora representing five languages. Braine concludes that in every instance in which a child frequently utters both possible orders of a pair of categories, either (a) both orders are found in the adult language, and the child has earned the two orders separately (evidence for this is the fact that one order typically predominates at first and then is supplemented by the alternative order); or (b) there is independent evidence that the utterances reflect a pregrammatical "groping pattern" in which the child wants to communicate a semantic relation, lacks the grammatical means to do so, and strings words together randomly in the hope of being understood. (The independent criteria for groping patterns include rarity, unproductivity, hesitation, "circular" repetition of constituents—e.g., *all wet . . . mommy . . . all wet*— and rapid suppletion by a strict ordering.) My own tabulations of Braine's English data indicate that about 95 percent of the utterances are in adult orders.

Reported Instances of Word Order Freedom in Fixed Order Languages

Brown (1973) does note three reports of apparent word order freedom in Stage I speech. One is from an unpublished colloquium delivered in 1971 and cannot be evaluated here. The second is from an earlier paper by Braine (1971b) in which he reports that his son Gregory passed through a brief stage (lasting about 1 to 1½ months) in which he used both orders of subject and verb, and of verb and object, with no apparent semantic contrast. No corpus is presented, but since Braine reexamined these corpora in his 1976 monograph and did not mention it as a counterexample to his claim that examples of word order freedom all meet the criteria of groping patterns, it is reasonable to assume that these criteria were met in this case and that Gregory had not yet mastered any rules expanding S or VP (he apparently did produce many NPs with the correct internal constituent order). The third example is from an unpublished paper by Park (1970a; also cited in Roeper, 1973) reporting that three German children often produced orders that were ungrammatical in adult German. Though Park's study has never been published and so the data are unavailable for close examination, it is possible that the so-called ungrammatical orders were ungrammatical only in simple matrix declarative sentences and would have been grammatical in subordinate clauses or sentences with modal auxiliaries, given German syntax. If so, the children may have learned phrase structure rules appropriate for subordinate clauses or sentences with preposed auxiliaries, but simply lacked the annotations on the rules and lexical entries that coordinate the choice of phrase structure expansions with embeddedness or presence of an auxiliary. In Chapter 7 I argue that a similar state of partial knowledge is responsible for several classes of errors in older English-speaking children.

Note that nothing in the hypothesis that ordered phrase structure rules are acquired makes predictions about the relative frequencies with which the child will use the various phrase structure rules that he or she has mastered. Phrase structure rules are templates specifying the permissible orders and compositions of phrases in a language. Their actual use in concrete situations will depend on a variety of pragmatic and processing factors that are not the subject of the acquisition theories considered here. Thus reports of children using word order to signal pragmatic relations such as *topic-comment* (e.g., Bates, 1976), or failing to match the relative frequencies of orders in adult speech, or exploiting the full flexibility of word order freedom allowed in the adult language, do not bear on the hypothesis that phrase structure rules are being acquired, so long as each order the child produces also may appear in adult speech.

Undergeneration of Constituent Order in Children's Speech

Turning now to the second column in Table 4.1, we find that there have indeed been reports of children acquiring free constituent order languages who use only a subset of the orders permissible. Park (1970b; described in Brown, 1973, and Roeper, 1973) reports that his daughter used only the SVO order while acquiring Korean, despite the appearance of SOV, OSV, and OVS orders in parental speech. Slobin (1966) notes that Gvozdev's Russian subject Zhenya at first used only the SOV order, later switching to SVO. Brown (1973) reports an unpublished study of the acquisition of Swedish whose author concludes that "word order is inflexible and conforms with the most dominant adult word order." Hakuta (1982) found that 98 percent of the utterances of a group of forty-eight Japanese children asked to describe a series of pictures were in SOV order; most of the children never used the OSV order. Undergeneration of word order in free constituent order languages is not universal (e.g., in Finnish, Bowerman, 1973; or Turkish, Slobin, 1982), but, as mentioned, it need not be for the phrase structure rule hypothesis, since multiple orders can be learned individually. Systematic undergeneration, however, is an embarrassment for the first-ID-then-LP hypothesis, since constituent order freedom is the default case and the statistical distribution of orders in adult speech would not provide evidence that the default should be rejected.

In sum, the available evidence seems to suggest that when a language has fixed constituent order the child rarely utters ungrammatical orders, but when a language has free constituent order the child may very well restrict himself or herself to a subset of the attested orders. This pattern suggests that the child records constituent orders from the start and relaxes it as the evidence warrants, rather than first recording only phrasal composition and then accumulating evidence for constituent order.

IDENTITY OF SYMBOLS ACROSS POSITIONS

One of the major reasons that phrase structure rules afford a grammar such economy and potential productivity is that common category symbols are used in different rules. For example, the NP symbol is introduced in subject, object, second object, complement, prepositional object, questioned constituent, topicalized constituent, possessor, and other positions. This feature allows a language user to know two things: (a) the class of words that can appear as the head of a phrase in one position may also appear as the head of a phrase in the other positions bearing that label; and (b) the internal structure of a phrase in one position is the same as the internal structure of a phrase in other positions bearing that label. These properties lead to advances in economy because they factor apart word class membership, the internal structure of a phrase, and the external distribution of a phrase. That is, if there are w words in a class, s ways in which the phrase can be expanded, and d external positions in which the phrase can appear, the use of common labels allows the grammar to contain $w + s + d$ pieces of information, rather than the $w \times s \times d$ pieces necessary otherwise.[10] Similarly, when a child learns a word in a given phrase, he can generalize it to the remaining $(s \times d) - 1$ phrases; when he or she hears a new expansion of the phrase, that expansion can be generalized to the $(w \times d) - 1$ remaining combinations of head noun and external position, and so on. For noun phrases alone, w is on the order of thousands and s and d are each on the order of ten (assuming that abbreviatory conventions are used); thus the savings in economy and learning time are prodigious. For this reason, the phrase structure acquisition procedures proposed in Chapter 3 make these generalizations as rapidly as possible. Words cannot be grouped into arbitrary classes on the basis of distributional similarity; they must be assigned to one of the small number of innately specified lexical categories. Likewise, phrases in various external positions cannot be given aritrary labels; they must be projections of one of the lexical categories. All nouns are given the same label, as are all noun phrases, regardless of differences in position among them in input sentences, and the size of the child's language can grow polynomially as the input sample increases linearly.

Before discussing the developmental evidence relevant to this claim, one must distinguish between two issues that can be easily confused: whether children's word classes are syntactic or semantic, and whether a word class that may appear in one syntactic position in children's grammar, however that word class is defined, is the same as a word class that may appear in some other position that is assigned the same label in the adult grammar. I consider only the latter issue here, deferring a full discussion of the former to the next section. In practice, of course, the issues can become conflated if the child appears to split an adult word class into two position-specific subclasses *and* if each of these subclasses is semantically cohesive.

I will concede at the outset that evidence firmly establishing the identity of symbols in young children's rules is difficult to come by. This becomes apparent when one considers what one would need in general to argue for identical symbols in two different rules. Two sorts of arguments are possible. First, one can present a person with a novel word and see if that person can use that new word in all of the possible external positions and internal structures of a category. (Alternatively, one can present the person with a novel external position for a category and see if it can be used with all the words in that category and all its possible expansions; or present a novel expansion and see if it can be used with all words and external positions.) If any of these is the case, the person could not simply list individual combinations of words, phrase structures, and positions; he or she must have the means to generalize from one such combination to the rest. Identical symbols that can be cross-referenced

by different rules is simply the traditional notation for such productive mechanisms. This can be called the *productivity-based
promiscuity* argument. Second, a similar argument can be made,
one that does not require the teaching of new forms, by taking
parsimony into account. If a speaker's grammar can generate all
$w \times s \times d$ combinations of the words, internal expansions, and
external positions manifested individually in the word combinations within his or her competence, it is more likely that his
or her grammar has $w + s + d$ rules (w word categorizations,
s expansions of the category, d rules introducing the category)
than each of the $w \times s \times d$ possibilities listed separately, especially since that product, as mentioned, is typically very large.
To establish the premises of the argument, which can be called
the *parsimony-based promiscuity* argument, one need only establish that all $w \times s \times d$ possibilities are acceptable to the speaker.
(The argument can be made even stronger by establishing that
for all $w \times s \times d$ combinations the head nouns have the same
properties of affixation, derivational morphology, pronominal-
izability, and extractability, yielding $w \times s \times d \times a \times m \times p
\times e$ combinations.)

In either of these arguments one must ascertain whether the
speaker in question accepts exemplars in the space of combinations formed by words, internal structures, and external positions. (These would include novel, taught forms for the
productivity argument, and forms attested at least once in the
prior speech of the speaker for the parsimony argument.) For
adults this is done by presenting an informant with a representative sample of possibilities and, if all receive assent, assuming that the rest of the space is also acceptable by induction,
usually with success. But for youngsters this cannot be done.
Children cannot judge the grammaticality of sentences in isolation until they are considerably beyond Stage I, which leaves
us with only their spontaneous speech as data. But for two
reasons one cannot simply examine which of the $w \times s \times d$
combinations are attested in a child's speech. First, $w \times s \times d$
will typically be a large number, and children, especially Stage
I children, do not utter vast numbers of sentences. Worse, those
sentences that they do utter will not be a representative sample
of the $w \times s \times d$ possibilities. Children do not try to exemplify
the space of possibilities allowed by their rule systems; they
communicate their intentions and observations, and often they
need only a small subset of the possible rule combinations in
their grammar to do so. Thus the absence of a given class of
combinations in children's speech can indicate either that the

child's rules do not generate that class or that his or her communicative intentions did not require that a particular rule sequence be exercised. Given that the gaps in a space of possibilities in children's speech are inconclusive, the best one can hope for in defending a theory positing phrase structure rules is to show that the gaps that have been observed are to be expected on independent grounds, and that as the sample size increases and the effects of these independent factors are lessened, the full space of possibilities begins to be filled. This would leave the debate over identical versus nonidentical symbols at a standoff, which itself would be an accomplishment, given the near-consensus that children lack adult-like phrase structure rules. I will attempt to make such an argument, and from here I will argue that the proposed theory is superior to its alternatives in accounting for the transition into the adult state.

Semantic and Lexical Differences

In this part of the chapter I will consider two well-attested generalizations that have been taken to indicate the use of different symbols in subject and object position in children's grammars. The first, which will be examined in this section, concerns semantic and lexical differences between subject and object noun phrases. Brown (1973), Bloom (1970), Bowerman (1973), and others have noted that in Stage I speech, preverbal elements tend to be drawn from the class of pronouns and nouns denoting animate beings, whereas postverbal elements tend to be drawn from the class of nouns denoting inanimate objects. Perhaps, then, the child has the rules $S \rightarrow YP_{SUBJ} VP$ and $VP \rightarrow V ZP_{OBJ}$, where Y and Z are distinct categories, as developmental grammar-writers (e.g., Bloom, 1970; Brown, n.d.; Macnamara, 1982) have suggested. I would argue that this conclusion is premature. In the proposed theory the child uses actionhood as a cue that a word is a verb, and agenthood and patienthood as cues that its arguments are expressed as subjects and objects, respectively. It follows that the child's first verbs (or, at least, first verb) will denote actions whose subject and object arguments are agents and patients. Agents are almost by definition animate, and patients will tend to be inanimate. Thus the absence of inanimate preverbal noun phrases in Stage I speech may be a consequence of the prevalence of action verbs. Children may not say things like *chair eat* simply because eating is not something that chairs typically do, not because their grammar forbids them to produce that combination. Indeed, Brown (n.d.) examined the speech of one of the mothers of his subjects (the girl he calls Sarah) and found that she—the mother—had a strong tendency to produce action verbs with animate subjects and inanimate objects, though her grammar surely had a single noun category. The account I am arguing for thus predicts that when non-action verbs are acquired, or when a patient of an action is plausibly animate, the animacy-position correspondence will freely be violated.

An examination of the Stage I speech of Brown's subject Adam bears this out.[11] Table 4.2 presents examples of Adam's preverbal inanimate nouns and postverbal animate nouns. Examples of this sort are, to be sure, a minority of cases, but they are a large enough minority to suggest that Adam's grammar was not incapable of generating animate and inanimate subjects and objects. It is the semantic selection restrictions of the first verbs acquired that make them rare, not the grammar itself. Though semantic classes are not as syntactically promiscuous for Brown's subject Eve as they are for Adam (e.g., almost all of Eve's subjects by the end of Stage II were pronouns or proper nouns), we still find *my graham cracker broke, my toy fall down,* and *my tushy make*

Table 4.2*

Animate object nouns	Inanimate subject nouns
me get John	towtruck come here
get you	shadow stay night
get kitty	horn playing
find kitty	paper go?
find doggie	shoe go?
find two tattoo man	bike go?
give doggie paper**	screwdriver hurt
give Cromer**	truck broken
throw Daddy**	windmill turn round
Dale get you pepper**	windmill turn on
see Daddy	tummy hurt
see Mommy	
pick Dale up	
hit mosquito	
move doggie	
hurt doggie	
call Daddy	

*Examples taken from tabulations of Adam's speech in Samples 1–3. Utterances referring to toy animals or dolls were excluded.

**In LFG, immediately postverbal indirect objects are assigned the function OBJECT.

more; Eve also productively used animate objects in such utterances as *Sue rocking Anna, see Anna, put dog away, put bird away, get the duck*, and *need another duck*.

Further evidence for the ability of Stage I grammar to generate animate objects comes from experiments on the comprehension of reversible active sentences (i.e., where both subject and object nouns are animate) in young children. Such experiments show that Stage II and late Stage I children correctly act out such sentences, or correctly choose a modeled action sequence exemplifying the sentences, in 80–95 percent of the trials in which their responses were clearly scorable as correct or incorrect (Bever, Mehler, and Valian, 1973; de Villiers and de Villiers, 1973b). Thus the animacy of a direct object does not prevent children from interpreting it appropriately.

Of course, the use of words with given semantic properties in both subject and object positions does not mean that the same individual words are used in both subject and object positions. Here we find that the amount of overlap is relatively small but still large enough to cast doubt on the hypothesis that preverbal and postverbal nouns are different syntactic categories in early speech. Brown (unpublished analyses; see n. 11) tabulated the number of words appearing in subject position, object position, and both positions in the first two samples of Adam's Stage I speech. He found that of fifty different nouns used in subject or object positions in Sample I, only five appeared in both positions; in Sample 2, seven out of fifty-three nouns appeared in both positions.[12] It is important to note, though, that one should not expect large numbers of nouns to be found in both positions in a small sample, even if the grammar permitted every noun to appear in both positions, because of the simple fact that conjunctions of events are rarer than single events. Brown's tables of utterances for Sample 1 indicate that there is a .30 probability of a noun's appearing in subject position in sentences containing a verb and a .80 probability of its appearing in object position; thus there would be a .24 expected probability of its appearing in both positions if the grammar made that possible. For Sample 2, the figures are .28, .85, and .24. For each sample, then, one would predict that about twelve words should appear in both positions. The observed numbers of promiscuous nouns, seven and five, do not appear to be as small relative to the sample size as one might have expected before calculating the expected frequencies. They are noticeably lower than the expected frequencies, to be sure, but that is not surprising given that in the world not all noun referents are equally well suited to serving as various verb arguments. I present these simple calculations to show that small sample sizes and asymmetric verbal argument structures can make small amounts of overlap in a corpus equivocal as far as the debate over children's syntactic categories is concerned.

Differences in Internal Structure

Let us now turn to a second question: are the *internal structures* of subject and object noun phrases in early word combinations the same? The claim has been that they are not: subject NPs tend to be bare nouns or pronouns; object NPs are the only ones that tend to be expanded as possessor-possessed, object-locative, modifier-object, article-object, and so on (e.g., Bloom, 1970; Bloom, Lightbown, and Hood, 1975; Brown, 1973). As a result, Bloom's and Brown's grammars for children's speech used special category symbols for subject NPs: *Nom* for Bloom (1970); *NP1* for Brown (n.d.); others would argue against the use of a syntactic category at all. Here I will follow the same tack as for lexical items: I will try to show that the subject-object asymmetry is a statistical tendency, not an absolute generalization, and that there are independent reasons to expect the statistical asymmetry to occur in the first place.

Differences in internal structure that are consistent with the acquisition procedures. Before examining the developmental data on differences in internal structure among noun phrases in different positions, it is necessary to determine which sorts of differences would be consistent with the acquisition mechanisms proposed in Chapter 3 and which would be inconsistent with them. Recall that in order to obtain more parsimonious children's grammars and to allow submaximal categories to be learnable, I proposed that children posit only as high a projection of a category as they need in a given position in the grammar. Thus if adults tend to utter bare nouns in subject position and full NPs in object position, which is a distinct possibility given some of the processing variables I will discuss below, the learning procedure could supply the child with the rules $S \rightarrow N_{SUBJ} \: VP$ and $VP \rightarrow V \: NP_{OBJ}$. These rules would generate the asymmetry observed in children's speech, and no further discussion would be needed.

Unfortunately, this account cannot predict the entire distributional pattern. The only differences it allows among internal expansions of a phrase when that phrase occurs in different positions is the existence of different levels of projection—for example, a bare noun in one position and the full NP or N″ in another. It would not allow the specifiers and complements appropriate to a given projection to appear at one position unless it also allowed the full expansion of the head at that level, and it would not allow one arbitrary subset of an expansion at a single level of projection to occur in one position and another subset in another position. For example, if the adult grammar generates a structure like Figure 4.7, the learning procedure as modified in the beginning of this chapter would allow the child to learn a rule that generated *A* alone in one position, (*C*)(*D*)*A* in a second, and (*B*)(*C*)(*D*)*A* in a third. However, no mixture of

Figure 4.7

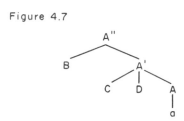

maximal and submaximal rules could generate *BA* in one external position and *CDA* in a second without also generating *BCDA* in the first position, nor could it generate *DA* in one position and *CDA* in a second without generating *CDA* in the first. The problem is, it seems that the asymmetries in children's speech may violate these restrictions in some instances. For example, in Stages I and II Brown's Eve uttered eight sentences in which the subject appeared to be composed of a possessor N and a head N; ten sentences in which the object had that composition; thirty sentences in which the object was composed of a modifier (adjectives or determiners) and a noun; but no sentences in which the subject was composed of a modifier and a noun. Whether the English NP has three levels of projection, as in (13a) and (13b) (see Jackendoff, 1977), or two levels of projection, as in (13c), there is no symbol that is expanded as a possessor-N sequence without also being expandable as an adjective-N sequence. Thus I am left with no way of accounting for the distribution of Eve's subject NPs, even using the theory of submaximal phrase structure acquisition advocated in the first section of this chapter.

(13) (a) $N''' \rightarrow (N'''_{POSS}) N''$
     (b) $N'' \rightarrow (A''') N''$
     (c) $N'' \rightarrow (N''_{POSS}) (A'') N$

Accounting for the asymmetries in children's speech that are inconsistent with the learning mechanisms. For cases such as Eve's subject noun phrases that cannot be explained by submaximal phrase acquisition, I argue that the absence of subjects with the full internal structure possessed by objects may be caused by factors extrinsic to the grammar. Bever (1970), Fodor, Bever, and Garrett (1974), Cooper and Ross (1975), Pinker and Birdsong (1979), Slobin (1973), and others point out that a "heavy" or elaborated construction is easier to produce and to comprehend if it comes at the end of a sentence. Presumably this is because there are more demands on cognitive processing capacity when elaborated constituents occur earlier; in that case, the possibilities for the integration of earlier units, or the planning of later ones, must be kept in working memory while the elaborated constituent is itself processed. (The precise prediction depends on a number of considerations such as whether processing is root-to-leaves or leaves-to-root and whether one is parsing or producing sentences, but the bias among language users to "save the heaviest for last" is well documented.) This predicts that children (and adults) would be biased to utter shorter subjects and longer objects in subject-initial languages like English, just what we observe. Since children presumably have less processing capacity than adults do, they would show the bias even for their very short sentences. In addition, if there is a tendency for speakers to have subjects express the "topic" or "given" information, and to have predicates express the "comment" or "new" information (see Clark and Haviland, 1977; MacWhinney, 1982), then one might expect there to be more lexical content in object NPs and a smaller probability that they would consist of pronouns, for pragmatic reasons. Thus both processing and pragmatic considerations lead one to expect more elaboration of object than of subject NPs in English even if the child's grammar, like the adult's, permitted subject and object NPs to have the same composition.

If so, one would expect elaborated subjects to be uncommon but not completely absent. This appears to be the case. For example, in Adam's Stage I and early Stage II speech, one finds possessor-N sequences not only in object position (e.g., *put Dale shoe on panda; see Daddy car*) but also as the subject of a verb (*Dale panda march*), the subject of a locative complement (*Dale shoe right there*), and as a predicate nominal (*look like Dale car; look like Dale truck*). One also finds modifier-N sequences not only as objects (*man drive busy bulldozer; I get that brush; read dat cowboy book; take a coat, Cromer*), but also as subjects of verbs (*what happen little cowboy fell down?; big doggie boot bit me shame; little boy sleeping*), subjects of predicate complements (*no pictures in here*) and predicate nominals (*yea, you busy bulldozer; here a hammer; here one*

Table 4.3

	Subject	Object	Total
Bare noun	36	163	199
Modified noun (possessor, determiner, or adjective)	8	42	50
Total	44	205	249

pencil; I a cowboy; I [am] *like a bulldozer*). Examples of modified subjects can also be found in other samples of early speech. For example, Bloom, Lightbown, and Hood (1975) report *any soda in there* and *his name a Johnny* (Eric, MLU 1.69), *funny man in* and *tiny bells in there* (Katherine, MLU 1.89), and *my pen down there* (Peter, MLU 1.75). Brown (n.d.) reports Sarah in Stage I saying *a bunny there; my horsie there; more tree there;* and so on.

How frequent are such constructions? In general, modified subjects are infrequent in Stage I speech but not necessarily less frequent proportionally than what we would expect given the relative rarity of subjects as a whole and modified within-sentence constituents as a whole. For example, Brown (n.d.) presents a tabulation of the frequencies of bare and modified subject and object NPs pooled from the Stage I speech of Adam, Eve, and Sarah. Table 4.3 summarizes the relevant frequencies. Even a casual inspection of the table shows that subjects are no rarer than the conjoined rarity of subjects per se and modified nouns per se; in fact, the expected frequencies of the four cells in the table under the hypothesis of no contingency between position and elaboration are in all cases within one utterance of the observed frequencies, and the chi-square is close to zero.

Brown (n.d.) presents another analysis of the intersubstitutability of constituents in Stage I and II speech. He asks whether his subjects' sentence-like utterances can be fit by the schema in Figure 4.8, in which pre- and postverbal elements are assumed to be selected from the same set of structural possibilities, and V + V sequences (complement-taking verbs like *gonna, hafta, wanna*) are assumed to have the same privileges of occurrence as bare Vs. (In the grammar that I am assuming, this is equivalent to the assumption that the main VP of a sentence is identical in internal structure to the VP complements of verbs, and that the main VP of a sentence is introduced by the same symbol regardless of its complement structure; see Chapter 6.) Note that the identity of the sets of braced elements before and after the

Figure 4.8
$$\left\{\begin{array}{l} \text{Pro} \\ \text{N + N} \\ \text{M + N} \\ \text{N} \end{array}\right\} \quad \left\{\begin{array}{l} \text{V + V} \\ \text{V} \end{array}\right\} \quad \left\{\begin{array}{l} \text{Pro} \\ \text{N + N} \\ \text{M + N} \\ \text{N} \end{array}\right\}$$

verbs means that both may be replaced by a common NP symbol that need be expanded only once. Under the assumption that something like this schema represents the child's syntactic competence, rather than a list of subschemas representing common utterance patterns, Brown calculates that the child should be able to produce fifty-four different utterance types: four types of isolated NPs, two types of isolated Vs, eight combinations of subject and verb, eight combinations of verb and object, and thirty-two combinations of subject, verb, and object. Of these fifty-four possibilities, though, sixteen are five or six words in length. Since mean length of utterance by Stage II is only 2.25 morphemes (by definition), it seems reasonable to exclude these from consideration because the child's processing capacity would prevent him or her from uttering long sentences even if the grammar would permit it (this is discussed in a later section). Of the remaining thirty-eight utterance types, Brown reports that thirty-two are to be found in the speech of Adam, Eve, and Sarah. (Of the six that are absent, three involve V + V combinations, which, as I will show in Chapter 6, require extra control mechanisms and are generally acquired somewhat later; and two involve pronominal objects.) Thus very near the full range of constructions generated by a simple set of rules is actually produced, lending support to the contention that maximally general grammatical rules provide a viable account of the young child's competence, statistical asymmetries notwithstanding.[13]

Thus far I have shown that nothing in the developmental data either strongly confirms or disconfirms the hypothesis that young children possess rules with identical symbols in subject and object positions. Children neither produce all of the combinations permitted by an adult grammar fragment, which would implicate adult-like rules, nor do they produce any sharply delineated subset of combinations that cannot be accounted for by extra-grammatical factors. The parsimony calculations thus fall in the intermediate range in which children could be said to have either a list of ad hoc rules spelling out every combination of constituents found in every position, or a set of maximally general rules together with pragmatic and processing factors that in practice delimit the combinations actually uttered. Deciding between these accounts at this time requires an appeal to criteria other than the children's language. As I argued in Chapter 1, learnability and extendibility are the most obvious ones to look to.

Both accounts posit rules that are easily learnable. The mechanisms in Chapter 3 acquire adultlike phrase structure rules, and one could devise similar algorithms that could acquire nongeneral rules via the following modification: rather than being categorized by one of the labels N, V, A, or P, words would be given arbitrary category symbols *A, B, C, . . .* , specific to the external position of the phrases they head. The rest of the learning procedures, including those that use X-bar theory to relate predicate-argument structure to head-complement configuration, could proceed apace. This would result in the grammar containing different symbols for noun phrases in different positions, and would thus allow these phrases to draw their heads from different word classes and to have different internal compositions.

What about extendibility to the adult state? Here we find differences between the theories. For the theory proposed in Chapter 3, extendibility is straightforward—the child immediately makes generalizations at the correct level of abstraction, and development into an adult phrase structure component only awaits adding other rules and collapsing them with existing ones, and learning the full set of functional annotations to the rules. Consider, now, the way in which a grammar with arbitrary category labels would be extended into an adult grammar. One possibility is that the adult grammar, too, has different category labels for, say, NPs in different positions but that the alternative categories have grown to have identical properties because with the passage of time all the relevant combinations of each phrase type in each position have been exemplified in the input. This hypothesis can easily be rejected. First, the number of combinations formed by multiplying the various possibilities of phrase structures, external positions, affixes, derived forms, extractions, and pronominalizations is in the millions. All are within the competence of adults, and the possibility that every adult has witnessed all of the millions of combinations is remote indeed. This number is large in part because of the large number of nouns in a person's vocabulary, but even if one allowed different noun phrase variants to be headed by the same lexical category (e.g., XP → A N B, YP → N C D), the number of combinations of internal structures and external positions that would have to be learned one by one would still be on the order of a thousand. Although the possibility that adults have witnessed every one in the input cannot be ruled out as confidently, it still seems highly improbable. Furthermore, adults can be shown to be productive in their use of nouns heard in one position. Having heard the sentence *the romatizer was broken,* any adult can generalize to *I fixed the romatizer; the ROMATIZER, I like; the romatizer's kadiddle; three romatizer-fixers;* and so on. Finally, it would be a mystery why languages almost invariably allow words within a class, internal phrase structures, external positions, affixation patterns, and so on, to combine promiscuously, given that it is easier to learn radically smaller subspaces of the possibilities than the entire space.

Somehow, then, the identity of different noun subclasses must be established. There are several ways that this might be done.[14] One way is to combine any two word classes that overlap to some minimum extent, then collapse the phrases headed by the formerly distinct categories. But this step is treacherous—it could easily combine classes like noun and verb that share vast numbers of words. A second possibility would be to collapse phrasal categories serving similar semantic functions, for example, expressing the same types of arguments. Unfortunately, this would fail to collapse subject and object noun phrases, to mention only the most blatant problematical case. A third possibility is to collapse phrases that share constituents, using procedures akin to P6. (The P6 procedures themselves, incidentally, could not apply, since they require that the two phrases to be collapsed have heads of the same category, and this is precisely what the learner does not yet know.) If a novel variant of P6 looked for correspondences of nonhead categories so as to combine subclasses, chaos might swiftly ensue. That is because any procedure that was clever enough to collapse two phrases that should be NPs on the basis of shared non-noun constituents would probably also collapse phrases that should be distinct—for example, verb phrases and adjective phrases, which both take PP complements (*John was aiming at the tree; John was angry at the man*), or adjective and adverb phrases, which both allow adverbial modifiers. A fourth possibility is that identical inflections on the heads of different phrases could cause the phrases to be united. Like semantic similarity, this would not in general help to unite phrases with different case markers, especially in synthetic languages with fusional morphology. Finally, a procedure could adopt as a collapsing criterion the very property that leads the P-procedures to hypothesize the appropriate syntactic categories to begin with—namely, notional properties such as being a person, thing, action, path, or attribute. It makes more sense, however, to have a learning procedure exploit syntax-semantics correspondences at the beginning of language acquisition rather than after a large set of rules has been learned, since the requisite correspondences in parental speech tend to weaken, not strengthen, as the child matures (Pinker and Hochberg, in preparation). The procedures I have proposed avoid these pitfalls by exploiting more reliable information: that words for physical objects used in talking to infants will all be nouns, and that words that occur in a position uniquely associated with previously learned nouns (the "uniquely" proviso is crucial) are also all nouns, regardless of the external positions of the phrases in which they are found. Furthermore, most errors that the procedure will make (e.g., learning a word for an action that is not a verb) will be misclassifications of words, not faulty analyses of entire phrases, and can be unlearned by procedures discussed in the first part of this chapter and in the next section.[15]

In sum, while the evidence from Stage I and II speech is ambiguous as to whether children have identical or nonidentical category symbols in different rules, a model that posits identical symbols from the start can account for the transition to adulthood in a straightforward manner, with a minimum of risky and unnecessary supplementary procedures. Thus I tentatively conclude that the identical-symbol account is to be preferred overall.

Syntactic versus Semantic or Word-Bound Rules

In the past section I considered whether children's rules use the same symbols or different ones in different positions for what are unified adult syntactic categories, ignoring the question of what those symbols actually are. In the acquisition theory the child learns rules containing syntactic categories from the very start (though the first evidence the child uses for assigning a word to one syntactic category versus another is largely semantic). In contrast, the past decade has seen influential arguments that the child's first rules lack syntactic categories, instead containing symbols for one or more of the three following entities: (1) broad semantic categories and relations such as *physical object,* or *agent-of-action* (e.g., S → *Actor Action*)—in the proposed theory these are used to trigger the hypothesizing of syntactic rules but do not enter into the rules themselves; (2) narrow semantic categories and relations, such as "vehicle," "temperature," or "custody of an object for the purpose of oral consumption" (e.g., S → *custody-for-consumption edible-object*); (3) individual words (e.g., S → *hurt X*). These arguments have been proposed by Bowerman (1973) and Braine (1976) and have been cited approvingly in several reviews of child language findings (e.g., MacWhinney, 1982; Maratsos, in press). The arguments have typically taken two forms: (a) that children's early word combinations provide no evidence *for* syntactic categories and relations, and (b) that children's early word combinations provide evidence *against* syntactic categories and relations. In this section, like the previous one, I examine the sort of evidence that could decide between the alternative accounts of children's language, examine the evidence in question, and then examine the alternatives in light of the learnability and extendibility criteria proposed in Chapter 1.

Criteria for the Attribution of Syntactic Categories to a Language User

What sort of evidence could decide whether a grammar representing a person's linguistic knowledge has syntactic or semantic categories? Let me begin by clearing away some red herrings that occasionally find their way into discussions of this issue in the context of children's language. First, the fact that certain types of word combinations have characteristic meanings or are used with a characteristic illocutionary force has nothing to do with whether syntactic categories are used or not; any theory of grammar positing a syntactic component for children or adults would also have semantic and pragmatic components which would pair syntactic structures with their appropriate readings. Second, the fact that a given word combination may have two meanings (e.g., *mommy sock*, which Bloom, 1970, reports was used by a child once to indicate possession and another time to indicate an agent-patient relation) is simply an example of an ambiguity, which for both children and adults can easily occur if a grammar has certain properties. And the fact that children use their syntactic abilities only to transduce meanings into sentences or vice versa simply means that a grammar representing their abilities must be embedded in a parser/producer that uses syntactic rules (and possibly other knowledge as well) to interpret or utter sentences on-line, just as for adults.

As in the previous section, I suggest that the relevant criteria for justifying particular symbols in rules concern "promiscuity": one must assess whether the entities represented by a putative symbol behave identically with respect to all combinations of rules that mention that symbol, or whether some entities or subsets of entities behave in one way and others behave in other ways. If the former is the case, and if the number of combinations is large, parsimony favors the use of a single symbol mentioned once by each rule, rather than n symbols each representing a smaller set of entities mentioned redundantly in n otherwise identical versions of each rule. Furthermore, any evidence of productivity—witnessing an entity used in one construction and then being able to use it in other constructions in the absence of evidence that doing so is possible—argues that that entity is in fact treated as an exemplar of a broader class. For example, if all verbs, regardless of their semantics, behaved identically with respect to inflectional rules, appeared in the same phrase types, appeared in phrases occupying the same positions, entered into the same lexical rules, and so on, one would need n times as many rules (and n times as many exemplars during learning) if one used n symbols representing the n verb subclasses (e.g., exhaustive lists of semantic subclasses, individual words) as one would need if one could use a single verb symbol. To decide among alternative symbols referring to word classes of various sizes, one picks the symbol that represents the largest set of words that behave identically with respect to the relevant linguistic phenomena. The rest of the story has a familiar ring to it: for adults, one can offer informants a random sample of the space of possible combinations for their approval; for children, limited metalinguistic abilities and lack of mastery of many of the constructions that the symbols in question enter into preclude this. Spontaneous speech is all we have to go on, and limited sample size and extragrammatical biases will produce ambiguous gaps in the space of possibilities attested in a corpus. Therefore I concede at the outset that I will be unable to present convincing evidence for the existence of syntactic categories and relations in early word combinations. What I will try to do instead is show that the data indeed *are* ambiguous, that the arguments that have been raised against phrase structure rules on the basis of early speech, and accepted by a large percentage of psycholinguists, are unsound. From there I argue that learnability considerations favor an account positing syntactic categories and relations.

Broad Semantic Categories and Relations

Melissa Bowerman (1973) was the first to construct a detailed argument against the unquestioning use of adult phrase structure rules to describe children's early speech. She noted that arguments of the sort I discussed above cannot be made for Stage I children because the constructions diagnostic of syntactic categories have not yet been mastered. Furthermore, infants' use of constructions putatively involving grammatical relations like "subject" are in fact restricted to a fairly small set of relations, mainly "agent action," but also "person-affected state," "object-involved action," "action object-created," and so on. A table presented in Bowerman (1973) pertaining to seven samples of children learning five languages shows that some children used only one semantic relation and others used no more than five in their subject-verb-object constructions. Bowerman concluded that the account of child speech that is most faithful to the data is one that posits rules containing symbols for thematic relations such as "agent" rather than grammatical relations such as "subject."

Bowerman also suggested, tentatively, that the prevalence of agentive subjects cannot be completely explained by parents' exclusive use of verbs taking agentive subjects. This is an important point, because SUBJ is not a category but rather a relation that is conditioned by the choice of verb. If all the verbs a child heard happened to take agentive subjects, it would immediately follow that all observed subjects in his or her speech would denote agents. Bowerman examined the speech of the mother of a Finnish-speaking boy named Seppo, a child who at first used only agentive subjects. Seppo's mother used the verb *fall*, which Seppo did not utter with subjects, more often than she used many verbs that Seppo did utter with subjects; eight other non-agentive verbs were modeled with frequencies equal to those of verbs Seppo uttered with subjects. (Overall, however, Seppo's mother did use verbs with agentive subjects 4.5 times as often as other types of verbs.) Thus Bowerman can argue that the semantic constraints on subjects are the product of the child, not just the mother.

My comments on Bowerman's arguments are the same as the comments on the differences in animacy between subject and object noun phrases. In order to account for the child's recognition of instances of universal categories and relations in the input, I proposed that he or she uses semantic categories and relations as evidence. Since actionhood is a likely semantic clue for verbhood, and agenthood for subjecthood, the child's first verbs will be action words with agentive subjects. The prevalence of agentive subjects in the child's speech may thus be a consequence of subjects and agents temporarily being in one-to-one correspondence in the child's grammar, not of there being no SUBJ symbol (Grimshaw, 1981).

This account predicts that when a child later learns verbs that do not take agentive subjects, he or she should have no trouble transferring the grammatical privileges that have been learned for agentive subjects to the new nonagentive subjects. By and large, this seems to be the case. For Stage I children learning English, the only syntactic privilege of subjects that has been acquired is their preverbal position. Interestingly, when non-agentive subjects appear in SVO sequences, they appear in their correct position as often as agentive subjects do in theirs. Table 4.4 shows the number of NVN sequences in Adam's first six samples (Stage I and early Stage II) in which the subjects were correctly ordered before the verb, for both agentive and non-agentive subjects (examples involving hesitations, *do it,* circular forms, routines, and uninterpretable relations were omitted). As one can see, when nonagentive subjects are used in sentences, they are correctly placed before the verb the same proportion of times as agentive subjects are.

Of course, with order alone as a diagnostic, it is impossible to rule out the possibility that a set of verb-specific argument placement rules were acquired (as Bowerman herself suggests), so a more conclusive case would require examination of other privileges of grammatical functions as they apply to agent and nonagent subjects or patient and nonpatient objects. Two trac-table examples are the expansion of the object noun phrase, which admits of the same possibilities regardless of its gram-matical, thematic, or semantic relation to the verb, and the agree-ment of a verb in number with its subject, which does not depend on the thematic or semantic relation of subject to verb. As for postverbal NP expansion, one can examine the expansions "bare noun," "pronoun," "article plus noun," "adjective plus noun," and "possessor plus noun" when the NP serves as a patient of an action verb, the experienced object of a perception or cog-nition verb, the location argument of a verb of motion or transfer, and the nominal predicate complement of a copular sentence or verb of resemblance. If the external position of an argument with a given thematic relation and its possibilities of internal expansion are learned separately, as a phrase structure account predicts, all twenty of these combinations should appear in early speech. In his first six samples (Stage I and early Stage II), Adam appeared to utter nineteen of the twenty possibilities (I found

Table 4.4

	Subject placed correctly	Subject placed incorrectly	Total
Agentive subject	83	7	90
Nonagentive subject	33	3	36
Total	116	10	126

no adjective-noun sequences used as objects of experience). Table 4.5 shows some examples. In later samples the promiscuity of internal expansions and thematic roles becomes even more complete.

As for agreement, Pinker, Stromswold, and Hochberg (in preparation) conducted four studies of the semantics of number agreement in children. We found that: (1) when Adam, Eve, and Sarah began using the third-person singular morpheme $-s$, they used it correctly equally often for action verbs and for various sorts of nonaction verbs; (2) 3- to 4-year-old experimental subjects correctly imitated the third-person present

Table 4.5

Noun Phrase Expansion

	N	Pro	Art + N	Adj + N	Poss + N
patient of action	get Bozo	tie dat	take a coat	drive busy bulldozer	pull Dale bike
	beat drum	turning that	kitty open the paper		
	change diaper	rock you	get that brush		
object of experience	want Bozo	read dat	see other one		like Dale bookshelf
	see sun	Dale see it	read dat train track		see Daddy car
	I like grapefruit	my see that	read dat cowboy book		
predicate nominal	dat knee	bed like dat	here a hammer	you busy bulldozer	look like Dale car
	dat lady	here one	here one pencil	here one pencil	look like Dale truck
	that man	milk like dat	I a cowboy	dat same way	dat Dale baby
locative	tractor go floor	drive up dere	Dale write the paper	go round sleeping dinosaur	spill Mommy face
	Cromer go School	put up dere			
	spill face	take off here			

indicative verb in sentences the same proportion of times whether the subject of the verb was an agent, experiencer, or instrument; (3) 4-year-old children, when judging which of two puppets described a picture better (the two puppets spoke identically except for number agreement), judged correctly as often when the subject was an agent as when it was an experiencer; (4) when 3- to 5-year-old children were taught two uninflected novel verbs, one denoting an action and one a spatial relation, they were able to apply the agreement marker equally easily in both cases (Stromswold, 1983). We found no evidence that when number agreement rules are acquired they apply in different ways to agentive and nonagentive subjects.[16]

Is there direct evidence against syntactic categories and relations? Martin Braine (1976) claims that Bowerman's argument can be taken even further. Not only is there, he claims, no evidence *for* grammatical relations in early speech, there is direct evidence *against* grammatical relations. His ingenious argument flows from the following prediction of a phrase structure account: "Thus, whenever an orthodox grammar has a set of rules of the form $A \rightarrow B + C, C \rightarrow D, E, F, \ldots$, then once a child has developed one of the patterns BD, BE, BF, none of the other patterns of the set should go through a groping stage as it emerges; nor should they emerge with their constituents consistently in the opposite order to those of the first pattern" (p. 75; ellipsis Braine's). In other words, with phrase structure rules, the order of constituents is distributive over the alternative internal expansions of one of those constituents. Braine claims to have found three classes of data that refute the prediction. Though I agree with Braine that he has pinpointed the type of empirical pattern that is relevant to answering questions about the presence of syntactic symbols in children's grammars, I will argue that in each of the cases where Braine applies his argument, there are alternative analyses of the data that are at least as compelling as Braine's analysis. Given that these are the only examples counting against grammatical relations that Braine reports in his painstaking examination of a dozen exhaustive corpora, I claim that by eliminating these examples I will have nullified the strongest arguments raised against grammatical relations in the grammars of Stage I children.

The first of Braine's examples concerns the subject-predicate distinction encoded by the rule $S \rightarrow NP_{SUBJ} \ VP$. The subject-predicate order, once learned for one expansion of VP, should apply to all others, if indeed NP_{SUBJ} and VP are the categories the child uses. Braine asks us to consider the two expansions VP → (V) (NP) and VP → Locative (in the present treatment, the latter expansion would be VP → V PP in the adult grammar). He finds in two corpora (Kendall I and Seppo) examples of children who have productive actor-action patterns but whose locative-entity relations are expressed by groping patterns (multiple short-lived nonproductive orders uttered with hesitations). He concludes that the children's rules ordered thematic relations like actor-action and entity-locative rather than subject NP and VP. However, as I have pointed out, if a child does not yet process the copular verb in subject-locative input sentences, he or she will have no evidence that the locatives in such statements are constituents of a verb phrase to begin with. Neither Kendall I nor Seppo produced copulas (nor for that matter, prepositions), so they were probably treating locative complements as simple NPs, or perhaps PPs (for prolocatives), and did not have either of them introduced in an expansion of VP in their grammars. Thus they could have had the rule S → NP$_{SUBJ}$ VP while lacking a rule like VP → V PP. Without a rule ordering locatives, the child would grope for an order whenever he or she had to express a locative relation. Eventually the rule S → NP$_{SUBJ}$?PP? or S → NP$_{SUBJ}$?NP? would be acquired, and, still later, VP → V PP$_{P-COMP}$), thanks to the mechanisms discussed at the beginning of this chapter.

One might ask, granted that it is *possible* for the child to have a phrase structure grammar ordering subjects and verbs but not ordering subjects and locatives, why, then, should the child not have *in fact* acquired a separate rule ordering subjects and locatives? Alas, I do not know. I take some comfort, however, in noting that a theorist pursuing Braine's argument would not know either. In his theory, presumably, the child would record the possible orders of thematic relations like actor and action or entity and locative as they were exemplified in the parental input. But in such an account, there is no reason why the child should not have recorded a positional pattern for entity and locative. Presumably it is because locative sentences are less plentiful in the input, or because the child does not attend to their order as often; whatever the reason, it would apply as easily to the acquisition of phrase structure rules as to the acquisition of semantic patterns.

Braine's other two putative counterexamples to phrase structure accounts concern the categorization of words rather than of entire phrases, so I will defer discussion of these examples to the following section.

Narrow Semantic Patterns and Word-Specific Patterns

Whenever a child limits his or her utterances to the semantic notions that enter into the semantic bootstrapping hypothesis, there is a principled explanation for the undergeneration. However, Braine has argued that even broad thematic relations like *agent-of-action* or *possessor* may be more abstract than the actual relations that govern children's word combinations. Braine points out that often children's speech does not even exemplify the full range of specific semantic relations exemplifying a thematic relation. For example, for one child almost all of the verb-object combinations expressed the movement of toy vehicles; for another two children most of their productive verb-object relations involved eating or having objects to be eaten; another expressed modifier-entity relations primarily when the modifier was a size word (*big* and *little*). And in some cases, even narrow semantic relations are too broad—some children appear to have productive patterns specifying the position of a single word in a two-word utterance, such as Bowerman's daughter Eva who uttered many verbs in isolation but used only the verb *want* in two-word combinations (Bowerman, 1976). In many cases in the corpora Braine (1976) examined, a syntactic category was exemplified by two to five words of various degrees of semantic relatedness, leaving it possible that the child had acquired either a small set of narrow semantic patterns or a somewhat larger set of word-based patterns.

Braine (also MacWhinney, 1982; Maratsos, in press) draw the narrowest possible conclusions from the data: that children's competence consists of positional patterns containing variables of arbitrary scope, ranging from single words to classes of words sharing some concrete semantic property to terms bearing some broad thematic relation to a predicate. Furthermore, individual children can differ from one another in arbitrary ways.

Like the logician who saw a black sheep through a train window on his first trip to Scotland and would conclude nothing more than that at least one sheep in Scotland was black on at least one side, these theorists have offered a hypothesis that is difficult to refute, given available evidence. Their argument that one *needs no more* than limited-scope formulae to account for children's earliest speech is impeccable; however, any argument that these data alone *belie* syntactic rules is unsound. That is because the proper empirical test for the existence of phrase structure rules—assessing the acceptability of sentences containing putative subclasses of a category when they enter into all combinations of rules mentioning that category—cannot be carried out because of limits on the size of corpora, range of constructions, range of interests, and metalinguistic abilities of infants. The data we have are precisely in the ambiguous region—children do not evidence full promiscuity of their categories; nor do they evidence the extreme limits of scope that some discussions imply (for example, an examination of Braine's corpora shows that patterns restricted to a *single* word or semantic subclass are extremely rare; most often the number ranges from two to five). Thus, I will argue, their speech can be described equally well by either account.

To be specific, a phrase structure theory can account for most of the observed undergeneration in children's speech in the following ways: (1) If a child simply never utters certain types of words in a category, he or she simply may never have acquired that word, because of its rarity in the input or because of his or her cognitive abilities and attentional biases. (2) If a child utters a word alone but never in combinations, he or she may simply have less interest in communicating the messages that the word would enter into. (Thus it would probably be no surprise to any parent that the first verb that enters into combinations is often *want* or that the first productive action-patient relations expressed involve eating.) Both of these accounts may also be applied to limitations in the range of grammatical relations expressed.

As Braine points out, the really difficult case for a phrase structure theory occurs when a child has acquired a word or set of words belonging to a putative category and does not encode it reliably in word combinations, and at the same time he or she does reliably encode other members of that category in word combinations (this is Braine's argument that order of constituents is distributive over their various individual expansions). Even these patterns, however, can be accounted for in cases where the child might know the meaning of two words but the syntactic categorization of only one. In that case, the child could utter the latter word in isolation but would not yet know which phrase structure rule dictated its position within a phrase. That is, even if the child knows that $A \rightarrow B + C$ and $C \rightarrow D, F$, for some E the child may not know that $C \rightarrow E$, hence he or she will not know that B precedes it, while still knowing that A precedes both D and F. For Braine to make his argument work, he needs independent evidence that the E in question is in fact already categorized as a C. In principle this could be done by showing that the child uses some third rule, either phrase structure or inflectional, that makes it clear that the child has in fact correctly classified E.

It is *possible*, therefore, for a child to have phrase structure rules and still know how to order only a subset of the members of an adult category. The question to be asked now is whether the current acquisition mechanism would ever create just that state. I have already shown that cases of undergeneration delineated by thematic or broad semantic criteria may be instances of an early stage in which all the exemplars of a category in the child's grammar happened to have been acquired by the semantic bootstrapping mechanisms. Let me now turn to the two examples of the narrower undergenerations that Braine argues refute phrase structure accounts.

The first comes from the child named Jonathan, who had productive subject-locative and actor-action patterns, presumably both involving the rule $S \rightarrow NP_{SUBJ} VP$ (actually I have argued that the former pattern involves a slightly different rule at this stage). At the same time, however, Jonathan productively expressed the subject-predicate relation in the opposite order, predicate-subject, for the predicates *boom-boom* and *allgone* (hence *boom-boom car; allgone stick*). It is not hard to see why Jonathan may not know the correct categorization of *boom-boom* and *allgone*, as my argument would require. Consider *boom-boom* first. Although the distribution of such terms in parental speech has never been studied, several parents of young children I have talked to felt that they would be most likely to use both *boom-boom* and *allgone* as isolated exclamations when talking to their children. If so, the child would have no way of knowing the words' categorizations. Note that in the learning procedures described in Chapter 3, even though words are tentatively categorized on semantic grounds, the categorizations are only added as permanent members of the lexicon by procedure L1 after a sentence containing them has been analyzed completely. No sentence, no permanent categorization. Without a categorization, there is no basis for any phrase structure rule of any sort to order the term relative to others, and the child is left to his or her own devices. Even in a modified model in which isolated words could be given categorizations on the basis of their semantic properties (e.g., in Chapter 8 I will argue for such a modification for the learning of subcategorizations), *boom-boom* and *allgone* do not clearly exemplify any of the semantic triggers listed in Chapter 2, so the child could still be at a loss as to how to categorize them. Given that a word remains uncategorized, the child might utter it in random positions, or at other times might search for some model from adult speech. I do not know what inspired Jonathan to order *boom-boom* consistently before the noun (Braine cannot say either), but expressions like *pop goes the weasel* and *ding ding ding goes the bell,* popular in children's songs and poems, seem as plausible a source as any. In the case of *allgone,* Michael Maratsos (personal communication) offers the not implausible conjecture that the child categorizes *allgone* as a Q (quantifier) on semantic grounds and thus orders it pre-nominally using the rule NP → QP N, hypothesized from examples like *more milk.* This predicts that every child who consistently orders *allgone* before the noun should also have mastered phrases like *more x, another x,* or *no x.* This was true of Jonathan, and also true of the child named Andrew (though he used *allgone* in both positions; the *x allgone* order is of course grammatical).

That leaves us with Braine's third example, in which Jonathan places the adjective *big, little, hot, blue, red,* and *old* at the beginning of utterances, but gropes for the proper position of *wet* and *all wet,* presumably also adjectives in a phrase structure account. Kathy Carpenter, a linguistics graduate student at Stanford, has pointed out to me that *wet* differs from all the other adjectives mastered by Jonathan in being syntactically ambiguous: one wets one's diapers, which are then wet, but one does not little or hot or old anything. One hardly needs to go to transcripts to make the case that parents use *wet* as a verb in the presence of their 2-year-old children. Given that both empirical evidence (Macnamara, 1982, Slobin, 1984a) and my account of the learning of misclassified words suggest that children only grudgingly categorize the same word as two different parts of speech, it is not implausible that Jonathan may have lacked a stable categorization for the word *wet.* This provides a reasonable alternative account for the last of Braine's three counterexamples to the phrase structure hypothesis, and so one can conclude that evidence from Stage I speech is consistent with the hypothesis that children use phrase structure rules.[17] Furthermore, it should be pointed out that regardless of how convincing the reader finds these accounts of the supposed counterexamples, they are the only accounts around—nothing in Braine's theory explains why Jonathan's combinations should have been misordered in the way that they were, nor why Jonathan, Kendall, and Seppo consistently ordered particular words and waffled in ordering the others.

As in the case of the internal expansion of subjects versus objects, the semantic properties of subjects versus objects, the expansion of different thematic postverbal noun phrases, the correct ordering of different thematic subject noun phrases, and the agreement of verbs with different thematic subjects, one finds that as the child advances and we are able to examine longer sentences and larger samples, a great range of combinatorial possibilities are realized in the child's speech. Consider again the different expansions of the noun phrase: bare noun, pronoun, adjective plus noun, article plus noun, possessor plus noun, and so on. In a phrase structure grammar, once the different expansions are learned they can be used as objects of any verb. In a severe limited-scope formula theory, the child would have to learn the within-NP ordering separately for each verb or semantic subclass. When children learn how to expand a phrase, do they do so promiscuously with a variety of verbs? Adam's data from Stage I and early Stage II suggest so. Adam used objects composed of an article plus a noun with fifteen different verbs, including verbs that denote actions (*get, open, touch*), possession (*have*), experiences (*see, read, like*), and states (*wear*), and those that take factitive objects (*make, draw*). He used objects composed of a possessor plus a noun for fourteen different verbs, including verbs that denote actions, experiences, and states (e.g., *look like, like*) and ones that take factitives (e.g., *write*). Objects consisting of adjectives plus nouns are less frequent, but still do not occur with just one or two verbs; one finds seven such types and the same number of tokens; and even with this small sample, there is semantic variety, including *like, go-round, put, find,* and *drive.* And of course there are dozens of verbs taking pronominal objects or bare noun objects. Again, one does not find the full set of combinatorial possibilities, but one does find many (considering the size of the sample of relevant utterances), and the ones found do not seem to be limited in any narrow semantic or word-bound way.[18]

Now that I have argued that phrase structure rules provide at least as good an account of the developmental data as narrow semantic or word-bound formulae, I turn to the question of whether phrase structure rules as descriptions of young children's competence provide an account of how the child learns the target language as a whole. The theory I presented is designed to make this as simple as possible. The child begins his linguistic career positing rules that are of the proper type for the adult language. Therefore, as far as learning the adult phrase structure component is concerned, the task before the child is simply to add, collapse, or uncollapse rules and to annotate functional equations to them where necessary according to the procedures outlined in Chapter 3 and amended in this chapter. Furthermore, any other acquisition procedures that are fed by the identification of grammatical relations or phrase structure configurations (rules governing control, auxiliary placement, complementizers, long-distance binding, and so on), can proceed apace. The rest of this book is an attempt to show how this can be done.

The learnability and extendibility of thematically based rules or limited-scope formulae, like other alternative accounts I have considered, is difficuilt to establish because no learning theory for them has ever been outlined. However, we can consider some likely candidates, and when we do, we find that all are wanting. One possibility is that there is no discontinuity between Stage I children and adults—adults, too, have learned a set of limited-scope formulae, just larger ones and more of them. This is easy to reject. The arguments raised earlier in this chapter against the use of arbitrary word class and phrasal category symbols is applicable here as well. The number of combinations of individual words (or even narrow semantic classes) with each of their morphological and syntactic privileges of occurrence is astronomical, and if each combination were simply listed separately, a newly learned word or semantic subclass could not be used productively with any construction other than the one it was first witnessed in. Furthermore, one would expect, contrary to fact, that languages would be more likely to allow each word to have different syntactic privileges than to insist that words fall into a small number of semantically nonhomogeneous categories and subcategories each with identical syntactic privileges. That is because if the human language acquisition process consisted of the accretion of limited-scope formulae, the former would be easier to learn than the latter.

So there must be some means of abstracting from lists of words or narrow semantic classes to syntactic categories. This is often assumed to be a trivial step, but it is not. One might think, for example, that the child could scan the list of individual words sharing some positional property and search for the least abstract semantic property that they all had in common. Then the positional property could be stated as being true of the entire semantic class, not of the individual words or semantic subclasses. As many people have pointed out, however, the members of a syntactic category or the set of predicate-argument relations expressible by a grammatical relation are semantically heterogeneous in adult grammars. Nouns can denote not only people, places, and things, but also actions, attributes, spatial relations, manners, tenses, aspects, abstract entities and relations, mean-ingless chunks of idioms, and so on. Subjects can be not only eaters and sitters and agents and experiencers and instruments, but patients and recipients and abstract arguments of any sort, not to mention idiom chunks, *it,* and *there.* Thus a rule stated in terms of some semantic attribute or function would exclude words that it should encompass and encompass words that it should exclude.

Perhaps, then, the child could converge on the *logical* function that all the members of a class enter into, such as being a pred-icate, argument, quantifier, and so on, and state the privilege formerly holding of the list as holding now of any item serving that logical function. Again this would lead to mischief as syn-tactic privileges are not invariably predictable from logical func-tions in adult languages. Nouns usually serve as referring expressions in subject position but need not do so, as in idiom chunks like *tabs* in *tabs were kept on the man from U.N.C.L.E.;* and nouns, verbs, adjectives, and prepositions can all denote pred-icates taking one or more arguments (e.g., *Sam's insistence on paying, Sam insisted on paying, Sam was insistent on paying*). Con-versely, any major phrasal category can serve as an argument of a predicate (e.g., *Bill appears to be sleeping/a fool/happy/underneath the desk*). Thus a rule stating the syntactic privileges of occurrence of all words serving some logical function would make a hash of the language (e.g., **the child seems sleeping, *John insistenced on paying*).

Perhaps, then, when the child observes that the set of ele-ments mentioned in a positional or morphological property have nothing in common semantically or logically, he or she replaces the list with an arbitrary symbol that can refer to any term what-soever. This would surely be a recipe for disaster, since it would eventually obliterate all the distinctions among words' privileges of occurrence, requiring negative evidence to undo the damage. In this connection, it is worth pointing out that many of Braine's formulae containing variable terms (e.g., *more x*) also would seem to require negative evidence to unlearn, since not all words can follow *more* in adult English even if it would make semantic sense (e.g., **I want more sunny*), and the child must somehow learn this.

A better strategy to use in the face of semantic heterogeneity of a list of similarly behaving elements is to replace the list with an arbitrary symbol in the rule and append that symbol to the lexical entry of each word formerly mentioned in the rule. But that still leaves the child with the task of recognizing the identity of the classes denoted by different arbitrary symbols in different positions, inflections, derivational rules, and so on. Unless the child takes this step, there is little gain in economy or productivity. But as I tried to show in the preceding section, without antecedent restrictions on the number of syntactic categories and the conditions under which they are hypothesized, it is not clear how this step could be taken reliably. Yet another possibility is that the child looks for some minimum degree of overlap between the elements mentioned in one rule and the elements mentioned in others, and if it is exceeded for some pair or *n*-tuple of rules, mentions of the list in each rule are replaced by an arbitrary symbol that is also appended to each of the former members of the lists. As I pointed out earlier, the degree of overlap of word membership between categories that should not be merged, such as nouns and verbs, is so large that a simple merge-if-you-find-overlap heuristic would do more harm than good (see also Pinker, 1979). If one were to try to salvage this heuristic by allowing any salient semantic difference between homonyms in different categories to block category mergers (e.g., if one avoided merging the privileges of occurrence of *hands* in the contexts *two* ____ and *John* ____ *the book to Mary* because the former refers to an object and the latter to an action), then one would find certain desirable mergers blocked, depending on the semantic properties deemed relevant, such as noun phrases in subject and object position (cf. *a man arrived* and *John is a man*) or the different senses of a verb (cf. *John gave the baby a toy* and *John gave the baby his name*). (In general, category merger based solely on common sets of words appearing in unconstrained "similar" sets of contexts has much in common with what I have called the "contingency table" theory of category formation and so suffers from the same set of problems discussed in connection with that proposal in Chapter 2.) If one were to restrict the relevant semantic properties that could block a merger, so that grammars would contain some set of intrinsically non-mergeable categories identified at first by certain semantic properties of their canonical members, then one would have arrived at a hypothesis that is very similar to the semantic bootstrapping hypothesis of syntactic category acquisition advocated here.

Similarly, one could take the current theory's criteria for initially positing certain syntactic categories and relations, namely certain semantic categories and relations, and have the child look for them among the list of elements in a rule. If one is found, it could be used as evidence that that list should be replaced by the syntactic category that the triggering element corresponds to. This could occur at some maturationally defined point, in accordance with the tadpole hypothesis. For example, if a rule states that terms serving as agents, experiencers, instruments, and several other arbitrary or abstract semantic roles all precede verbs (of course "verb" here is itself simply shorthand for a list of words or semantic subclasses), the child could notice the presence of *agent* on the list and as a result replace the list with the term SUBJ. Because SUBJ would also be mentioned in other appropriate rules and acquisition procedures, this would lead to the correct type of generalization. However, this variant of the proposed procedures has the disadvantage that by the time the child has amassed a large enough set of rules, he or she may also have heard the triggering semantic element in noncanonical syntactic constructions and so would make incorrect replacements of semantic symbols with syntactic symbols. For example, if the child hears a passive sentence with an action verb, the relation *patient* will be listed as one of the preverbal semantic roles, and that list could then mistakenly be replaced by the symbol OBJ. The child misses his or her chance to exploit syntax-semantics correspondences if he or she waits too long; in the current procedure, these correspondences are exploited at the beginning of language learning when they are presumably strongest, and only then.

The basic problem with accounts that have the child create syntactic categories via a general cognitive process of inductive generalization is that grammatical relations (and for that matter, grammatical categories) do not fall into any natural inclusiveness hierarchy with individual words nested within semantic classes which in turn are nested within syntactic classes. Syntactic entities may be correlated with semantic properties in basic structures, but they do not represent a superset or disjunction of semantic properties. Any learner who finds evidence in the input that violates a semantic or word-based hypothesis must make a generalization that does not seem to be defined by any obvious category in a general cognitive repertoire—he or she must conclude that previous hypotheses were of the wrong sort, and that the correct generalization involves classes of elements or relations that are defined by their participation in a restricted set of complex and abstract phenomena (phrase structure, inflection, control, anaphora, and so on). The child must have just this sort of hypothesis available to him or her as something to turn to when a semantic or word-based hypothesis fails. Whether such correct hypotheses occur to the child *only* when the wrong-headed ones fail, or whether the child entertains them as soon as some semantic property signals their presence in basic structures (as I have been proposing), correct sorts of hypotheses about syntactic categories and relations must be a part of the child's language acquisition mechanisms; they are unlikely to emerge from the simpler sorts of inductive mechanisms examining lists of words or semantic features. The principal developmental question, then, is *when* the child exercises this capability to form linguistic generalizations that refer to specific syntactic categories and relations. If the discussion in this section is correct, there may be no reason to reject the simplest hypothesis, namely, that the child uses syntactic categories and relations even in the early stages of acquisition.

To sum up the claims of this section: (a) An examination of corpora of children's speech is unlikely to provide the sort of evidence that one ordinarily needs to justify phrase structure rules unambiguously. (b) However, it is possible to write phrase structure grammars for children's corpora that undergenerate along broad semantic or thematic lines, narrow semantic lines, or with respect to individual words, by restricting the lexicon in the appropriate way. (c) The proposed acquisition procedures predict that broad semantic and thematic undergeneration can occur at the very earliest stage of language acquisition, and under certain reasonable assumptions they can account for the cases of word-bound undergeneration that Braine cites as evidence against phrase structure rules (examples that Braine himself provides no account for). (d) Evidence primarily from late Stage I and early Stage II speech suggests that these children are already heading in the direction of allowing word classes, semantic roles, external positions, internal phrase structures, and inflections to combine promiscuously, as a phrase structure account predicts. (e) The phrase structure acquisition hypothesis yields a straightforward account of how the child attains the adult state, whereas for semantically-based or word-based accounts, it is unclear how this can be achieved. Thus all things considered, the best theory at this time appears to be the one that attributes syntactic categories and relations to the child from the start (or, at the very worst, attributes them to the child as an innately specified hypothesis to turn to when certain other hypotheses fail).

LENGTH LIMITATIONS IN STAGE I SPEECH

A final example of overgeneration by my phrase structure grammar for Stage I speech is its production of complete sentences, ones that invariably contain a subject, a verb, and the noun phrase and locative arguments that the verb subcategorizes for. Young children, of course, are not so fastidious. Individual utterances often appear to be missing subjects, objects, verbs, indirect objects, locative complements, and head nouns that tend to appear intact in other utterances or utterance fragments. In this section, I briefly consider four hypotheses about the fragmentary nature of early word combinations.

Deletion Rules

An influential hypothesis about apparent deletions in children's speech is that they are not just apparent. Rather, there exists a level of representation in the child's grammar that includes the full set of lexical items in a grammatical sentence, plus a rule of grammar that deletes items in specific configurations (e.g., Bloom, 1970; Bowerman, 1973). Usually the level at which the sentence is complete is assumed to be some sort of underlying constituent structure, such as the deep structure of the Standard Theory of transformational grammar or Fillmore's case grammar, and the deletion rule is considered to be one of a set of transformational rules that map between underlying structure and surface structure. Since LFG has neither multiple levels of constituent structure nor rules that delete constituent structure, this option is closed to the proposed acquisition model on theoretical grounds, so I will try to argue against deletion rules on independent grounds and then propose an alternative to them.

There are four arguments against deletion rules. First, most formulations of deletion hypotheses do not account for the full set of apparent deletions in the data (Braine, 1976). Second, a grammar with deletion rules of the sort proposed violates the formal property of "recoverability of deletion" (Chomsky, 1965) that usually is enforced on transformational components, and hence introduces a needless discontinuity between the formal properties of children's and adults' grammars (Atkinson, 1982). Third, it is unclear which sort of learning mechanism and input sequence would have led the child to hypothesize a deletion rule in the first place. If adult sentences were fully processed by the child, they would not exemplify deletion rules of this sort in any way. And even if we assume that the child processes only parts of the adults' sentences, the parts that pass through the child's input filters would not exemplify the sorts of deletion rules that the child is claimed to have. That is because the input filters that are commonly used to explain the degeneracy of children's speech, often motivated by processing limitations known to hold for adults, block out unstressed and sentence-initial or sentence-medial segments (e.g., Slobin, 1973; Gleitman and Wanner, 1982a; Newport, Gleitman, and Gleitman, 1977). However, Stage I children frequently omit major, stressed, sentence-final constituents as well (e.g., *Mama doing; other blue*). Thus it is unlikely that the child's fragmentary representation of the input sentence inspires him or her to coin a deletion rule to generate those fragments.

A fourth argument against deletion rules, also based on learnability, is that it is unclear how the child would progress to the adult state. Somehow he or she would have to "unlearn" rules that were unnecessary in the first place. Worse, if such rules are ever optional (which Bloom, 1970, claims is the case for a certain stage of development), the child would need negative evidence to discard them. Adult sentences would mostly not exhibit the operation of such rules, but since the child's rule is optional, his or her grammar could parse complete sentences simply by not applying the rule and no change to the grammar would ever have to be made. This would leave the child deleting obligatory constituents all his life. Of course, one might argue that the adoption and discarding of deletion rules are not evidence-driven learning processes but rather are arbitrary maturationally imposed processes. However, this is just the sort of process that would unnecessarily complicate the child's primitive computational machinery, and so is not to be adopted unless necessary according to the parsimony metric outlined in Chapter 1.

Incomplete Rules

In theories like Braine's, the constituents that appear to be missing would simply not be listed in the relevant rules. For example, the child might have an *action + object* formula that simply did not include a subject term; likewise *actor + action* has a slot for action terms, including transitive verbs, but none for objects. A similar account could be adapted to phrase structure rules, by having the child posit rules like $S \rightarrow VP$, $S \rightarrow NP_{SUBJ} V$, $S \rightarrow NP_{SUBJ} NP_{OBJ}$, $S \rightarrow A N$, $S \rightarrow NP_{POSS} N$, and so on. One difficulty with this approach is that it is not entirely clear how the child would learn, short of relying on negative evidence, that the initially absent elements such as subjects were in fact obligatory. But the main problem with this approach is that usually one finds in children's speech a set of related sentences each missing a different constituent but with the remaining constituents all correctly ordered with respect to one another and admitting of the same possibilities for internal expansion. For example, Bloom (1970) notes the presence of subject-verb, verb-object, and subject-object sequences followed shortly by subject-verb-object sequences; Brown (1973) considers the schema *agent-action-dative-object-locative* and notes that seven types of two-word subsets, four types of three-word subsets, and a four-word subset of the sequence appeared in Adam, Eve, and Sarah's Stage I samples, with the within-subset order virtually always correct. Often the different fragments are uttered in close succession in "replacement sequences" (Bloom, 1970; Brown, 1973). Similarly, I summarized above unpublished data on Stage I and II speech from Roger Brown which show that the way an object noun phrase can be expanded (as a bare noun, pronoun, modifier + N, or possessor + N) is the same whether or not a subject or verb or both are mentioned in the sentences, and that the way a subject noun phrase can be expanded is the same whether or not an object or verb or both are included (of course, one would want to show that the latter was true for transitive verbs per se). If one used individual mini-rules to represent all the possibilities, in the latter case different rules would redundantly specify that the modifier preceded the noun and that the possessor preceded the noun when the noun phrase was uttered in isolation, when the noun phrase was preceded by a subject and a verb, when the noun phrase was followed by a verb, and when the noun phrase was followed by a verb and an object. These expansions would also have to be specified redundantly for the noun phrase that occurred with a predicate nominal or locative; Brown did not tabulate these sentence types but it is likely that they would be attested as well. For example, in Adam I and II we find *I a cowboy; yeah, you busy bulldozer; look like Dale car; put tractor Dale bike; put dat innere; put innere; put hat; put train ball; here one pencil;* and other examples of correctly ordered elaborated noun phrases in appropriate positions within fragments of miscellaneous sentence types.

Thus a mere listing of all the sequences of constituents found in children's speech, one rule per sequence, seems to miss the generalization that the orders within the set of related sequences are all mutually consistent, and taken together form a larger sequence that itself emerges shortly after the child starts uttering sequences of the requisite length. As Bloom (1970) and Brown (1973) have noted, the data seem to be telling us that the child at some level knows the order of the entire sequence and that something with the same effect as a deletion rule is preventing him or her from realizing the entire sequence in overt speech.

Let us consider two other sets of alternatives that try to account for this.[19]

Optionality

Perhaps in the child's phrase structure rules all symbols are at first optional: S → (NP) (VP), VP → (V) (NP), and so on. Incomplete fragments could then be generated directly by the grammar. There are two problems with this tack. First, the criticisms I leveled against the learnability and expungeability of deletion rules holds in full force here as well. Second, as Bloom (1970) and Brown (1973) note, if all symbols were optional, one would expect full sequences like *agent-action-dative-object-locative* to be uttered at least occasionally at the same stage as the two-word subsets are uttered, and this virtually never occurs. One could say in reply to Bloom and Brown that if there is a fixed small probability p that a category will be expanded as an overt word, then the likelihood of all five categories in a sequence being expanded is p^5 whereas the probability of only two being expanded is $10p^2(1 - p)^3$, a much larger number when p is small. However, if one is to invoke small fixed probabilities of expansion of categories, a nongrammatical property, one is likely to attribute them to some processing mechanism that finds it "costly" to do the equivalent of expanding categories. If one is willing to posit a processor that has trouble expanding categories as words, then why not forget about optionality in the rules themselves, with all the learnability problems that accompany it, and simply say that the processor's limited capacities result in the child producing fragments that his or her grammar by itself would deem ungrammatical? This would allow maximum continuity in the sequence of the child's intermediate grammars, would account for the observed systematicity of order within fragments, and would not invoke any mechanism that would not also be needed in the optionality account. This is the account I will pursue.

Processing Limitations

I suggest that the child may utter incomplete sentences at first for the following reasons: (1) He or she may not have learned certain unstressed closed-class morphemes, and so will not say them; see the section "Three Learnability Problems" (above) for an account of how the reanalyses that become necessary when they are learned may be accomplished. (2) He or she has learned the fact that in the adult language noun phrases can be uttered in isolation in certain discourse contexts (Brown, 1973, makes this suggestion). The child certainly has ample evidence for this in parental speech (Snow and Ferguson, 1977), and a learning theory more complete than the present one would have to have mechanisms for learning discourse-sensitive rules of ellipsis. (3) The child's processing mechanisms are limited in capacity and so can coordinate only a fixed number of lexical items at some stage in the chain of transduction from communicative intention to semantic structure to f-structure to c-structure to actual utterance.

In the absence of systematic experimental evidence on children's speech production it is impossible to say precisely where this bottleneck lies. Certain options can be eliminated, however. Because the noun phrases are ordered by phrase structure rules according to the grammatical functions (relations) they assume, an NP must be assigned a grammatical function before it can be ordered. However, NPs can be assigned appropriate functions only by verbs or other predicates according to the proposed theory (i.e., there is nothing like an "actor-first" rule). Therefore, whenever NPs are correctly ordered in a verbless sentence the verb must still be represented at some level prior to the insertion of NPs in phrase structure slots. For the same reason, if a verbless sentence has the same semantic interpretation as it would have had with the verb, the verb must be represented at some underlying level since the verb determines the semantic role that an NP with a given grammatical function plays. Thus a possible locus for the processing bottleneck, initially proposed by David Lebeaux in Pinker and Lebeaux (1981), is the mapping from functional structure to constituent structure. The processing mechanism that realizes predicates as full words occupying terminal nodes in the tree might be unable to handle more than a certain number (like all cognitive processing limitations, the limits could be probabilistic and not absolute). Thus the representations underlying *Mommy* [draws an] *eye* could be like those shown in Figure 4.9.

Because all elements necessary for semantic interpretation are present in the functional structure, these sentences are interpreted, and the noun phrases ordered, in precisely the same way as would happen for a full sentence.

This account avoids the counterintuitiveness (for whatever that is worth) of deletion rules. Bloom and Bowerman were forced to posit such rules because in the Standard Theory of transformational grammar and in the theory of Case Grammar, unlike LFG, a verb is needed in an underlying constituent structure for the assignment of grammatical relations. David Lebeaux

Figure 4.9

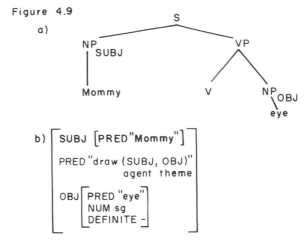

a)

b)
$$\begin{bmatrix} \text{SUBJ} \begin{bmatrix} \text{PRED "Mommy"} \end{bmatrix} \\ \text{PRED "draw (SUBJ, OBJ)"} \\ \qquad\qquad \text{agent theme} \\ \text{OBJ} \begin{bmatrix} \text{PRED "eye"} \\ \text{NUM sg} \\ \text{DEFINITE} - \end{bmatrix} \end{bmatrix}$$

points out that the reason a deletion rule is especially counter-intuitive in the case of a standard transformational grammar is that an identity mapping (between deep and surface structure) is intuitively the simplest to compute, and hence any additional operation (such as a deletion) would add to the set of computations that the child had to perform. As the child matured, he or she would then have to discard computational operations. However, in an LFG, because there is no identity mapping between functional structure and phrase structure, a surface structure with unrealized nodes would instead be "easier" to compute. Developmentally, then, the so-called deletion would disappear as the child was able to handle more computational operations as he or she grew older (Pinker and Lebeaux, 1981).

This particular version of the processing limitation hypothesis is highly speculative, and plausible alternative versions could also be formulated so long as the bottleneck is "downstream" from the f-structure (e.g., constituent structure might also be intact, but a word buffer accessed just prior to articulation might have a smaller number of slots than there are words in the tree). However, both learnability considerations and developmental evidence suggest, I think, that the best theory of the fragmentary nature of early speech would place the limitation not in the child's rule system itself but in the procedures that utilize the rules in speech production.

UNIVERSAL SYMBOLS IN CHILDREN'S RULES

In the preceding four sections I have argued that children's early rules are similar to the phrase structure rules created by the learning mechanisms (as amended earlier in this chapter) in the following ways: they must express the order of constituents; they use the same category symbols for noun phrases in different positions; they use category symbols that are not restricted to broad thematic roles and semantic categories, to narrow semantic categories and roles, or to word-bound categories and roles; and they specify complete sequences of categories within phrases and the sentence. (Incidentally, one aspect of phrase structure rules I will ignore is the precise geometry of children's trees, such as whether there exists a branching VP node or not. Bowerman, 1973, showed that earlier arguments for a VP node were unsound; and I think that the sort of evidence necessary even for making tentative hypotheses about a VP node for children, or other detailed aspects of their tree geometry, does not currently exist.) These properties cover the major theoretical commitments implied by the use of phrase structure rules, but there is one remaining: the use of category and function symbols with cross-linguistic significance imputed to them, such as N, V, SUBJ, and OBJ. All the arguments I have made in this chapter apply equally well to a theory in which the child's rules are identical to those that were postulated except for the substitution of CATEGORY-α and CATEGORY-β for N and V and FUNCTION-γ and FUNCTION-δ for SUBJ and OBJ, where α, β, and so on are arbitrary symbols for entities that are similar to grammatical categories and relations but that need have no relation to any symbols in grammars for children acquiring other languages. As I argued in Chapter 2, this question is meaningful to the extent that there exists a set of universal acquisition mechanisms that cross-reference certain symbols (see also Steele, 1981, 1982). For example, the mechanisms that acquire annotated phrase structure rules and lexical entries will posit certain symbols (what I have referred to as SUBJ and OBJ) that, under certain conditions, will trigger other procedures to go into action (e.g., those acquiring agreement, control relations, and anaphora). It is because those other procedures are biased to "look for" symbols of a given sort that one considers those symbol names meaningful—the names in effect refer to the potential cross-referencing or triggering relations among the subsystems of rules created by a universal set of acquisition procedures.

   How could one establish that young children's rules draw their symbols from the universally defined set that their other acquisition procedures will subsequently recognize? One way would be to show that some universal unlearnable property, like nonextractability from complex noun phrases, simply emerges as a

consequence of the child's having learned the requisite constructions (in this case, complex noun phrases and extraction). Since
the child could not have learned such a property directly from
positive evidence, it must have been triggered by a procedure
that recognized that the property should apply. And for the
procedure to recognize that the property should apply to a given
construction, the construction that it applies to must have been
labeled with the appropriate symbols. It is clear that I will not
be able to make such an argument for very early grammars.
Most of the putatively universal and unlearnable properties of
grammar are only manifested in complex constructions that children of this age simply do not utter and cannot give grammaticality judgments about (Maratsos, in press).

A second but less convincing demonstration would be to identify a set of properties that were not strictly unlearnable but
would be learned much more quickly if their acquisition procedures could recognize certain antecedently defined symbols
in existing rules, and show that children indeed learn those
properties very rapidly. An illustrative example is agreement.
According to the substantive portion of the theory of Lexical
Functional Grammar, verbs may agree in number, gender, and
so on with any of the grammatical functions subcategorized by
the verb. Thus a language may force verbs to agree with their
subjects, or objects, or second objects, but no language can force
a verb to agree with its nearest neighbor or the second constituent following it regardless of its function, or with the heaviest
noun phrase in the sentence, or with the possessor of a certain
noun phrase, or with the sister of a preposition in a locative
adjunct. Correspondingly, the hypothesis-testing procedures for
agreement markers (see Chapter 5) look for properties only of
SUBJs, OBJs, and so on of the verb in trying to determine which
properties the affix agrees with; it does not even test for properties of the constituents that do not bear symbols for subcategorized grammatical functions. If it did, it would still eventually
learn the correct rules, because the hypothesization procedure
is designed to reject all incorrect hypotheses, but it would take
longer to do so, since it would have to await disconfirming
evidence for a variety of hypotheses that are universally incorrect. Now, if it can be shown that children in fact never entertain
such hypotheses but entertain instead only potentially correct
ones (and if there is no alternative explanation for their selec-
tivity, such as nonlinguistic cognitive biases), one can conclude
that their affixation mechanisms must have recognized the set

of symbols that universally can support agreement (namely, the set including SUBJ, OBJ, and so on), and therefore that symbols of just that sort were present in the grammar beforehand.

Thus one can argue that when children rapidly converge on a rule and entertain only hypotheses that are definable in terms of universal symbols in previously acquired rules, those prior rules must indeed have contained the universal symbols. Again, such data will not be easy to obtain. It would take some experimental ingenuity, and considerable luck, to show that a given child at a given stage was entertaining some hypothesis not sanctioned by Universal Grammar, such as having verbs agree with their preceding noun phrase's possessors. A still weaker but more feasible demonstration would be to show that when children begin to acquire new sorts of rule systems, they do not take any obvious blind alleys, but rapidly arrive at the correct hypothesis consistent with previously learned rules and with Universal Grammar. While not demonstrative (since one has not shown which hypotheses may have been tested and discarded along the way), findings of rapid and cumulative development lend prima facie support to a model that exploits language universals to acquire grammars with a minimum of false starts. In the rest of this book I discuss several cases in which what appear to be bizarre detours on the road to adult competence in fact turn out to be quite reasonable first steps, considering the learnability task facing the child. To the extent that these arguments are successful for each example of apparent noncumulativeness, I will have shown that a model attributing universal symbols to the child is viable.

No doubt many people will wonder what I could possibly mean, then, when I say that a child has (say) a SUBJ symbol in his or her grammar at a time when there is still only one privilege of occurrence for subjects, namely appearing preverbally, and when the other procedures that it triggers have not yet gone into action. In such cases the symbol itself is not doing any of the work that we normally expect of an entity before associating linguistic symbols like SUBJ to it. Any symbol would do, and whether we call the symbol used at that degenerate stage SUBJ or some other name appears to be purely academic. This objection has a grain of truth to it, in that all I am demanding of the symbol is that it automatically enter into the phenomena we associate with SUBJs as soon as such phenomena begin to be learned. In calling a part of a rule SUBJ, I am simply asserting that *in the future* it will interact with certain mechanisms in predetermined ways, regardless of its limited role at that time. If some theory claimed that the initial symbol was not called SUBJ (since it wasn't doing much that was subjectlike) but instead *turned into* SUBJ automatically at some stage, that theory would essentially be indistinguishable from the one I have been arguing for (though it would, I have argued, be less parsimonious). The use of universal adult symbols in children's first rules, then, is simply the theoretical commitment that the child's early rules are continuous with their later ones and with adult ones.

An analogy with embryology may help. While an embryo is still a mostly undifferentiated mass of cells, it is possible to identify regions that will develop into mature organs. A clump of cells absorbing a large amount of some stain, or forming a slight bulge, may turn into the wing of a bird. Would one say that the bulge is "really" a wing? In one sense, no; in another, yes. It is not a wing because it has none of the properties that mature wings have. On the other hand, its intrinsic structure, location within the cell mass, and so on, are such that it will inevitably turn into what is uncontroversially a wing. (For such reasons one would also say that mammalian embryonic gills are not lungs in *any* sense, regardless of similarities in function or even structure with mature lungs.) One says that a collection of cells "is" a wing in order to express the claim that there is continuity of mechanism, and it is for precisely this reason that I say that young children's rules have symbols that "are" SUBJs.

5 | Inflection

ASIDE FROM constituent order, case and agreement inflections are the principal grammatical means of expressing predicate-argument relations in the world's languages. In this chapter I discuss the acquisition of inflectional systems, such as the affixes and closed-class morphemes encoding case, number, gender, person, tense, aspect, and so on. First I will discuss a simple hypothesis-sampling model for the acquisition of closed-class morphemes outlined in Pinker (1982), point out its deficiencies in terms of learnability and empirical support, and present a somewhat more complex but more promising model of their acquisition.

A Simple Learning Theory for Inflections

What Must Be Learned

In the theory of Lexical Functional Grammar, the rules governing the use of grammatical morphemes are assumed to be stored in the lexical entries for the particular morphemes as sets of functional or feature equations. These equations assert what must be true of the sentence in which the morpheme is found. For example, the lexical entry for the English third-person singular verb inflection (the *-s* in *Fred dances*) forcing agreement between verb and subject will contain syntactic information in something like the following format:

(1) -s: V affix: TENSE = present
            ASPECT = imperfective
            SUBJ's NUMBER = sg
            SUBJ's PERSON = 3

A noun affix for a nominal marker encoding accusative case, definiteness, and animacy in some hypothetical language would look like (2).

(2) -dax: N affix: CASE = acc
DEFINITE = +
ANIMACY = +

The equations in the entries for affixes would be merged with the equations in the entries for stems by a lexical rule of affixation, resulting in an entry like (3) which could then be inserted in the appropriate slot in a phrase marker.

(3) eats: V: PRED = "eat"
TENSE = present
ASPECT = imperfective
SUBJ's NUMBER = sg
SUBJ's PERSON = 3

Constraints on Inflection

Several formal and substantive conditions constrain which equations are possible in the lexical entry of an affix. The first is Kaplan and Bresnan's (1982) Functional Locality Constraint, which restricts each side of an equation to chains of two symbols. Thus SUBJ's NUMBER = *sg* is a possible equation, but not SUBJ's MOD's NUMBER = *sg*. The second is Bresnan's (1982c) constraint that an affixed predicate may enforce agreement with those of its arguments bearing subcategorizable grammatical functions. Thus SUBJ's NUMBER = *sg* is possible, but not AD-JUNCT's TENSE = *past* or ADJACENT-NP's NUMBER = *sg*. The third constraint (Bresnan, 1982c) is that only minor categories and heads of phrases (i.e., constituents annotated with the equation ↑ = ↓) may contain affixes bearing equations that constrain the features of other constituents of their phrases. Thus an equation on a head preposition may constrain the case of its object, but an equation on a direct object cannot constrain the case of a second object or an oblique object. This constraint is an immediate consequence of the requirement that the equation ↑ = ↓ be appended to heads and minor categories (see Bresnan, 1982c for details).

Finally, there must be a set of substantive constraints on the set of features that can enter into these equations. It has often been noted that not just any semantic notion can be encoded by an affix (e.g., Slobin, 1979, 1982, 1984a; Bybee, in press, a, b; Greenberg, 1963; Talmy, 1978). For example, affixes in the world's languages can obligatorily encode tense, aspect, number, gender, case, person, animacy, definiteness, humanness, rough shape, relative proximity, and perhaps twenty or so other notions; but no language obligatorily encodes temperature, time of day, prettiness, interestingness, Euclidean distance, texture, weight, degree of effort, natural versus man-made, familiarity of objects, value, and so on. Furthermore these constraints not only delimit what can be encoded in an equation, but which equations can be encoded in affixes to which categories. For example, aspect and tense can be encoded on verbs but not nouns; the features encoding whether an event is hypothetical versus actually occurring can be encoded in complementizers and verbs but not adjectives or prepositions, and so on.

A First Approximation: Exhaustive Hypothesization

In the learning procedure first proposed in Pinker (1982), it was assumed that the child already knew the syntactic categorization of some words, and, in the case of verbs, the grammatical roles of their arguments (e.g., that a given verb's agent is a subject, its patient an object). It was also assumed that the child had segmented the affix from the stem. The model was addressed to an interesting problem pointed out by Dan Slobin (1979; 1982). The principal difficulty that a learning mechanism for affixation faces is that different languages grammaticize different aspects of an event, and when they do, they do so *obligatorily*. Thus the child cannot encode the pragmatically salient notions in his or her interpretation of an input sentence containing inflections and work on the assumption that the inflections are encoding only those notions. For example, whether or not an adult wishes to communicate the information that an event is present or past, or that the subject argument of a verb is singular or plural, the language leaves him or her no choice: tense and subject number must be encoded in English. And the child not only cannot use the situation to determine which notions are encoded, he or she cannot use a priori knowledge either, since for all the child knows, it could be subject animacy or object number that an affix is encoding. In other words, in determining which notions are encoded in a language's morphology, the child is faced with a formidable search problem.

Thus the first part of the learning mechanism of Pinker (1982) was a procedure that hypothesized *all* the equations that were (a) consistent with the situation; (b) consistent with Kaplan and

Bresnan's formal and substantive conditions on functional equations as they applied to the child's analysis of the input sentence; and (c) composed of the primitive symbols encoding Slobin's taxonomy of grammaticizable notions. For example, when the child hears a sentence like *the boy eats an orange* and simultaneously constructs a semantic representation for it by attending to the accompanying scene, he or she could consider any of the following equations (and a number of others as well) as candidates to be added to the lexical entry for *-s*:

(4) (1) SUBJ's NUMBER = sg
     (2) SUBJ's GENDER = masc
     (3) SUBJ's PERSON = 3
     (4) SUBJ's ANIMACY = +
     (5) SUBJ's HUMANNESS = +
     (6) ASPECT = imperfective
     (7) TENSE = present
     (8) EVIDENTIAL-STATUS = witnessed
     (9) OBJ's NUMBER = sg
    (10) OBJ's PERSON = 3
    (11) OBJ's ANIMACY = −
    (12) OBJ's HUMANNESS = −
    (13) OBJ's SHAPE = globular

Let us call the set of equations that are simultaneously consistent with the inferred interpretation of a particular scene, the grammatical analysis of a particular sentence, and the universal constraints on feature equations the "permissible equation set." In Pinker (1982) I proposed that the child obeys the following two procedures: (1) Append all the equations in the permissible equation set of the input sentence to the lexical entry of the morpheme. (2) If any equation previously added to the morpheme is inconsistent with the current input sentence-plus-meaning, expunge it permanently from the lexical entry. Since the number of possible equations sanctioned by the constraints mentioned earlier is finite (see Pinker, 1982, Appendix 1, for a simple proof), the child, by following this procedure, will eventually converge on the correct equations for the morpheme to be learned. In the present example, the child would repeatedly add equations 1, 3, 6, and 7 to the lexical entry for *-s* when sentences with that morpheme are encountered, and would at one point or another encounter meaning-sentence pairs that contradict each equation in 2, 4, 5, and 8–13. For example, *the mama bear licks her cubs* is cause to delete equations 2, 5, 9, 11, and 13; *the sign bothers us* is cause to delete 4, 5, 9, 10, 11, 12, and 13; and so on. Thus the child will eventually arrive at the correct lexical entry for the morpheme -s.[1]

This model has a lot of problems. First, the number of equations in a permissible set, though a finite subset of the cognitively possible equations, is still quite large. Even if we were confident that the list of encodable notions for nouns had only 30 members, the child would have to form on the order of $30n$ ($ei + m$) equations for a single clause, where n is the number of noun phrases, e is the number of inflectable elements per noun phrase (including the noun itself, plus its adjectives, determiners, and possessors), i is the number of inflections per inflectable element in the noun phrase (e.g., in an agglutinating language), and m is the number of inflections on the verb (since verb inflections can also agree with the properties of the verb's subcategorized noun phrases). Even for simple sentences, this number can be quite large; for example, it is on the order of 120 in the previous example if we assume that the child knows that only *the, a,* and -*s* are grammatical morphemes. This seems to be an implausible number of equations to have the child keep in mind at once.

In any case, the empirical facts about the acquisition of closed-class morphemes are devastating to this model. The model predicts that affixes that are sensitive to a full set of grammatical features (e.g., an affix used only on plural, masculine, animate, accusative nouns) would be learned more quickly than an affix that is sensitive to only one feature (e.g., number), because in the latter case it would take more time for incorrectly hypothesized features to drop out. In contrast, it has been found that the more semantic or syntactic features that are encoded in an English grammatical morpheme, the later the child comes to use it in obligatory contexts (Brown, 1973; de Villiers and de Villiers, 1973a; Pinker, 1981c).[2] Similarly, affixes in agglutinating languages (e.g., Turkish), each of which encodes only one feature, are learned far more rapidly than affixes in fusional languages (e.g., Serbo-Croatian), each of which encodes several features (Slobin, 1979, 1982). Finally, the account makes the prediction that children should first undergeneralize the use of their morphemes at the stage at which they have not driven out the incorrect equations (e.g., they might restrict a nominative case marker to nouns with animate singular globular definite proximal referents), and then gradually expand their usage until it matches that of adults. In fact, children the world over do the opposite: they quite frequently overgeneralize the use of individual morphemes to words that do not allow them in the adult language, respecting one distinction encoded by that morpheme while ignoring a second distinction also encoded by it. This is often true even if the child respects that very distinction in the use of some other morpheme. For example, Slobin (1984a) summarizes reports of children respecting case but ignoring gender, respecting gender but ignoring case, respecting case but ignoring polarity, respecting case but ignoring animacy, respecting tense but ignoring mood, respecting number but ignoring gender, and several other examples; these reports concern languages as different as Hebrew, German, Russian, Spanish, Japanese, and Hungarian.[3]

A Second Approximation: Hypothesis Sampling

In Pinker (1982) I discussed some of these problems and suggested a modification that solved them. Instead of having the child hypothesize all the permissible equations consistent with an input sentence, the child could sample one equation randomly selected from the permissible set. For each sentence, a different equation could be hypothesized. If an existing equation is hypothesized again, it would be strengthened; if an existing equation is contradicted by a newly hypothesized equation, both would be permanently expunged. Eventually all and only the correct equations would be appended to the affix. This would allow development to go from simple to complex and from general to specific, as mandated by the data. It would not involve large amounts of on-line computation.[4] And, by imposing a weighting on the child's hypotheses, one could account for the large disparities in the prevalence of various grammatical encodings in the world's languages, and in the speed of acquisition of various encodings by children. Many languages encode number, gender, case, and person; fewer encode shape, witness-versus-hearsay, or relative position in a social/biological hierarchy (see Greenberg, 1963; Slobin, 1979, 1984a). Children learn how to encode the aspect of a verb with ease (e.g., in Czech, Polish, Russian, and Serbo-Croatian) but have great difficulty in learning verbal affixes that agree with the definiteness of the verb's object (in Hungarian). They also have more difficulty learning to inflect conditional and negation markers for tense or person than they have for verbs that bear such markers (in Japanese; all examples from Slobin, 1984a). These disparities can be explained if we assume that the probability with which the child hypothesizes an equation encoding number is higher than the probability with which he or she hypothesizes an equation encoding shape, or that the probability of hypothesizing equations on a verb encoding aspect is smaller than for equations on a verb encoding the definiteness of nominal arguments, and so on. In fact, many of Joseph Greenberg's linguistic universals (see Greenberg, 1963) can be translated into weightings of classes of hypotheses, each such translation making a developmental prediction.

Problems for the Second Approximation

Unfortunately, the revised model still has some serious problems. First, there is no account whatsoever of how the segmentation of affixes from their stems occurs; clearly this is a nontrivial step that cannot be accomplished by an examination of individual inflected words. Furthermore, many of the developmental phenomena surrounding the acquisition of affixes seem to involve variables to which segmentation is sensitive—for example, syllabic affixes are acquired more quickly than nonsyllabic ones, and inflections in analytic languages are acquired more quickly than those in synthetic languages (Slobin, 1977, 1982). Without an account of segmentation, tests of the model against specific developmental data will be difficult.

A second problem, related to the absence of a segmentation mechanism, is how the child discovers zero morphemes such as the English present-tense marker for the first and second persons (e.g., *I walk/*I walks/*he walk*). Since there is no acoustic cue for zero morphemes, it is not clear what would prompt the child to set up lexical entries for such morphemes. Perhaps the child sets up zero morphemes for *all* words and then eliminates those that do not end up with a stable set of equations, but this seems extremely wasteful. To be sure, children often have trouble learning zero morphemes (Slobin, 1973), but the theory must provide some means by which the child can eventually learn them.

Third, the model has no means of acquiring gender classes and arbitrary declensional and conjugational classes (e.g., in Latin). In Pinker (1982) it was suggested that the child uses the sex of human referents as a semantic cue for the feature name GENDER and the feature values *masc* and *fem*, with the gender of inanimate nouns learned distributionally via their similarity in inflection to words denoting humans. This predicts that the first affixes sensitive to gender that the child masters should be used with personal pronouns or human nouns, and that gender errors should be very common at first for nonhuman nouns. Although there have been reports of children making gender errors while getting case right (e.g., Slobin, 1973), the converse has also been observed (MacWhinney, 1978; Maratsos and Chalkley, 1981; Maratsos, in press), and children also have been shown to be insensitive to the sex of a noun's referent when assigning grammatical gender to it (Karmiloff-Smith, 1979). Furthermore, such an account could not work at all for affixes sensitive to membership in completely arbitrary classes with no semantic correlates even in the pronominal system; nor for affixes sensitive to the phonological properties of their stems.

Fourth, Lebeaux (1982, in preparation) and Pinker and Lebeaux (1981) point out that the model would be unable to account for the acquisition of affixes in languages displaying *syncretism*, the use of one affix to encode different sets of features. For example, if a particular affix marked both nominative masculine and genitive masculine nouns but not accusative and dative masculine nouns, the two case features would come in conflict and cancel each other, leaving only the information that the affix marked masculine nouns. This would lead the child to use the affix, incorrectly, to mark the accusative and dative cases.

Fifth, this model makes the implausible assumption that the child sooner or later hypothesizes out of thin air every feature equation that languages in the world can use. Thus an English-speaking child will at some point hypothesize equations suitable for Navajo shape classifiers, for the Turkish distinction between witnessed events and those learned about through hearsay, for alienable versus inalienable possession, and so on, albeit not very often and very briefly. It seems more plausible that some mechanism would draw the child's attention to distinctions made by the target language in cases where those distinctions are uncommon cross-linguistically or cognitively nonsalient.

Sixth, there is a striking developmental pattern called "morphological imperialism" that this model cannot account for. Children acquiring Russian (Slobin, 1973) and Polish (Slobin, 1984a) have been observed to use a single morpheme to express a certain case, ignoring gender distinctions, and then to cease using that morpheme completely and instead use a morpheme of a different gender to mark that case. The model can account for the failure to distinguish among the genders (the gender equation could simply not yet have been hypothesized), but why children would replace one morpheme with another to encode the same set of equations remains a mystery.

Seventh, it is not clear in the model what would impel an English-speaking child to replace his or her overgeneralized forms (e.g., *breaked, *foots*) with the correct forms as they get older. Clearly some version of the Uniqueness Principle could be relevant to this suppletion process, but the versions proposed in Chapter 4 would not accomplish what is needed here.

A New Learning Theory for Inflection: Paradigm Formation

WHAT MUST BE LEARNED

Paradigm Representation

I will begin by presenting a characterization of the adult state which differs from the one just described by its essential use of the traditional grammatical notion of a *paradigm* for representing sets of related affixes. Instead of classifying declensional information solely by appending grammatical features to the lexical entries for each affix (and thus having the affixes serve as indexes to that information), the grammatical information itself can also serve as an indexing system, under which particular affixes are listed. I assume that the adult grammar represents information about affixes in a paradigm or matrix representation, such as is shown in Figure 5.1. In addition, the paradigm would contain a symbol indicating which syntactic category it was appropriate

Figure 5.1

a) First declension masculine nouns in Latin

NUMBER

CASE	Singular	Plural
Nom	-a	-ae
Acc	-am	-as
Dative	-ae	-is
Abl	-a	-is
Genitive	-ae	-arum

b) German articles

GENDER

NUMBER		CASE	Masc	Neut	Fem
Sing		Nom	der	das	die
		Acc	den	das	die
		Dative	dem	dem	der
		Genitive	des	des	der
Plural		Nom	die	die	die
		Acc	die	die	die
		Dative	den	den	den
		Genitive	der	der	der

to, and the lexical entry of each noun would contain a feature equation specifying the gender or declensional class it belongs to, so that the correct paradigm can be associated with each noun. Finally, there would have to be a representation associating the position of affixes within the word with the set of features that they denote, like that in (5), where (a) would be characteristic of an agglutinating language, and (b) characteristic of a fusional language.

(5) (a) [$_N$Stem + affix + affix]
            GENDER CASE
  (b) [$_N$Stem + affix]
            CASE
            GENDER

The paradigm representation is related to the lexical entry representation used in (1) and (2) by the following convention: the term on the left-hand side of an equation (e.g., CASE, GENDER) becomes a *dimension* of the matrix representing the paradigm; each of its possible right-hand-side values (e.g., *nom, acc, masc, fem*) becomes a *level* of that dimension; the name of the affix (or word) is listed inside the *cell* representing a conjunction of levels of different dimensions. One can think of the "paradigm" and "lexical entry" notations as emphasizing different indexes or access routes within the same set of information. The paradigm is an appropriate representation to use in sentence production, where the speaker has grammatical information in mind and must find the affix that encodes it; lexical entries are an appropriate representation to use in sentence comprehension, where the hearer has the affix in mind and must find the information that it encodes.

General and Specific Paradigms

In Figure 5.1 I showed a paradigm containing only the closed-class morphemes. It is also possible to represent entire inflected words in paradigms specific to that word; indeed, this must be done for irregularly inflected words. Fragments of specific word paradigms are shown in Figure 5.2. Part (a) would belong to a paradigm for an irregular verb, and part (b) would belong to a paradigm for a regular verb. Note that in this representation these verbs may be stored in the correct cells of their paradigms without ever having undergone morphological analysis.

There is reason to believe that both general (e.g., Figure 5.1)

Figure 5.2

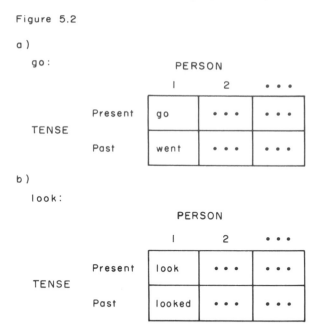

a)

go:

and word-specific (e.g., Figure 5.2) paradigms are necessary in the adult grammar. In accord with "full entry theories" (see Halle, 1973; Lieber, 1981; and Bresnan, 1982b), I will assume that in this model, as in its predecessor, the fully inflected word can simply be stored in the lexicon, and that it is inserted into the phrase marker when lexical insertion takes place. But it is insufficient simply to have individual lexical paradigms. The inflectional system is productive—the adult, having heard the dative of a new noun in a case-marking language, must be able to deduce its nominative form. In other words, there must be a general rule schema to derive new forms from old ones. This would for example sanction the entrance of *apteryxes* into the lexicon if the form *apteryx* had been heard; it would allow *insulam* to be entered given *insula*. This can be accomplished by having the general paradigm listing of affixes in Figure 5.1 apply to a partially filled word paradigm to fill out the rest of its cells. Thus the partial word paradigm in part (a) of Figure 5.3 could be combined with the general affix paradigm in part (b) to yield the full word paradigm shown in part (c). The full word-specific paradigm would be formed by substituting for the affix in the known case (in this instance *-am*) the affixes corresponding to the other cases, keeping the stem constant. In this account, as in the previous model of the adult state, the separate listing of

Figure 5.3

a)   CASE

Nom	Acc	Dat	Gen
	insulam		

b)   CASE

Nom	Acc	Dat	Gen
-a	-am	-ae	-ae

c)   CASE

Nom	Acc	Dat	Gen
insula	insulam	insulae	insulae

affixes is essentially part of the word formation component; the actual full lexical entry is what is inserted in the phrase marker.

The Unique Entry Principle

There is an important constraint on affixation that can be stated easily in terms of the paradigm representation: no complete set of grammatical feature values may be encoded by two or more distinct morphemes. This can be translated into the constraint that no cell in a paradigm may be filled with more than one affix. I will call this the "one entry per cell" or "Unique Entry" principle. (In Pinker and Lebeaux, 1981, and Lebeaux, 1982, it is called the "Cell Uniqueness" principle.) Constraints similar to this principle have been proposed (e.g., by Aronoff, 1976; Lapointe, 1980, 1981c) to account for the fact that irregularly inflected forms do not coexist with their regular counterparts; if an irregular form exists in a word-specific paradigm, its regular alternative formed by the general affix paradigm is blocked. It has also often been noted in this connection that when irregular and regular forms do appear in the same language community, such as when two dialects are mixed, the regular and irregular forms come to take on different meanings. As we shall see, the Unique Entry principle will play a significant role in the acquisition theory.

Syncretism and Paradigms

Lebeaux (1982; see also Pinker and Lebeaux, 1981) points out another advantage of the paradigm as a representation of the adult state: it allows a perspicuous account for patterns of syncretism across the world's languages. Recall that syncretism is the use of a single inflection to register distinct sets of syntactic features. Thus in Latin *-um* is used to mark both nominative singular and accusative singular in declension II; in German the article *die* is used for all nominative plurals. Syncretism does not occur randomly within a paradigm, but rather tends to occur in certain patterns. For example, according to Williams (1981b), the syncretism of nominative singular and accusative singular is "natural," but not that between nominative singular and accusative plural, nor, more interestingly, that between nominative singular and nominative plural. (See also Greenberg, 1963, who summarizes many such patterns across languages.) In a paradigm one may nest some dimensions within others. "Natural classes" would then consist of contiguous cells within the paradigm if one nests particular dimensions within others, and if one assumes that contiguous cells may actually be subclasses of a superordinate. For example, Williams classifies nominative and accusative as *direct* cases, and dative and ablative as *oblique* cases. If the number dimension is superordinate to the case dimension, the cells for singular nominative and accusative case would be contiguous and could be described as being a single cell bearing the "direct" label—a cell that could contain a single affix. Thus a paradigm in which the same affix encoded nominative plural and accusative plural could be represented as in Figure 5.4. Similarly, a slice of a paradigm in which gender was neutralized entirely within the plural number (English is as good an example as any) would be represented as in Figure 5.5. With a paradigm notation, then, the "natural" patterns of syncretism are repre-

Figure 5.4

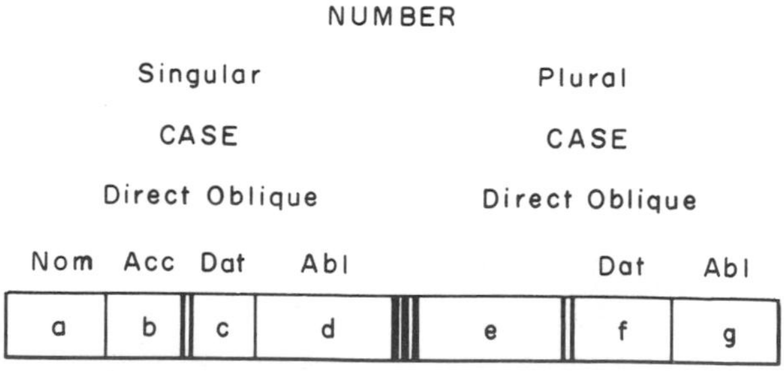

Figure 5.5

NUMBER

Singular   Plural

GENDER

M   F

he	she		they

sented as requiring fewer distinct cells than "unnatural" patterns—for example, one cannot draw a single cell comprising
only nominative, accusative, and dative; nor a cell comprising
nominative singular and accusative plural; nor a cell comprising
nominative singular and accusative singular.[5] Thus "natural-
ness" becomes equated with a certain form of paradigm economy. As we shall see, the syncretism patterns will be related to
certain properties of the acquisition mechanisms when these
mechanisms are discussed later in the chapter.

So far, I have simply presented an alternative formulation of
the adult state and some of its advantages. In the rest of this
chapter I describe a revised acquisition theory for affixation based
on ideas developed in collaboration with David Lebeaux (Pinker
and Lebeaux, 1981, Lebeaux, 1982, in preparation; some of the
hypotheses have been independently proposed by Mac-
Whinney, 1978). Specifically, the proposal has the following features: (1) a hypothesization procedure similar to that of the
previous model; (2) formation of one-dimensional and then *n*-
dimensional paradigms of related sets of affixes; (3) a progression
from word-specific to general paradigms; and (4) extensive use
of the Unique Entry principle to inspire changes in the paradigm.
In outlining the modified theory I will show how it solves the
problems that plagued the original one, and I will mention the
developmental evidence relevant to each mechanism.

Initial Learning of Word-Specific Paradigms

This step is essentially similar to its counterpart in the previous
model, except that I do not assume that segmentation has taken
place, and I have the child enter the hypothesized equations
into the grammar in the form of word-specific paradigms, in
addition to lexical entries for the individual items, using the
feature name = dimension, feature value = level translation scheme
mentioned earlier.[6] The proposal that the child begins with word-

specific paradigms is motivated by two main considerations. First, given the near-impossibility of computing morpheme boundaries based on a word's acoustic properties (e.g., Cole and Jakimik, 1980), one has little choice but to propose a process whereby the child first creates word-specific mini-paradigms and only later abstracts the patterns of inflection contained within them to create general inflectional paradigms (Lebeaux, 1982, in preparation). Furthermore, the developmental evidence supports a progression from word-specific to general paradigms. Children initially use inflections such as *-ing, -s,* and *-ed* only on a tiny subset of the words that allow those inflections, and then gradually expand their usage to more and more verbs (Bloom, Lifter, and Hafitz, 1978; Brown, 1973; Cazden, 1968; Kuczaj, 1977, 1981). They learn inflected irregular forms just as easily as regular ones at first; overregularization of irregular forms tends to occur at a later stage (Brown, 1973; Kuczaj, 1977). Children also make many segmentation errors in their early speech (Brown, 1973; MacWhinney, 1982).

There is another reason why the child should be capable of appending equations to entire words rather than just to affixes. Many distinctions that are encoded as affixes in one language are encoded in other languages as sets of morphologically unrelated verbs whose meanings contrast minimally according to that distinction (for examples see Bybee, in press, a, b; Gentner, 1982; and Talmy, 1975, 1978). These minimal contrasts play an important role in disambiguating sentences in those uncommon languages that lack any grammatical means of signaling predicate-argument relations (Li and Thompson, 1976). By first hypothesizing equations for entire verbs and only later trying to generalize inflectional patterns if that can be done, the child could use a single process to learn how to express semantic features whether the language encodes them in affixes or in verb alternations.

The procedure that sets up these paradigms is I1:

I1. Choose a linguistically relevant feature from among the features contained in the inferred sentence meaning. Create an equation expressing the value of that feature, such that the equation is also consistent with formal and substantive constraints. Append that equation to the lexical entry of the word to which it is relevant according to those constraints, and enter the word itself in a paradigm defined by the equation. If such a paradigm already exists and the relevant cell is already filled with a different form, allow only a single entry to fill that cell unless the lexical entries of both forms are high in strength.

A child following this procedure and choosing case as the relevant feature (exploiting the syntax-semantics correspondences such as *agent* = *nominative, patient* = *accusative*) could end up with a one-dimensional paradigm like that shown in Figure 5.6, where *a, b,* and *c* refer to inflected nouns. The child can create multidimensional paradigms by following I2:

I2. When the lexical entry for a word that is already in a paradigm is then given a new hypothesized equation involving a different feature, encode that equation as a new dimension in the paradigm.

Thus if the child now sampled equations for number, he or she would eventually build the paradigm shown in Figure 5.7.

Use of the Unique Entry Principle

In general, languages use no more than one inflection for each combination of their grammaticized features; in other words, each adult paradigm cell may contain no more than a single entry. The procedures avoid such violations of the Unique Entry principle at first by only adding a second entry to a cell if the lexical entries of both forms exceed a certain strength value (recall that I am assuming that affixes still have entries in the lexicon distinct from their listings within paradigms). This provision has a Bayesian flavor to it: the child requires more evidence to accept an a priori unlikely hypothesis (i.e., a paradigm with a uniqueness violation) than an a priori likely hypothesis. It also makes the procedure more robust in the face of possible ungrammatical or misanalyzed inputs, since a single input that is inconsistent with a learned form will cause no permanent change. If two forms competing for a cell both have strong entries, then procedures that I will propose later in the chapter attempt to restore uniqueness by changing the structure of the paradigm itself. Thus the Unique Entry principle itself is not explicitly stated in a single procedure; the procedures taken together yield paradigms with unique filled cells as the only stable final state.

Figure 5.6

	CASE	
Nom	Acc	Dat
a	b	c

Figure 5.7

		CASE		
		Nom	Acc	Dat
NUMBER	Sg	a	b	c
	Pl	d	e	f

Developmental evidence concerning the Unique Entry principle. As I have mentioned, there are many reports in the developmental literature of children failing to respect some features when choosing a morpheme—for example, using a marker that is appropriate in case but inappropriate in gender. Interestingly, in the initial stages of using a morpheme the child is more likely to use a single morpheme in all contexts than a full set of morphemes in free variation (Slobin, 1973, 1984a). At first this might seem to be a natural consequence of the child's having an underdifferentiated matrix, such as the ones in Figure 5.6 or Figure 5.7 (assuming that the language also differentiated case markers according to a third dimension such as definiteness): the matrix would simply lack a dimension because of the child's failure to hypothesize a feature at first. But this cannot account for the child's use of only a single morpheme for a given combination of cells in his or her provisional paradigm, since as far as the child is concerned the input contains evidence for more than one morpheme. In the example in Figure 5.7, the child will hear at least two markers for the nominative singular (one for definite nouns, one for indefinites), two markers for the accusative singular, and so on. Thus a simple failure to notice a feature could in principle lead the child to use alternate sets of affixes in free variation at first, but, as mentioned, usually this does not occur. The Unique Entry principle, or, more specifically, its instantiation in the last provision of procedure I1, is a necessary part of the explanation. The complete explanation would be stated in two parts: first, the child is unlikely to hypothesize certain semantic dimensions at first, that is, those that are low on the hierarchy of accessible notions relevant to a particular type of affixation, or those that have no semantic correlates, such as gender or declensional class. (And, in fact, Slobin reports that underdifferentiation tends to occur for certain features but not for others; it usually occurs for features that are perceptually less salient or that are rare cross-linguistically; Slobin, 1984a). Second (crucially), the Unique Entry provision of I1 makes it difficult for the child to place two morphemes in the same cell, even if the child hears a second morpheme for which he or she has hypothesized the same feature values as an existing morpheme. In other words, a failure to hypothesize a dimension will yield a single cell for a particular case; the Unique Entry principle then prevents the child from entering a second affix into that cell.

I have been discussing a scenario in which the child fails to enter a case marker that he or she has heard because of the

Unique Entry principle. However, there is nothing in procedures I1 or I2 that dictates that an existing affix must be retained and evidence for alternative affixes ignored. The competition between two forms could also result in the old one being eliminated and the new one replacing it. This would result in the phenomenon sometimes referred to as "inflectional imperialism." Imperialism is not widespread but it is quite persistent when it occurs (Slobin, 1984a). In the reported cases the driven-out affixes have had some property that appears to make them susceptible to replacement. In Slobin's reports of Russian children using single case markers to encode accusative case and instrumental case, ignoring gender, the driven-out forms were either zero morphemes or affixes with several homonyms in the language's inflectional system (e.g., *-a*, which is used in the neuter and feminine citation forms and as a diminutive masculine suffix). In Smoczynska's report of imperialism in Polish (in the Slobin 1984b volume), the driven-out morpheme was a zero form. Interestingly, Slobin (1973, 1984a) reports that homonymity and silentness are also properties that in other languages cause morphemes not to be acquired in the earliest stages. Thus it appears that certain properties of an affix, such as homonymity with other affixes, lack of phonological substance, and perhaps low frequency, will cause it to lose the competition for cell occupancy, either by not being hypothesized to begin with or by being driven out by a later form.[7] If an affix occupying a paradigm cell does not have these unfortunate properties, then it will remain in that cell despite evidence for a rival affix and the result will be the singleminded use of one affix that Slobin describes.

The Problem of Gender

In order to explain why children initially fail to mark certain distinctions, I postulated that the child is unlikely to sample certain feature values because they are low on the hierarchy of availability or because they have no semantic correlates. According to that formulation, affixes encoding grammatical gender, then, would have to be heard first for personal pronouns, where sex of referent is a salient feature. Then the child could assign gender features to sexless entities by noting which of the previously learned affixes they bore. This predicts that children should first learn gender agreement and concord for personal pronouns and then extend it to other nouns, and also that gender is more likely to be absent from early paradigms than the more semantically transparent features like case and number. It also would explain why all languages that have a system of grammatical gender for nouns also have a personal pronoun system differentiating gender in at least one person (Greenberg, 1963).

Unfortunately, neither of the developmental predictions appears to be true in general. For example, German children make case errors while respecting gender (MacWhinney, 1978, Maratsos, in press; see also Slobin, 1984a, which summarizes other reports of early learning of gender markers). Furthermore, children show no strong tendency to associate masculine nouns with male referents or feminine nouns with female referents (Karmiloff-Smith, 1979), in contrast to their tendency to associate other quasi-semantic noun features with the corresponding attributes of their referents (e.g., count-mass, Brown, 1957, though see also Gordon, 1982; proper-common, Katz, Baker, and Macnamara, 1973; Gelman and Taylor, 1983). In cases where there is concord between article and noun and nouns rarely appear without an article (e.g., French), correct use of gender is no mystery—the child would simply store the article-plus-noun combination in a cell in the paradigm, as if the article were a bound definiteness prefix (I discuss the stripping of affixes from stems later in the chapter, and the discovery of free versus bound morphemes in n. 12).[8] In cases of subject-verb agreement, however, it is unlikely that the child would store every combination of subject and inflected verb, and in cases where the child productively extended an affix to a novel bare noun (for German children as young as three in MacWhinney's 1978 experiment), stored unanalyzed units would be of no help. These findings seem somewhat paradoxical from the standpoint of the acquisition model—why would the child as a first hypothesis assume that an affix encoded the membership of a noun in one of a set of opaque classes, and how does the child do so well so early?

Slobin (1984a, and personal communication) points out that in most cases of early acquisition of gender systems, gender in fact correlates extremely highly with certain phonological properties of the stem, such as having an open or closed final syllable, or ending in a certain vowel. Furthermore, even when gender seems to be learned quickly, children will make errors on irregular nouns whose gender differs from what their phonological properties suggest. For example, Hebrew-speaking children treat all nouns ending in -*a* as feminine (Slobin, 1984a), and French-speaking children consistently guess the appropriate gender of rare and concocted nouns on the basis of their phonological properties (Tucker, Lambert, Rigault, and Segalowitz, 1968). They can even do so when the referent of the concocted noun is of a different sex than the one corresponding to the phonologically indicated gender (Karmiloff-Smith, 1979).

It appears that gender in such languages is almost a surrogate for phonological features. Slobin suggests that the child hypothesizes phonological features in parallel with hypothesizing semantic features and consequently succeeds at respecting gender categories. Translated into the present theory, that means that procedure I1 would be modified to add equations to affixes stating phonological properties of the items they can govern (this would constitute the same class as the semantically governable items). For example, SUBJ's FINAL-SYLLABLE = *open*, STEMVOWEL = *long*, STEM-FINAL-CONSONANT = *voiced*, and so on, would be possible equations (the actual feature names and feature values would, of course, be drawn from the theory of morphology and phonology). As in the case of semantically based equations, the set of values for a feature could define the cells of a dimension in a paradigm; and if the hypothesis was incorrect, that dimension could be eliminated by the same mechanism that eliminates incorrect dimensions based on semantic features (that mechanism, I3, will be discussed in the next section).[9]

As with semantically based equations, the sampling likelihood of various features and values would be arranged in a hierarchy, usually reflecting (and in part causing) their relative prevalence in languages. For example, equations enforcing vowel harmony or voicing assimilation between stems and sets of suffixes would be highly accessible, but not equations specifying the number of syllables in the stem (Slobin, 1984a).

This modification brings with it several advantages. An account in which phonological features are hypothesized in parallel with semantic ones predicts that gender can come to be respected either early or late in acquisition depending on its correlation with accessible phonological features in the language. Slobin (1984a) reports that this is the case cross-linguistically (e.g., gender categories correlating poorly with phonological properties, such as in Slavic languages, are acquired late). In addition, the I-procedures, as amended to attend to phonological properties, could also serve to learn strictly allomorphic variation among affixes with no further additions to those procedures; for example, they could learn the allomorphs -*s*, -*z*, and -*iz* variously coding plurality in English as a function of the final voicing and manner of articulation of their stems. But the procedures still cannot learn gender classes whose common phonological properties are so unusual that it is unlikely that a child would ever hypothesize them out of the blue, or learn arbitrary declensional or conjugational classes with no phonological properties in common whatsoever nor any reflexes in common with the personal pronouns. As we shall see, these sorts of learning will be accomplished by mechanisms that make use of the paradigm notation and the Unique Entry principle.

Eliminating Incorrect Hypotheses

One problem of the earlier model, discussed at the beginning of the chapter, can now easily be solved. By entering different forms in cells constituting a row of a paradigm, the child is implicitly "expecting" the language to have forms for feature values other than the first one hypothesized. When the child hears the same marker encoding a different feature value, he or she simply enters the marker into its appropriate cell. In the first version of the model, this would lead to the permanent deletion of the feature equation, even if some third feature value was marked by a different form. In the revised model I am considering here, the child only eliminates a feature if the *entire row* of cells corresponding to the possible values of that feature contains the same affix; otherwise the cell entries, and corresponding lexical entries for affixes, are kept distinct. I3 accomplishes this step, which is still necessary whenever the child hypothesizes a dimension not encoded by the target language.

I3. If the same affix appears in all the cells defining a dimension across a given combination of values of the other dimensions, and this is true for every possible combination of values of the other dimensions, eliminate that entire dimension from the paradigm.[10]

Imagine, for example, that the child attempting to learn the paradigm in Figure 5.7 had mistakenly hypothesized humanness as the feature crossed with case because he or she had often heard form *a* referring to a singular nominative entity that also happened to be human, and form *d* referring to a plural nominative entity that also happened to be nonhuman. Figure 5.8 would be the result.

Figure 5.8

		CASE		
		Nom	Acc	Dat
HUMAN	+	a	b	c
	–	d		

Figure 5.9

		CASE		
		Nom	Acc	Dat
HUMAN	+	a	b/e	c
	–	a/d	b/e	c

However, the child would also hear *a* used with a nonhuman referent many times, *b, c,* and *e* used with both human and nonhuman referents many times, and so on, and would end up with a paradigm like Figure 5.9 (exactly which forms would be in the paradigm at that point would depend on frequency, phonetic substance, and so on). Since the same affixed forms appear for both values of the feature HUMAN, and this is true for all cases, procedure I3 eliminates it as a paradigm dimension. When the correct feature NUMBER is hypothesized, it will define rows with distinct features and so I3 will never eliminate it. Since the procedure awaits complete rows and columns containing the same forms, it will not be fooled into eliminating legitimate dimensions when there are forms appearing in two out of *n* cells in a row or column, for example, a language that used one affix for nominative case and a second one for the accusative and dative case.

One might wonder why I am assuming that competing forms of high strength can temporarily coexist in a paradigm cell, given the Unique Entry principle, and why procedure I3 is stated so as to collapse a dimension whenever a form appears in all cells in a row or column, rather than insisting that all rows and columns be filled with identical forms. The reason is that if the child were only able to retain a single form for each cell over the short term, he or she could choose forms from different levels of an as-yet-unhypothesized dimension (e.g., *a* and *d* above) and hence fail to recognize that each form could be used in all levels of the first dimension, which is what he or she must do in order to remove that dimension. By allowing multiple forms to be retained pending procedures that alter the dimensionality of the paradigm (to be discussed later), one can give the child the means to recognize incorrect hypotheses quickly.[11]

STEM-AFFIX SEGMENTATION AND THE LEARNING OF GENERAL PARADIGMS

So far I have had the child form word-specific mini-paradigms, but we cannot leave the child in that state for long. We know that English children by the age of 5 can inflect novel bare nouns productively for number, and verbs for tense (i.e., they can pass the "wug" test; Berko, 1958; Pinker et al., in preparation; Stromswold, 1983). Similarly, some German 3-year-olds can choose articles correctly for novel nouns even though the choice involves respecting arbitrary grammatical gender (MacWhinney, 1978). Furthermore, in agglutinating languages like Turkish the number of possible combinations of stems and inflections would be too numerous to learn one by one (and in fact Turkish children can inflect nouns productively by the age of 2; see Slobin, 1977, 1982). Therefore, it is important to show how children generalize from many mini-paradigms, specific to individual words, to a general paradigm embodying knowledge of exactly what each affix encodes when it inflects any stem.

A First Approximation

The following procedures, developed in collaboration with David Lebeaux (Lebeaux, 1982, in preparation; Pinker and Lebeaux, 1981), are first approximations of a theory of how the child strips stems from affixes and forms general paradigms and word structure templates.

I4. Find the phonetic material in common among all the cells in a word-specific paradigm. Enter that material in the lexicon with the feature "STEM" or "ROOT" and as a label for the word-specific paradigm from which it was extracted.

I use the phrase "phonetic material in common" as a placeholder for more precise notions to be taken from a theory of phonology. This "material" would consist of the contiguous string of segments that make up the stem in languages with prefixing or suffixing, and the triconsonantal root in Semitic languages using patterns of vowel alternations. An example of I4's operation is illustrated in Figure 5.10, where parts (a) and (b) are paradigms

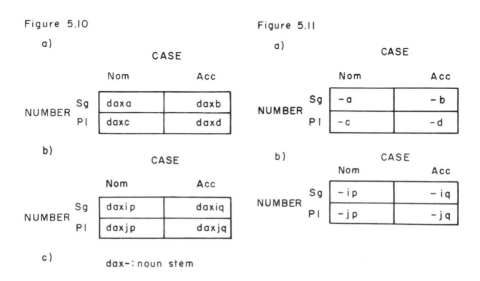

Figure 5.10

a)

CASE

		Nom	Acc
NUMBER	Sg	daxa	daxb
	Pl	daxc	daxd

b)

CASE

		Nom	Acc
NUMBER	Sg	daxip	daxiq
	Pl	daxjp	daxjq

c)   dax-: noun stem

Figure 5.11

a)

CASE

		Nom	Acc
NUMBER	Sg	-a	-b
	Pl	-c	-d

b)

CASE

		Nom	Acc
NUMBER	Sg	-ip	-iq
	Pl	-jp	-jq

for hypothetical fusional and agglutinating languages, respectively, and (c) is the stem extracted (this would then be attached as a label of the relevant paradigm).

Procedure I4 has simply isolated the stem or root of a word; it is also necessary to analyze the affixes left after the stem is extracted to determine which affixes encode particular cases, numbers, and so on. At first glance, this would seem to be trivial—just subtract the stem discovered by I4 from each of the entries in the paradigm, and the residue in each cell would be the exact affix or combination of affixes appropriate to its row and column. Thus after subtracting part (c) of Figure 5.10 from parts (a) and (b), one would be left with the general paradigms shown in parts (a) and (b) of Figure 5.11, respectively. Zero morphemes would be discovered when paradigms contain entries of the form *m* and *mn*; after the common material *m* is subtracted, a zero entry is left in the former cell.

Some problems and a revised learning procedure for general paradigms. Simple though this procedure is, it does not seem correct. The problem is that it treats fusional and agglutinating languages identically—in each case, an unanalyzed affix would be listed in a cell as encoding the combination of feature values specified by the position of the cell in the matrix. Such a formulation ignores the highly systematic internal structure of affix strings in agglutinating languages, and would make it mysterious indeed why such languages would violate Zipf's Law for hundreds of years by retaining multisyllabic affixes (e.g., Turkish—Slobin, 1978). Furthermore, by learning the inflectional morphology of fusional and agglutinating languages with equal ease such a procedure leaves unexplained the dramatic differences in acquisition rates for the inflectional systems of the two sorts of languages (e.g., mastery by the age of 2 for Turkish, versus 5 and beyond for a fusional language like Serbo-Croatian; Slobin, 1977, 1982, 1984a). The account would also be unable to explain the greater likelihood that agglutinating as opposed to fusional inflections will be carried over into pidgins and creoles (Slobin, 1977). Clearly the internal structure of affix strings in fusional languages is analyzed in the minds of speakers, and the simple procedure just mentioned would not easily allow this to happen.

Consider instead procedures I5 and I6:

I5. Choose a dimension from a multidimensional word-specific paradigm and a level for that dimension. Examine all the cells of the paradigm specified for that level, and extract the common phonetic material exclusive of the stem. Enter that material in a cell of a unidimensional general paradigm corresponding to that level. Repeat the process for the other levels of that dimension to complete that paradigm, and then repeat the entire process for other dimensions to build unidimensional paradigms for them. If for any level there is no common phonetic material in all its cells, recursively increase the number of dimensions chosen, apply the procedure to sets of cells defined by levels of pairs (triples, *n*-tuples, etc.) of the dimensions instead of to cells defined by levels of a single dimension, and put the common material found therein into the cells of a general paradigm with the same number of dimensions.

I6. Create a word structure template of the form

$$[_X\text{Stem} + \text{affix} (+ \text{affix} + \ldots)]$$
$$\quad\quad\quad \text{DIM-1} \quad \text{DIM-2}$$

where *X* is the category of the paradigm, and DIM-*i* is the dimension (or *n*-tuple of dimensions) successfully analyzed by I5. The position of the new affix symbol in the affix list is determined by an examination of the position of the newly discovered affix in the words containing it relative to the positions of the affixes already listed in the word structure template and general paradigm.[12]

Applied to the paradigm in part (b) of Figure 5.10 and selecting number as the dimension examined, procedure I5 would create the general paradigm in part (a) of Figure 5.12; I6 would create the word structure template in part (b). When case is chosen as a dimension, I5 and I6 will create Figure 5.13 (a) and (b), respectively.

Let us now turn to the acquisition of fusional paradigms. When I5 chooses number as a dimension and tries to apply the procedure to the paradigm in Figure 5.10 (a), it finds nothing in common (other than the stem) and so cannot create a general paradigm. It now has to choose two dimensions simultaneously, considering in turn all four combinations of the levels of the two dimensions and searching for common nonstem material. In this case the paradigm has only two dimensions and so the nonstem

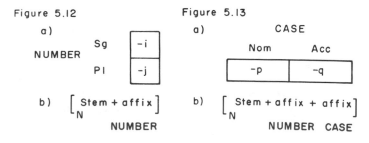

Figure 5.12

a)

NUMBER   Sg | -i
         Pl | -j

b)   [Stem + affix]_N
              NUMBER

Figure 5.13

a)   CASE
         Nom   Acc
         | -p | -q |

b)   [Stem + affix + affix]_N
              NUMBER CASE

material in Figure 5.10 (a) is simply extracted and placed in a two-dimensional paradigm resembling Figure 5.11 (a). The corresponding word structure template would be (6):

(6) $[_N$Stem + affix]
      NUMBER
      CASE

Note that in executing I5 the child must perform a more complex set of calculations for fusional than for agglutinating languages. The first part of the procedure must be tried and recognized to fail, then the second part must be tried with an increased number of dimensions; for more complex fusional systems, the process must be repeated again and again, increasing the number of dimensions each time. Worse, the more dimensions the child is forced to consider simultaneously when entering affixes into a general paradigm, the greater the demands on his or her short-term processing capacity—at any time in applying I5 the child must keep track of his or her place in a temporary list of m^n cells (where n is the number of dimensions being considered and m is an average of the number of levels per dimension), as compared to only m elements to be kept in mind temporarily for an agglutinating language. Procedure I5 spares the child from unnecessary examination of combinatorially expanding numbers of cells: the child need only process simultaneously the number of dimensions actually fused by the target language's inflectional morphology, a number discovered during successive searches for common phonetic material in sets of cells defined by the fewest possible dimensions.[13] The difference between the ease of acquisition of agglutinating and fusional languages is then a by-product of this computationally efficient mechanism.[14]

Not only will the child have to expend greater amounts of processing capacity when coordinating the transfer of information from specific to general paradigms in a fusional language, but even if he or she can muster enough capacity to complete the process, the resulting general paradigm will be relatively weak. For an agglutinating language, the one-dimensional general paradigm is strengthened several times in the course of one complete pass through the word-specific paradigm; for a fusional language it would only be strengthened once in the course of a complete pass. Thus a greater number of successful applications of I5 and I6 would be needed to create a general paradigm of equivalent strength.

The most important general point here is that the paradigm representation allows one to state straightforward procedures for the segmentation of affixes and stems. This is because the representation allows the child to index all the inflected words containing the same stem for the purpose of extracting that stem, which appears as the common material throughout the paradigm. Furthermore, they allow the child to index all the inflected words marked for a given case (or number, or feature value, or combination of feature values) for the purpose of extracting the marker indicating that case alone (or number, feature value, etc.). And this can be done for any pattern of fusion in a computationally efficient way.

Application of General Paradigms

Once a general paradigm has been formed it can be applied to incomplete word-specific paradigms to fill in empty cells in the way described earlier in this chapter. However, the procedure that executes this process must be capable of handling certain complexities inherent in the task. First, if it is applied to an empty cell in a paradigm for an irregular verb, overregularization errors will occur (e.g., if the cell for the first-person singular past of *go* is empty, a general verb paradigm will fill in the cell as *goed*). As anyone with the least bit of familiarity with children's language knows, this is in fact a very frequent error (e.g., see Ervin, 1964; Kuczaj, 1977). But how, then, are such forms unlearned? The Unique Entry principle ensures that no verb may have two past tense forms in free variation. This in itself does not solve the learnability problem, however, since in response to an apparent violation of the principle the child could take several courses of action. He or she could, for example, ignore the correct form altogether when it is heard in parental speech, and keep the overregularized form as the sole occupant of the relevant cell. In fact, I have argued that this is what happens in the case where the child uses one morpheme at first to signal a certain distinction, ignoring a second distinction. As mentioned, in those cases, ignoring an input form is most likely to happen when one form is zero-inflected or homonymous with other members of the paradigm. What makes overregularization treacherous is that just these dangerous factors could be at play for many irregular forms in English (e.g., the past tense of *hit* is zero-inflected; the past tense of *hear*, among many other verbs, is homonymous with its past participle). Thus one must show how the child eventually realizes that the input forms must be heeded and his or her own forms discarded. A second, equally incorrect option for the child would be to split the paradigm by adding a new dimension to it, following procedures that I will outline later in the chapter. Here too we must ensure that the child ignores this possible course of action in the case of over-regularization.

Somehow the child must know that when a regularized form and a form that is heard in the input compete for a paradigm cell, the correct course of action to ensure satisfaction of the Unique Entry constraint is to drive out the regularized form. This in turn implies that the child can distinguish a paradigm entry that was created by the application of a general paradigm and one that was heard directly in the input. The preemptability symbol "?" introduced in Chapter 4 (and to be invoked again in Chapters 6 and 8) can serve precisely that function. I propose that any word-specific paradigm entry created by a general paradigm be annotated as in Figure 5.14(a) or (b). In particular, entries so annotated are preemptable by forms that can be entered into their cells by Procedure I1, that is, appropriate forms that are directly witnessed in the input. Thus *feet* will preempt *foots* when it is heard, but no alternative to *anteaters* will ever appear and so the form will remain unchanged indefinitely (albeit be preemptable at any time).[15]

Such an account could work for cases in which a general paradigm filled in an empty cell in a word-specific paradigm. But it does not explain cases in which a correct irregular form was used at first, followed by an overregularized form, followed in turn by the correct irregular form (see Ervin, 1964; Kuczaj, 1977). Why should children ever replace ostensibly correct forms, forms that were directly attested in the input? One possibility is that this, too, is an example of preemption, and that all forms entered into word-specific paradigms before a general paradigm is created would be annotated with the "?" symbol. However, this

Figure 5.14

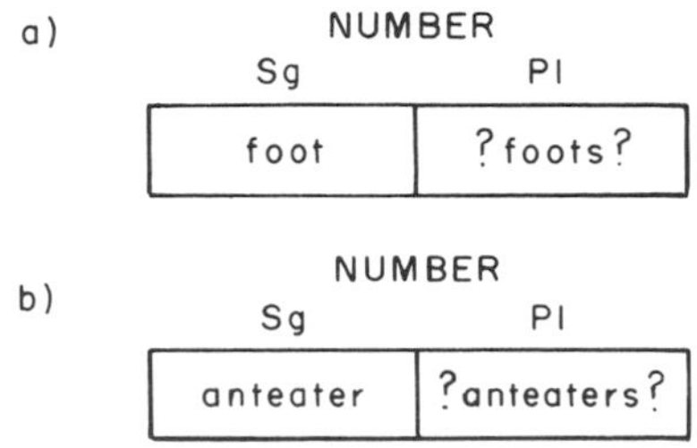

a)

	NUMBER	
	Sg	Pl
	foot	?foots?

b)

	NUMBER	
	Sg	Pl
	anteater	?anteaters?

would be unlike my other uses of preemptability, where the "?" symbol always signals potentially incorrect rules. Here there is no learnability-inspired motivation to build in a mechanism that allows initial paradigm entries to be unlearned—they should in general be correct the first time around. Fortunately, I am spared from having to take such an ad hoc step. Kuczaj (1977, 1981) has pointed out that the initially learned irregular forms are never driven out; they generally coexist with the overregularized forms in the child's speech and are comprehended well through-out the period of overregularization. Furthermore, children si-multaneously overregularize stems and their irregular forms, producing *went, wented,* and *wenting* as well as *go, goed,* and *going*. Kuczaj's explanation is that the child simply does not recognize that *go* and *went* even belong to the same paradigm— they may simply be unrelated forms in the child's lexicon. If Kuczaj is right, the Unique Entry principle is not violated and no preemption actually occurs. (I have not paid attention to the factors causing the child to recognize that distinct inflected words belong to the same paradigm, but presumably some conjunction of phonetic and semantic similarity is involved; the phonetic dissimilarity of *go* and *went* may at first prevent the child from combining them into a single paradigm, requiring a correspond-ingly greater amount of semantic evidence before the child can do so. When he or she does, preemption of *goed, wented,* and *wenting* will occur because these forms will have been marked as preemptable.)

There is a variant of Kuczaj's account, one that would also work in cases where the overregularized forms are morpho-logically similar to the correct forms. According to this variant the child would simply be unable to access the paradigm dis-tinctions telling him or her which item belonged in a given cell, because of processing limitations and an inadequately strength-ened paradigm. That is, he or she would be unable to access the "pointer" indicating that the past tense cell of the *break* par-adigm contains *broke*. Thus *broke* would not block the derivation of *breaked* and could itself undergo inflection. All this could hap-pen without the child actually storing (as Kuczaj proposed) sep-arate paradigms for *broke* and *break*. An advantage of this alternative is that it is consistent with the fact that adults often make over-regularizing errors in their speech (Merrill Garrett, personal com-munication; Stemberger, 1982). Assuming that inaccessibility of paradigm distinctions is inversely related to paradigm strength which in turn is directly related to frequency, this alternative would also account for the well-known fact that irregularly inflected forms are almost always frequent.[16] In either case, the entry of overregularized forms into the child's language would not cause preemption of some strong form stored in the child's paradigm; if either account is correct, then, there is no need to invoke some version of preemptability that does not serve a learning function.

What happens, now, when the language does contain alternative inflected forms in free variation, such as *dived/dove, has proven/has proved, leaped/leapt, cactuses/cacti,* and so on? (These examples are taken from Wasow, 1981.) The answer is simple. Since both forms are exemplified in the input, neither will be assigned the preemptability feature "?"; thus neither will drive out the other, and the child will retain both.

Retroactive Constraint Enforcement

We are not yet out of the woods. Imagine a child who has not learned that an affix is sensitive to some feature of its stem noun (e.g., animacy) and who has created a general noun paradigm lacking this feature as well. Imagine also that he or she has used the general paradigm productively to fill in empty cells in the word-specific paradigm for some noun, but has applied the wrong affix as a result of being oblivious to animacy (e.g., an affix specific to animate nouns is applied to an inanimate noun). Eventually the fully differentiated general paradigm, in which animacy is correctly specified, will be acquired (by a combination of procedures already discussed and procedures to be proposed shortly), but the damage has been done: before the full general paradigm is acquired, the child may already have added ungrammatical forms to his or her lexicon. Since no cells in those bad word-specific paradigms are empty, the full final general paradigm will not be called in, and so no uniqueness violations will impel the child to expunge the incorrect form generated by the earlier underdifferentiated general paradigm. This situation is diagrammed in Figure 5.15.

Somehow, the child must coordinate word-specific paradigms with general paradigms not only when the word-specific paradigm has empty cells but also after it is filled in, so that consistency with the language's full affixing regularities can be enforced. This can be accomplished by a straightforward extension of the process of applying general paradigms, and the entire procedure we require can be expressed as procedure I7:

I7. Whenever an inflected form is accessed, also access the general paradigm indexed by the set of features belonging to the inflected

Figure 5.15

a) incorrect general paradigm:

CASE

Nom   Acc

– w	– x

b) filled – in word – specific paradigm:

bif : N
    animate = –

CASE

Nom   Acc

bif y	? bifx ?

c) correct general paradigm:

CASE

Nom   Acc

ANIMATE

+	– w	– x
–	–y	–z

form. Juxtapose the cells corresponding to the desired conjunction of features in the general and word-specific paradigms, and make them consistent in the following way: If the relevant cell of the word-specific paradigm is empty, fill it using the general paradigm. If the relevant cell of the word-specific paradigm contains a preemptable affix different from the one specified by the general paradigm (taking the full set of features into account), use the general paradigm to replace the affix in the word-specific paradigm with the one in the general paradigm. If the relevant cell in the word-specific paradigm contains a nonpreemptable form distinct from the form specified by the general paradigm, leave the word-specific paradigm alone.

In the example under consideration, I7 would compare the paradigms in Figure 5.15(b) and (c), take note of the "animate = –" feature on the word stem, and replace the incorrect form *bifx* with the correct form *bifz*. In general, procedure I7 ensures that any change to a general paradigm will eventually make itself felt in all the relevant word-specific paradigms. This process of retroactive constraint enforcement is a natural extension of the use of general paradigms to alter word-specific ones, requiring only the additional assumption that general paradigms are *always* invoked when an inflected form is accessed, not just when a desired form is absent.

PARADIGM SPLITTING AND THE SEARCH FOR MISSING FEATURES

I still have not shown how the child acquires arbitrary declensional and conjugational classes (i.e., those not predictable from the phonological shape of the stem) or affixes sensitive to less accessible semantic and phonological features. David Lebeaux and I (Lebeaux, 1982, in preparation; Pinker and Lebeaux, 1981) have found that the paradigm representation and the Unique Entry principle allow one to formulate plausible mechanisms that accomplish this step. Consider what happens when a language differentiates case markers according to arbitrary declensional classes, say, "Declension I" and "Declension II" nouns. When the child applies I5 to paradigms for various Declension I nouns, he or she will create a general case paradigm listing those case markers. When the child applies I5 to paradigms for Declension II nouns, however, he or she will be forced to hypothesize a second set of case markers competing for the case cells in the general paradigm. The Unique Entry principle applies both to general and to specific paradigms and prevents the child from keeping both markers for a particular case within the same cell. But this unstable state is just the information the child needs to deduce that a dimension is missing from his or her paradigm. The child can use the temptation to violate the Unique Entry principle to search for the missing dimension, thanks to I8 and I9.

I8. If I5 finds a set of affixes to insert into a general paradigm, and the relevant cells are already filled with different affixes, then generate a new dimension for that paradigm, the contents of the original paradigm occupying the cells corresponding to one level of the new dimension, and the newly discovered affixes occupying the cells corresponding to the other level.

Procedure I9 labels the new dimension created by I8 and the levels of that dimension.

I9. Examine the word-specific paradigms in the lexicon containing the old set of affixes, and those containing the new set.

(a) If the stems corresponding to one set have a common value of some semantic or phonological feature which contrasts with the value of that feature among the stems corresponding to the other set, label the new dimension with the feature name, and its levels with the contrasting values of that feature corresponding to the two sets.

(b) If no common property is found, give the new dimension a set of arbitrary labels (e.g., the dimension DECLENSION with values I, II, . . .) and append the corresponding feature equation (e.g., DECLENSION = I) to the lexical entry of the stem for each word-specific paradigm, depending on which of the two sets of affixes it contains.

(c) If only a small number of word-specific paradigms are found containing one of the sets of affixes, do not add a new dimension to the general paradigm.

This procedure would allow the child to learn, for example, stem-conditioned inflectional subclasses, such as the inflection of past tense by ablaut that applies to English verbs ending in *-ing* (and which children use productively: e.g., *brang*). In general, the procedure would discover nonsalient or improbable semantic and phonological features of words encoded in the morphology of the language, as a response to the discovery that the language was making a previously unnoticed distinction. This would spare American children from spontaneously having to hypothesize features appropriate to, say, Navajo shape classifiers. Instead, the Navajo child would notice, thanks to I9, that all the nouns marked with one set of affixes denoted extended shapes whereas those marked with another set denoted globular shapes (thus procedure I9 has a Whorfian flavor; see also Schlesinger, 1977). In addition, the procedure could learn completely arbitrary declensional and conjugational classes, and exceptional words that are not affixed according to a general paradigm. Thus the difference between common inflectional features such as number, gender, and case, and rare ones such as shape and relative position in a supernatural hierarchy, would correspond to the distinction between features that are spontaneously hypothesized and features that are noticed only as a result of uniqueness violations.

Stem-Specific and Context-Specific Features

The I9 procedure, as I have stated it, would not be able to discover features that are defined by the situation or discourse context rather than by the intrinsic properties of the stem. Consider a fusional language with markers for case and definiteness.

If the child had not hypothesized that definiteness was a paradigm dimension, then he or she would be faced with inexplicable duplication in the case-marker system, just as for gender, arbitrary declensions, and so on as discussed above. But here an examination of the semantic and phonological properties of the words found to be affixed one way or another would turn up nothing. Definiteness is not something that is true or false of individual nouns, but of nouns used in specific discourse contexts. Thus the noun paradigms in the child's lexicon would bear case markers haphazardly, depending on whether the nouns were initially heard in definite or indefinite contexts. However, the difficulty of finding context-specific as opposed to stem-specific features by examining the lexicon is offset by the fact that only discourse-specific features will lead to violations of the Unique Entry principle *within word-specific paradigms*. Before definiteness is hypothesized as a dimension, a given word will sometimes be heard with one nominative case marker, sometimes with another, and this violation, unlike those caused by failure to hypothesize gender, can be discovered before a general paradigm is created. Whether a uniqueness violation occurs in a word-specific or a general paradigm is thus diagnostic of whether a missing dimension is stem-specific or context-specific. Procedures I10 and I11 incorporate this principle.

I10. If an inflected form with some minimum degree of strength is entered into a paradigm cell that is already occupied by a distinct nonpreemptable inflected form with some minimum degree of strength, split the contested cell into two cells by adding a dimension (e.g., rows) to the paradigm, and place the new form in the newly created cell. Choose a context-specific feature pertaining to the use of that form in the current discourse context, then label the new dimension with the name of that feature, and label the level specific to the new cell with the name of the appropriate value of that feature. Place the other entries in the paradigm into arbitrary cells along the new dimension, and append the "?" symbol to them.

I11. Whenever an inflected form is heard that is appropriate to a level of a paradigm dimension (e.g., a given column), and there is an orthogonal context-specific dimension (e.g., rows) that is only partially filled, then (a) if the cell that is appropriate to the role of the item in the current discourse context is empty, place the form in that cell; (b) if the appropriate cell is filled with a preemptable form, displace that form into a different cell and place the current one in the vacated cell; (c) if the appropriate cell is filled with a preemptable version of the current form, then remove the preemptability symbol. If for every column all the rows are filled with a single affix, allow I3 to eliminate that label for the row dimension, choose another context-specific feature pertaining to the referent of the current form, and hypothesize it as a new row dimension. Apply this procedure iteratively.[17]

Procedures I10 and I11 thus do for context-specific features what I8 and I9 did for stem-intrinsic features: they impel the child to search for a previously ignored dimension that could explain the apparent violation of the Unique Entry principle. Furthermore, they constrain the search to features that differentiate the contexts in which the different forms are used, rather than all the features that are currently true of a single form. The principal difference between the operation of I10/I11 and the operation of I8/I9 is that for the former, search is extended in time and conducted over a series of inputs, rather than over a set of stored entries. This difference is motivated by an assumption about the child's long-term memory: although the child must store information about words' sounds and meanings above and beyond that required by a current set of grammatical rules (i.e., semantic properties are necessary for inference making, and phonological properties are necessary for the pronunciation and recognition of the word), it is unlikely that the child would have stored many features about the discourse contexts of inflected forms in past inputs before the features had been hypothesized as dimensions of the paradigm. (See Tulving, 1972, and Anderson, 1976, for discussion of this distinction between "semantic" and "episodic" memory.) Thus the child has little choice but to begin his search for the missing feature in a non-unique word-specific paradigm from that moment on, and must also be capable of recognizing when a situation-specific hypothesis turns out to be incorrect and has to be replaced by an alternative.

With these procedures specified, one is now in a position to account for the complete developmental sequence commonly found for the acquisition of productive fusional paradigms, as summarized by Slobin (1973): (1) use of a single form to encode one feature, ignoring distinctions in a second feature, sometimes with one form replacing another; (2) often a brief period of free variation among the allomorphs encoding the second feature; (3) correct usage with respect to both features (see Pinker and Lebeaux, 1981; Lebeaux, 1982, in preparation). Stage (1) I have already discussed; it corresponds to an underdifferentiated matrix occurring when the second feature is low on the grammaticizability hierarchy for semantic or phonological features or lacking a semantic or phonological correlate entirely. At this point, the strength of individual inflected forms (as determined by phonological substantiveness, nonhomonymity, and possibly frequency) will determine which gets to occupy the single relevant cell in the paradigm, and which form can imperialistically drive out another. When an existing form in a paradigm and its rival (stored in the interim in a lexical entry but not in the paradigm) both attain sufficient strength, they both become eligible for entry into the same cell in the paradigm, and procedure I10 is triggered (or I8, for general paradigms if any exist), and the paradigm will be split. However, until I9 or I11 has successfully sorted the newly split cells according to their correct level in the new dimension, or, in the case of stem-specific features, classified the nouns into their correct classes, apparent free variation will occur, corresponding to stage (2). This is because procedures I9 and I11 may not have successfully concluded their tasks at the time that the paradigm is initially split. (Whether the correct dimension labels will be hypothesized when the paradigm is split will depend on many factors; for example, the correct choice could be delayed because not enough word-specific paradigms exist in the lexicon to demonstrate the correct stem-specific semantic or phonological contrasts; those contrasts may be too subtle for the child to grasp at first; an incorrect context-specific feature may have been hypothesized; or the correct context-specific contrast may be too subtle for the child to grasp.) When procedures I9 or I11 do arrive at the correct dimension label, the third stage—complete mastery—will be the result. (See Lebeaux, in preparation, for further discussion of learnability-theoretic explanations of this and other developmental sequences.)

The Unique Entry Principle and Negative Evidence

It is worth making the general point that the use of the Unique Entry principle to hypothesize new paradigm dimensions assures the learnability of inflectional systems in the absence of negative evidence (Pinker and Lebeaux, 1981; Lebeaux, 1982, in preparation). Suppose that there were no constraint limiting a cell in the paradigm to containing one affix. Then consider the case of a child learning German who would have to acquire the paradigm in Figure 5.16. The problem is that there is nothing to stop the child from creating the less detailed paradigm in Figure 5.17 in which the articles are simply used in free variation within each case. That is, the parental input to the child can be

Figure 5.16

CASE

		Nom	Acc	Dat
	M	der	den	dem
GENDER	N	das	das	dem
	F	die	die	der

Figure 5.17

CASE

Nom	Acc	Dat
der/die/das	das/die/den	dem/der

described by Figure 5.17 as well as by Figure 5.16, and as long as the child either does not hear or does not use negative evidence to amend his or her grammar, there will be nothing to prevent the child from adopting the more inclusive grammar in which choice of article is not contingent on the choice of head noun. But if the Unique Entry principle is enforced, this possibility is excluded. The representational constraint thus operates in lieu of negative evidence, to ensure that the grammar of the language is learnable (see also Lasnik, 1981; Wexler, 1979, 1981; Lebeaux, in preparation; Pinker, 1981b).

Extent of Paradigm Splitting

When a paradigm is split in response to a violation of the Unique Entry principle for a given cell, the child in effect "expects" to find alternative entries for each of his or her other existing affixes that do not already have alternatives with strong lexical entries. In particular, the child will search for affixes or affixed forms that differ from the existing ones according to some semantic, phonological, or context-dependent property of those forms. Since in a completely crossed matrix the number of cells increases exponentially with the number of dimensions, an instance of paradigm splitting could imply that the child would have to engage in great amounts of further learning. For example, when the child discovers that a past tense form has two allomorphs depending on the gender of the subject, and splits the paradigm accordingly, he or she is faced with having to learn new affixed forms for every combination of number, person, tense, aspect, etc., so as to fill in the rest of the paradigm. In fact it is extremely rare for a language to require children to learn a distinct morpheme for every cell in the cross-product of its features (Greenberg, 1963). Instead, the neutralization of one dimension for a given level or levels of another dimension is a very common phenomenon. This implies that a split made in a matrix need not be orthogonal to every other dimension, in turn raising the question of which cells, and how many cells, should be split by I8 or I10 along with the cell that is discovered to violate the Unique Entry principle.

One possibility already alluded to in the discussion of syncretism stems from the hypothesis that some dimensions are universally "nested" within others. For example, in the paradigm representation for the number, case, and gender of German articles shown in Figure 5.18, case and gender are nested within number but crossed with each other. In this notation the different gender categories are specified both for singular and plural. In fact, one could exploit the nesting relation to achieve greater economy in the paradigm, as in Figure 5.19. This difference in economy may be trying to tell us something: instead of the child learning the same plural article, *die*, three different times for masculine, neuter, and feminine nouns in nominative case and three more times for masculine, neuter and feminine nouns in accusative case, and learning *den* three times for masculine, neuter, and feminine nouns in the dative case, he or she may simply have learned the separate case forms for the plural, ignoring the gender dimension entirely. Since the child must have attended to gender in order to acquire the singular paradigm, it seems that the discovery of a gender dimension defined for singular number may not lead the child to expect that dimension to be defined for the plural number. In other words, when I10 originally discovered three nominative singular articles, it may have split the other two case levels into three cells apiece, expecting to find gender differences in them, but may

Figure 5.18

NUMBER

		Sg						Pl		
		GENDER						GENDER		
		M	N	F				M	N	F
CASE	Nom	der	das	die		CASE	Nom	die	die	die
	Acc	den	das	die			Acc	die	die	die
	Dat	dem	dem	der			Dat	den	den	den

Figure 5.19

NUMBER

Sg   Pl

GENDER

		M	N	F
	Nom	der	das	die
CASE	Acc	den	das	die
	Dat	dem	dem	der

	Nom	die
CASE	Acc	die
	Dat	den

have left the case dimension for the plural sector of the paradigm unsplit, pending evidence that it should be. In general, then, I propose that when a cell of a paradigm is split by I10 or I8, only the cells crossed with it or nested under it are also split, not those corresponding to the other level of the dimension under which it is nested. This would save the child from expanding his or her paradigm combinatorially only to find that large numbers of distinct cells contained the same entry. At the same time it would explain why certain features are very often neutralized within certain values of others across languages (Greenberg, 1963): the child would need more information to learn that there existed distinctions in all levels of a nesting dimension as compared to a crossing dimension.

What determines the hierarchy of nesting of dimensions? Greenberg (1963; see also Bybee, in press, a, b) point out that the frequently neutralizing dimensions, as opposed to the frequently neutralized dimensions, are also the dimensions most frequently encoded to begin with. In other words, they are the dimensions that are presumably higher in the grammaticizability hierarchy. It turns out that the paradigm-splitting model explains why the correlation between cross-linguistic prevalence and neutralizing powers should occur: earlier hypothesization of a neutralizing (nesting) dimension leads to more efficient acquisition of an inflectional paradigm. To see why this might be so, consider the two possible orders of hypothesization of number and gender for English third-person pronouns, ignoring case and person for now. If the child hypothesized gender first, he or she would first have the paradigm in Figure 5.20. When the child discovers that the pronoun *he* has an alternative plural entry, *they*, the child would add the number dimension to the paradigm and would then have to fill the empty cell for feminine plural with *they* when it was heard in the input referring to a

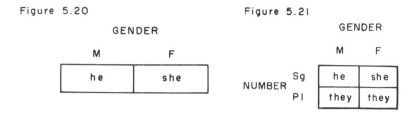

Figure 5.20

	GENDER	
	M	F
	he	she

Figure 5.21

		GENDER	
		M	F
NUMBER	Sg	he	she
	Pl	they	they

set of females. The child could instead not split the feminine cell in two, but then soon enough an alternative to *she* would be discovered—namely, *they*—and the feminine cell would have to be split anyway. Thus, in either case the result would be the paradigm shown in Figure 5.21, and four input exemplars would have been necessary to learn it: *they* must be learned as the masculine plural, and it separately must be learned as the feminine plural.

Now consider what would happen if the child hypothesizes number first, which is more likely if number is higher than gender on the grammaticizability hierarchy. The first paradigm would be Figure 5.22. When *she* is encountered (or *he,* if *she* was entered as the first singular pronoun), it will force a split of the singular cell. However, in this case, if that cell alone is split, the child would already have reached the adult state shown in Figure 5.23, with no further learning being necessary. The child would in effect have learned that *they* is the third-person plural, applicable to the third-person masculine plural, the third-person feminine plural (and, for that matter, the third-person neuter plural), all with a single exemplar. Of course, in those languages that do differentiate gender in the plural, a violation of the Unique Entry principle will occur, causing the plural cells to be split at that point as well.

Thus early hypothesization of a neutralizing or nesting dimension results in more efficient learning under a limited paradigm-splitting model. Imagine an alternative model, which, rather than selectively splitting the paradigm within a level of a nesting dimension, instead automatically copied the contents of the new entry of the duplicated cell throughout the appropriate level of the neutralizing dimension (e.g., in Figure 5.21 *they*

Figure 5.22

NUMBER	Sg	he
	Pl	they

Figure 5.23

NUMBER	Sg	GENDER	M	he
			F	she
	Pl			they

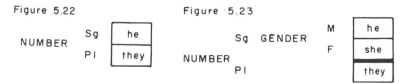

would be copied from the masculine plural cell to a newly created feminine plural cell). This would be as efficient in exploiting prevalent neutralization patterns as the limited-split model I have proposed. However, the copying model would work equally well regardless of whether the neutralizing or the neutralized dimension was hypothesized first. This would leave unexplained the correlation between neutralizing powers and grammaticizability in general, unlike the limited paradigm-splitting model.

The developmental prediction of limited paradigm splitting would be that when children first encode a new feature in a language that crosses the values of that feature completely with an earlier learned feature (i.e., a language that does not neutralize the less prominent dimensions), the child could pass through a stage in which he or she respected that new feature only for one of the levels of the old feature, using a single affix to encode that feature in its other levels (as usual, ceteris paribus). Such data are not easy to find in the published literature because often inflectional errors for a particular part of a paradigm are reported without information about the encoding of that feature in the rest of the paradigm. However, Slobin (1984a) does cite data from Smoczynska showing that Polish children use the masculine genitive marker for all genders. Since he reports that it is "an extremely persistent, late error," it seems likely that these children were respecting gender for other cases in the paradigm at the same time. Another shred of evidence in this regard is the fact that an English child studied by Huxley (1970) incorrectly used accusative pronouns in nominative contexts 69 percent of the time for plural pronouns (i.e., *us* and *them* instead of *we* and *they*, respectively), but only 4 percent of the time for singular pronouns (i.e., *me* and *him* or *her* instead of *I* and *he* or *she*, respectively). These data are fragmentary indeed; clearly this is an area in need of further empirical investigation.

SUMMARY OF ADVANTAGES OF THE PARADIGM ACQUISITION MODEL

Earlier in this chapter I listed seven problems with the simple equation sampling model outlined there and in Pinker (1982). I then proposed as an alternative, in an attempt to solve those problems, a paradigm acquisition model conforming to the Unique Entry principle. How did the new model solve those problems? (It should go without saying that I am using the term "solve" somewhat loosely in this summary, given the complexity of the issues involved.)

The problem of features being spuriously eliminated in cases of syncretism was solved by setting up rows of cells specific to all the possible values of a given feature, and eliminating the feature only when *all* the cells contained the same affix, rather than when the same affix encoded only two values of the feature. Later in the chapter I also showed both how a limited paradigm-splitting operation could result in efficient acquisition of inflectional systems given prevalent patterns of syncretism, and why neutralizing dimensions should also be the dimensions that appear most frequently in languages' inflectional systems.

The problem of accounting for inflectional imperialism was solved by proposing that certain dimensions are unlikely to be hypothesized at first, that certain affixes are intrinsically low in "strength" or "staying power" because of lack of phonetic substance and homonymity, and that the Unique Entry principle dictates that no exhaustive conjunction of feature values may be encoded by more than one affix.

The problem of gender and arbitrary declensional and conjugational classes was solved by two separate mechanisms: (a) the hypothesization of salient phonological features in parallel with the hypothesization of semantic features, and (b) the creation of new stem classes when a general paradigm is split in response to violations of the Unique Entry principle and when no phonological or semantic property common to the stems inflecting similarly can be found.

This same mechanism also accounts for the ability to hypothesize cross-linguistically rare features only when the target language demands it. Such features will lead to violations of the Unique Entry principle that will in turn inspire a search for stem-specific properties, if the violation is in a general paradigm, or context-specific properties, if the violation is in a word-based paradigm.

The problem of accounting for segmentation was solved by using the paradigm as a means of comparing all the inflected forms of a word so as to isolate the stem and extract the individual inflections. This process is also capable of discovering zero morphemes, another problem for its predecessor. The procedure proposed to accomplish segmentation used the dimensional organization of the paradigm to learn any possible pattern of fusion in the computationally simplest manner. The mechanism also exploits the simplicity of inflection in agglutinating languages to learn them more quickly than fusional languages. The result of these operations was a general paradigm that could be used productively to generate novel inflected forms, and to eliminate incorrect forms that were generated prematurely.

Finally, the problem of suppletion of overregularized forms by their irregular counterparts was solved by proposing that forms generated by the application of a general paradigm to an incomplete word-specific paradigm were distinguished from inflected forms witnessed directly in the input, the former bearing a symbol that sanctions preemption by the latter.

6 | Complementation and Control

ANY VERBS have as one of their logical arguments a complete proposition, which appears in the sentence as a complement consisting either of a complete sentence or of some part of a sentence. Which arguments may be present in a complement, and how those missing are interpreted, depends on properties of the matrix verb. In LFG (see Bresnan, 1982c) different types of complement-taking verbs have different types of lexical entries, specifying how many logical arguments the verb takes, the syntactic category of the complement, and which matrix argument is to be interpreted as coreferring with a missing argument in the complement. Some examples, with their lexical entries, appear in (1); constituent structures for (1a) and (1c), (1b) and (1d), and (1e) are shown in parts (a), (b), and (c) of Figure 6.1, respectively.

(1) (a) John *tried* to leave. ("subject-equi")
        try: V: PRED = "try (SUBJ, V-COMP)"
              SUBJ = V-COMP's SUBJ

   (b) John *told* Bill to leave. ("object-equi")
        tell: V: PRED = "tell (SUBJ, OBJ, V-COMP)"
             OBJ = V-COMP's SUBJ

   (c) John *tends* to leave. ("raising-to-subject")
        tend: V: PRED = "tend (V-COMP)"
              SUBJ = V-COMP's SUBJ

   (d) John *believes* Bill to have left. ("raising-to-object")
        believe: V: PRED = "believe (SUBJ, V-COMP)"
               OBJ = V-COMP's SUBJ

   (e) John *thought* that Bill left.
        thought: V: PRED = "think (SUBJ, S-COMP)"

Figure 6.1

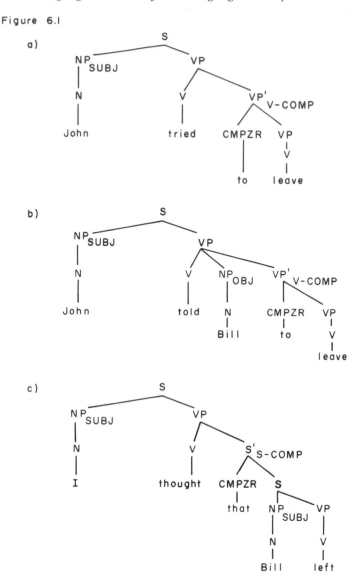

Example (1a) represents a *subject-equi* verb and has the logical structure *try (John, (John leaves))*. That is, the verb has two arguments: the tryer, expressed as a subject, and the deed attempted, expressed as a complement headed by a verb. This is indicated by the first line in the lexical entry for *try*. The complement lacks an overt subject, and the argument that would have been expressed by the subject of the complement verb is interpreted as being identical in reference to the subject of the matrix verb. This is indicated by the equation SUBJ = V-COMP's SUBJ listed in the second part of the entry. In an *object-equi* verb like *tell* in (1b), on the other hand, there are three arguments: the teller, the hearer, and the command; hence the logical structure is *tell (John, Bill, (Bill leaves))*. The lexical entry for *tell* listed in (1b) indicates that these are expressed as a SUBJ, OBJ, and V-COMP, respectively, and that here the missing complement subject is to be interpreted as coreferring with the object. So-called *raising* verbs have the same constituent structure (see part (b) of Figure 6.1) as equi verbs, but in each case, one of their surface syntactic constituents does not serve as a direct logical argument of the matrix verb; their logical structures are *tend (John leaves)* (*John* not an argument of *tend*) and *believe (John, (Bill leaves))* (*Bill* not an argument of *believe*), respectively. The matrix NPs that do not serve as matrix verb arguments nonetheless serve as controllers of the missing complement subjects, as the equations in (1c) and (d) indicate. Two good diagnostics of whether a verb is equi or raising include, first, the admissibility of dummy elements or idiom chunks in the matrix clause: raising verbs can have them (*it tends to rain in Spain; tabs tend to be kept on subversives; I believe there to be seven species of carp inhabiting the Charles River; I expect tabs to be kept on football players from now on*); equi-verbs cannot (**there tried to be a parade; *tabs tried to be kept on subversives*); and, second, the rough synonymity of active and passive versions of the complement: only with raising verbs are the two versions synonymous (*I expect John to defeat Bill* equals *I expect Bill to be defeated by John;* but *I told John to defeat Bill* does not equal *I told Bill to be defeated by John*). Both these tests are consequences of the single fact that all syntactic arguments are logical arguments of the matrix verb in equi sentences but not in raising sentences (see Bresnan, 1982c). A final type of complement-taking verb takes a sentential complement or S-COMP, as in (1e); here the complement has all its arguments expressed overtly within the complement and so it needs no control equations.

Not all complement-taking verbs have infinitival verbs as the heads of their complements. For example, *consider* and *seem* can have an adjectival complement or A-COMP (*I consider John foolish; John seems foolish*); *call, consider,* and other verbs can have a nominal complement or N-COMP (*I consider John a fool; I called John a fool*); and *want* and other verbs can have a prepositional complement or P-COMP (*I want flowers on the table tonight*). In addition, complement-taking verbs can specify whether or not the complement must contain a complementizer (CMPZR, in the notation I will use) and if so which one. For example, the difference between *make* and *force* in *I made John leave/*to leave* and *I forced John *leave/to leave* is enforced by the equation V-COMP's CMPZR $=_c \emptyset$ or V-COMP's CMPZR $= to$ appended to the matrix verbs' entries (similar equations could mandate the use of *as* or *that* for verbs like *regard* or *recall*). An additional equation in lexical entries can specify whether the complement verb must be tensed, infinitival, or a participle (past or present). This differentiates verbs like *keep* in *John kept running* (V-COMP's MORPH $= progpart$, where *progpart* means "progressive participle") from *desire* in *John desired to run* (V-COMP's MORPH $= inf$). Also, it differentiates *arrange* in *John arranged for Bill to win* (S-COMP's MORPH $= inf$) from *ensure* in *John ensured that Bill won* (S-COMP's MORPH $= fin$).[1] As we shall see in Chapter 7, such equations play an important role in rules for auxiliaries, which in LFG are treated as similar to raising-to-subject verbs (see also Gazdar, Pullum, and Sag, 1982; Lapointe, 1980, 1981a; and Baker, 1981).

Two important substantive constraints on control are that the argument that may be absent in the complement is always the subject, never an argument bearing some other function, and that the missing subject is interpreted as being identical to the matrix's second object, if there is one (via the equation OBJ2 $=$ V-COMP's SUBJ); if not, as being identical to the matrix object, if there is one (via the equation OBJ $=$ V-COMP's SUBJ); and if not, as identical to the matrix subject (via the equation SUBJ $=$ V-COMP's SUBJ). This pattern holds cross-linguistically regardless of whether grammatical functions are encoded configurationally or morphologically, and for virtually all the English complement-takers. There are, nonetheless, some exceptions, such as *promise* in *John promised Bill to leave* (but not *John promised to leave* or *John promised that Bill would leave*, which follow the rule) and a handful of others (one sense of *ask* in *the boy asked the teacher to leave the room; strike* in *John strikes me as pompous; impress* in a similar context, and *make* as in *John made Mary a fine husband*). In these two cases, the missing subject is controlled by the matrix subject even though an object is present. Thus it is possible to omit the control equation from the lexical entries of most predicates, listing them only for exceptional predicates like *promise,* and allowing a general principle of control to supply the interpretation unless the predicate was explicitly annotated with its own control equation. For clarity's sake, I will display both exceptional and nonexceptional predicates as having explicit control equations in the discussion to follow.

Acquiring Complement Structure and Control Relations

Pinker (1982) proposed the following procedure (modified slightly here) for the acquisition of complement-taking predicates.

Whenever a predicate takes an argument which is itself a complete proposition, and when that proposition is represented in the tree without its subject by a phrasal category X:

C1. Connect X as a sister of the predicate that contains the propositional argument.[2] (This may be a special case of P4(b).)

C2. Create a lexical entry for the predicate, in which the propositional argument is encoded as the function X-COMP where X is the category label of the subjectless proposition.

C3. Add to the lexical entry of the complement-taking predicate the equation X-COMP's SUBJ = (FUNCTION), where (FUNCTION) is the grammatical function annotated to the matrix argument that is coindexed with the missing complement subject in the contextually inferred semantic representation.

The operation of these mechanisms can be seen in the example shown in Figure 6.2, where (a) is an f-structure representation encoding the semantic information inferred from the context, (b) is the input sentence, and (c) is the tree built by the phrase-building procedures outlined in an earlier chapter. Jointly (a) and (c) trigger the C-procedures because a propositional argument is found in the string sans subject; (d) is the completed tree. The phrase structure rule and lexical entry that are induced are shown in (2):

(2) $\text{VP} \rightarrow \text{V NP}_{\text{OBJ}} \text{VP}'_{\text{V-COMP}}$
     convince: V: PRED = "convince (SUBJ, OBJ, V-COMP)"
                OBJ = V-COMP's SUBJ

Another procedure (not mentioned in Pinker, 1982) is needed to acquire the annotations whereby matrix verbs specify the formal properties of their complements, such as being finite or infinitival, and whether and which complementizers must be present in the complements. This procedure, triggered by the same conditions that triggered the other C-procedures, is as follows:

C4. Add two equations to the lexical entry of the complement-taking verb. The first should have the form

Figure 6.2

a) f-structure

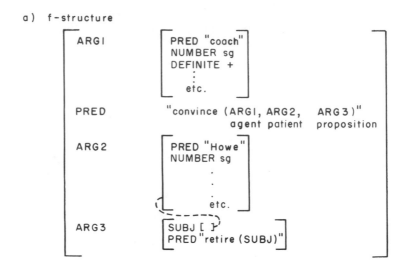

b) Sentence: "The coach convinced Howe to retire".

c)

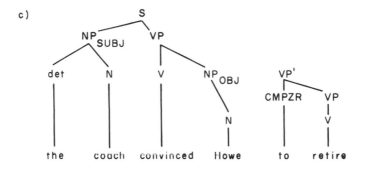

d)

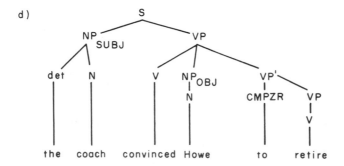

$$\text{X-COMP's MORPH} = \alpha$$

where α is *inf, fin, perfpart* (perfect participle), *progpart* (progressive participle), etc., depending on the morphology of the embedded verb (see Chapter 7 for proposals on how these feature values are recognized).[3]

The second should have the form

$$\text{X-COMP's CMPZR} = \beta$$

where β is the word found in complementizer position (i.e., specifier of X' in the complement). If there is no such word, define β to be $\emptyset$. If there already exists a similar entry with a conflicting equation, both forms will be maintained in separate lexical entries (e.g., S-COMP's COMPZR $=$ *that* versus $\emptyset$ for the entries of *think* in *I think he left* versus *I think that he left*).

Developmental Evidence:
The First Complement-Taking Verbs

Complement-taking verbs are rare in early word combinations. The only examples among the hundreds of utterances listed in the corpora examined by Braine (1976) are *want* + V or *want* + V + N in Sipili, Tofi, David, and Embla; *I can't* + V (+ N) and *can I* + V (+ N) in David; and a small number of others for Embla, a Swedish-speaking child, including (*Embla* +) *go* + V; (*Embla* +) *may* + V, and *look fall*).[4] It is not even certain that these instances are really examples of equi-constructions; these children were also occasionally expressing action demands or refusals in expressions like *more* + V or *no* + V, even though *more* and *no* do not ordinarily take verbs in English. Thus the proper analysis of the similar expressions *want* + V and *I can't* + V is not clear; both *more walk* and *want walk* may be action demands that are either ad hoc combinations strung together in the absence of an appropriate rule, or forms containing a verb misclassified as a nominal (see Chapter 4). Brown (1973) notes that complement-taking verbs are relatively rare in Stage I speech; recall that his unpublished analyses (cited in Chapter 4) showed that of the thirty-eight short word combinations which one might expect to appear in Stage I and II speech, three of the six unattested examples involved V + V sequences. Limber (1973) and Bloom, Lightbown, and Hood (1975) also note that these verbs are rare in early speech.

It does not take long, however, for the child to begin learning them. By the time children are regularly combining words in three- and four-word sequences, they seem to acquire a variety of complement-taking verbs quickly. Bloom, Lightbown, and Hood (1975) report the correct use of subject-equi verbs like *want* in *I want sit down* (*gonna* and *hafta* were used similarly) in children about 2 years old (MLU 1.3–2.6); they also note that they could find no errors of control (e.g., *I want comb hair* with someone other than *I* as intended subject, or *hotdog wanna eat*, meaning *I want to eat the hotdog*).[5] Limber (1973) reports that within a month of a complement-taking verb's first appearance in a child's speech, it is used correctly with its complement (so long as the child is producing four-word utterances at all). He reports about twenty-five different verbs of this sort used before the third birthday, including subject-equi verbs (*want, like*) and a raising-to-subject verb (*need*); then object-equi verbs (*watch, see, help, tell*) and a raising-to-object verb (*want* NP VP—the status of this example is not obvious and will be discussed in detail later in this chapter). Shortly afterward, modals and auxiliaries appear, which in LFG are treated as raising-to-subject verbs (*is, will, may, can*), and, finally, verbs taking full sentential complements with their subjects present (*think, know*). Bloom, Lahey, Hood, Lifter, and Fiess (1980) report a similar list (including *know, think, see, look, show, watch, tell, ask, teach*, and *explain*) at a similar age for their four subjects.

My own analyses of Eve's and Adam's acquisitions of these verbs reveals a similar pattern. In the first sample I examined (MLU = 2.65), Eve used four verbs that could be classified as raising-to-subject (*can't*, auxiliary *have, don't*, and *go* used in the sense of *gonna*), and two subject-equi verbs (*forget* and *try*). (When I say "use a verb," I mean "use it in a sentence with the relevant arguments," of course.) In the succeeding four biweekly samples Eve used one additional raising-to-subject verb in each successive sample: *gotta, may, will*, and *shall*; and used one other subject-equi verb: *wanta*. In the same period she used *let, see*, and *watch*, all object-equi verbs, but always with *me* as an object, so it is not certain that these were treated as verb-object constructions; the first object-equi verb used with any other object was *look at*, a full four months later (MLU = 3.2). Verbs taking sentential complements appeared two samples after the first one (*think, see if*), augmented by *remember* three samples after that. What may be a raising-to-object verb (*want Mommy read*; to be discussed later) appeared first in a very early sample (MLU = 1.68) and then not again until six months later when Eve said *I want it off so that it'll get well* and *want have some tapioca in it*. Adam showed a similar pattern, using raising-to-subject verbs (*gonna, don't have* [to]), subject-equi verbs (*want*), and object-equi verbs by Stage II (MLU = 2.26). Verbs taking sentential complements (*know, heard, see*) and productive use of the possible raising-to-object verb *want* appear considerably later (Stage V, MLU = 4.0–4.5). Thus a rough ordering of acquisition, collapsing across these analyses, would be: (1) subject-equi and raising-to-subject; (2) object-equi; (3) sentential complement; and (4) raising-to-object (discussed below). Not too much weight should be placed on this ordering, since except for the unclear case of raising-to-object verbs, the time span covering the first appearances of the forms is often short (six weeks in the case of Eve), and the ordering could be a simple result of the length of the respective utterances (shortest for subject-equi and raising-to-subject, a bit longer for object-equi when the object is a pronoun, and longer still for full sentential complements). In all the samples I have seen, the various forms all appear relatively early (though later than Stage I), and I have seen no reports of control errors in spontaneous complete sentences (though see n. 5).

In experiments on the comprehension of object-equi verbs, children have been reported to be somewhat less competent. Goodluck and Roeper (1978) report that 3-year-olds correctly act out reversible sentences with *watch* and *see* about 61 percent of the time, increasing to 85 percent by the age of 6–7 (chance is 50 percent; I have computed these approximate percentages from their tables). Tavakolian (1978, 1981) observed chance performance for 3-year-olds acting out *tell* sentences (46 percent object control and 46 percent subject control, by my calculations), increasing to 58 percent for 4-year-olds and 71 percent for 5-year-olds. Kessel (1970) found virtually error-free performance in the acting-out of sentences with *tell* in children 5 years old and older. As for the poor performance of the younger children, it should be noted that comprehension data from act-out experiments with young children are fairly noisy even when the construction in question is always used correctly in spontaneous speech. For example, the order of subject and object is almost always correct in spontaneous speech (see Chapter 4) but interpreted correctly more intermittently in act-out experiments (see de Villiers and de Villiers, 1973b; note that the high comprehension rates I reported in Chapter 4 concern the percentage of codable responses that were correct, not the percentage of responses in general that were correct). Furthermore, in act-out experiments there is a bias for children to use the same toy as the actor of the first and second actions designated by the stimulus sentence (Legum, 1975). This response bias could operate against the child's production of a correct action sequence for object-equi sentences even if the child had mastered their lexical entries. Thus the comprehension results give us little reason to doubt what the production data show: that complement-taking verbs of the classes considered are learned with relative ease.

Why do children seldom use complement structures at first, then within a short span acquire a variety of productive equi and raising forms? Several simple possibilities can be ruled out. It is not solely because children's sentences are short at first; even two-word sequences such as *want* + V, *try* + V, and *hafta* + V, or the three-word sequences like *want* + N + V, *see* + N + V, or *know* + N + V are sufficient to suggest that complement structures are beginning to be acquired, but such sequences are nonetheless rare (as mentioned, *want* + V is not uncommon but it is about as frequent as the ungrammatical *more* + V; hence its analysis is equivocal). Moreover, the reason that complement structures are initially rare is not that the semantics of the predicates of the individual verbs makes them hard for a toddler to learn. The verbs themselves often appear productively in non-complement structures at very early stages (e.g., *want* + N, *see* + N, *look at* + N, *help it, I can't, I like it*—all from Braine, 1976). Similarly, it is doubtful that the propositional contents of complement structures are all so sophisticated that Stage I children cannot handle them: Bloom et al. (1980) report that "notice" or calling attention to an object is one of the semantic functions of children's complement structures (e.g., *look birdie fly*); but "notice" is also one of the "major meanings" expressed in earliest word combinations (Brown, 1973; Braine, 1976). Likewise, the meaning of *stop* in *I stop crying* (Adam, Stage V) is not significantly different from the cessation or disappearance meaning expressed early on by *allgone* + *x* or *no* + *x* (Brown, 1973); NP *can't* VP and NP *don't* VP are not radically different in meaning for a child from *no* NP VP or NP *no* VP, even though *can't* and *don't* are used later than *no* to express negation (Bellugi, 1967). Similarly, *keep* as in *keep it on* (Adam IV–V) expresses a "recurrence" meaning similar to Stage I *more* and *other*; and so on. No doubt semantic complexity plays a role in the acquisition of complementation, but if it were the only determinant of acquisition order, one would expect complement structures to be more prominent among early Stage I constructions than they are.

An intriguing possibility suggests itself when the acquisition procedures for control and complementation are examined. The child must notice that a predicate takes a complete proposition as an argument, and also that the SUBJ argument of the embedded predicate is unexpressed in the surface sentence and coreferential with a matrix function. As for the first triggering condition, we do not know enough about the cognitive abilities of infants to conclude that they can or cannot mentally represent complete propositions as arguments of predicates, but the expression of recurrence, negation, notice, and action demands in early speech suggests that they indeed can. What about the second condition, the perception of subjectlessness? To recognize that a SUBJ is "missing," the child must know which of the arguments of the embedded verb is the SUBJ argument, and which phrase structure position or case marker expresses the SUBJ. Similarly, to recognize that the missing embedded SUBJ is coreferential with a matrix phrase bearing a potentially controlling grammatical function (i.e., SUBJ, OBJ, or OBJ2), the child must know the phrase structure or affixational reflexes of those relations in the language. In Chapter 4, I argued that phrase structure rules and lexical entries containing symbols for syntactic categories and grammatical relations are the Stage I child's principal acquisitions. Thus it is possible that the onset of the acquisition of functional control must await the acquisition of stable rules indicating the syntactic or morphological expression of grammatical relations in the language. This "awaiting" need not be an extrinsic ordering of the C-procedures relative to the P- and I-acquisition procedures; it may just be that the C-procedures are ready to apply from the start but their triggering conditions require that some threshold of strength of rules containing grammatical functions be exceeded before these conditions are considered to be met.

This hypothesis involves no extra assumptions about the acquisition mechanisms, and would explain why complement structures are not among the child's first utterances but begin to appear very shortly afterward, around the time that the first phrase structure rules introducing SUBJ and OBJ functions appear to be consolidated. Furthermore, if the appearance of complement structures awaits only the acquisition of phrase structure rules (in English; case markers in other languages), one would expect that exemplars of both raising and equi-verbs should be acquired at roughly the same time, since both are present in parental speech (Pinker and Hochberg, in preparation) and both are acquired by the same acquisition procedure. (This is possible because in LFG raising and equi constructions differ only in the number of arguments listed in the PRED statement in their lexical entries; they do not differ in their surface structures or control equations—see Bresnan, 1982c.) As mentioned, this seems to be the case: subject-equi and raising-to-subject constructions (the latter in the form of modals, auxiliaries, and catenatives) appear at about the same time, usually followed shortly afterward by object-equi constructions (the raising-to-object construction involving *want* often appears at the same time; see the next section).

There is also evidence that once the C-procedures are triggered, they operate smoothly. First, errors involving the ordering of verb and complement (e.g., *eat wanna*) are nonexistent. Second, when complement structures appear, control errors are virtually nonexistent in spontaneous speech. The C-procedures use the same triggering conditions to coin the phrase structure rules generating the subjectless complement phrase and the equations governing control of the missing subject, so the correct surface structures and control relations should (and do) appear in tandem. (This feature is made possible by the fact that in LFG the X-COMP functions appended to subjectless phrases must be accompanied by a control equation on the matrix verb conforming to the near-universal conditions on control discussed earlier—see Bresnan, 1982c). In sum, the acquisition procedures as stated are consistent with the fact that complement structures are rare at first and then are quickly acquired with both raising and equi verbs, with no reported errors of ordering or control.

Note that not all acquisition theories predict this error-free acquisition pattern. A model in which the learning of the surface structures of the complements was triggered by one set of conditions (e.g., the surface sequence of nouns and verbs) and the learning of control relations by another set (e.g., the semantics of the verb) could lead to errors of control at some intermediate stage. A model in which all complements are first generated as embedded sentences, whose subjects are then deleted by a transformation in the presence of subject-equi verbs (Chomsky, 1965), would, under the simplest set of assumptions, incorrectly predict that before the transformation was acquired, errors such as *I tried me* [or *I*] *to go* could occur,[6] and also that subject-equi sentences would be mastered after sentential complement or object-equi sentences (Maratsos, 1978, in press; but note that Chomsky's, 1981, most recent theory of equi-constructions addresses these problems). Finally, consider an account involving the statistical tabulation of linguistic properties in which children would overgeneralize from simple, early constructions to later and more complex constructions. Such an account would falsely predict that children would generalize from early acquired subject-equi and raising verbs like *gonna* and *wanna* and *hafta* that matrix subjects are always controllers, leading to control errors in sentences with objects such as *tell* NP *to* VP.

A final pattern of evidence supporting the proposed acquisition procedures for complementation and control comes from a set of phenomena that at first would seem to disconfirm them. I have argued for the plausibility of the procedures on the grounds that as soon as children reach the state of knowledge at which these procedures could be triggered, the children correctly produce a wide range of structures that the procedures can acquire. However, Carol Chomsky (1969) reports three systematic error patterns in the comprehension of complement structures in children far older (5–10 years) than the ones I have been discussing. If the acquisition procedures for control can be triggered early, why should older children persist in making control errors? The answer is that each of the poorly comprehended constructions involves some grammatical phenomenon that is systematically different from ordinary lexically governed functional control, according to independently motivated analyses of adults' judgments of such sentences. One of the constructions involves *"tough-movement"* complements such as *Donald is hard to see*, which children interpret as if the matrix subject also served as the complement subject rather than as the object. However, the interpretation of the missing object in such sentences is governed in LFG by a set of mechanisms with very different properties from functional control: namely, the "constituent control" or "long-distance trace binding" mechanisms, also involved in relative clauses, *wh*-questions, and interrogative complements (Kaplan and Bresnan, 1982). In constituent control, the missing phrase can bear any grammatical relation (including OBJ, OBJ2, and any of the OBL objects), whereas in functional control, only SUBJs may be missing. In constituent control, arbitrary distances and structures may separate the position of the missing phrase from its antecedent (subject to subjacency constraints), whereas in functional control, only a specific verb or chain of verbs with the lexical property of controlling missing complement subjects may intervene. *Tough*-movement in both regards follows the constituent control pattern (e.g., one can say *a book is easy to give Donald*, or *Donald is easy to talk to*, or *Donald is easy to pass over*, or *Donald is easy to fool yourself into thinking you like*). *Tough*-movement constructions cannot be acquired by the C-procedures because they don't involve the functional control mechanisms that the C-procedures acquire; rather, they must be learned at least in part by procedures for the acquisition of constituent control, which is sensitive to different input properties (see Pinker, 1982, and Chapter 7). Thus it is no surprise that children err on these sentences at an age far past the age at which functional control is mastered (in fact, their errors suggest that they had mistakenly applied the C-procedures to those constructions, leading them to interpret them as having subject-equi verbs).

The second putative control construction that befuddled children in Chomsky's experiments was *ask Donald what to do,* which children interpreted as if the object *Donald* was the subject of the matrix verb *do* (the children also misinterpreted *ask* as meaning *order* or *command,* but this is simply a confusion in word meaning). Again, we are not dealing with functional control here, but with a different set of mechanisms that Bresnan (1982c) calls *anaphoric control.* Anaphoric control differs from functional control in allowing the interpretation of the missing subjects to be arbitrary; for example, *ask Donald what to do* can be synonymous with *ask Donald what one should do* [*in such circumstances*]; in *tell Donald to leave,* on the other hand, no such interpretation of the complement subject is possible. Furthermore, in anaphoric control, unlike functional control, functions other than OBJ2, OBJ, or SUBJ can serve as controllers; and in anaphoric control, only referential identity between missing phrase and antecedent is implied, whereas in functional control, both referential identity and consistency of case and other grammatical features must be ensured (these can best be illustrated in languages other than English; see Bresnan, 1982c, for the relevant arguments). Thus here again, a construction that children have trouble understanding is also a construction that, according to independent arguments, is not handled by the functional control mechanisms that the C-procedures acquire.

The final example of a misunderstood construction is the verb *promise* in the structure *Donald promised Mickey to do a somersault,* which many children mistakenly interpret as if the object, *Mickey,* were coreferential with the missing complement subject. This is indeed a bona fide example of functional control, but is one of the rare violations of the near-universal principle of functional control stating that a matrix object if present must be the controller of a missing complement subject (Bresnan, 1982c). I discuss the learning and unlearning of this anomalous verb in detail in the "Marked Control Relations" section below; suffice it to say here that in each of Chomsky's demonstrations of failure to master complement structures, normal functional control as acquired by the C-procedures is not implicated in the adult state. Thus verbs allowing functional control form a "natural class" both within LFG and in language development: a full range of structures within the class is acquired in a relatively short period of time, and the structures that are not acquired in this period do not fall within the class. These data thus support the conjunction of the acquisition theory that treats those constructions as a natural class and the grammatical theory according to which such an acquisition theory is in fact acquiring the right rules for the adult language.

Developmental Evidence: Co-occurrence Restrictions

The C4 procedures that acquire the equations governing the finiteness, mood, and complementizers of a verb's complement are triggered by the same conditions as the C1–C3 procedures, which acquire complement phrase structure and control relations. In order to add an equation to a complement-taking verb, however, C4 must recognize the relevant properties of the complement in an input sentence containing the verb so that it can conclude that it is those properties that the verb forces its complement to have. Thus until the child recognizes that *to* or *that* are complementizers of verb phrases, he or she will be unable to add equations stating that *want* or *argue*, respectively, take those complementizers. Similarly, until the child can distinguish between finite and infinitival forms, he or she will be unable to learn that *know* takes only finite sentential complements, whereas *arrange* takes infinitival complements (the acquisition of tense markers would proceed according to the procedures outlined in Chapters 5 and 7). Thus once complement structures are acquired, the acquisition of complement co-occurrence restrictions should proceed as soon as the relevant complement properties can be recognized.

I know of no systematic studies of the inflectional morphology of embedded verbs as a function of their matrix verbs. Bloom, Tackeff, and Lahey (in press) report that embedded verbs were almost always bare at first in the speech of the children they studied, which is also the case for Adam and Eve. However, this is also true of children's early verbs in general (Brown, 1973), and since most of the complement-taking verbs first learned require infinitival complements, bare verbs in English are the correct forms. Later one finds a small number of inflected complements, some correct, some incorrect, some ambiguous: Bloom et al. report *I want a dumped out*, though this could have been a transcription of *I want it dumped out* or *I want to dump it out*; Adam in Stage III said *I like going take a pie* and *I like going sleep*, the latter of which Brown (n.d.) interprets as a gerund closer to *I like going to sleep* than to *I'd like to go to sleep*. Adam also produced the correct forms *I stop crying, see me walking*, and *heard you talking* (all in Stage IV) and *look at dat big truck goin somewhere* and *I saw a duck swimming in the water* (Stage V), and the incorrect forms *let it spilled* and *make it walks* (Stage V). In addition, there are errors with complements to auxiliaries of the form *can it rolls?*; I discuss both such errors in detail in the next chapter. It is not surprising that inflected verb complements appear later than bare ones, since that is true of verbs in general; and the late appearance of verb inflections with *-s* and *-ed* is consistent with their late mastery in simple sentences (Stages IV–V; Brown, 1973). However, it is not clear why complement-taking verbs with *-ing* should first appear in the samples I examined a full year later than the point at which *-ing* was supplied in obligatory contexts in general over 90 percent of the time (Brown, 1973). Not much more can be said at this point since the rarity of complement structures with progressive verbs could be a consequence of the children's parents rarely exemplifying them in their own speech, or simply of sampling error.

In contrast to the paucity of data on complement verb inflection, Bloom, Tackeff, and Lahey (in press) have conducted an extensive survey of the acquisition of the complementizer *to* in young children. They found, in accord with Brown (1973), that children at first seem to learn the contracted V + *to* form as an unanalyzed verb in certain subject-equi and raising-to-subject cases (*wanna, hafta, gonna,* etc.), resulting in one case in the later form *hafta to*. This is not surprising, given that the adult form is phonologically contracted to begin with. Children also omit the fully pronounced *to* altogether in all forms. However, by the age of 30 to 32 months, all four of Bloom et al.'s subjects were supplying *to* 85–100 percent of the time. Bloom et al. also made three intriguing discoveries that support the prediction that the acquisition of complementizer selection awaits only the perceptual isolation of complementizer words and the realization that they are complementizers. *To,* like other unstressed, monosyllabic closed-class morphemes, is perceptually nonsalient, unlikely to be uttered in isolation or in sentence-initial or sentence-final position (though elliptical expressions such as *I don't want to* are an exception), and semantically empty. For these reasons it will be difficult for the child to segment them (see Chapters 2, 4, and 5; also Slobin, 1973; Newport, Gleitman, and Gleitman, 1977; Gleitman and Wanner, 1982). Therefore, it will in effect not be part of the input to the child at first. Interestingly, Bloom et al.'s data suggest that this does not seem to prevent the C4 mechanisms from drawing conclusions about whether a complementizer is present in a given input. Bloom et al. discovered that complement-taking verbs that were acquired early were then persistently uttered without *to* during the same period of time that newly acquired verbs were accompanied by *to* (or a phonologically reduced version of it) from their first usages. This suggests that the learning mechanisms had previously recorded in the lexical entries of those early verbs the (false) information that the verb requires no complementizer—otherwise the complementizers would be used with old verbs and new verbs alike as soon as the acquisition mechanisms noted their existence in the input. It is as if the child did not hear the presence of a complementizer and thus concluded that there was no complementizer; that is, he or she invariably appended the equation V-COMP's CMPZR = $\emptyset$ to the early complement-taking verbs. Subsequent evidence from parental input that there was in fact an overt complementizer would then take time to drive out the earlier, incorrect equation.

How could this "driving out" be accomplished? I suggest that the mechanisms that replace the old equation by the new one would be the same sort as outlined in Chapter 4. Recall that the phrase structure acquisition mechanisms are able to learn the positions of predicate complement and locative phrases even when the morphemes defining the categorization of those phrases are not processed. The procedures can indicate that the categorizations they make are tentative and preemptable by subsequent acquisitions by using the "?" symbol. One can account for the learnability of complementizer selection despite early mistakes in the same way. Say that all equations specifying a null complementizer, like several other rules hinging on the detection of a closed-class element, included the preemptability symbol, hence: V-COMP's CMPZR = ?$\emptyset$?. In this case any non-null complementizer subsequently encountered would preempt the $\emptyset$ equation. As in Chapter 4, if the null complementizer were then hypothesized a second time, after there was an equation calling for the non-null complementizer in place, the new null complementizer equation would not be preemptable. This is necessary for the child to acquire verbs that have optional complementizers (e.g., *I helped him leave/to leave; I think he left/that he left*) and hence two complementizer equations (e.g., V-COMP's CMPZR = *to*; V-COMP's CMPZR = $\emptyset$).[7] This convention should be reliable because once the child's vocabulary and perceptual abilities are sufficiently powerful to recognize and hypothesize non-null complementizers, then a subsequent temptation to hypothesize a null complementizer is likely to have been caused by the genuine absence of a complementizer in an input sentence and not a failure to recognize one that is there.[8]

Note also that if the preempting process is computationally

costly, it would explain why verbs taking no complementizers in adult English tend to be the simpler, more frequent forms that children are likely to have learned early when they did not process complementizers. Compare, for example, *see* and *hear* (*I saw/heard him leave*) with *perceive* (*I perceived him *leave/to leave*); *make* (*I made him leave*) with *force* or *compel* (*I compelled/forced him *leave/to leave*); *say* (*John said he left*) with *proclaim* or *argue* (*John argued/proclaimed *he left/that he left*; *think* and *believe* (*I think/believe John left*) versus *conclude, profess, maintain,* and so on (*I concluded *John left/that John left*). (See Roeper, 1982, for the first description of a version of this hypothesis.)

What eventually allows the child to recognize the presence of a complementizer? Again, Bloom et al.'s data (in press) provide part of an answer. They found that children use the complementizer *to* only after they have begun to use the spatial preposition *to* (as in *to the door*), and their mastery of the complementizer form of *to* lags behind their mastery of the preposition. It is plausible that the semantically transparent preposition *to* can be learned when it appears in an interpretable context (e.g., the child witnessing something moving toward a destination, and hearing a phrase with *to* and the destination's name) and that it is also sometimes heard in salient sentence positions (e.g., *to bed!, that's the one I was pointing to; hit it TO me, not away from me!*). All of these factors would make the preposition *to* easier to segment from the auditory stream than the complementizer *to*. Since in Chapter 2 I proposed that segmentation is accomplished in part by the fitting of templates for known words onto the sound stream, the prior acquisition of a homonymous element would facilitate the segmentation of an otherwise nonsalient word like the complementizer *to*. That is why children would start using *to* as a complementizer only after they were using it as a preposition. This account is related to one of my early accounts of the recognition of the agentive preposition *by* in Chapter 3 and would account for the fact that other complementizers in English (e.g., *that, from, for*) also have noncomplementizer homonyms. (Note as well that many English complementizers evolved historically from prepositions—Jesperson, 1964.)

While this account would show how children segmented the complementizer word *to*, it would not explain how that word was recognized as *being* a complementizer. One possibility is that any preverbal or presentential word that has been independently categorized as a preposition is thereafter given the categorization CMPZR as well. Other complementizers without prepositional homonyms would then be acquired by the distributional analysis procedures (possibly supplemented by a procedure that made distributional generalizations from S to VP or vice versa). Bowerman (1982a) presents some evidence that children use such a procedure: she found that her two daughters often mistakenly used prepositions in complementizer positions, such as *you make me cry with putting that up there*, and *I made a noise from taking my diaper out*. Whether this procedure will work in general will depend on whether *every* language has prepositional homonyms for at least one of its complementizers. If not, the child could hypothesize the existence of a complementizer by the following rule: if a phrase bearing an X-COMP function (as recognized by procedures C1–C3) contains a meaningless phrase-initial morpheme, categorize that morpheme as the complementizer for that phrase type. Possibly a combination of these two procedures would be the correct acquisition mechanism for recognizing complementizers.[9] In either case, the word in question must be isolated as a word beforehand, and Bloom et al.'s data suggest that this is the step that the acquisition of overt complementizers in English awaits (as opposed to the acquisition of null complementizers, which seems to get under way as soon as the first complements are acquired).

Once complementizers are recognized, are they immediately entered into equations of the proper form, as the present theory predicts, or might the child test for various correlations between the presence of a complementizer and a variety of other phenomena in complement sentences? Bloom et al.'s data suggest that at least one sort of potential hypothesis-testing or correlation-sampling operation does not take place. They examined whether children's use of *to* was contingent on the choice of matrix verb (as in the adult language, and as procedure C4 mandates) or on the choice of the embedded verb (which is closer to it in the phrase structure tree and in serial position when an object is present). They found overwhelmingly that the presence of *to* was conditioned by the choice of matrix verb, and that there was no dependency, nor any developmental trends, involving the embedded verb. This suggests that the acquisition mechanisms for complementizers draws the correct conclusions about where to append the equations governing their presence.

Thus it is possible to conclude that the acquisition procedures as I have stated them for complement phrase structure, complement-taking verbs and their control relations, and complementizers may very well be active from the onset of language acquisition, the rate-limiting step being the prior acquisition of the elements that enter into the procedures' triggering conditions (rules mentioning grammatical functions in the case of complement-taking verbs; isolation of the complementizer word in the case of complementizers). This is what the theory would predict, since there is no extrinsic ordering or built-in maturational delays on the activation of the various sets of acquisition procedures (in many cases the steps within a set of procedures are ordered—e.g., the P-procedures—though it is unclear to what extent even that is necessary). It would certainly be possible to impose such orderings or delays, but that would result in a less constrained and less explanatory theory. It is welcome news that the data do not force one to do so in this case, and it would be an intriguing discovery if that were found to be the case in language acquisition in general.

I will conclude this chapter with discussions of the acquisition of two sorts of complement-taking verbs that are relatively rare in the world's languages, and that pose certain learnability problems for theories of complement acquisition: raising-to-object verbs, and transitive verbs with subject control.

The Acquisition of Raising-to-Object Constructions

The acquisition mechanisms for complements hinge on the child's recognizing that the subject of the embedded verb is "missing," that is, not in the phrase structure position or with the case markers that normally tag a noun phrase as being the subject of a particular verb. It is not clear, however, how the child can recognize that the subject of the complement is missing in the case of so-called raising-to-object verbs (also called "exceptional case-marking" verbs in Chomsky, 1981; e.g., *expect* as in *I expect John to leave*). Since the object of the matrix verb is not one of its logical arguments but in fact expresses the subject argument of the embedded verb, the child might assume that a verb like *expect* takes a full sentential complement (S-COMP), expressed as [$_S$NP to VP] or [$_S$NP VP'], as opposed to the (OBJ, V-COMP) analysis proposed by the theory of LFG. (In an alternative theory such as that of Chomsky, 1981, the same learnability problem would appear in the guise of how the child recognizes that *expect* is able to assign case to the subject of its complement.) This is not just a matter of conforming to a formalism: an incorrect analysis here would eventually prevent the child from passivizing such constructions (as in *John was expected to leave*), would yield errors in the case assignment of pronouns (resulting in **I expected he to leave*), and would cause trouble for any other rules sensitive to the label OBJ. How, then, does the child recognize that OBJ V-COMP, and not S-COMP, is the proper analysis? I present three alternatives below. Each alternative makes predictions about language universals and about developmental sequences.

Hypothesis 1: Raising Depends on Equi

The solution proposed in Pinker (1982) exploited the fact that the first P-procedure conservatively attempts to parse incoming sentences with existing phrase structure rules to as great an extent as possible before any other procedure coins new phrase structure rules. In particular, I proposed that before being exposed to raising-to-object constructions, the child had already acquired object-equi constructions (e.g., *I told Harry to sing*). As mentioned, such constructions have phrase structures that are identical to those of raising-to-object constructions, but they assign a semantic role (e.g., person affected) to their objects. As a result, when the child first encounters an object-equi construction, he or she could assign the postverbal noun phrase the function OBJ on semantic grounds. This would leave the complement subjectless, since a given phrase cannot subtend two branches in the constituent structure, and the complement/control acquisition procedures would be correctly triggered. This in turn would result in the coining of the phrase structure rule VP → V NP_{OBJ} $VP'_{V\text{-}COMP}$. Once acquired from these equi cases, that would be the preferred analysis for the raising sentences when they are encountered, because there would be no rule at that point expanding S as NP-*to*-VP. And once the raising sentence was parsed in this fashion, the complement/control acquisition procedure would be triggered by the presence of a subjectless propositional argument of the matrix verb. This makes three predictions: (1) no language may have raising-to-object constructions unless it also has object-equi constructions (otherwise, the raising constructions would be unlearnable); (2) object-equi constructions should be acquired by the child before raising-to-object constructions; and (3) object-equi constructions should be present in parental speech before raising-to-object constructions.[10]

I do not know whether the cross-linguistic provision is true but I suspect it is, given that object-equi constructions are common but raising-to-object constructions are rare across languages (Chomsky, 1981). However, the developmental predictions do not receive clear-cut support. It is true that most raising-to-object verbs (*expect, consider, believe, regard,* and so on) did not appear in the speech of the children I have considered in this chapter, whereas all the children used object-equi constructions at or shortly after they used complements in general. But there is a single possible raising-to-object verb, *want,* that is prevalent in children's first sentences with complements (and in their parents' speech; Pinker and Hochberg, in preparation). Bloom, Tackeff, and Lahey (in press) report *I want this doll to stay here* and *want me to do it?*; Menyuk (1969) reports *want the fire engine to talk* from a child of 2 years 9 months; and Limber (1973) reports that sentences such as *I don't want you read that book* are common in the speech of the 2-year-old he studied. Brown's Eve in Stage I said *want Mommy read* and *want Mommy you read* (the latter immediately followed her mother's sentence *you read to me,* and Brown interpreted *you read* to be a single unanalyzed verb). Brown's Adam said in Stage IV *want car to go . . . go dat way?* plus a variety of questions beginning with *want me* or *d'you want me,* and in Stage V said *I want this to go on there; I want this to have a wheel on it; I want him to play . . . play with this* (transcription of *him* uncertain); and *you want Ursula to see.* For some children (e.g., Eve and Limber's subject), *want* NP *to* VP occurred simultaneously with or prior to the first object-equi verbs.

The first question one must ask is whether *want* NP *to* VP is really a raising-to-object verb in adult English. The evidence is that it is definitely closer to a raising than to an equi construction. The postverbal NP can be a dummy subject, as in *I want there to be flowers on the table,* or an idiom chunk, as in *I want tabs to be kept on all expenditures from now on,* and passivizing the complement does not change the predicate-argument relations in the meaning of the sentence: compare *I want a doctor to examine John* with *I want John to be examined by a doctor.* Furthermore, it seems closer to raising-to-object verbs than to S-COMP verbs, since the postverbal NP receives accusative case marking (*I want him to go/*he to go/*that he goes;* cf. *I think that he went/*him to go*). In LFG a verb cannot specify the case of a particular argument within its complement; that would require the equation V-COMP's SUBJ's CASE = *acc,* which violates Kaplan and Bresnan's Functional Locality Condition in having three non-nested terms on one side of an equation. Furthermore, in LFG there can be no deletion operations on phrase structures (as there is in Chomsky, 1981), nor null constituents other than traces (e.g., there cannot be a phonetically null case-assigning preposition in the phrase structure). Therefore, within the current framework *want* NP *to* VP should be a raising-to-object construction in the adult grammar. (One hitch is that *want,* unlike other raising-to-object verbs, cannot undergo passivization: *John is expected/*wanted to leave.*

However, that is also true for the simple transitive version of *want*: *an ice cream cone is wanted by Sally*).

The second question we must ask is whether children in fact have acquired a raising-to-object entry for *want* when they use it with an NP and a VP following it. Perhaps *want* is in fact an equi-verb for children, the direct object serving as an argument of *want* as well as of the complement verb (perhaps as some kind of instrument, i.e., the person whom the child intends to satisfy his or her desire). It would be difficult to rule out this hypothesis since children of this age do not produce the dummy subjects, idiom chunks, or passives that take part in the equi-versus-raising test (in any case *want* does not allow passivization). However, there is no independent motivation for this suggestion, and the examples in the literature (e.g., *want the man stand up, I don't want you read that book*) certainly do not compel an observer to interpret the object as an intended argument of *want*. A second possibility is that the postverbal NP-VP configuration at first serves as a sentential complement for children. Again, there is no decisive argument against this claim, but it is unparsimonious in requiring the child to unlearn this analysis at a later stage. The only evidence relevant to settling this issue is whether children give pronouns following *want* the nominative case marking appropriate to subjects or the accusative marking appropriate to objects. In the published literature we find that Bloom et al. (in press) report *want me to do it?* (i.e., correct accusative case marking); in contrast, when children produce unambiguous S-COMPs shortly afterward, they seem to use the correct nominative case marking. Limber reports, *I guess she's sick, I think I want grape juice,* and *do you think he wants some?*, and no incorrect uses. My own examination of *want + personal pronoun + VP* construction in the speech of Adam shows that he used accusative case marking 102 times (one of them an uncertain transcription) and nominative case marking only 3 times (one of them uncertain). Unfortunately, this analysis is less than conclusive because (a) all but one of the relevant constructions in Adam's speech were examples of *d'you want me VP?, do want me VP?,* or *want me VP?*, which may have been unanalyzed question-markers for Adam; and (b) Adam was not consistent in his case marking even in the unproblematic object-equi cases; for example, we find *let he walk* in his Stage V speech. To complicate matters further, Tom Wasow (personal communication) has recorded his daughter saying *I don't want she + VP* several times. Thus the issue of whether young children have acquired raising-to-object verbs at the same time as or before object-equi verbs is currently unsettled, and furthermore is likely to be settled by evidence from experiments rather than from spontaneous speech. However, the data do alert us to the strong possibility that the prediction that object-equi constructions invariably precede raising-to-object constructions in children's speech is false, and therefore it is important to explore alternative mechanisms for the acquisition of raising-to-object verbs.

Hypothesis 2: Raising Depends on Simple Transitives

This hypothesis depends on the continuity assumption as it applies to children's parsing mechanisms (see Chapter 1). Ford, Bresnan, and Kaplan (1982) provide evidence that when adults parse ambiguous sentences, they have a bias to give as yet unlabeled constituents the category labels that would satisfy the subcategorization requirements of the "strongest" (usually, the highest frequency) lexical entry of the verb. For example, Ford et al. show that in (3a) the phrase *that they couldn't hear* tends to be interpreted as a relative clause modifying *the guide*, whereas in (3b) it is interpreted as a sentential complement.

(3) (a) The tourists objected to the guide that they couldn't hear.
    (b) The tourists signaled to the guide that they couldn't hear.

They argue that the biases are caused by the relative strengths of the alternative lexical entries for the verbs: *object* (SUBJ, OBL$_{goal}$) is stronger than *object* (SUBJ, OBL$_{goal}$, S-COMP); whereas *signal* (SUBJ, OBL$_{goal}$, S-COMP) is stronger than *signal* (SUBJ, OBL$_{goal}$) (see Ford, Bresnan, and Kaplan, 1982, for experimental evidence). They call this the principle of *lexical preference*.

Returning now to the acquisition of raising-to-object verbs, note that *want* NP *to* VP has a counterpart in English, *want* NP (e.g., *I want a Gulf credit card*). If the child, when applying P1, parses the postverbal NP as an object because that is what *want* wants, the remaining VP, which is an argument of *want*, will have no expressed subject. These are just the conditions that spring procedures C1–C4 into action. One can now propose that the existence of a single transitive verb, combined with Ford et al.'s principle of lexical preference, is what allows children to realize that raising-to-object complements can be analyzed as consisting of an object and a VP. Note that I am not claiming that the parsing bias is itself responsible for the form of the raising-to-object verbs; this is determined by the fact that the C-procedures are designed to enter complement structures into the grammar in response to subjectless propositional arguments in the input. However, the parsing bias is what ensures that the child will *find* the particular parse of the input string, from among the set of possible parses, that serves as the trigger for those procedures.[11]

This hypothesis makes two predictions. One is that every language that has raising-to-object verbs should also have simple transitive counterparts to those verbs. This is true for English: we have *I expect John to leave* and *I expect an earthquake; I consider John a fool* and *I considered the offer; I believe him to be brilliant* and *I believe his story;* and so on. Second, it predicts that children should acquire the simple transitive forms of these verbs before their raising-to-object counterparts. That, too, seems to be true: each of the children that I discussed as uttering an instance of *want* NP *to* VP had previously used the simple *want* NP construction (e.g., *I want juice*).

Hypothesis 3: Case Marking and Passivization

David Lebeaux has suggested a third possibility to me: the child could use just the evidence that a linguist would use to determine that a predicate has raising-to-object properties—the passivizability, or accusative case marking, of the object. That is, parental sentences like *John is considered to be crazy* and *I consider him brilliant* or *I want him to leave* would force the child to analyze those verbs as taking an object and a V-COMP. Once one of these properties was encountered, the ability to use the other (i.e., passivization or assigning accusative case marking to the object) would follow automatically. The use of passivizability would require that passivized subject NPs are reliably related to objects in an alternate lexical entry; given that in LFG passivization is universally stated to apply to objects (see Chapter 8), this assumption is unproblematic. For *want*, which does not passivize in adult English, only case marking could serve as a clue.

These variants of Hypothesis 3, like the two hypotheses discussed before it, make cross-linguistic and developmental predictions. First, no language may have raising-to-object verbs unless it also has passivization, according to one variant, or accusative case marking, according to the other. Second, children should not acquire raising-to-object verbs before they have acquired passivization, according to one variant, or accusative case marking, according to the other. I do not know the relevant facts about other languages, but children do have a productive passive rule by the age of 4 (Lebeaux and Pinker, 1981; see also Chapter 8), and reliably use the accusative pronouns in object position at differing rates but no later than the early school years (Huxley, 1970; Tanz, 1974). These ages, though relatively advanced, probably precede the acquisition of raising-to-object verbs like *believe, expect,* and *consider.* (Of course, experimental evidence would be needed to show that children *could not* acquire these verbs before the accusative case or passive had been mastered.) However, *want* is used before the reliable use of either passivization (Bever, 1970) or accusative pronouns (Huxley, 1970; Tanz, 1974); if *want* is indeed a raising-to-object verb for children, Hypothesis 2 would seem more plausible as the source of its acquisition. In fact, it would not be surprising if some combination of Hypotheses 1, 2, and 3 were shown to be what children use to acquire these constructions. The implications of such redundant cues to the language will be discussed in Chapter 9.

Marked Control Relations

The acquisition procedures for complementation and control proposed in Pinker (1982) and reproduced here can learn any controller for a missing subject with equal ease, as long as the child witnesses the relevant sentence in a context in which the coreference between the subject argument of the embedded verb and one of the matrix arguments is perceivable. This is empirically untenable: children in fact do not learn all control relations with equal ease. Carol Chomsky (1969) was the first to demonstrate that many children up to the age of 9 (25 percent of those she tested) consistently interpret object-equi sentences with *promise* as having the matrix object control the missing complement subject, rather than the matrix subject controlling it (another 22.5 percent were inconsistent in their responses to such sentences). That is, these children interpreted *Donald promises Bozo to lie down* to mean *Donald promises Bozo that Bozo will lie down*, rather than the correct interpretation in which it is Donald who will lie down. Similar sentences with *tell* rather than *promise* were acted out correctly, and in a separate test, all children were shown to understand the meaning of the word *promise.* Children's difficulty with *promise* has also been documented in replications of Chomsky's experiments by Sherman (1983) and Kramer, Koff, and Luria (1972). Similar errors have been reported for children learning the equivalent of *promise* in Arabic (Aller, Aller, and Saad, 1977).

All that procedures C1–C3 need in order to learn a correct entry for *promise* is to witness a sentence like *John promised Bill to leave* in a context in which it was clear that it was John, not Bill, who was committed to leaving. Thus, the only way in which the current theory could be consistent with Chomsky's results is if her experimental subjects had never before heard *promise* in such a context. At first glance, this hypothesis would seem to have been refuted by Chomsky's demonstration that the children understood the meaning of *promise* in a separate test. However, in LFG, there are in fact several distinct lexical entries for *promise*, specific to the configuration of grammatical functions that accompany *promise* in the sentence. Three different entries are listed in (4), together with sample sentences.

(4) (a) promise (SUBJ, S-COMP): I promise that John will leave.

    (b) promise (SUBJ, V-COMP): I promise to leave.
       SUBJ = V-COMP's SUBJ

    (c) promise (SUBJ, OBJ, V-COMP): I promise John to leave.
       SUBJ = V-COMP's SUBJ

Since there is no lexical rule that converts one of the members of (4a), (b), or (c) into either of the other two members, the child will have to learn each entry individually when he or she hears it in adult speech. It was the (c) form that Chomsky's subjects erred on in the experiment, but the (a) and (b) forms that they were mostly tested on in the pretest demonstrating their comprehension of the word *promise*. Therefore, it is indeed possible that they had never before heard the (c) form in an interpretable context.

This hypothesis is not as implausible as it first may appear. *Promise* NP *to* VP is an extremely rare construction even in adult-to-adult speech; and in our study of a large sample of parent-to-child speech (Pinker and Hochberg, in preparation) we have not encountered a single instance. In fact, many adults find the construction ungrammatical altogether (for example, Tom Wasow, personal communication, has found that many of his undergraduate students in linguistics courses give such judgments when *promise* NP *to* VP is discussed). Furthermore, the individual children in Chomsky's experiment were very idiosyncratic in whether or not they made errors, and their mean competence rose very slowly with increasing age over a range of 5 years. In particular, 25 percent, with a mean age of 6 years 9 months and a range from 5,0 to 8,10, invariably were wrong; 22.5 percent, with a mean age of 7 years 4 months and a range from 5,1 to 9,7, were inconsistent; and 52.5 percent, with a mean age of 7 years 11 months and a range from 5,2 to 10,0, invariably were right. Tavakolian (1978) also found a great deal of variability in her subjects, with 57 percent of her 4-year-old subjects erring on *promise* NP *to* VP sentences and 43 percent acting them out correctly; for her 5-year-olds the corresponding figures were 37 and 62.5 percent. Thus, while performance improves slightly with age, there are large individual differences within an age range, and even the slight age trend may simply reflect the increasing likelihood of a child's having heard *promise* NP *to* VP in an interpretable context at least once as he or she lives longer.

Unfortunately, this hypothesis fails in two other ways. First, it does not account for why so many of the error-prone children consistently interpreted the *promise* sentences as having the object corefer with the missing complement subject rather than giving the sentence random interpretations. Second, it does not account for why transitive verbs whose matrix subjects control their complement subjects are so rare in English and other languages. Many observers, including Chomsky herself, have pointed out that children's errors in these experiments exemplified the very control relations that the vast majority of object-equi verbs conform to. Presumably, both facts should be predictable from some property of the child's acquisition mechanisms for control relations. At present, the learning mechanisms for complementation do not have any such property.[12]

The acquisition procedure, it appears, must be modified, and a replacement for C3 that I will call C3(a) is one possibility:

C3(a). Add to the lexical entry of the complement-taking predicate the equation X-COMP's SUBJ = OBJ2 if there is a second object present in the matrix clause; if not, add the equation X-COMP's SUBJ = OBJ if there is an object present; if not, add the equation X-COMP's SUBJ = SUBJ.

This procedure does not even need coreference information inferred from the context to coin the control equation; the universal generalization about control relations provides the needed information. As it stands, however, the procedure could *never* learn the correct control equations for marked verbs like *promise* NP *to* VP, *strike* NP *as* XP, and *impress* NP *as* XP. Thus it must be supplemented with C3(b).

C3(b) If the complement subject in the contextually inferred f-structure is coindexed with an argument of the matrix predicate other than that indicated by C3(a), alter the function in the right-hand side of the control equation to make it consistent with the coreference information in the f-structure.

A child equipped with both C3(a) and C3(b) can acquire unmarked control equations with or without contextual information, and marked control equations with it.[13] Because C3(a) needs less information, it can be applied more easily, explaining why the unmarked forms that it acquires are more prevalent. Furthermore, it explains the behavior of the children in Chomsky's experiment, who were old enough to parse the sentence and recognize it as having a complement but had no contextual information about who was to carry out the promised action. Unable to apply C3(b), they could still apply C3(a), and would make the error of having the matrix object of *promise* control the missing embedded subject.

This account still requires that the error-prone children had never heard *promise* NP *to* VP in an interpretable context before entering the lab, not even once, because if they had, C3(b) would have acquired the correct entry. This is strictly an empirical question, one that can be settled in principle by exposing such children to a *promise* NP *to* VP sentence in a highly redundant nonlinguistic context, and (controlling for attention and the like) seeing if that single exposure is sufficient to teach them the correct marked form.[14]

There is an alternative hypothesis, first suggested to me by David Lebeaux, that does not make these rather extreme empirical predictions. This hypothesis involves mechanisms I will call C3(a)' and C3(b)', which are the same as C3(a) and C3(b), respectively, except that the equations hypothesized are not added in an all-or-none fashion to the lexical entry. Instead, they are assigned a strength value ranging from 0 to 1 that is incremented with each input exemplar of the relevant type according to a learning function such as $s = 1 - e^{-ji}$, where s represents strength, i is the number of input exemplars that cause C3(a)' or (b)' to be triggered, and j is a rate parameter. In this model C3(b)' could also strengthen a control equation set up by C3(a)' if the semantics of a sentence were available and agreed with the unmarked control equation (in the original model, C3(b) was only used if the semantics contradicted the equation set up by C3(a)). Crucially, the rate parameter j would depend on the form of the equation relative to the arguments present in the sentence. When the equation is of a marked form (e.g., subject control when there is a matrix object present), the rate parameter is smaller than when the equation violates those constraints. In other words, I have kept the C3(a) and (b) procedures intact but have made the marked forms "harder" to learn: a greater number of input exemplars is needed to learn a marked form to a given level of strength than un unmarked form. Thus the marked forms are at a double disadvantage: the child needs an additional type of information to learn them, and he or she needs more of it. This hypothesis does not make the questionable prediction that Chomsky's error-prone subjects had never heard *promise* NP *to* VP in an interpretable context before entering the lab, nor that such a child would instantly learn the marked form, all other things being equal, if exposed to a single exemplar. Instead, it merely predicts that these error-prone children must not have heard *promise* NP *to* VP very many times beforehand, and that they would need more exemplars of it in interpretable contexts than they would need for unmarked verbs. However, the somewhat greater plausibility of its predictions comes at the price of decreased parsimony—the addition of two rate parameters—and hence I will tentatively adopt the stronger hypothesis embodied in C3(a–b) pending the relevant experimental evidence.

Note that I have invoked two different interpretations of the "markedness" of *promise*-type verbs in presenting the last versions of the complementation learning mechanisms. According to the first variant, a marked rule is one that cannot be specified by default—the learner must encounter some relevant piece of evidence before coining the rule (contextually inferred semantic information, in this case). However, once that bit of evidence is encountered, the learning of the marked rule should proceed without impediment. According to the second variant of markedness, a marked rule is one that is in some sense harder to learn—the learner must encounter more evidence for such a rule than he or she would need for its unmarked counterpart. This distinction is quite general, and applies to any case in which the concept of markedness is invoked in linguistics (and, accordingly, in any case in the present learning theory in which there are mechanisms that define an unmarked form plus mechanisms that can learn their marked alternatives—such as X-bar violations in Chapter 3, or Unique Entry violations in Chapter 5). The distinction must be addressed when one brings markedness to bear on developmental data, or vice versa, because only if one adopts the second version of markedness can one take lateness or difficulty in acquisition as being diagnostic of a rule's being marked. Under the first version, the child could learn a marked rule on a single "trial" so long as the relevant evidence against the default was available. See Pinker (in press, b) for further discussion.

Replacing Incorrect Control Equations

According to each of the last two hypotheses I have presented, a child in Chomsky's experiment would have acquired, during the course of the experiment, a lexical entry for the verb *promise* containing the equation V-COMP's SUBJ = OBJ rather than V-COMP's SUBJ = SUBJ. This leaves us with the problem of explaining how the child would unlearn this entry when he or she eventually encountered the semantic and syntactic evidence showing what the correct entry should be.[15] Learning a correct formulation of *promise*'s lexical entry is not in itself sufficient, since the child must know to discard his or her earlier incorrect usage rather than using the verb in both the correct and incorrect ways. As in other cases in which I have wanted to show how the child unlearns a bad rule, one can appeal to a version of the Uniqueness Principle. A first approximation of the necessary principle might be (5).

(5) No predicate may have two or more lexical entries differing only in their control equations.

If the child used this principle, then when he or she encountered evidence that *promise* required subject control, the newly created equation would drive out the earlier one specifying object control. However, (5) is too strong: there seems to exist at least one English verb, *ask*, which comes in two forms differing in control. For many people *John asked Bill to leave* is ambiguous, with either the matrix subject *John* or the matrix object *Bill* serving as the subject of *leave* (the subject control reading is more noticeable in *John asked Bill to be allowed to leave*). In LFG this would correspond to having two lexical entries for *ask*, one with an equation specifying subject control, one with an equation specifying object control. (Another possible verb in this category is *beg*, which behaves like *ask* in some dialects; and also *make*, as in *John made Mary a good wife* versus *John made Mary a good husband*, mentioned in Bresnan, 1982c, though other analyses may be possible here as well). The problem is that according to principle (5) a child would alternately adopt one equation and discard the other as each of the two forms was heard.[16]

What could make a child discard the incorrect control equation for *promise* when the correct one was coined, but not discard one of the correct equations for *ask* when the other was coined? The answer is clear: for *ask*, evidence for both control relations is present in the input when the child hears *ask* sentences in contexts in which it is clear that the matrix subject, in one episode, and the matrix object, in another, corefers with the missing subject. With *promise,* on the other hand, there is never any semantic evidence for object control: the object control equation is only formulated as a default option in the absence of semantic evidence, by procedure C3(a). Somehow this difference must be registered in the control equations.

This can be done by appealing to the principle that I have used several times in this book (and will use again in Chapter 8) stating that forms created by general productive mechanisms, but not forms witnessed in the input, are marked as being preemptable by witnessed forms that fall into the same equivalence class. In this case, any equation hypothesized by C3(a) alone would be marked as preemptable using the "?" symbol, e.g., (6) below. What would not be preemptable, but would instead have the power to preempt, would be an equation justified by semantic evidence—that is, one whose control relations were witnessed to be true in the nonlinguistic context of some input sentence, e.g., (7).

(6) V-COMP's SUBJ = ?OBJ?

(7) V-COMP's SUBJ = OBJ

All marked equations acquired by C3(b) would have this property.

Note, however, that as it stands an unmarked equation acquired by C3(a) would forever be marked as preemptable, since contextually induced semantic information is never brought to bear on it. This suggests an interesting and unanticipated feature of the acquisition mechanisms for control. Even though semantic information is not *necessary* to learn unmarked control relations, it should be brought to bear on those control relations even when the information merely confirms the unmarked case. Specifically, when the context of an utterance is consistent with the control equation that was created by C3(a), the "?" symbol should be erased, making the equation nonpreemptable. For example, when a sentence like *ask Daddy to drive you* is heard in context, the lexical entry for *ask* is transformed from having equation (6) to having equation (7); at this point a sentence such as *I asked her to be allowed to leave* no longer has the power to drive out the control equation.

The final version of the C3 procedures, then, would be as follows:

C3(a). Add to the lexical entry of the complement-taking predicate the equation X-COMP's SUBJ = OBJ2 if there is a second object present in the matrix clause; if not, add the equation X-COMP's SUBJ = OBJ if there is an object present; if not, add the equation X-COMP's SUBJ = SUBJ. Append "?" to the equation.

C3(b). Examine the coreference information pertaining to the matrix and complement arguments in the contextually induced f-structure. If the complement subject is coindexed with an argument of the matrix verb other than that mandated by the predicate's current control equation, and if that equation bears the "?" feature, replace the equation with a new one that is consistent with the coreference information in the f-structure. If the contradicted equation does not bear the "?" feature, retain it and add a second equation that is consistent with the coreference information. If the existing equation is consistent with the coreference information, remove its "?" feature if it bears one.

The C-mechanisms as amended above (or similarly amended C'-mechanisms that perform the same operations but on rules of graded strength) can now account for (a) the failure of children to comprehend *promise*-type verbs, (b) the mistakes the children make when they fail, (c) their ability to learn the correct versions, (d) their ability to unlearn the incorrect versions, and (e) the within-language and between-language prevalence of object-control transitive verbs.

The account sketched here has several advantages over those proposed in the literature. Chomsky proposed that children interpret "the implicit subject of the complement verb [as] the NP most closely preceding it," a strategy that would work for unmarked but not marked object-equi verbs. However, as Maratsos (1974a) points out, this predicts that children will misinterpret the missing subject in the passive of object-equi sentences such as *John was told by Mary to leave*. In an elegant set of experiments, he showed that if a 4- or 5-year-old child has mastered the simple passive, he or she will interpret these sentences correctly. This is an automatic consequence of the functioning of lexical rules in LFG: the passive, in replacing the OBJ argument by SUBJ in a lexical form, also executes this replacement in the control equations associated with the form, converting OBJ = V-COMP's SUBJ in the active entry into SUBJ = V-COMP's SUBJ in the passive entry. (There are languages that do not obey this pattern—see Keenan, 1976—but they can be learned via the application of procedure C3(b), which can examine contextually inferred patterns of coreference and override the control equations created by productive mechanisms.) Maratsos's own account, based on Jackendoff (1972), has the child control the missing subject by the argument of the predicate with the thematic role *goal*. This account is similar in important respects to the present one but is somewhat less general because *any* grammatical object, if present, will control the missing subject in complement structures, not just objects that semantically are goals (for example, objects in raising-to-object complements such as *I expect there to be fireworks tonight* or *there struck me as being too many lawyers in parliament*). Tavakolian's (1978) claim that children first pass through a stage in which they "select the subject of the first clause as the referent of the missing subject in the second clause" contrasts with the present claim that the child's default hypothesis is that matrix objects control missing subjects. But Tavakolian's data do not support her interpretation: as mentioned, her 3-year-old subjects were simply performing at a level near chance for both *tell* and *promise* sentences. Finally, the informal account that children simply overgeneralize the control relations from *tell* verbs to *promise* (e.g., Dale, 1976) does not explain why children do not similarly overgeneralize from *want to, going to, need to,* and so on, and conclude that subjects are always controllers, leading them to misuse object-control sentences (with *see, tell,* and so on) when they first learn them. The overgeneralization hypothesis also does not explain why subject controllers in sentences with both objects and complements would be so rare in the world's languages.[17] In the present account, the high relative frequency of object-control verbs does not lead the child to err on *promise*; rather, the acquisition process that leads him to err on *promise* is also what causes object-control verbs to be easy to learn and hence more frequent. Finally, none of these hypotheses accounts for how the marked forms are eventually learned, nor for how the unmarked forms are unlearned.

7 | Auxiliaries

THE ENGLISH auxiliary system, and its interactions with tense, modality, mood, constituent order, inflection, and ellipsis, is notorious for its intricacy, and I cannot hope to present anything like a complete acquisition theory for it. The auxiliary system is, however, an important topic for any theory of language acquisition. Historically, it was one of the first areas of language that motivated the theory of transformational-generative grammar (Chomsky, 1957), and since then it has frequently been offered as a paradigm case of the explanatory advantages of the transformational approach (see Gazdar, Pullum, and Sag, 1982). It also has played an important historical role in the study of children's language. Several aspects of the auxiliary system were discovered to emerge in a systematic sequence (Brown and Hanlon, 1970), and children exhibit several striking error patterns in their use of auxiliaries that have figured in accounts purporting to demonstrate the partial or abnormal use of syntactic transformations in children's speech (Bellugi, 1965, 1967, 1971; Brown, 1968; Hurford, 1975; Mayer, Erreich, and Valian, 1978). Since the theory developed in this book forbids both the use of syntactic transformations and the postulation of arbitrary children's rule systems not motivated by a learning theory, these data would seem to challenge the particulars of the theory. Therefore, the ability to provide a motivated account of the source of auxiliary errors is a significant criterion in the evaluation of the approach.

In addition, there are positive reasons for dealing with the auxiliary system. Despite its complexity, many of the rules governing the system are learnable by mechanisms that have been introduced for other purposes. Furthermore, children learn their first auxiliaries early (see Chapter 6) and master a good part of the system in the preschool years in a sequence that is as notable for the absence of imaginable errors (Maratsos, in press; Maratsos and Kuczaj, 1978) as for the errors that do occur.

I will focus on two sets of grammatical phenomena that come into play in well-formed English sentences. First, I discuss the English auxiliary system itself: the order of auxiliary elements, the co-occurrence restrictions among them, and their sensitivity to sentence modality. Second, I discuss the interaction between auxiliary placement and *wh*-words in constituent questions and interrogative complements. In doing so, I also touch briefly on the subject of gaps or traces and their antecedents as they enter into *wh*-questions. For each of these phenomena, I will discuss what the child must learn, how he or she learns it according to the theory, and the relevant developmental patterns.

The Structure of the English Auxiliary

WHAT IS LEARNED

English auxiliaries can be subdivided into the modals (*can, could, will, must, should,* etc.), perfect *have,* progressive *be,* and passive *be.* Each imposes different constraints on the verb that appears in its clause, as can be seen in (1).

(1) (a) John might eat/*ate/*eaten/*eating.
   (b) John has eaten/*eat/*ate/*eating.
   (c) John is eating/*eat/*eaten/*ate from twelve to one.
   (d) John was eaten/*eat/*eating/*ate by a wolverine.

These co-occurrence restrictions hold not only between auxiliaries and adjacent main verbs but also between auxiliaries and other adjacent auxiliaries, as shown in (2).

(2) (a) John might have left/*has left/*having left/*had left.
   (b) John might be leaving/*is leaving/*being leaving/*been leaving.
   (c) John has been leaving/*be leaving/*is leaving/*being leaving.
   (d) John might have been leaving/*has been leaving/*have is leaving/etc.

In addition, there is the auxiliary *do,* whose co-occurrence restrictions are similar to those of the modals (3), and which is obligatory when there are no other auxiliaries in questions, negations, and emphatic assertions (i.e., those denying a previous negation), as in (4).

(3) (a) Could John go/*went/*going/*gone?
    (b) Did John go/*went/*going/*gone?

(4) (a) Did John leave?
    (b) *Left John?
    (c) John did not leave.
    (d) *John left not.
    (e) Yes, John *did* leave!
    (f) *Yes, John *left!*

Transformational and Lexical Accounts

In Chomsky's (1957) famous analysis of the auxiliary system, these facts are handled by proposing that there is an *Aux* constituent in deep structure which is expanded as *Tense (Modal) (Have en) (Be ing).* An "affix-hopping" transformation then adjoins any affix (*Tense, en, ing*) to the right of the verb immediately following it in deep structure; if there is no verb immediately following the *Tense* affix, the element *do* is inserted, thanks to a "*do*-support" transformation. Though this account is elegant in certain respects, both the *Aux* constituent and the affix-hopping transformation have a number of properties that seem inconsistent with formal constraints on standard transformational grammars (see Gazdar, Pullum, and Sag, 1982, for an enumeration). Furthermore, C. L. Baker (1981) has argued that the affix-hopping account has certain intractable learnability problems; these will be addressed in detail below. Alternatives to the affix-hopping account have been proposed that treat auxiliaries as complement-taking verbs that are subcategorized for complements with specific grammatical features. According to these accounts it is the subcategorization restrictions, rather than a movement transformation, that enforce co-occurrence constraints between an auxiliary and its adjacent verb (e.g., Baker, 1981; Falk, 1980b; Gazdar, Pullum, and Sag, 1982; Lapointe, 1981a; Kaplan and Bresnan, 1982; Pullum and Wilson, 1977; also, certain aspects of Akmajian, Steele, and Wasow, 1979). Since this class of theories is formally compatible with LFG and avoids the difficulties facing the traditional accounts, it is the one I will adopt as a theory of what the child must acquire. Unlike other domains of LFG, however, no single treatment of the auxiliary has been defended as the optimal one, and certain phenomena (e.g., inversion in *wh*-questions) have not been discussed at all. Hence I am forced to propose my own version of a lexical theory of auxiliaries here, drawing from the various theories just cited and adding some novel proposals.

In most lexical theories of the auxiliary, auxiliaries are treated as main verbs taking complements, analogous to raising-to-subject verbs. The lexical entry of each auxiliary dictates which morphological feature (i.e., pertaining to finiteness and participlehood) the complement verb must have, and consistency-enforcing mechanisms rule out verb choices that contradict those constraints. Lexical entries for five sorts of auxiliaries—modals, *do, have, be* (progressive) and *be* (passive), are shown in (5), and a tree for an auxiliary structure, generated recursively by the rules VP → V VP'$_{V\text{-COMP}}$ and VP' → (CMPZR) VP, is shown in Figure 7.1.

(5) (a) might: V: PRED = "might (V-COMP)"
           SUBJ = V-COMP's SUBJ
           V-COMP's MORPH =$_c$ inf
           AUX = +

   (b) do: V: SUBJ = V-COMP's SUBJ
           V-COMP's MORPH =$_c$ inf
           AUX = +

   (c) have: V: PRED = "perfect (V-COMP)"
           SUBJ = V-COMP's SUBJ
           V-COMP's MORPH =$_c$ perfpart
           AUX = +

   (d) be: V: PRED = "progressive (V-COMP)"
           SUBJ = V-COMP's SUBJ
           V-COMP's MORPH =$_c$ progpart
           AUX = +

   (e) be: V: PRED = "be (V-COMP)"
           SUBJ = V-COMP's SUBJ
           V-COMP's MORPH =$_c$ passivepart
           AUX = +

The lexical entries for the various verbs, including the auxiliaries themselves in multiple auxiliary sequences such as in Figure 7.1, supply the correct morphological form; the formal constraints on the completeness, coherence, and consistency of f-structures rule out various ungrammatical constructions. The ↑ TENSE annotation on the matrix VP in the rule S → NP$_{SUBJ}$ VP $_{↑TENSE}$ ensures that the head verb in the matrix sentence will always be tensed. Interrogatives can be generated by a rule that allows a verb bearing an AUX feature to appear optionally in the fronted position, and that allows a V-COMP to alternate with the tensed VP. These rules, in simplified form, are shown in Figure 7.2.[1]

Figure 7.1

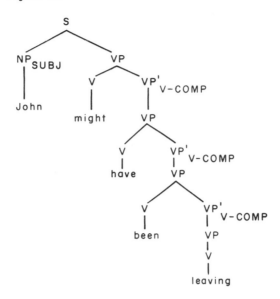

Figure 7.2

a) $S \rightarrow (V_{AUX=_c+})NP_{SUBJ} \left\{ \begin{array}{c} VP_{\uparrow TENSE} \\ \\ VP'_{V-COMP} \end{array} \right\}$
   $\uparrow TENSE$

b) $VP \rightarrow V \ (NP_{OBJ}) \ (VP'_{V-COMP})$

c) $VP' \rightarrow (CMPZR) \ VP$

Figure 7.3

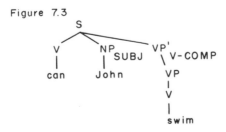

Figure 7.3 shows the structure of an interrogative sentence generated by these rules. Ungrammatical questions with fronted

main verbs (e.g., **swam John?*) are blocked by the AUX $=_c$ + constraint on the fronted verb position. Since *do* has the AUX feature and does not add unwanted meaning, it is the only verb that can be chosen for inverted questions lacking any other auxiliary. Ungrammatical sentences with both a fronted and a medial auxiliary (e.g., **can he can go?*) are blocked by the consistency requirement: all tokens of a given semantic predicate are given distinct indices in f-structures. In these double-auxiliary non-sentences there are two separate entries, PRED = *can* (V-COMP)$_i$ and PRED = *can* (V-COMP)$_j$, at the same level of f-structure (they are at the same level because the second *can* is not separated from the first by a V-COMP level of f-structure), and consistency is thus violated (see Kaplan and Bresnan, 1982).

Three Complications for the Simple Complementation Theory of Auxiliaries

Of course, life is never that easy. Baker (1981) and Lapointe (1981a) have pointed out that any simple set of rules generating English auxiliary sequences is likely to generate several classes of ungrammatical sentences as well. Since it is natural to assume that children adopt simple grammars in preference to complex ones if the simple ones can account for the input, these theories predict that children should produce these ungrammatical sentences when acquiring the auxiliary system and in the absence of negative evidence should continue to produce them as adults. Baker was referring primarily to the affix-hopping account of auxiliaries, but it is easy to show that any simple learning theory accompanying the account of auxiliaries sketched above is subject to the same problems of overgeneration (for example, the theory presented in Pinker and Lebeaux, 1981, and in Pinker, in press, a, presupposed that simple grammar for auxiliaries, and thus also would run into these problems). In this section I briefly review Baker's examples of auxiliary overgeneration and show how an extended lexical theory of the adult state can handle them; in the following two sections I propose an acquisition theory for the auxiliary system and consider the developmental evidence relevant to it.

The first complication: order of auxiliary elements. Auxiliary elements must be sub-sequences of the schema *Modal-have-progressive be-passive be.* No member of this schema may be repeated, as is done in (6a–c), nor can any pair of members occur out of order, as in (6d–f).

(6) (a) *John must can swim.
   (b) *John has had left.
   (c) *John is being seeing Sharon.
   (d) *John is can(ning) go.
   (e) *John is having eaten.
   (f) *John has could go.

A natural way of handling these examples is to point to the equations in the lexical entries of the auxiliaries constraining the inflectional forms of their complement verbs, and to propose that certain auxiliary verbs lack certain of the inflectional forms that other auxiliaries require (Baker, 1981; Pullum and Wilson, 1977; Gazdar, Pullum, and Sag, 1982). *Must* and other modals require infinitival complements—see (5a)—so (6a) can be blocked if modals themselves lack infinitival lexical entries; this would be consistent with the defectiveness of paradigms for modals in general (*cans; *canning; *to can go*). *Has* requires that its complement verb be a perfect participle (see 5c), so (6b) and (6f) can be blocked if neither the auxiliary *have* nor the modals come in perfect participle versions. Finally, *be* requires its complement verb to be a progressive participle, so (6c–e) can be blocked if neither the modals, *have*, nor progressive *be* itself may assume progressive participle forms (passive auxiliary *be*, distinct from progressive auxiliary *be*, does have a progressive participle, as is shown by *he was being tickled*). Partial paradigms for auxiliary and main verbs according to this analysis are shown in Figure 7.4.[2] (Person and number dimensions would be nested within the levels *present* and *past*, which themselves would be nested within the *fin* level; see the discussion of nesting in

Figure 7.4

MORPH

		Inf	Perfpart	Progpart	Fin
a.	can :	–	–	–	can
b.	have: (perfect)	have	–	–	has
c.	be : (progressive)	be	been	–	is
d.	be: (passive)	be	been	being	is
e.	walk:	walk	walked	walking	walks

Figure 7.5

MORPH

Inf	Perfpart	Progpart	Fin
-∅	-en	-ing	-s

Inf   Perfpart Progpart   Fin

Chapter 5. Here I list the present third-person singular forms for simplicity.)

Baker points out that this "defective paradigm" analysis of auxiliaries requires two assumptions. First, productive inflection (in terms of the present theory, the application of general paradigms; see Chapter 5) must somehow be blocked for auxiliary verbs. Otherwise, a speaker would create the general paradigm in Figure 7.5 from the many word-specific paradigms like Figure 7.4(e) and fill out the incomplete paradigms in Figure 7.4(a–c), vitiating the defective paradigm analysis. Second, Baker points out that there must be distinct paradigms for auxiliary and non-auxiliary forms of a given verb, with no generalization from one to another. That is because nonauxiliary forms of *have* (e.g., possessive and raising-to-object), *be* (e.g., copula), and *do* (e.g., pro-verb) have full paradigms (*John is being stubborn today; I am having a manicure; I have had three husbands; I am doing something about it*). Thus there must be a general principle forbidding paradigms for auxiliaries to be filled out by general paradigms or by paradigms for homonymous forms.

Baker proposes that these prohibitions be stated so as to apply to verbs in general: no productive inflection may be applied to verbs whose partial paradigms are already irregular; no paradigm sharing may occur among homonymous verbs. Wasow (1981) offers counterexamples to these claims and suggests that the prohibitions be stated in terms of their relevance to auxiliaries per se, citing arguments that the auxiliary category is a substantive linguistic universal (Akmajian, Steele, and Wasow, 1979; Steele, 1981). Given Wasow's counterexamples and the general principle within the proposed theory that the child looks for and exploits substantive universals (see Chapter 2), I adopt Baker's prohibitions as amended by Wasow: the prohibitions apply to verbs having the feature AUX = +.

The second complication: "do" in the neutral sentence modality. Do must appear in inverted, negated, or emphatic sentences with nonauxiliary verbs; at the same time, it *cannot* appear in non-inverted, non-negated, nonemphatic sentences (e.g., *I do go to school*). I will call this conjunction the "neutral sentence modality."[3] The equation AUX = + appended to auxiliary verbs, and AUX =$_c$ + appended to the phrase structure position of the inverted verb and of the morpheme *not*, will rule out the absence of *do* when it is obligatory (e.g., **goes he to school?*). However, it will not rule out the presence of *do* in cases where it should not appear.

Baker proposes a solution to this problem in which every verb would have two forms: "type A" forms for the neutral sentence modality, and "type B" forms for inverted, emphatic, or negated sentence modalities. For main verbs, the type A forms would be tensed and the type B forms would consist of a tensed form of *do* plus an infinitival form of the verb, and this relationship would be productive. For auxiliaries, on the other hand, the type A and type B forms would be identical to one another. Thus the speaker, when accessing a neutral (e.g., type A) form of main verbs, would never have occasion to access a *do* + V form because such forms are only listed as type B.

Baker's proposal has an additional benefit: it would rule out the third class of ungrammatical constructions otherwise allowed by the simple complementation theory of auxiliaries: sequences of *do* plus another auxiliary (**did he must go?*, **does she have gone?*, **does John be going home?*; these are discussed in the next section). Baker proposes that the suppletion of regular by irregular forms (which is part of the Unique Entry principle) applies to the A-B paradigm; hence the presence of a tensed type B form for auxiliaries (which happens to be identical to their A forms) blocks the application of the productive general paradigm which otherwise would derive the *do* + *infinitive* type B form from its type A counterpart.

Though Baker's theory represents a major advance beyond the simple complementation theory, it has some problems. First, by appealing to suppletion or uniqueness principles in order to rule out *do* + AUX sequences, Baker cannot explain why certain auxiliaries and quasi-auxiliaries can neither invert nor enter into constructions with inverted *do*. For example, *better* behaves in many respects like a modal auxiliary, as in (7a), but has no type B form with *do*, as shown in (7b), even though it also lacks the inverted type B form, (7c), that would have to block the creation of (7b).

(7) (a) You better not pout.
    (b) *Does he better pout?
    (c) *Better he pout?

Likewise, *used to* seems to have no type B form in certain dialects (e.g., that of the author: *used he to pout?*, ?*did he used to pout?*), and even certain standard modals fail to be acceptable to many American speakers when inverted (e.g., ?*ought John to leave?*, ?*might Mary go?*). Second, as Baker notes, nothing in the theory rules out the possibility that *do* will be entered as a legitimate complement-taking verb, allowing it to appear in neutral sentence modalities after all. Finally, the theory is stated in a highly informal way, leaving it unclear how to represent the lexical entries corresponding to the *do* + V construction in terms of some grammatical formalism. Thus I will adopt a modification of Baker's theory which remedies some of these problems but which preserves the descriptive, and, as we shall see, learnability-theoretic advantages of his account.

Specifically, I propose that verb paradigms have a dimension whose levels correspond to syntactically distinguishable sentence modalities such as negation, inversion, emphasis, and neutral, and that this dimension is crossed with the morphology dimension differentiating finite from nonfinite forms. The levels of the sentence modality dimension are defined by features introduced by phrase structure rules, lexical entries, and prosodic rules; for example, SENT-MOD = *inv* would be appended to the fronted verb position in the expansion of S shown in Figure 7.2; SENT-MOD = *neg* could be appended to the lexical entry for *not* or to the phrase structure node introducing it. The equation AUX $=_c$ + would now be superfluous for English, but does no harm and would be necessary in other languages where certain phrase structure positions are specific to auxiliaries but not necessarily specific to sentence modalities. The feature value

Figure 7.6

			Neut	Inv	Neg	Emph
a)	walk :					
	MORPH	Fin	walks	–	–	–
		Inf	walk	walk	walk.	walk
b)	can :					
	MORPH	Fin	can	can	can't	can
		Inf	–	–	–	–
c)	do :					
	MORPH	Fin	–	does	doesn't	does
		Inf	–	–	–	–

SENTENCE - MODALITY

neutral could be supplied automatically as the unmarked sentence modality wherever no other sentence modality was defined (see Baker, 1981).[4]

As mentioned, incomplete paradigms for auxiliary verbs may not be filled out by general paradigms. Furthermore, every verb would be constrained to appear only in sentences containing the features corresponding to filled cells in its paradigm (via equations like SENT-MOD $=_c$ *inv, neg, neut*, in their lexical entries). Hence, the prohibition against main verbs appearing in type B constructions (here, the Inv, Neg, and Emph cells), and against *do* appearing in type B constructions, would be a consequence of the unfilled cells in their paradigms, as illustrated in Figure 7.6(a–c); I omit the participle levels and the person, number, and tense dimensions for simplicity's sake. When a speaker wishes to query (via inversion), negate, or emphasize a proposition whose main predicate is not realized as an auxiliary, he or she will have no choice but to use *do* (assuming that the speaker does not want to add surplus meaning to the proposition by using another auxiliary), because matrix clauses must be finite and nonauxiliaries lack finite forms compatible with non-neutral sentence modalities.

Apart from its ability to account for the distribution of auxiliary and main verbs in different sentence modalities and its ability to be stated explicitly using a familiar grammatical formalism, this theory has several other descriptive advantages. It has often been noted that various modals occur in some but not all sentence modalities (e.g., Twadell, 1963). For example, modal *need* and *dare* may not occur in affirmative sentences, emphatic or not, though they may occur in negations and inversions.

(8) (a) *John need go.
    (b) John need not go.
    (c) Need I say more?
    (d) *Yes, I *need* buy a smoke detector!

Since the paradigms in Figure 7.6 list all the sentence modalities a verb can appear in, combinations of permissible modalities other than those actually listed in Figure 7.6 can be represented easily, as the paradigm for modal *need* in Figure 7.7 shows.[5] Modal *better* has still another pattern (see (7); also note the acceptability of *you better go* and *you BETTER go!*). These facts can be handled if *better* has the paradigm shown in Figure 7.8. Finally, in the dialect in which *he didn't used to go* and *did he used*

Figure 7.7

SENTENCE – MODALITY

need:

MORPH

		Neut	Inv	Neg	Emph
	Fin	–	need	need	–
	Inf	–	–	–	–

Figure 7.8

SENTENCE – MODALITY

better:

MORPH

		Neut	Inv	Neg	Emph
	Fin	better	–	better	better
	Inf	–	–	–	–

Figure 7.9

SENTENCE – MODALITY

used to:

MORPH

		Neut	Inv	Neg	Emph
	Fin	used to	–	–	–
	Inf	–	–	–	–

to go? are ungrammatical, *used to* would have a paradigm with yet a different pattern, as shown in Figure 7.9.

In other words, by having each auxiliary listed in its own paradigm with sentence modality and morphology as dimensions, and by prohibiting such paradigms from being filled in productively, the auxiliaries' idiosyncrasies as to which modalities they can appear in can be captured. This is also true for the many idiosyncrasies revealed in the interactions between the morphology of auxiliaries and their sentence modality. For example, the first-person singular present-tense version of *be* is *are* only in negated inversions (e.g., *aren't I/*amn't I/*are I/*I are/*I aren't going*). The contractability of negations varies from auxiliary to auxiliary (e.g., *won't/*willn't; shan't/*shalln't*); and the negation of the meaning of certain modals is often not what the morphologically negated form of those modals actually expresses (e.g., the negation of the meaning of *must* is not expressed by *must not* but by *doesn't have to*). See Gazdar, Pullum, and Sag (1982) for further examples. All of these facts favor the analysis that is needed on independent grounds to handle the distribution of *do*, namely, one in which auxiliaries' privileges of occurrence for combinations of finiteness and sentence modality are spelled out separately for each auxiliary.

The third complication: "do" + auxiliary. The account sketched above can also account for the third of Baker's cases of auxiliary overgeneration: constructions containing *do* plus auxiliary *have* or *be*. (*Do* plus *modal* constructions are independently blocked by the fact that *do* requires an infinitival verb in its complement, and modals lack infinitival forms.)

(9) (a) *John doesn't have left yet.
    (b) *Does John have left yet?
    (c) *John doesn't be running anymore.
    (d) *Does John be running now?

Sentences (9a–d) can be blocked by the paradigms for *have* and *be* shown in Figure 7.10(a–b); there are no available infinitival

Figure 7.10

		SENTENCE – MODALITY			
		Neut	Inv	Neg	Emph
a) have:					
MORPH	Fin	has	has	hasn't	has
	Inf	have	–	–	–
b) be:					
MORPH	Fin	is	is	isn't	is
	Inf	be	–	–	–

forms of *have* and *be* to co-occur with *do*.[6]

To sum up this section: Baker's examples of overgeneration can be handled by a hybrid of his own proposals and the version of LFG I have been using and developing in this book. Specifically, one needs only two assumptions. (1) All verbs, including auxiliary verbs, enter into paradigms with a dimension differentiating infinitival, participial, and finite forms, crossed with a dimension differentiating neutral, inverted, negated, and emphatic sentence modalities. (2) Incomplete paradigms for auxiliary verbs may not be filled in by general paradigms or paradigms for homonymous verbs (nor, I might add, may *any* incomplete paradigm be filled in by virtue of its partial similarity to a pattern found in a word-specific paradigm of an auxiliary verb).

A LEARNING THEORY FOR AUXILIARIES

Given the extended lexical theory of adult competence outlined in the preceding section, surprisingly little need be added to the existing learning mechanisms to account for the acquisition of the English auxiliary system. As mentioned, auxiliaries are treated as complement-taking verbs (specifically, as raising-to-subject verbs), so procedures C1–C4 can learn their proper phrase structure and functional analysis and the constraints they impose on the morphology of their complement verbs as soon as the auxiliaries are recognized to take propositional arguments and as soon as those arguments are recognized to lack syntactically realized subjects. A modal like *can*, for example, takes as its argument the entire proposition whose possibility is being asserted; that proposition appears in the sentence without its subject (since *can* intervenes). *Can* thus triggers procedures C1–C4, just like a raising-to-subject verb, and those procedures acquire *can*'s subcategorization for a V-COMP, control of the missing complement subject by its own subject, and the constraint that the complement verb be infinitival. Similar conditions would lead to the acquisition of entries for *have* and the *be*'s. Furthermore, the paradigms that spell out which verbs have which morphological forms, and which verbs may co-occur with which syntactic realizations of sentence modalities, may be learned via the I-procedures for the acquisition of inflectional paradigms proposed in Chapter 5. Finally, the acquisition of the phrase structure of inverted sentences (see Figure 7.2(a)) can be acquired by the P-procedures outlined in Chapter 3, as I shall illustrate in the second major section ("Inversion of Auxiliaries in *Wh*-Questions") in this chapter.

Thus, unlike what I do in Chapters 3, 5, 6, and 8, I will not propose in this chapter a new set of acquisition procedures for the grammatical phenomena discussed here. The learning theory for auxiliaries basically consists of the claims that children analyze auxiliaries as complement-taking verbs, that they create verb paradigms with sentence modality and morphology as dimensions, and, crucially, that cells in such paradigms for auxiliaries may not be filled in by productive operations based on nonauxiliary paradigms (or on homonymous forms), only by direct positive evidence (and, conversely, that nonauxiliary paradigms may not be filled in by processes generalizing patterns found in auxiliary paradigms). I now need two things to complete the account: (1) a theory of how the child recognizes that a verb is an auxiliary, so that he or she will know not to generalize from its paradigm to those of other verbs or vice versa; (2) a theory of how the child hypothesizes the various features defining the paradigms.

Recognition of "Aux"

Auxiliary verbs must be distinguished from nonauxiliaries by some equation such as AUX = + so that their partial word-specific paradigms will not be productively filled. Steele (1981) and her colleagues have examined auxiliaries in a number of languages and have proposed a universal characterization of them. This characterization specifies that auxiliaries (a) must contain elements expressing tense or modality or both; (b) may express sentence and discourse level notions, such as question, evidential status, emphasis, negation (what I have been calling "sentence modality"), and also aspect and deontic notions and agreement with subject or object; (c) consist of a small, fixed, nonproductive set; (d) occur in specific phrase structure positions, especially the first, second, or last constituent positions; (e) tend to be inflections or elements that may be phonologically reduced by contraction or cliticization (I take this particular summary from Wasow, 1981).

Given the semantic bootstrapping hypothesis of the recognition of grammatical universals defended in Chapter 2, the next step is obvious: I propose that the child probabilistically categorizes an element as an auxiliary if it encodes tense or modality (see (a) above) and if it encodes some combination of sentence modality, aspect, and deontic notions (see (b) above). The more such notions an element encodes, the more likely it will be hypothesized as an auxiliary. The child learns that an element encodes such notions, of course, by attending to relevant features of a sentence's perceptual and discourse context and by hypothesizing paradigms defined by those features using the I-procedures. The discovery of nonidentical cells for levels of the tense, aspect, and sentence modality dimensions then corresponds to an element's "encoding a notion." In addition, phonological reduction (e) and sentence-peripheral position (d), in conjunction with these recognizable semantic features, could also induce the child to posit the AUX feature.

Syntactic conclusions licensed by the recognition of "Aux." According to the bootstrapping hypothesis (Chapter 2), after a child recognizes an element as belonging to a universal syntactic category by virtue of its having a certain semantic property, he or she can predict that it must have or that it is likely to have certain syntactic properties. In the case of elements recognized as being auxiliaries, the child first of all can deduce that the paradigms for such elements may not be productively filled-in (c), as the present account requires. Furthermore, he or she can hypothesize that the sentence-peripheral phrase structure positions that the elements appear in (in English, verb positions) may be specific to just those elements (d). Specifically, I propose that the child would add the equation $AUX =_c +$ to any phrase structure position (i.e., a symbol in the right-hand side of a phrase structure rule) that a recognized auxiliary is found to appear in; if subsequently a nonauxiliary is found to appear in that position, the equation is expunged. Finally, the child will actively hypothesize features like aspect, tense, and modality if they have not yet been acquired for an auxiliary (b); these hypotheses would then be subject to confirmation or disconfirmation according to the I-procedures proposed in Chapter 5.

In other words, once the child recognizes that an element is an auxiliary by virtue of its having recognizable properties from among (a–e), he or she can narrow down the search for the element's other syntactic properties to the remaining properties listed in (a–e).

Hypothesization of Auxiliary-Relevant Paradigm Dimensions

To complete the account of the acquisition of auxiliaries, it is necessary to say a few words about how the dimensions defining auxiliary paradigms themselves are recognized, a step I have taken for granted thus far. Two dimensions are relevant here: the one differentiating finite, infinitival, and participial forms of the verb, and the sentence modality dimension or dimensions differentiating negation, emphasis, inversion, and so on. The semantics of these features are far too complex for me to provide anything like a detailed account of their perceptual bases here (see Steele, 1981); instead I will simply provide brief first approximations to show that the present theory of auxiliary acquisition does not beg the question of how they are recognized.

As for the first feature, what I have been calling MORPH for convenience, I assume that the child is sensitive to the immediate completedness versus ongoing nature versus imminence of an event (see Bickerton, 1981, in press; Kuczaj, 1977; Slobin, 1984a) and eventually to the relative times of occurrence of the utterance of a sentence, the event referred to, and a reference point (Hornstein, 1977b). These notions form the basis for the tense feature and its values *present, past, future,* and so on. As for distinguishing the tense feature values in general from infinitives, I suggest that a verb form whose temporal reference is undefined, or whose temporal reference is conceptually dependent on the temporal reference of another predicate of which it is an argument, could be assigned the feature value *inf*. The participle features could be assigned to any verb form with a special morphology specific to its appearing as a complement to an auxiliary verb (once again, this would have the child making inferences based on prior recognition of the AUX feature); and its specific realizations *prog-part*, *perfpart*, etc., would be taken from the predicate (or other features listed in (a–b) above) of the auxiliary that it is a complement of.

Finally, I propose that the child can infer from a sentence's discourse context the illocutionary force intended by the speaker— that is, whether the proposition expressed in the sentence is being asserted, denied, questioned, exclaimed, emphasized in contrast to a presupposed negation, offered as only a hearsay report, commanded, etc. As a result he or she posits the SENT-MOD feature with values *neut, neg, emph*, and so on. Feature equations of the form SENT-MOD $= x$ are appended to the lexical entries, phrase structure positions, and prosodic templates that are found to express these modalities, and corresponding constraining equations of the form SENT-MOD $=_c x$ define a paradigm dimension for auxiliaries and main verbs.[7] (See Chapter 2 for an explanation of the distinction between defining and constraining equations.)

The proposal that the child posits sentence modality features corresponding to contextually induced semantic and pragmatic features leaves it somewhat mysterious why the child would posit the formal feature *inverted* rather than something like *interrogative*, which would be closer to the pragmatic feature that the child is perceiving. One possibility is that the child is innately prepared to look specifically for verb inversion in the input. He or she would learn the verb position for neutral sentences, and if an interrogative sentence with its verb in initial position was then encountered, the equation SENT-MOD $= inv$ would be appended to the initial verb position, and a paradigm level corresponding to the equation SENT-MOD $=_c inv$ would be added to the verb's paradigms. Though the feature is initially learned for the interrogative sentence modality (that is the only way that preschool children use inversion), the feature could then be extended to other inverted constructions, involving negative polarity, exclamation, comparatives, *so*, and the like, via some combination of structure-dependent distributional analysis of the input and generalization along the semantic continuum that may relate all the uses of inversion (see Steele, 1981; and n. 4). This account is motivated by the fact that inversion is a common means of encoding the interrogative modality across languages (Chomsky, 1975; Greenberg, 1963; Steele, 1981). An alternative account would have inversion be part of a more general class of rearrangements of constituents of the root sentence signaling non-neutral sentence modalities (Emonds, 1976). On this account, the child would attend to differences in the positions of phrases in neutral versus non-neutral root sentence expansions, and append an equation for a particular sentence modality to the relevant alternative phrase structure position in the rule expanding S. As before, a constraining version of this equation would define a paradigm level for the element occupying that position. (I return to this learning process later in this chapter.)

As I have stressed, there is no doubt that many refinements will be needed for the preceding account of the acquisition of tense and sentence modality features. Nonetheless, all that is required is that *some* account along these lines be plausible. If so, the rest of the theory for the acquisition of auxiliaries, depending as it does on the creation of the proper paradigms, would seen viable.

Developmental Evidence

In this section I consider several aspects of the theory of the acquisition of auxiliaries sketched above and examine evidence on the development of auxiliaries in English-speaking children relevant to evaluating it. The theory has three key features, so the discussion of auxiliary acquisition will be divided into three parts: similarities between the acquisition of auxiliaries and of nonauxiliary complement-taking verbs; conservatism in the use of auxiliaries in different morphological forms; and conservatism in the use of auxiliaries in different sentence modalities.

Before discussing the developmental evidence, however, I would like to make a methodological point. The English auxiliary system is complex, with scores of different types of errors that children can make. Often the literature will contain reports of small numbers of errors of a particular type. Some writers will draw theoretical conclusions from the existence of an error (e.g., Mayer, Erreich, and Valian, 1978; Prideaux, 1976; Menyuk, 1969; MacWhinney, 1982; Hurford, 1975), while other writers draw very different conclusions from the rarity of an error (e.g., Maratsos and Kuczaj, 1978; Baker, 1981), sometimes referring to the very same data. There are dangers with both sorts of conclusions: an isolated error may reflect a slip of the tongue or an idiosyncratic conclusion reached by a creative or metalinguistically precocious child; the rarity of an error may simply reflect a rarity of opportunities for the child to utter the form or for an observer to notice it. If progress is to be made, researchers must summarize the data far less glibly.

I try to take a step in that direction in the discussion to follow by citing the actual examples found of any error pattern that is brought to bear on the hypotheses, examining a large number of studies and data on auxiliary development, and citing *experimental* studies of auxiliary development when such studies exist (all too rarely, alas). The sources I have examined, nonetheless, seem comprehensive enough for one to make reasonable tentative summaries. They include the spontaneous speech (catalogued by sentence type) of Adam (twenty-three samples) and Eve (sixteen samples); Brown's (n.d.) grammars for Adam, Eve, and Sarah at each of five linguistic stages, including stages not included in the categorized samples listed above; examples of errors cited by Menyuk (1969), Hurford (1975), Mayer, Erreich, and Valian (1978), Erreich, Valian, and Winzemer (1980), Kuczaj (1976), Maratsos and Kuczaj (1978), Wells (1979), Bloom, Lightbown, and Hood (1975), and Fletcher (1979); and the results of Major's (1974) experiment eliciting a variety of auxiliary forms from children. When I say that a potential error has not been reported, it will mean that I was unable to find instances from any of these sources; the size of that data base will also allow me to consider an error as basically nonexistent if I find (say) only a single attested instance despite frequent opportunities for it to appear. Finally, I will not count contracted auxiliaries (e.g., *he's, I'll, it's*) as auxiliaries at all, since there is abundant evidence (Brown, 1973; Kuczaj, 1976; MacWhinney, 1982) that many children simply fail to segment these contractions into pronouns plus auxiliaries and use them as pure pronouns.

Auxiliaries as Complement-Taking Verbs

Since the core of the present account is that auxiliaries are similar to raising-to-subject verbs and acquired by mechanisms designed to acquire verbs of functional control in general (i.e., those proposed in Chapter 6), it would be reassuring (though not, of course, conclusive) to discover that they followed similar developmental courses. This seems to be true. As mentioned in Chapter 6, the first auxiliaries appear in children's speech at about the same time as complement-taking verbs such as *want* and *try*—that is, subsequent to the mastery of simple constructions involving subject, verb, and object in Stage II or in the third year. Wells (1979), for example, reports that there is a set of five auxiliaries that were each used by more than half of the twenty-eight children in his sample before the third birthday. Furthermore, many of the developmental patterns are similar. Children never misorder a verb of functional control and its complement (e.g., *I leave wanna*), nor do they misorder an auxiliary and its main verb as in, e.g., *I go can't* (Slobin, 1973; Maratsos and Kuczaj, 1978; see also Kuczaj and Maratsos, 1975, for experimental evidence bolstering this conclusion). There are no reports of children using a subject of an auxiliary verb which did not also express the subject argument of its complement (e.g., *he can't see*, where *he* refers to the object of *see*), just as in the case of functional control verbs (see Chapter 6). Finally, children show certain errors in their ability to coordinate the choice of auxiliary and the morphology of its complement that can be explained quite naturally on the assumption that auxiliaries are complement-taking verbs. Since these errors have received considerable attention in the literature, entering into the debate over whether language acquisition is best characterized as a process of hypothesizing components of grammatical transformations, I will examine them in some detail.

Overtensing errors. Hurford (1975), Fay (1978), and Mayer, Erreich, and Valian (1978) have noted that children make errors such as those in (10), in which an auxiliary appears together with a tensed verb rather than an infinitive or participle, as mandated by (5a–e).

(10) (a) Does it rolls?
     (b) What are you did?
     (c) Can you broke those?
     (d) I did fell when I got blood.
     (e) What's that is?

These authors have taken these errors as evidence of defective acquisition of grammatical transformations, arguing as follows. Adult movement transformations decompose into two "basic operations," one copying an element to a new position, and the second deleting the original occurrence of the element. Children at first hypothesize incomplete versions of one or more of the following adult transformations: (a) the transformation that "inverts" the auxiliary, placing it to the left of the subject noun phrase for a question (Hurford, 1975; Mayer, Erreich, and Valian, 1978); (b) the transformation that moves the auxiliary to the left of a negation element of a negated declarative (Fay, 1978); or (c) the transformation that hops an affix or TENSE element onto the end of a following word (Mayer, Erreich, and Valian, 1978).

Specifically, children are claimed to have acquired the copying part of the transformation but not the deletion part. As a result, their transformation leaves two identical elements in different places in the sentence. In the case of, say, (10a), the element is the present-tense feature which marks the main verb *roll* as *rolls* in its sentence-medial occurrence, and which, after being copied into sentence-initial position by an auxiliary-copying (rather than movement) operation, is transformed into *does* by a *do*-support transformation. Similarly, in (10d) the tense element is left behind in preverbal position by a tense-copying (rather than hopping) operation, then supported by *do* (Mayer et al., 1978). In (10e) the auxiliary *be* together with its accompanying auxiliary TENSE element is copied (rather than moved) before the subject (Hurford, 1975).

As Kuczaj (1976), Maratsos and Kuczaj (1978), Prideaux (1976), and Goodluck and Solan (1979) point out, "aux-copying" analyses have many problems. First, they predict other copy-without-deletion errors that do not occur, such as *he ising leaving*. Hurford's and Fay's versions fail to account for the fact that overtensing occurs in declaratives (e.g., (10d)), where no auxiliary movement takes place, or in sentences where an overt auxiliary occurs in sentence-initial position with only a tensed verb in medial position (e.g., (10c)). Purported examples of copied *be* (e.g., (10e)) are better explained as segmentation errors, given the frequency of errors such as *that's what's the witch says to her brother* (Kuczaj, 1976). Often the tense of the auxiliary and the tense of the main verb are different, belying a "copying" analysis (e.g., *it didn't has any*; Kuczaj, 1976). Many children do not ever make overtensing errors or make them very rarely; no child invariably makes them (see Maratsos and Kuczaj, 1978; in the samples I have examined, for example, Adam made only two such errors and Eve made only one). Finally, the adult models on which the analysis are based are suspect: Fay's analysis of the deep structures and transformations subserving negation are linguistically unmotivated (Maratsos and Kuczaj, 1978); most current theories of transformational grammar treat movement as a primitive operation, not as a concatenation of copying and deletion (e.g., Chomsky, 1981); the affix-hopping transformation upon which Mayer et al.'s analysis is based is incompatible with many formal properties of commonly held grammatical theories (Gazdar, Pullum, and Sag, 1982).

It is fortunate for the present theory that the empirical facts speak against the auxiliary-copying hypothesis, since if it had stood up to critical scrutiny the hypothesis would severely challenge the theory. The hypothesis, of course, invokes a class of mechanisms that the theory disallows. But even if that were not true, the hypothesis attributes a rule to the child that he or she would have no occasion to hypothesize on the basis of the evidence available to him or her: all the parental inputs exemplify auxiliary movement and tense hopping, and none exemplify auxiliary copying or tense copying. In the same vein, it is unclear how the child would give up his or her copying analysis (barring negative evidence) rather than keeping both copying *and* movement in the grammar.[8] Since the theory holds that the child does not take arbitrary sidesteps on the tortuous path to adult competence, it is comforting that the account is implausible on narrow empirical grounds. In the next few paragraphs, I show how the complementation theory of auxiliary acquisition can handle the same data without having to posit unmotivated descriptions of the child's abilities.

As mentioned, co-occurrence restrictions between an auxiliary and its complement verb are enforced by equations such as V-COMP's MORPH $=_c$ *inf* appended to the lexical entries of auxiliary verbs. Overtensing errors such as those listed in (10) are simply violations of these restrictions. Furthermore, auxiliaries are special cases of complement-taking verbs subject to functional control, and the constraining equations enforcing their co-occurrence restrictions are identical to those used by standard f-control verbs. Hence the theory predicts that children's mistaken marking of complement verbs should extend to complements of standard f-control verbs as well as to complements of auxiliaries. This prediction is strongly confirmed, as shown in (11).

(11) (a) going being careful (J. Sachs, cited in Erreich, Valian, and Winzemer, 1980)
   (b) Daddy's going taking nap (J. Sachs, cited in Erreich, Valian, and Winzemer, 1980)
   (c) We've got to pasting (Menyuk, 1969)
   (d) Next year, I'd like to bowling (Menyuk, 1969)
   (e) Make it walks (Adam, Sample 19)
   (f) She gonna fell out (Adam, Sample 21)
   (g) D'you wan'me fell in them? (Adam, Sample 21)
   (h) It's gonna falling near Paul (Adam, Sample 21)
   (i) Lemme sleeps (Adam, Sample 19)
   (j) I can let it spilled (Adam, Sample 19, said twice)
   (k) Mommy, d'you wan'me kick you down and broke your crown? (Adam, Sample 22)
   (l) Fraser go sitting in that chair (Eve, Sample 12)

(m) I gonna saw it (Maratsos and Kuczaj, 1978)

(n) Then I'm going to sit on him and made him broken (Bowerman, 1982b)

Six of these examples involve the use of a participle rather than an infinitive (which is also an error made with auxiliaries: Eve said *you will gone away* in her eighteenth sample); the remaining eight involve the use of a tensed form. The number of examples may seem small, but it is greater than the total number of auxiliary overmarking errors found in the literature plus Brown's samples with auxiliaries other than *do*. (The greater frequency of errors with *do* will be discussed later.) Thus we have evidence that overtensing with auxiliaries is part of a larger pattern whereby children fail to apply a constraining equation (e.g., V-COMP's MORPH $=_c$ *inf*) that should be appended to a complement-taking verb.

Why should such constraints fail to be enforced? Given that the children seemed to treat the constructions as verb-complement structures (i.e., the children who made the errors placed the auxiliary and main verb in their correct positions, and the elements of their utterances seemed to be composed in a semantically appropriate way given their contexts), the co-occurrence errors could have come about for three reasons: (a) the morphology of the particular embedded verb was not identified correctly as signifying an infinitive, participle, etc.; (b) the constraining equation failed to be applied in the production of the sentence for performance reasons; or (c) the constraining equation was not learned to begin with. By examining the factors affecting the frequency of overtensing errors, it is possible to argue that (a), (b), and (c) all help to explain why the errors occur.

Maratsos and Kuczaj (1978) point out that the majority of errors like those shown in (10) occur when the complement verb has an irregular tensed form. That is, errors of the form *did I broke it?* are more common than those of the form *did I fixed it?*[9] This is also true of the errors with nonauxiliary verbs: five of the examples cited in (11) involve irregular pasts, and one more involves a regular present form of a verb whose past is irregular. Presumably this is because verbs like *broke* are not analyzed as *break* + *past tense* at this stage; that is, the child has not entered *broke* into the correct past-tense cell of a paradigm for *break*. This hypothesis is supported by Kuczaj's (1981) observations of inflected irregular forms like *broked* and *wenting* and by the standard overregularizations such as *breaked* if the Unique Entry principle holds (as argued in Chapter 5). Of course, if *broke* does not contribute a *fin* feature value to the complement it appears in but instead contributes an *inf* feature value, the equation V-COMP's MORPH $=_c$ *inf* forbidding the complement to define any tense will not rule out *broke* in the complement, and the child will not be prevented from selecting that word as he or she speaks. However, this cannot be the whole story, since overtensing errors also occur, though less often, with regular tensed forms (e.g., *does it opens?* in Adam's twenty-second sample; *did you turned it?* in Eve's fifth sample).

A second interesting fact about overtensing errors is that they occur far more frequently (though not exclusively) in questions and negations than in simple declaratives (Maratsos and Kuczaj, 1978). That is, errors like *can you broke those?* and *you can not broke those* are more frequent than errors like *you can broke those*. This supports Maratsos and Kuczaj's hypothesis that transient "slip of the tongue" errors, independent of the child's linguistic knowledge, are in part responsible for overtensing errors. Further support for this possibility comes from the fact that adults occasionally make such errors in their speech (Merrill Garrett, personal communication; Stemberger, 1982).[10] In the sentence production model accompanying LFG (see Ford, 1982; Ford, Bresnan, and Kaplan, 1982), before a verb is uttered, its lexical entry is activated, and the equations in the entry are kept active in an "f-description" with which all subsequent word and rule choices must be consistent. Since this is a short-term memory representation, it is reasonable to suppose that information in it begins to decay as soon as it is activated (Anderson, 1976). The longer the interval between activating the equation and using it to constrain a word choice, or the more other concurrent tasks must be processed, the more likely it is that the equation will have decayed by the time the word choice must be made. A noun phrase or negation element interposed between the auxiliary and the complement verb may have just that effect; the equation V-COMP's MORPH $=_c$ *inf* may be inaccessible by the time the embedded verb is chosen and so nothing may prevent a tensed form from being chosen. This account is consistent with the notion that sentence processing is in part capacity-limited (Wanner and Maratsos, 1978; Kaplan, 1974, 1975; Ford, 1983), and with the general observation that the frequency of speech errors is affected by the number of words intervening between the two elements entering into the error (Garrett, 1980). Similarly, it is consistent with Mulford and Morgan's finding (1983) that gender errors in Icelandic children's and adults' speech are more likely when the element coreferential with the incorrect form is separated from it by a greater amount of intervening material. Note that since these accounts attribute children's errors to the failure to apply a rule, rather than an incorrect rule, explaining children's recovery from the errors poses no problem. The errors will disappear as soon as the impediments to the application of the rule are lifted (in this case, the inflectional analysis of irregular verbs and the growth of processing capacity).

Why are there so many overtensing errors with "do"? The final observation relevant to this discussion is that overtensing errors occur far more often with a *do* form as the auxiliary than with other auxiliaries such as *be* or the modals. In fact, the number of *do* errors dwarfs the number of errors with other auxiliaries and with nonauxiliary complement-taking verbs.[11] Since both *do* and the other auxiliaries appear with complement verbs with either regular or irregular tensed forms, and since both types appear in the same position in questions and the same position in negations, neither of the accounts presented above can account for this difference.

Given these facts, the difference between *do* and other auxiliaries may be traced to the different degree of strength or accessibility of the constraining equation V-COMP's MORPH $=_c$ *inf* appended to *do* versus the other auxiliaries (I say "accessibility" rather than "presence" since no child makes overtensing errors anywhere near 100 percent of the time). Something about *do* makes the constraining equation particularly hard to consolidate into the lexical entry.

One possibility, proposed in Pinker (in press, a), is that the left-to-right nature of sentence processing affects both the comprehension process *and* the acquisition process. *Do*, unlike other modals, never appears adjacent to its complement verb (except for the relatively infrequent emphatic construction such as *I DID eat it!*). Procedure C4 (which coins constraining equations) must keep the lexical entry for the auxiliary "open" or activated while it waits for the complement verb, which appears later in the sentence. When the procedure finds the verb, it then must analyze it so that it can complete the equation V-COMP's MORPH $=_c \alpha$. If the open lexical entry, or the as-yet-uncompleted constraining equation, decays before the verb is found, nothing can be added to the entry. The more often this occurs, the less often the equation will be strengthened and the weaker the equation will be. For auxiliaries other than *do*, part of the time the auxiliary will be adjacent to the main verb (and hence will still probably be active when the complement verb is analyzed), and part of the time it will be fronted or separated by a negation element (and hence will be more decayed when the verb is found). *Do*, however, *only* appears in the more decay-prone fronted position, and so its constraining equation will not reach criterion strength as quickly even if the total number of input exemplars is the same as for other auxiliaries. With a weaker equation in its entry, tensed forms are less likely to be ruled out during sentence production, and overtensing errors will be more likely. A similar account will explain Slobin's observation (1973) that in many languages discontinuous elements that constrain each other are acquired slowly. However, there is a slight difference between Slobin's examples and the present one. Thanks to the contrast between the frequency of overtensing errors with modals and with *do*, this is one of the few cases in which one can attribute the "discontinuous morpheme effect" to difficulties in acquisition, rather than to difficulties in speech production.

Unfortunately, two plausibility arguments weaken this proposal. First, it is hard to believe that a single interposed morpheme, and a monosyllabic or subsyllabic one at that (e.g., *I don't like her, d'you like her?*), would add enough of a delay or increase in processing load to interfere with the recording of co-occurrence restrictions to such a degree that there would be so massive an asymmetry of errors with *do* versus errors with modals. Second, Newport, Gleitman, and Gleitman (1977) found that the more that parents used yes-no questions when speaking to a child, the faster the child increased the use of auxiliaries in her own speech—even though most such uses by the child were in declaratives rather than questions. (Newport et al. demonstrated that this conclusion holds even with the child's age and initial usage of auxiliaries partialed out.) Newport et al. point out that in English yes-no questions, an auxiliary is obligatory in the perceptually salient sentence-initial position, possibly making auxiliaries easier for the child to attend to, in turn facilitating auxiliary acquisition. Though the finding bears only indirectly on the account sketched in the previous paragraph, it does suggest that input frequency in the fronted rather than medial position is the crucial variable for auxiliary acquisition per se, and thus that the failure of *do* to appear adjacent to its complement should be balanced or outweighed by its greater salience whenever it appears in the sentence-initial position.

An alternative and intuitively more plausible account of the *do* effect follows from an examination of the input conditions for the C-procedures that acquire auxiliaries and their co-occurrence restrictions. The procedures for the acquisition of complement-taking verbs are triggered by the following condition: "a predicate takes an argument which is itself a complete proposition, and that proposition is represented in the input tree without its subject" (see Chapter 6). Clearly, from the child's point of view, a sentence with auxiliary *do* cannot be characterized as such: *do* has no predicate of which the proposition expressed in the sentence is an argument; rather, *do* is a meaningless verb carrying features for tense and sentence modality. (For an adult, *do* has the harmless entry PRED = "*do* (V-COMP)" according to LFG, but of course it does no semantic work.) Thus the child may not recognize that sentences with *do* are verb-complement structures, since they do not fulfill the necessary semantic requirements. To add to the child's confusion, the frequency of *do* in inverted position also vitiates a second clue for complementation and control in many input sentences: the absence of an overt subject for the complement verb. Thus the child may parse input sentences with *do* as in Figure 7.11(b) rather than as in 7.11(a).

Figure 7.11

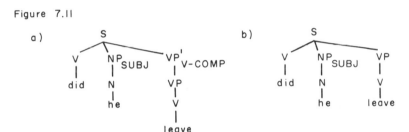

The relevance of the meaninglessness of *do* is as follows. In the proposed theory, the child learns complement co-occurrence restrictions not by correlating every property in a sentence with every other property (see Chapter 2), but by applying the specific procedure C4 when it is appropriately triggered. If, as I have suggested, C4 is ordinarily triggered by the semantics of complementation and hence is not easily triggered in the case of *do*, the child will not examine the morphology of the verb and append an equation to *do* constraining it to be that way. With less of a chance of that *do* will be recognized as a complement-taking verb, and hence less of a chance that the equation V-COMP's MORPH $=_c$ *inf* will be appended to it, there will be a greater likelihood that *do* will be used with a tensed verb.

To provide independent motivation for the hypothesis that the child treats *do* as lacking a PRED = "do (V-COMP)" semantic representation, we need to find some other grammatical consequence of the absence of PRED, and show that there is evidence for that consequence in children's speech. Kaplan and Bresnan (1982), in discussing the ability of LFG phrase structure rules to overgenerate sentences with auxiliary verbs in inverted and medial positions, point out that "the f-description for (*is a girl is handing the baby a toy?*) is inconsistent because the separately instantiated semantic forms for *is* are both assigned as its PRED." In other words, a matrix sentence may have only one predicate; if the fronted V position in the rule expanding S is filled by a verb, the matrix VP position must not be filled because it would define a second conflicting predicate. Thus if *do* is often predicateless for the child, one would expect to find cases of children using fronted *do* in questions containing filled VPs, i.e., having the structure of Figure 7.11(b). Though I have found nothing that could be interpreted as such in children's spontaneous speech, there are relevant data from an experiment by Major (1974). Major subjected children to a task in which they had to convert declarative sentences with modal auxiliaries into yes-no questions. She found thirty-six instances of children forming questions with *do* and a modal, e.g., *do you must eat spinach?* These are prima facie cases of the child filling both tensed V positions in the matrix clause, one with *do,* the other with a modal. Since children never had to question sentences lacking auxiliaries, these errors cannot be explained away as consequences of the child's mindlessly falling into the habit of forming questions with *do* in the task. Furthermore, children *never* made errors of the form *you don't must eat spinach* in a comparable task requiring them to convert affirmative declarative sentences into negative declarative sentences. Thus the errors in question cannot simply be yet another manifestation of the phenomenon being explained, namely, children ignoring co-occurrence restrictions imposed by *do,* since that would predict the occurrence of such *don't + modal* errors (just as children overtense both in negations and in questions). Further evidence that the modal is in the matrix VP clause and not the VP' complement is the fact that I have found no instances of children using modals in nonauxiliary complements (e.g., *I want to can go*[12]).

To recapitulate the argument concerning the frequency of overtensing errors with *do:* co-occurrence restrictions are acquired by a procedure triggered by the recognition of a predicate taking a propositional argument lacking its subject. *Do* lacks such a predicate, hence is less likely to trigger those procedures, hence lacks the equation expressing the co-occurrence restrictions. Independent evidence for *do* lacking a predicate in the child's grammar is its appearance in inverted questions (but not negations) containing modals: such a construction is ruled out in the adult grammar by the PRED entry of the inverted auxiliary.[13]

With the frequency of *do* in overtensing errors accounted for (and I know of no other account in the literature), we have a coherent theory of overtensing errors in general. The theory, which follows from the analysis of auxiliaries as complement-taking verbs, accounts for the genesis of and recovery from such errors, the absence of certain other types of errors (e.g., stranded inflections, which one would not expect if overtensing errors result from the failure to learn or apply a co-occurrence restriction), the distribution of the errors that do occur, and the existence of parallel errors in which no auxiliary is involved.[14] The ability to account for overtensing errors thus eliminates the challenge posed to the theory whereby a developmental phenomenon at first glance seemed to exemplify a useless sidestep in language learning, and a sidestep that seemed to call for a transformational explanation at that.

This discussion of overtensing errors was a digression (though an important one, given previous claims) from the examination of developmental data relevant to the proposed theory of auxiliary acquisition. I now return to that examination by briefly considering two remaining developmental corollaries of the theory: conservative acquisition of auxiliary morphology, and conservative acquisition of auxiliaries' privileges of occurrence with various sentence modalities.

Inflection of Auxiliaries

The theory I have been defending holds that the inflectional paradigm for any element recognized as an auxiliary must be filled in cell by cell as each cell is exemplified in the input; no general paradigms may productively complete a partial auxiliary paradigm. This prediction is strongly confirmed: I have found no instances of Modal + *ed* (e.g., *canned*), Modal + *ing* (*canning*), Modal + *s* (*cans*), Modal + *en* (*cannen* or *shoulden* or *mighten*), *to* Modal (e.g., *to can*, though see n.12), perfect *have* + *en* (*I have had gone* or *I have haven gone* or *I have haved gone*), perfect *have* + *ing* (*I am having gone*), or progressive *be* + *ing* (*I am being going*).[15] This is true despite the fact that children are notorious overregularizers, saying *goed*, *wented*, *chasen*, *haved* (possessive), and so on with abandon (see Chapter 5; Ervin, 1964).

The account simultaneously predicts that children should not make the sorts of ordering and co-occurrence errors with auxiliaries that the defective paradigm hypothesis rules out—for example, Modal + Modal, *have* + Modal, *be* + Modal, *be* + *have* (perfect), *be* + *be* (progressive), *do* + *auxiliary, auxiliary* + *do*, and so on. Again, there are virtually no reports of such errors in children's spontaneous speech, and I have found no examples in the samples available to me. In fact, several authors have claimed explicitly that such errors are nonexistent (e.g., Slobin, 1973; Maratsos and Kuczaj, 1978).[16]

Possible systematic counterexamples: experimental evidence. In Major's (1974) experiment, children did make many auxiliary combination errors (though in no case did such errors constitute the majority of responses). The vast majority of the errors consisted of using an inverted auxiliary together with a modal in main verb position. As I have argued in several places in this chapter, such errors seem best analyzed as redundant expansions of the initial and medial verb positions, rather than as verb and verb-complement constructions disobeying co-occurrence restrictions, since the errors did not occur in the negation or imitation tasks and were most likely to occur when the task forced the child to form questions with noninvertible or rarely inverted modals such as *might, ought, better,* and *must.* Three additional instances of auxiliary combination errors consisted of contracted *have* co-occurring with uncontracted *have* (see n. 15). Examples of uncontracted declarative auxiliary combination errors also occurred when strict compliance with the task would have called for the child to utter ungrammatical sentences. Given the possibility that in such cases the child tossed out his or her best guess as to how to say the sentence even if that guess was not countenanced by the child's grammar, and given the rarity of declarative auxiliary combination errors altogether (about 10 instances out of 1,600 opportunities in Major's experiment), it seems wisest not to make too much of these errors, pending further experimentation.[17]

Auxiliary inflection errors and auxiliary combination errors, then, are virtually absent from children's spontaneous speech, and (aside from questions with a surplus auxiliary in inverted position when the simple inverted form would be ungrammatical), auxiliary combination errors can be elicited in experimental situations only rarely and in special cases. Therefore I tentatively conclude that the child is conservative in filling the paradigm cells corresponding to different inflectional forms of auxiliary verbs. This supports the acquisition theory proposed by Baker (1981) and developed in this chapter.

Use of Auxiliaries in Different Sentence Modalities

My account of auxiliary structure focuses on two paradigm dimensions: the "morphology" dimension distinguishing tensed from infinitival from participial forms, and the sentence modality dimension. I predicted that the child should be conservative in filling in the cells defined by both dimensions. In the previous section I examined children's conservatism with respect to the former dimension; here I examine children's conservatism with respect to sentence modalities.

Conservatism in inversion. The first testable prediction is that children should never invert verbs that they do not hear in inverted position. This prediction is strikingly confirmed. First, children virtually *never* invert nonauxiliary verbs. From the thousands of utterances that I and others have examined, the only examples I could find are *goes paci*[fier] *in mouth?* (J. Sachs, cited by Erreich, Valian, and Winzemer, 1980), *where's going to be the school?* (Menyuk, 1969), and *where goes the wheel?* (which the child immediately followed with *where the wheel do go?* and *where does the wheel goes?*—Menyuk, 1969).[18]

Children's reluctance to invert words that they have not heard in inverted position extends even to modals and quasi-modals like *better* that are semantically and (apart from noninvertibility) distributionally similar to standard modals (e.g., *you better not pout*). Kuczaj and Maratsos (1979) report that their intensively studied subject never inverted modal *better* (e.g., **better you go?*), despite his inverting the semantically similar *should*. Likewise, *gotta* and *hafta*, which are semantically eligible to be modals but are not in English, are also never inverted. Major (1974) obtained the same result experimentally: not a single child from her sample of forty-four ever inverted *better* or *d'rather* when told to ask questions corresponding to *he'd better go home now* or *he'd rather be a dog.*

Finally, children are often unwilling to invert auxiliaries that are invertible in the adult grammar. This occurs most notably for auxiliaries that invert in formal but not conversational speech (e.g., *might Mary go?, may he play today?, ought Sam to eat?, shall Jim leave?*). Major found that none of her subjects ever inverted *might, ought to,* modal *dare,* or modal *need* when the task demanded that they form questions with them, and that *must, may,* and *shall* were inverted only by a small minority. At the same time they freely inverted *can, will, would,* and so on. Non-inversion of certain invertible auxiliaries at the same time that other auxiliaries are inverted can also be seen in children's spontaneous speech with more common auxiliaries. Kuczaj and Maratsos (1979) report that their subject used *could* and *would* only in declaratives, using *can* and *will* instead for the corresponding inverted questions. Fletcher (1979) reports that his subject used *willn't* and *can't* only in declaratives while freely inverting *can* and *will*. Brown (n.d.) reports that Adam inverted only *be* in Stage IV, and almost invariably inverted *do* in Stage V while failing to invert other auxiliaries, including *doesn't*.

Conservatism in negation. There is also evidence for conservatism in the use of auxiliaries with sentence modalities other than inversion. I have found no examples or reports of examples of children negating a main verb as they would an auxiliary (e.g., **I ate not the cracker*). Major found various age groups reluctant to negate *shall, may, might, ought to, done,* and *need* when required to do so in the task; at the same time they imitated these auxiliaries in declaratives easily, and negated other auxiliaries easily.

Conservatism in the neutral sentence modality. There is also some evidence for avoidance of the use of an auxiliary in the neutral sentence modality: Fletcher (1979) describes a child who used *shall* in inverted questions only, never in declaratives; and Brown (n.d.) reports that Adam frequently used *don't* and *can't* in Stage III without ever using *do* or *can*.

Unfortunately, there is one possible exception to children's conservatism in using verbs only in the sentence modalities that they have heard them in. According to the present analysis, *do* is ruled out in neutral sentence modalities (e.g., *I did go*) because there is no entry in its paradigm cell defined by finite morphology and the neutral sentence modality. There is no such entry because the child, filling cells as they are attested in the input, never hears *do* in the neutral sentence modality. By the same logic that led to the predictions that children should not invert or directly negate nonauxiliaries, one must predict that children should not use *do* in the neutral sentence modality. Here are the counterexamples I have found:

(12) (a) I did broke it (Mayer, Erreich, and Valian, 1978)
      (b) Jenni did left with Daddy (Erreich, Valian, and Winzemer, 1980)
      (c) I did rode my bike (Erreich, Valian, and Winzemer, 1980)
      (d) He's do take his, take his clean pants off (Kuczaj, 1976)
      (e) I did read that motor boat book (Menyuk, 1969)
      (f) You did hurt me (Fletcher, 1979)
      (g) Lisa did hurt me (Fletcher, 1979)
      (h) My balloon did pop (Fletcher, 1979)

(i) I do got (Adam, Sample 6)
(j) I do wash hands (Adam, Sample 11)
(k) I did see it (Adam, Sample 16)
(l) I did catch him (Adam, Sample 19)
(m) What you did eat? (Kuczaj, 1976)
(n) Where the wheel do go? (Menyuk, 1969)
(o) Oh no, they do fly? (Adam, Sample 11)

What should one make of these sentences? Some may have been intended as emphatic constructions whose stressed intonation was not recorded in the transcripts, but it is unlikely that this happened in all these cases, and it certainly did not occur in the last three. There are enough recorded instances that one cannot dismiss the phenomenon, yet there are also more opportunities for this error to occur than for almost any other error: whenever the child utters a nonemphatic affirmative declarative sentence. Perhaps one should be surprised instead by how *rare* the error is, given the number of opportunities for it to occur and the seductiveness of the generalization that would produce it. (That is, if negations are formed with *do not,* and questions with inverted *do,* and emphatic sentences with stressed *do,* why shouldn't neutral sentences contain noninverted, unstressed, non-negated *do?*)

If one were to try to account for these errors, one might suggest that *Neutral* is the unmarked sentence modality—that is, any verb whose SENT-MOD feature is absent (e.g., because it has decayed or is inaccessible) is automatically assumed to permit the neutral sentence modality. This might be the case for *do* at certain points in development, but as the modality features for *do* become stronger, it will no longer lack such a feature, and the unmarked convention will never apply to it. Alternatively, one might suggest that certain children might occasionally be oblivious to the emphatic nature of an affirmative declarative input with *do,* mistakenly interpreting the input as having the neutral modality. In the absence of evidence for or against these conjectures, and given the uncertainty as to whether (12a–o) represents an error pattern sufficiently widespread to try to account for, I choose to leave the question open at present. Neutral *do* thus stands as a possible counterexample to the theory, but no more than that.

Inversion of Auxiliaries in Wh-Questions

I conclude this chapter with a discussion of an aspect of the English auxiliary system that children are known to have trouble with. As Bellugi (1965) has documented, children frequently fail to invert subject and auxiliary in *wh*-questions, producing sentences like *what he can ride in?* (see also Brown 1968; Labov and Labov, 1978; Kuczaj and Brannick, 1979; Erreich, 1980; Tyack and Ingram, 1979; also Slobin, 1984a, who reports that noninversion also occurs in the speech of children learning German). The problem is not that children lack inversion altogether, because the same children who produce these errors can invert in yes-no questions.

As in the case of auxiliary overmarking, this error pattern may be seen as evidence for viewing language acquisition as the accretion of transformations. Perhaps children at that age have mastered both the transformation that fronts the *wh*-word and the transformation that inverts the subject and auxiliary. Though these children can apply each transformation singly, together the transformations may tax a child's processing capacity and so only *wh*-fronting is applied in *wh*-questions. Yes-no questions do not require *wh*-movement; hence there is enough capacity left to apply inversion (Bellugi, 1965). Further support for such an account is the finding that noninversion errors are even more frequent in negated questions (Bellugi, 1971), which were thought to involve yet another transformation, one that is specific to the negation element.

Since such syntactic transformations are not available to the present theory for use in describing children's abilities, it is fortunate that there are arguments against the transformational account of noninversion. First, the account predicts that children should also occasionally apply subject-auxiliary inversion while neglecting to apply *wh*-movement, leading to some echo questions such as *can she see what?*; however, such constructions are extremely rare in children's speech (Brown, 1968). Second, there is evidence that if grammatical transformations are applied during sentence comprehension and production, they do not in general consume processing capacity (Fodor, Bever, and Garrett, 1974; Berwick and Weinberg, 1983). In any case, later I will review developmental evidence that is inconsistent with the transformational account.

In the next section I propose a theory for the acquisition of inversion in *wh*-questions and similar constructions in other languages, and show how it accounts for noninversion in children and the circumstances in which it is likely to occur. However, since there is at present no LFG description of the distribution of inversion and *wh*-words in the adult grammar, I must begin by proposing such a description.

A GRAMMAR FOR INVERSION IN WH-QUESTIONS

Near-Independence of Inversion and Wh-Words

The most striking fact about inversion and *wh*-questions in English is that they are almost, but not quite, independent of one another (Grimshaw, 1977; 1979b). Consider the sixteen possible sentences defined by the orthogonal combination of *wh*-word present or absent, subject-auxiliary versus auxiliary-subject order, matrix versus embedded clause, and question versus non-question sentence modality:

(13) (a) She can sing (*wh* absent, noninverted, matrix, nonquestion)
  (b) She can sing? (*wh* absent, noninverted, matrix, question)
  (c) I know she can sing (*wh* absent, noninverted, embedded, nonquestion)
  (d) I wonder if she can sing (*wh* absent, noninverted, embedded, question)
  (e) Can she sing! (*wh* absent, inverted, matrix, nonquestion)
  (f) Can she sing? (*wh* absent, inverted, matrix, question)
  (g) *I know can she sing (*wh* absent, inverted, embedded, nonquestion)
  (h) *I wonder if can she sing (*wh* absent, inverted, embedded, question)
  (i) What songs she can sing! (*wh* present, noninverted, matrix, nonquestion)
  (j) *What songs she can sing? (*wh* present, noninverted, matrix, question)
  (k) I know what songs she can sing (*wh* present, noninverted, embedded, nonquestion)
  (l) I wonder what songs she can sing (*wh* present, noninverted, embedded, question)
  (m) *What songs can she sing! (*wh* present, inverted, matrix, nonquestion)
  (n) What songs can she sing? (*wh* present, inverted, matrix, question)
  (o) *I know what songs can she sing (*wh* present, inverted, embedded, nonquestion)
  (p) *I wonder what songs can she sing (*wh* present, inverted, embedded, question).

Of the sixteen combinations, six are ungrammatical. Of those six, four (13g, h, o, p) are ungrammatical because they contain inverted auxiliaries in embedded sentences. This leaves only two (13j, m): a noninverted matrix *wh*-question, and an inverted matrix *wh*-exclamative.

Ruling Out Inversion in Embedded Sentences

The ungrammaticality of inverted auxiliaries in embedded clauses can be handled by introducing a feature ROOT whose value is defined as + in matrix or root clauses and as − in embedded clauses. The feature is then constrained to have the value + by the category symbol in the right side of the phrase structure rule expanding S specifying the position of the inverted verb, as in Figure 7.12. The ROOT feature annotated to V in Figure 7.12 is motivated by Emonds's (1976) generalization that there is a set of category permutations and deletions, often involving the categories that signal non-neutral sentence modalities, that are restricted to root clauses (though see also Grimshaw, 1979a, for an alternative formulation of Emonds's generalization).

Figure 7.12

$$S \rightarrow (V)_{\substack{ROOT =_c + \\ SENT-MOD = inv}} \quad NP_{SUBJ} \quad \left\{ \begin{array}{l} VP \\ VP'_{V-COMP} \end{array} \right\}$$

Phrase Structure of Wh-Constituents and Inversion

Since *wh*-words occur with and without inversion, and vice versa—see (13a), (f), (i), and (n)—it seems most economical to assume that the two phenomena are independent as far as the phrase structure rules are concerned. Thus to generate all the phrase structures, one would simply need a rule generating preposed *wh*-phrases, such as the one presented in Figure 7.13. The XP position (actually, a disjunction of NP, PP, and AP) is for the focused or questioned element in interrogatives, relative clauses, and so on (see Kaplan and Bresnan, 1982). It is constrained to contain some word contributing a *wh*-feature (viz., a *wh*-word), and is defined as the controller of a gap or trace elsewhere in the sentence. For example, in *who did you see?*, the question constituent containing *who* fulfills the role of the object of *see*; in LFG this is accomplished by allowing a phrase structure rule to generate a null element or trace in the object position,

Figure 7.13

$$S' \rightarrow (XP)_{wh =_c +} \quad S$$
$$\downarrow = \downarrow\downarrow$$

annotated by $\uparrow = \Uparrow$. A binding mechanism then links the constituent defined by the trace with the XP constituent in the focused position using the respective equations $\uparrow = \Uparrow$ and $\downarrow = \Downarrow$ annotated to them (see Chapter 2, and Kaplan and Bresnan, 1982, for details). For the present purposes, what is important is that both the presence of the *wh*-word in Figure 7.13 and the presence of the inverted verb in Figure 7.12 are optional, generating all four combinations of inversion versus noninversion and presence versus absence of *wh*. In the subsection describing the acquisition of these phrase structure rules, we will see that the child has little choice but to posit such rules, given the input and the phrase structure acquisition procedures.

One might think that, to rule out the ungrammatical examples in (13), equations should be added to the *wh*-constituent in Figure 7.13 coordinating the choice of interrogative versus exclamative sentence modality with the presence of the *inv* feature value in the S. However, several considerations argue for an alternative treatment. First, *how come* is a question word that is semantically similar to *wh*-words, and appears in the same sentence-initial position, but does not allow inversion, as shown in (14).

(14) (a) How come I can't go?
    (b) *How come can't I go?
    (c) Why can't I go?
    (d) *Why I can't go?

Second, not all *wh*-words can appear in exclamatives—see (15)—so the interrogative-exclamative difference that one might be tempted to encode into the phrase structure rule in Figure 7.13 must be specified in the lexical entries for *wh*-words in any case.

(15) (a) What characters she picks up in bars!
    (b) *Who she picks up in bars!
    (c) What dives he hangs out in!
    (d) *Where he hangs out!

Thus a straightforward alternative way to account for the co-occurrence restriction between *wh*-words and inversion is to encode the restrictions that are specific to a *wh*-word in the lexical entries of the *wh*-words themselves, as in (16).

(16) (a) what: PRED = "for which x"
  wh = +
  SENT-MOD $\neq_c$ noninv
  (b) what: PRED = "behold x"
  wh = +
  SENT-MOD $=_c$ noninv
  (c) why: PRED = "why"
  wh = +
  SENT-MOD $\neq_c$ noninv
  (d) how come: PRED = "why"
  wh = +
  SENT-MOD $=_c$ noninv

The equation SENT-MOD $\neq_c$ *noninv* appended to (16a) and (16c) requires that the sentence modality not be defind as *noninv*, that is, that there must be inversion. (Here I use *noninv* as a feature value within which is nested *neut*, *emph*, and *neg*; alternatively, there could be an INV = $+/-$ feature crossed with binary *neg*, *neut*, and *emph* features; see also n. 5.) The reason that such equations are formally preferable to the more intuitive equation SENT-MOD $=_c$ *inv* will become clear in the next paragraph. Presumably some similar equation could appear in the lexical entries of "negative-polarity" words such as *never* in *never would I consent to such a thing*. Lexical rules (see Chapter 8) could license or encourage the generalization that *wh*-question words or negative-polarity words with sentential scope are accompanied by equations constraining inversion.

Some Technical Complications Raised by the Grammar for Inversion

Before the learnability and development of the rules shown in Figures 7.12 and 7.13 and in (16) can be discussed, there is a potential problem with them that must be addressed. Part (a) of (16) dictates that interrogative *what* may occur only in inverted sentences, but (17) shows three sorts of counterexamples to this restriction: echo questions (17a), double questions (17b), and subject questions (17c, d).

(17) (a) You can eat *what* in 30 seconds?
  (b) Who should see whom?
  (c) Who can leave at 5?
  (d) Who left at 5?

One might object that (17c) is in fact inverted, since there could be a trace in subject position between *can* and *leave*. However,

(17d) cannot be interpreted in that way, since nonauxiliary verbs do not invert, so the corresponding inverted sentence would have to be *who did leave at 5?*.

These counterexamples can be ruled out by two well-motivated formal properties of Lexical Functional Grammar. First, the SENT-MOD $\neq_c$ *noninv* equation introduced by the *wh*-words cannot be checked for consistency with the SENT-MOD = *inv* equation defined by the verb position when those *wh*-words are introduced in positions assigned grammatical functions like SUBJ and OBJ. This is clearly the case in (17a) and (17b), where the *wh*-words are in subject and object positions, but not in (13j) and (13n), where the *wh*-words are in the S-complementizer position. Thus violations of the equation can be checked in the latter, but not the former, as the empirical facts require. This restriction on the scope of application of constraining equations is an immediate consequence of the formal machinery of LFG: constraints introduced by lexical items percolate up the tree through any nodes annotated by $\uparrow = \downarrow$, but this percolation stops at any node annotated by $\uparrow$ FUNCTION = $\downarrow$, i.e., any constituent annotated with a grammatical function (see Kaplan and Bresnan, 1982). Thus a SUBJ, OBJ, OBL, or X-COMP will seal off the inversion constraint introduced by the *wh*-word in (17a) and (17b) from access to the verb position that defines whether or not the sentence is in fact inverted.[19] Thus (17a) and (17b) are permitted despite the constraint.[20]

A second provision, one that is needed to account for (17d), is that subject *wh*-questions are gapless. That is, the *wh*-word is generated directly in subject position, forming the structure in part (a) of Figure 7.14 rather than the one in part (b). See Gazdar (1981) for arguments for this analysis. With the *wh*-word appearing directly in subject position, its inversion constraint is

Figure 7.14

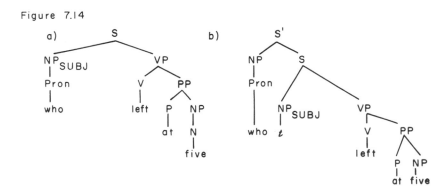

denied access to the V's inversion features by the same mechanisms at work in (17a, b), and so subject questions remain noninverted (their counterparts with *do* such as *who did leave?* are ruled out by the sentence modality constraints on *do* discussed earlier in the chapter).

Aside from allowing one to account for the facts of (17) using a single set of mechanisms, this gapless analysis of subject *wh*-questions is consistent with certain learning considerations. The child cannot assume that all *wh*-questions involve traces, since that is not true in many languages (e.g., Chinese). Thus he or she must be equipped with a procedure for discovering the presence and distribution of traces in languages that allow them. The procedure for learning traces posited in Pinker (1982), and, I imagine, most other plausible learning theories for trace binding, would have the child look for places in the input string where an obligatory constituent is missing and for elements in designated positions outside that S that quantify over a variable corresponding to the grammatical role that the missing constituent would have played had it been present (see Chomsky, 1981, for concrete proposals as to constraints on where traces and their antecedents may occur). In sentences like (17d), it is unclear why the child would assign such an analysis (i.e., the one in part (b) of Figure 7.14) given that the simpler analysis in Figure 7.14(a), in which nothing is missing, would be available. The child would posit a gapless analysis of subject *wh*-questions, and according to the present account he or she would be correct (alternatively, one reason that Figure 7.14(a) is correct may be that the child cannot help but learn it).[21]

LEARNING INVERSION CONSTRAINTS

Now that I have given a partial account of the adult grammar of inversion that meets the formal requirements demanded of such an account, we can turn to how the child acquires that grammar. Three pieces of information must be learned: (1) the inverted verb position in the phrase structure rule expanding S; (2) the equation defining that as an "inverted" position and restricting it to root sentences; and (3) the constraining equation in the lexical entries of *wh*-words preventing the verb from remaining noninverted.

Learning the Phrase Structure Position of the Inverted Verb

The phrase structure position of the inverted verb itself can be learned straightforwardly by the existing P-procedures (as amended in Chapter 3 to posit submaximal category projections) when input sentences with S-initial verbs are processed. Crucially, the child ends up with rules in which both the *wh*-constituent and the inverted verb are optional constituents. This is partially because X-bar theory posits two levels of projection of S (S and S'), with the binding XP position specified to be in the complementizer position of S'. But more importantly, it is because the range of *wh*-constructions in the input spelled out in (13) trigger the P6 procedures to place optionality parentheses around the fronted *wh*-phrase position and around the inverted verb. Regardless of how the phrase structure rules are constructed, for every sequence of constituents in a rule containing a *wh*-word (or an inverted verb), (13) shows that there will be an input sequence identical to it except lacking the *wh*-word (or the inverted verb). Minimal pairs consisting of a rule plus an input sequence lacking one of the constituents in that rule are the exact triggering conditions for P6 to declare that constituent optional. Thus the phrase structure acquisition procedures by themselves leave the child with a set of phrase structure rules that permit all four combinations of (*wh*-phrase present versus absent) × (inversion versus noninversion).

Learning the "Inv" Feature on the Inverted Verb Position

Inversion of the main verb is not an uncommon means of forming questions in the world's languages (Greenberg, 1963; Steele, 1981), and I see no reason why the child should not be equipped with a mechanism explicitly designed to recognize it. Specifically, the inversion equation could be acquired by the following procedures:

M1. Append the equation SENT-MOD = *inv* and ROOT =$_c$ + to an S-initial verb position in a phrase structure rule expanding S if that S-initial position is used exclusively for non-neutral sentence modalities pertaining to the degree of epistemic certainty of the proposition (see Steele, 1981).

M2. Append SENT-MOD = *noninv* to the verb position used for neutral sentence modalities. If an embedded non-neutral clause is encountered with an S-initial verb, and there are no rules permitting that position to be used for the neutral sentence modality, expunge the ROOT =$_c$ + equation from the rule expanding S.

(Incidentally, the ROOT =$_c$ + equation appended to that category may be so appended as a special case of the application of a procedure that, in the unmarked case, restricts alternative expansions of S for non-neutral sentence modalities to root sentences; see Emonds, 1976.)

Note that procedure M1 is stated so that the acquisition of the full rule for inverted sentences presupposes that the noninverted sentence rule for the neutral sentence modality is acquired beforehand, but not vice versa. That is, the child must know that an initial V position is used exclusively for non-neutral sentence modalities, hence he or she must know that the neutral sentence modality is expressed by some *other* verb position, hence he or she must already know the rule expressing the neutral sentence modality. This is necessary to prevent the child from applying the *inv* or ROOT features to verb positions that are not restricted to non-neutral sentence modalities in root sentences (e.g., in VSO languages), or to verb positions that alternate from the standard ones for stylistic or pragmatic reasons. In other words, the acquisition of a canonical rule expanding neutral sentences is a prerequisite to the acquisition of non-neutral expansions, so that the child can safely append the inversion feature only to expansions known to signal non-neutral modalities.

This provision also has the happy consequence of making the procedure consistent with the fact that children fail to use inversion in their early stages (Kuczaj and Maratsos, 1979; Bowerman, 1973), even when they ask questions (in English they use rising intonation instead—Bellugi, 1971; Brown, 1973). This occurs despite the fact that inverted questions actually constitute the plurality or majority of parental inputs (Newport et al., 1977). There are also examples of children learning other languages who are delayed at using phrase structure positions that correlate with non-neutral sentence modalities. For example, Japanese children fail to alternate the positions of the past-tense particle contingent on negation properly; French children fail to place the object pronoun in its proper position in imperatives contingent on negation; Hungarian children fail to use the proper verb particle order contingent on negation, modality, and imperative, and fail to place person markers in their proper positions contingent on the conditional (all examples from Slobin, 1984a). In fact, Slobin summarizes a widespread cross-linguistic pattern of development by characterizing the child as using the following heuristic: "if a clause has to be reduced or deformed when not functioning as a canonical main clause (active, declarative, affirmative clause with full noun arguments and finite verb), attempt to use or approximate the full or canonical form of the clause."

One final observation relevant to this procedure for the ac-

quisition of inversion constraints is that the procedure automatically restricts inverted verbs to matrix or root sentences barring
evidence to the contrary, a property motivated by Emonds (1976).
This predicts that once children learn inversion, they should
restrict it to matrix clauses. Erreich (1980) found that only two
out of eighteen children made inversion errors (two apiece) in
embedded *wh*-questions in a task designed to elicit them; I have
found only a single such error in Brown's data (*I don't know what
are dey*, from Adam's nineteenth sample), as compared to five
or so correct embedded questions with noninverted auxiliaries.
Thus children do seem to restrict inversion to root questions,
despite the fact that the rules expanding root and embedded
questions are otherwise virtually identical, and despite the fact
that children, as we shall see, are rather cavalier at inverting
versus not inverting when the choice is dictated by other grammatical features (viz., presence of a *wh*-word).

Coordinating Inversion with Wh-words

I propose that the child learns the constraints imposed on
inversion by *wh*-words in the same way that he or she learns
other grammatical properties of closed-class items: by the sampling procedure outlined in Chapter 5. That is, the child hypothesizes equations in the lexical entries of various items such
that (a) the equations are permissible according to universal principles of government (both in terms of their form and in terms
of the types of elements whose lexical entries they can appear
in); (b) the equations pertain to grammaticizable features; and
(c) they are instantiated in the current input sentence. Mutually
contradictory sets of equations accumulated over many inputs
(i.e., $X = A, B, \ldots, H$ where A to H exhaust the possible values
of the feature X) are expunged. In the present example, I have
already argued that *inv* and *noninv* are grammaticizable feature
values; all that must be added here is that *wh*-words are among
the elements in whose lexical entries the child is capable of
hypothesizing the equation SENT-MOD $\neq_c$ *noninv*. Other elements with that property would include complementizers, adverbs, and, of course, auxiliaries. Naturally, this is only a rough
characterization of the set of hypothesizable equations for the
child in this domain; presumably more elegant characterizations
can be given of the set of sentence modality-relevant features
that includes *inv*, and of the set of potential inversion constrainers that includes *wh*-words, complementizers, adverbs, and
auxiliaries (see, e.g., Greenberg, 1963; Steele, 1981). For the present purposes it suffices to say that the child is capable of hy-

pothesizing that *wh*-words constrain the presence or absence of the *inv* feature value when he or she hears inverted *wh*-questions.

DEVELOPMENTAL EVIDENCE ON THE ACQUISITION OF INVERSION

It is now possible to characterize what is wrong with the child's grammar when he or she fails to invert in *wh*-questions. What is wrong is simply this: the child lacks the SENT-MOD $\neq_c$ *noninv* equation in the lexical entries of *wh*-words. The child lacks the question because he or she has not yet hypothesized it (or has not hypothesized it on enough occasions to give it sufficient strength), and has not hypothesized it because it is relatively inaccessible on the hierarchy of available feature constraints (see Chapter 5). This account makes a number of empirical predictions, and I will conclude the chapter by examining the evidence relevant to each one.

Independence of Inversion and Preposed Wh-Words

First, if children simply lack a constraining equation in the lexical entries of *wh*-words, nothing should *prevent* them from inverting in *wh*-questions (so long as they invert at all); they just would not be *required* to invert in *wh*-questions. That is because they would have an optional phrase structure position for inverted verbs and an optional phrase structure position for preposed *wh*-words, and these positions are independent as far as the phrase structure rules are concerned. As argued earlier, independence of *wh*-word and inversion is almost the case in the adult grammar, and during the time at which the child is not yet hypothesizing the constraining equation, yes-no questions, *wh*-questions, and *wh*-exclamatives would all be consistent with those rules. Thus we would expect that all four possibilities of (*wh*-word present versus absent) × (inverted versus noninverted auxiliary) should appear in the speech of the supposed noninverters. This is exactly what happens. Tyack and Ingram (1977) found that not a single one of the twenty-one children in their study failed to invert only in *wh*-questions in spontaneous speech. Most inverted properly, and those that failed to invert did so sporadically, and both in yes-no questions and *wh*-questions. Erreich (1980) selected eighteen children who used auxiliaries frequently and who made noninversion errors, and had them participate in a question elicitation task. No child failed to invert in *wh*-questions without also failing to invert in yes-no questions;

all but one inverted at least occasionally in *wh*-questions; most inverted optionally both in yes-no and *wh*-questions. Thus the supposed syndrome of inverting in yes-no questions but not in *wh*-questions either does not exist or exists only rarely. The common error pattern is to invert optionally in all questions, just what one would expect if children had optional positions for inverted auxiliaries and for preposed *wh*-words, and had not yet learned the constraining equation that rules out the single logical possibility for expansion that is ungrammatical.

Lexical Specificity of Inversion

The proposed account of *wh*-questions localizes the inversion constraint in the lexical entries of individual *wh*-words, and attributes noninversion errors to the absence of such constraints. Therefore the child should pass through a stage in which he or she has acquired the constraint for some but not all *wh*-words, and so should systematically invert some *wh*-questions but not others, depending on the particular *wh*-word. Exactly this pattern has been documented in several ways. Labov and Labov (1978) report that their daughter first inverted *how* questions, then, in addition, *what*, *when*, and *where* questions, and finally *why* questions. Kuczaj and Brannick (1979) found that children tended at first to invert only *what* questions, *where* questions, or both in their spontaneous speech. Experimental data from Kuczaj and Brannick support this pattern of lexical specificity: when their 3- and 4-year-old subjects distorted inverted questions into noninverted questions while imitating them, they did so with varying likelihoods depending on the *wh*-word, ranging from 54 percent to 18 percent for the 3-year-olds, and from 26 percent to 4 percent for the 4-year-olds. Similar results were found in a second experiment.

Inverting When One Shouldn't

If children's problem is that they think that *wh*-words and inversion are completely (rather than mostly) independent, then they should not only fail to invert where they must but should also invert where they must not—for example, in *wh*-exclamatives or in *how come* questions. I have found no instances of young children using *wh*-exclamatives of any sort. However, Kuczaj and Brannick (1979) have found that children will often invert *how come* questions (e.g., *how come will you paint that?*) both in their spontaneous speech and when imitating noninverted models; the distortions occurred in approximately half the sentences in which the 3- and 4-year-old children repeated an auxiliary at all.

Kuczaj and Brannick interpreted such errors as examples of the child's overgeneralizing a productive inversion rule from the *wh*-words that permit it to *how come,* which does not. However, the data actually support the simpler hypothesis that inversion errors are cases of the child's simply failing to note any contingency at all between most *wh*-words and inversion. According to the account I have been discussing, *how come* would be just one more example of a *wh*-word lacking its inversion constraining equation, rather than a case of overapplication of a productive rule. First, children inverted *how come* questions even at the youngest ages, during which they were failing to invert questions with other *wh*-phrases. That is, in the children for whom *how come* triggered inversion in 32 percent of the imitations, *why, who,* and *how long* triggered inversion in only 38, 36, and 24 percent of the imitations, compared to 72 percent for *what* and *where.* If children had developed a productive inversion rule that was mistakenly applied to *how come,* inverted *how come* questions should only have appeared in later stages after the child had begun to invert *wh*-questions reliably in general. Second, Kuczaj and Brannick, in a clever control condition, had the children imitate *why* and *how come* questions lacking an auxiliary altogether (e.g., *why/how come the turtle fell on the ground?*). Many children spontaneously inserted an auxiliary when imitating the *why* questions, since *why* requires inversion and main verbs are noninvertible. If children who inverted *how come* questions in general did so because they overextended the privileges of *why* to *how come,* then they should have inserted auxiliaries into auxiliaryless *how come* questions, since their lexical entries for *how come* would have demanded inversion. If, on the other hand, they inverted *how come* questions because their lexical entires for *how come* didn't care one way or another about inversion, then they should have imitated auxiliaryless *how come* questions verbatim. In fact, a majority of the children who inverted *how come* questions did *not* insert extraneous auxiliaries into *how come* stimulus questions lacking them. This suggests that their deficit consisted of having an entry for *how come* with too little information, rather than the wrong kind of information, about inversion.[22] This supports the account whereby noninversion is the product of *wh*-words that lack an equation constraining inversion.

Evidence on the Hypothesizability of Inversion Constraints

Though I have presented evidence that children's *wh*-words simply lack inversion constraints at a certain point, I have offered no explanation as to why that constraint should be missing, while other co-occurrence constraints (e.g., between *to* and the morphology of its infinitive verb) are usually obeyed. The account requires that the hypothesis that *wh*-words constrain inversion be relatively inaccessible to the child, in the same way that direct object definiteness is less accessible as a hypothesis for verb inflections than aspect (see Chapter 5, and Slobin, 1984a, for discussion of hierarchies of accessibility of grammatical hypotheses). In other words, I must claim that the hypothesis is accessible enough to be hypothesized eventually, but not accessible enough to be hypothesized early in development. Obviously, simply stipulating that the inversion feature is relatively inaccessible as something for *wh*-words to constrain would be ad hoc. What is needed is independent evidence that hypotheses of that general sort are relatively inaccessible, taken from studies of the acquisition of similar constraints in English and other languages.

Though it is difficult to delineate precisely the class of features and the class of potential constrainers across languages that are "similar" to the English inversion constraint by *wh*-words, a preliminary characterization of the claim might be the following: sentence modality features introduced in specific positions by phrase structure rules are moderately inaccessible to being constrained by words outside that clause or verb phrase. Fortunately, there is evidence for this claim from the acquisition of many languages. Slobin (1984a) characterizes children the world over as tacitly conforming to the injunction "an operator that affects a whole phrase or clause should not be placed within that phrase or clause, nor should it require the changing of elements within that phrase or clause." For example, children acquiring Hebrew and French have trouble selecting the sentence complementizer that is appropriate to the semantic relation between the embedded proposition and the matrix proposition. English children have trouble suppressing the negation particle of auxiliaries when the subject is inherently negative (e.g., they will say *no one didn't go*), or suppressing negation in complements when the complement-taking verb expresses negated complements by being negated itself (e.g., they will say *I think it's not fulled up to the top* rather than the more common *I don't think it's filled up to the top*). Hungarian children at a certain stage fail to suppress the present conditional particle attached to the verb when they use a past conditional postposition. And Turkish children have trouble learning those complementizers and conjunctions that require complement clauses with altered orders or forms. Examples such as these provide independent motivation for the claim that it does not easily occur to the child to hypothesize constraints between modality-relevant clause alterations and elements external to the clause or VP being altered.

8 | Lexical Entries and Lexical Rules

DURING the past twenty-five years the lexicon has assumed an increasingly important role in theories of generative grammar. Many phenomena once thought to be governed by phrase structure or transformational rules were later discovered to be better explained by rules associated with particular lexical entries or sets of entries (see Chomsky, 1965, 1970, 1981; Jackendoff, 1977; Bresnan, 1978, 1982b; Baker, 1979). Though current grammatical theories differ as to exactly which rules are assigned to the lexicon versus other grammatical components, the lexicon plays a major role in all of these theories, and for that reason any comprehensive theory of language acquisition must address in some detail the problem of how the child learns lexical entries and lexical rules. In this chapter I propose a theory in which the child can learn lexical entries by using four related mechanisms. In addition, I examine the problem of how the child can keep these mechanisms from running amok and creating entries that do not belong in the language, a problem that has received considerable attention in recent discussions of language learnability. As I have done throughout, I will discuss what the child has to learn, how the child might learn it according to the acquisition theory, and evidence from developmental psycholinguistics relevant to evaluating the theory.

What Must Be Learned

LEXICAL ENTRIES

The lexical entries of words in major categories (nouns, verbs, adjectives, and prepositions) must specify how many arguments can appear with the word, the thematic roles of the arguments, and how these arguments may be encoded syntactically. For example, in (1) the verb takes an agent subject and a patient or theme object; in (2) the verb takes a theme subject and a location object.

(1) John hit Bill.

(2) John occupied the chair.

In LFG the argument frames of these verbs are represented as in (3) and (4), with the thematic role assignments of particular arguments paired with particular grammatical functions.[1]

(3) hit (SUBJ , OBJ)
　　　　 agent theme

(4) occupy (SUBJ , OBJ)
　　　　　　theme location

Different predicates allow different arguments to be expressed syntactically and use different grammatical functions to do so, under the constraint that no argument may be expressed by two different functions (e.g., *Reagan looked his wife at Nancy*) and no function may express two different arguments (e.g., *John washed* cannot be synonymous with *John$_i$ washed John$_j$*; see Bresnan, 1982d). These different classes are called *subcategorizations* of the verb category; examples of different verb subcategorizations are shown in (5), and their LFG argument frame representations (omitting thematic roles) are shown in (6).

(5) (a)　John fell/*fell the floor.
　　 (b)　John ate/ate the steak.
　　 (c)　John devoured the steak/*devoured.
　　 (d)　John put the steak on the plate/*put the steak/*put on the plate.
　　 (e)　John darted into the room/*darted.
　　 (f)　John gave a book to Mary.
　　 (g)　John begrudged Sam his good fortune.
　　 (h)　John told Mary to go/that she should go.
　　 (i)　John thought that Mary should go/*Mary to go.

(6) (a)　fall (SUBJ)
　　 (b)　eat (SUBJ, ∅)/eat (SUBJ, OBJ)
　　 (c)　devour (SUBJ, OBJ)
　　 (d)　put (SUBJ, OBJ, OBL$_{loc}$)
　　 (e)　dart (SUBJ, OBL$_{goal}$)
　　 (f)　give (SUBJ, OBJ, OBL$_{goal}$)
　　 (g)　begrudge (SUBJ, OBJ2, OBJ)

(h) tell (SUBJ, OBJ, V-COMP)/tell (SUBJ, OBJ, S-COMP)
(i) think (SUBJ, S-COMP)

As these examples show, individual verbs dictate which syntactic structures they may appear in. Thus one important piece of information for the child to learn is the argument frame associated with each verb (or, more generally, argument-taking predicate) in its lexical entry.[2]

LEXICAL RULES

Lexical redundancy rules, or lexical rules, have been proposed as a mechanism that relates entries in the mental lexicon (Aronoff, 1976, Jackendoff, 1975, Bresnan, 1978, 1982b, d). Lexical rules have an obvious use in characterizing related words like *tie* and *untie* or *buckle* and *unbuckle,* and Bresnan (1978) has shown how they might be used to relate parallel sets of verb subcategorizations as well. For example, each pair of entries in (7) is a member of a large class of verbs with similar alternations, and such alternations can be summarized by the lexical rules listed in (8).

(7) (a) John ordered a martini.
        order (SUBJ, OBJ)
        A martini was ordered by John.
        order (OBL$_{agent}$, SUBJ)

    (b) Irving gave a ring to Sheila.
        give (SUBJ, OBJ, OBL$_{goal}$)
        Irving gave Sheila a ring.
        give (SUBJ, OBJ2, OBJ)

    (c) The computer crashed.
        crash (SUBJ)
        Scott crashed the computer.
        crash (SUBJ, OBJ)

    (d) John expects that the Celtics will win.
        expect (SUBJ, S-COMP)
        John expects the Celtics to win.
        expect (SUBJ, OBJ, V-COMP)

(8) (a) *Passive*
        Syntactic change: OBJ $\mapsto$ SUBJ
                          SUBJ $\mapsto$ OBL$_{agent}$
        Morphological change: $\mapsto$ MORPH = passivepart

    (b) *Dative*
        Syntactic change: OBJ $\mapsto$ OBJ2
                          OBL$_{goal}$ $\mapsto$ OBJ

(c) *Causative*
Semantic change: PRED (   ) ↦ CAUSE (, PRED (   ))
                theme   agent   theme
Syntactic change: SUBJ ↦ OBJ
                  (agent) ↦ SUBJ

(d) *Subject-to-object raising*
Syntactic change: S-COMP ↦ OBJ, V-COMP

As these examples show, lexical rules can specify syntactic, semantic, and morphological differences between related verbs. (See Bresnan, 1978, 1982b, d, for more precise formulations.) They can be interpreted as operations that take one lexical entry as input, and alter or supplement that entry with new information to create a second entry. Thanks to this mechanism, it is not strictly necessary to list both versions of every verb that enters into alternations like those shown in (7); only a single entry plus the lexical rule need be stored in the lexicon. Thus lexical rules, in addition to lexical entries, are structures that the child must learn.

Different grammatical theories attribute different phenomena to the operation of lexical rules. For example, in relational grammar (e.g., Perlmutter, 1980), neither dativization nor passivization nor raising is lexical. In Chomsky's (1981) Government-Binding theory, dativization is lexical, raising is a lexically specified structure deletion rule, and the English passive is both lexical and transformational. (A lexical rule creates a passive participle, which, lacking a feature that assigns case to its object noun phase, forces a movement transformation to place the object in the empty subject position.) In LFG, dative, passive, causative, and raising are all lexical. Since all theories admit of the need for lexical rules in some domains, and all theories need rules that induce lexical entries from surface input, the acquisition theory outlined below should be relevant to all theories at least in part, though its relevance to particular constructions or particular aspects of those constructions should differ from theory to theory.

Learning Lexical Entries: Four Mechanisms

DIRECT LEARNING FROM POSITIVE EVIDENCE

In Chapter 3 I proposed a mechanism, called L1, for the acquisition of lexical entries. I will repeat a description of that mechanism here as the first of four to be discussed. The child encodes the argument-taking predicate of the sentence, and cognitive abilities allow him or her to know how many arguments the predicate takes and which thematic role each argument bears. The child parses the incoming sentence using a combination of existing phrase structure rules and the tree-building procedures P1–P6. Once the sentence is parsed, the child applies the following procedure:

L1. Add subcategorization information to the lexical entries of argument-taking predicates by examining the functions encoding its arguments in the tree and listing those functions in the PRED equation for that entry. If an argument is not encoded by any phrase in the tree, assign it the symbol ∅ in the PRED equation.

For example, suppose that the child heard a hypothetical sentence such as (9a) while at the same time witnessing the relevant act of transfer so that the child could tell that *glimpf* had the argument structure in (9b).

(9) (a) I glimpfed the bone to the dog.
     (b) glimpf (,   ,   )
                 agent theme goal

The child could construct a phrase structure tree from already-acquired phrase structure rules, yielding Figure 8.1. The child could use this tree to determine the lexical entry of the unknown verb, by entering the grammatical functions of the nodes dominating the words expressing the arguments into the corresponding places in the lexical form. The result is shown in (10).

(10) glimpf (SUBJ, OBJ , OBL_{goal})
            agent theme goal

Note that the input sentence in which the phrase structure rules *themselves* are first learned represents a degenerate case of the operation of this mechanism: the thematic roles of the verb predict the ultimate lexical entry of that verb perfectly, with the phrase structure tree doing no work. That is because the P-procedures induce the grammatical functions annotating the tree by examining the verb's thematic structure, and the lexical entry for the verb then is created by reading those very same grammatical functions off that tree. However, in all sentences other than the one in which the phrase structure rules were first learned, it is the phrase structure tree that this mechanism uses to de-

Figure 8.1

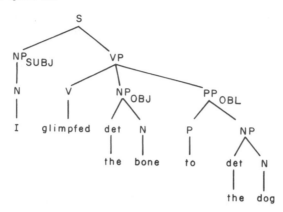

termine the verb's lexical entry, not its thematic structure. The procedures were built this way so that whenever the canonical correspondences between thematic structure and grammatical structure broke down in intermediate and late stages of acquisition (e.g., verbs like *receive*, or passives), the child would learn the correct grammatical structure exemplified in the sentence and not be led astray by syntax-semantics correspondences that did not hold. Thus once phrase structure rules are learned, mechanism L1, which I will also call *direct learning from positive evidence*, allows the child to learn any association whatsoever between a verb's arguments and grammatical functions.

Canonical Mapping

There is a second way in which the child could learn lexical subcategorization, which can best be illustrated by a thought experiment suggested to me by David Lebeaux. Suppose that one is shown a particular action that obviously involves an agent operating on a patient, and one is told that this is a case of *thwicking*. It is a good bet that any adult could use the verb productively, supplying the arguments in their correct positions, without having heard it first modeled in a sentence. Thus, seeing a cat performing an act of thwicking on a dog, one says *the cat is thwicking the dog* rather than the conceivable alternative **the dog is thwicking the cat*. What creates this asymmetry, given that the input is ambiguous as to which of the two orderings is the one used in the language and that L1 would do nothing in this case? Presumably there is some principle operating in English-speaking adults such as (11), leading to a process of word formation like that illustrated in (12).

(11) If a verb takes an agent and a patient, associate the agent with the subject and the patient with the object.

(12) thwick (,   ) → thwick (SUBJ, OBJ)
      agent patient   agent patient

It is possible to perform this induction of lexical subcategorization from thematic roles without parsing or even hearing a sentence with the verb used, as long as one is able to determine the morphological shape of the verb and recover the thematic roles inherent in the described action. Presumably something like the thought experiment described above occurs when new verbs enter the language (e.g., *to foul Kareem, to crash the computer*). If the procedure could be formulated in some way that would work universally, not just in English, it would be easy to imagine that a child could learn a new verb this way. Thus we have a second mechanism for learning lexical entries for argument-taking predicates: by using a *canonical mapping* between a predicate's thematic roles and canonical grammatical functions corresponding to them.

The injunction in (11) is of course far too simple minded. A more accurate portrayal of correspondences between thematic roles and grammatical relations is the following. In a language's "basic forms" (roughly, simple, active, affirmative, declarative, minimally presuppositional, and pragmatically neutral sentences; see Keenan, 1976), agents (if present) are realized as subjects, themes are realized as subjects if there is no agent and as objects otherwise, and sources, locations, and goals are realized as oblique objects if there is an agent or a theme or both, or as objects if there is only a theme. David Lebeaux has suggested to me that these regularities can be stated in terms of a constraint on how two ordered tiers may be associated, one for thematic relations, one for grammatical functions. The tiers are listed in Figure 8.2, the constraint in (13) (see Bresnan, 1982d; Fillmore, 1968; Keenan, 1976; Keenan and Comrie, 1977; Perlmutter, 1980; for related formulations and evidence concerning the cross-linguistic validity of such a constraint).

Figure 8.2

SUBJ	OBJ	OBLIQUE	(grammatical functions)
agent	theme/patient	goal/source/location	(thematic relations)

(13) Lexical entries in basic structures must have the thematic roles of their arguments associated with their grammatical functions without crossing links between the tiers of Figure 8.2, and with exactly one thematic role linked to SUBJ.[3]

Predicates that respect the no-crossing-links provision of (13) may be called *canonical*; those that violate it are *noncanonical*. For example, a normal active predicate like *pound* would exemplify a canonical mapping, since SUBJ is paired with the agent thematic role and OBJ is paired with the theme (in this case, a patient), as is shown in Figure 8.3. Consider, on the other hand, the impossible English verb *shmound*, exemplified in Figure 8.4(a). This noncanonical verb would violate (13), since the links associating the tiers for thematic and grammatical relations would cross, as shown in part (b) of Figure 8.4.

Lebeaux's constraint for basic lexical forms is easily translated into a learning procedure for canonical mapping that can be called L2: namely, create a lexical entry for a predicate by assigning grammatical functions to its thematic roles in such a way that (13) is respected. By defining this learning mechanism in terms of constraints on the association of tiers, we arrive at a more accurate formulation than one that simply says "associate agents with subjects, themes with objects." That is because certain thematic roles, such as theme, are associated with either subjects or objects, depending on what other arguments are present in the sentence. The associations required by some other existing and impossible English verbs (Figures 8.5–8.10) illus-

Figure 8.3

a) John pounded the wall.

pound (SUBJ , OBJ)
      agent   theme

b) SUBJ OBJ   OBLIQUE
     | |
  agent theme goal/source/location

Figure 8.4

a) *The wall shmounded John.
     theme   agent

*shmound (OBJ , SUBJ)
        agent theme

b)  SUBJ   OBJ   OBLIQUE

  agent   theme   goal / source /location

Figure 8.5

    a) The sun is shining.

               shine (SUBJ)
                    theme

    b)  SUBJ   OBJ   OBLIQUE

        agent   theme   goal / source / location

Figure 8.6

    a) Ian occupied the chair.

               occupy (SUBJ, OBJ)
                    theme location

    b) 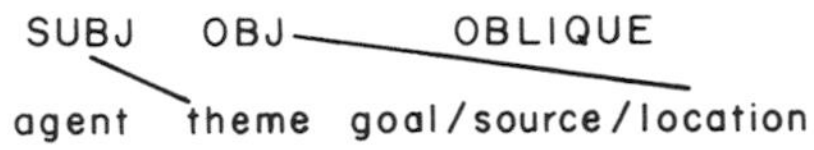 SUBJ   OBJ———   OBLIQUE

        agent   theme goal / source / location

Figure 8.7

    a) John stayed in the park.

               stay (SUBJ, OBL_{loc})
                 theme location

    h) SUBJ   OBJ   OBLIQUE

        agent theme goal / source /location

Figure 8.8

    a) *The park shmayed in John

              *shmay (OBL , SUBJ)
                  theme location

    b)  SUBJ   OBJ   OBLIQUE

        agent theme goal / source / location

Figure 8.9

    a) John fled from the scene of the crime.

               flee (SUBJ, OBL_{source})

               agent source

    b) 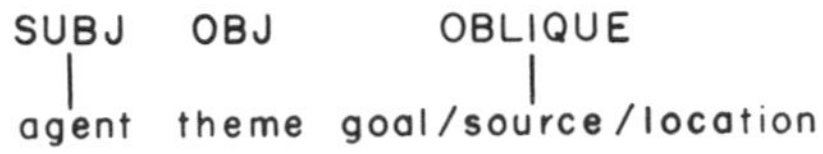 SUBJ   OBJ   OBLIQUE

        agent theme goal / source / location

Figure 8.10   a) *The scene of the crime shmled from John.

$$*\text{shmlee (OBL}_{\text{source}}, \text{SUBJ)}$$

agent   source

b) SUBJ   OBJ   OBLIQUE

agent theme goal/source/location

trate this point. The constraint that SUBJ be linked to one argument rules out argument-taking verbs that lack subjects altogether—for example, *fell John* and *shined [by] the sun* (but see n. 1 to Chapter 5).

Note, finally, that passives, and certain verbs such as *receive, please,* and *strike as,* fail to respect canonical correspondences between thematic roles and grammatical functions, since the association lines cross; see Figures 8.11 and 8.12.[4] In order to learn nonbasic verb forms such as passives, exceptional verbs like *receive,* and verbs without clearly defined thematic relations (e.g., *Sam's data underdetermine the theory he wants to argue for*), the child must rely on the first mechanism, direct learning from positive evidence (L1), and in fact must allow L1 to override the mechanism exploiting canonical mapping, L2. Thus L2 cannot replace L1; in fact L2 is not necessary for solving the learnability problems in lexical subcategorization at all. I propose the canonical mapping process here to account for near-universal regularities in lexical subcategorization for basic forms, for productive word formation in adults, and because it is a natural

Figure 8.11   a)   The wall was pounded by John.

$$\text{pound (OBL}_{\text{agent}}, \text{SUBJ)}$$

agent   patient

b)   SUBJ   OBJ   OBLIQUE

agent   theme   source/goal/location

Figure 8.12

a)   Harry received a ticket from Sgt. McGinniss

$$\text{receive (SUBJ, OBJ, OBL}_{\text{source}})$$

goal   theme   source

b)   SUBJ   OBJ   OBLIQUE

agent   theme   source/location/goal

extension of the mechanisms discussed in Chapters 2, 3, and 5 that use thematic roles to learn phrase structure rules and case markers (see Lebeaux, 1983, in preparation, for further arguments). In a later section I will show in addition that there is developmental evidence that suggests that children use something like this canonical mapping mechanism.

APPLICATION OF LEXICAL RULES

In Chapter 2 and early in this chapter, I pointed out how lexical rules can be used to derive new lexical entries from old ones. An example is passivization, as shown in (14).

(14) Old entry: thwick (SUBJ, OBJ)
                  agent theme

  Lexical rule: SUBJ $\mapsto$ OBL$_{agent}$
              OBJ $\mapsto$ SUBJ
              $\mapsto$ MORPH $=$ passivepart

  New entry: thwicked (OBL$_{agent}$, SUBJ)
                 agent   theme
                 MORPH $=$ passivepart

The application of lexical rules is a third way in which the child could acquire lexical entries. Naturally, this begs the question of how lexical rules themselves are learned. Here is a mechanism proposed in Pinker (1982), which I will call L3:

L3. If a predicate has two lexical entries each with the same number and type of arguments but with different grammatical functions encoding these arguments, coin a lexical rule that specifies the replacement of each function in the first lexical entry by its counterpart in the second. The lexical rule also should add or delete any feature equations that distinguish the two entries.

L3 as stated is extremely powerful, but its power is limited in practice by the lexical forms that may appear in the input, and these are constrained by principle (13) and similar constraints on nonbasic forms to be discussed later.

    Once the child has learned an active entry for a given verb (via either direct learning or canonical mapping) and a passive entry (via direct learning) for that verb, he or she could apply L3 to create a lexical rule of passivization. Once the rule is itself learned, it could then be applied to active lexical entries to yield their passive counterparts (or vice versa). The process whereby new entries are added to the lexicon via the application of lexical rules can be called L4.

A more perspicuous way of representing this process is to borrow a notational convention used extensively in Chapter 5: the paradigm or matrix representation for related verb forms. Here we can have a dimension (or set of mutually crossed dimensions) called, for convenience, CONSTRUCTION, with entries for various versions of a verb such as active, passive, causative, reflexive, dative, inchoative, reciprocal, ergative, middle, and so on. When a child has acquired separate lexical entries for active and passive entries of a verb (via direct learning or canonical mapping), he or she might have a verb-specific paradigm like the one shown in Figure 8.13. As in Chapter 5, a *general paradigm* could be derived from a *word-specific paradigm* (or, more realistically, from a set of parallel word-specific paradigms). This general paradigm, shown in Figure 8.14, is simply an alternative notation for a lexical rule, and the process of creating it is identical to procedure L3. The general paradigm/lexical rule could then be applied to partially filled word-specific paradigms like Figure 8.15(a) (i.e., verbs for which the child has acquired only an active entry), to yield the fully filled paradigm in Figure 8.15(b).

So far, the use of paradigms to represent lexical entries and lexical rules is just a notational device, but we shall see in the second half of this chapter that the device allows one to propose a perspicuous theory of how the child learns constraints on the domain of productivity of lexical rules, using mechanisms al-

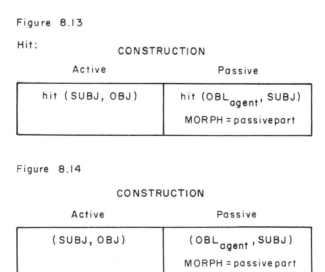

Figure 8.13

Hit: CONSTRUCTION

Active   Passive

| hit (SUBJ, OBJ) | hit (OBL$_{agent}$, SUBJ) |
| | MORPH = passivepart |

Figure 8.14

CONSTRUCTION

Active   Passive

| (SUBJ, OBJ) | (OBL$_{agent}$, SUBJ) |
| | MORPH = passivepart |

Figure 8.15

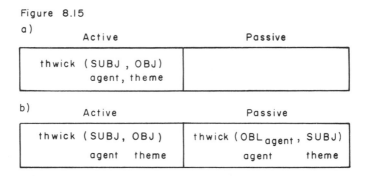

ready proposed for the learning of inflectional systems in Chapter 5. In addition, one could define superordinate levels for various sets of forms, to capture various morphological and syntactic regularities pertaining to them (as was done in Chapter 5 to express patterns of syncretism). For example, CONSTRUCTION could first subdivide into the levels *Transitive,* embracing active, transitive, and causative, and *Intransitive,* embracing passive, intransitive, inchoative, middle, reflexive, and reciprocal, if the language assigned similar properties to these two classes (see Berman's contribution to Slobin, 1984b, for an argument that children respect this superordinate transitive/intransitive distinction in Hebrew before they learn to subdivide each of these classes). Similarly, some of the regularities documented by Perlmutter (1980) could perhaps be captured using this formalism. I will not discuss these possibilities further; I simply raise them to point out that the paradigm representation may well be motivated by considerations other than the learnability problems I will use them for in this chapter.

NONCANONICAL MAPPING

There is a variant of the third acquisition mechanism for lexical entries. When a child learns a nonbasic verb form such as a passive, he or she could use a modified version of L3 to note how that form encodes its thematic roles grammatically, and could then generalize that other verbs may map their thematic roles onto grammatical functions in the same way. One can call this the method of *noncanonical mapping* or L5; see Williams (1981c) for arguments that adult grammars may contain a mechanism of this sort. The device used to effect this learning might be a general construction paradigm identical to Figure 8.14 but with thematic roles explicitly labeled, as in Figure 8.16. (In fact, the labels would not be "agent" and "theme" linked in one-to-one correspondence with grammatical functions, but tiers such as

Figure 8.16

CONSTRUCTION

Active	Passive
(SUBJ, OBJ) agent　theme	$(OBL_{agent}, SUBJ)$ agent　　　theme MORPH = passivepart

those shown in Figure 8.2 and their passive counterparts to be discussed later in the chapter. The simpler lists are shown for clarity.)

There are two differences between the application of lexical rules, L4, and of noncanonical mapping, L5. First, lexical rules require that one version of a given verb be acquired before the other can be derived from it; with noncanonical mapping, in contrast, the child could invent a passive form for a verb with agent and patient arguments heard in isolation without ever acquiring the active version of that verb. Noncanonical mapping also is applicable only in certain circumstances, ones that do not affect the operation of lexical rules. Specifically, it requires that a verb have clearly identifiable thematic roles so that these roles can be mapped onto the proper grammatical relations; this would not work for passivizable constructions lacking such roles—for instance, idioms (e.g., *John made headway in his quest for a perpetual motion machine/Not much headway was made yesterday in that quest*)— and lexical rules would still be needed for such cases.

Summary of Acquisition Mechanisms for Lexical Entries

I have proposed four mechanisms that acquire lexical entries: L1, L2, L4, and L5 (recall that L3 acquires the general paradigms used by L4 and L5). These procedures can be organized into a taxonomy that will become useful when we examine the evidence concerning lexical development. The taxonomy, displayed in Figure 8.17, classifies the procedures in terms of whether they are productive or unproductive (i.e., whether they can create subcategorization frames that are not exemplified in the input), whether they are lexically or thematically based (i.e., whether a particular lexical entry or a particular set of thematic roles serves as input to the procedure), and whether they are canonical or noncanonical (i.e., whether or not they obey provision (13)).

Note that the set of acquisition mechanisms I have proposed need not be considered an arbitrary list. Rather, all but L1 can

Figure 8.17

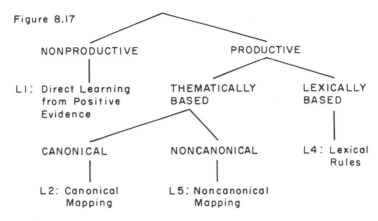

be considered to be variants of a single procedure that uses the redundancy implicit in a single general paradigm such as that in Figure 8.16 to make different sorts of inductive leaps. L2 uses the lower line in the Active cell in Figure 8.16 to predict the corresponding upper line in a word-specific paradigm for an incompletely learned word; L4 uses the upper line in the Active cell to predict the upper and lower lines in the Passive cell; L5 uses the middle line in the Passive cell to predict the upper and lower lines in that cell. One can imagine yet another procedure that used the lower line in the Passive cell to predict its upper line. The general point is that Figure 8.16 captures the regularities in the lexicon of a language, and that it can support several different inferences by a language learner depending on which part the learner uses as a premise and which part he or she uses as a conclusion.

Development of the Lexicon

By and large, children acquire verbs with their proper subcategorization frames. For example, Brown (n.d.) reports that Adam, Eve, and Sarah respected the intransitive/transitive distinction in their use of verbs from the very first stages. The only incorrect uses were the omission of objects from transitive verbs and prepositions from oblique arguments during the stage in which all sorts of obligatory constituents were absent. Even in Stage I there was a massive statistical tendency to use direct objects only for transitive verbs, and telegraphic errors disappeared monotonically from stage to stage with few errors of any sort in the later stages. Maratsos and Chalkley (1981) also point out that children of all ages make few subcategorization errors.

Most of this evidence, however, is ambiguous as to which learning mechanism accomplished the learning. That is because of massive confoundings in the lexicon of English and other languages. Take the sentence *he pushed the truck*. A child who acquired the verb *push* from that sentence could have done so by noting that the pusher argument, *he,* was in the subject position as defined by the phrase structure of English, and that the pushee argument, *the truck,* was in the object position (that is, he or she could have used L1, direct learning from positive evidence). Alternatively, the child could have noted that the concept *push* involves an agent argument and a patient argument, and that according to L2 the canonical lexical entry for that verb, given its thematic structure, should call for SUBJ and OBJ functions, respectively. Likewise, a passive participle in the sentence *Sheila was licked by the cat* could be learned by inspecting the phrase structure of the sentence and noting the presence of OBL and SUBJ functions annotating the arguments of *lick* (L1), by applying a lexical rule to an already acquired active entry for *lick* (L4), or by mapping *lick's* agent and patient arguments directly onto OBL and SUBJ, respectively (L5).

Thus the evidence that would implicate a particular acquisition mechanism must involve verbs that break the confounds between canonicalness and presence in the language, between derivability by lexical rules and presence in the language, and between derivability by lexical rules and the use of noncanonical thematic roles. Such verbs include those that display noncanonical correspondences between thematic and grammatical relations, those that the child invents, and those that an experimenter concocts. Fortunately, enough such cases exist for one to bring developmental evidence to bear on the four acquisition mechanisms. In particular, I will examine three classes of developmental evidence: differences between the ease of acquisition of canonical and noncanonical verbs; examples of productivity in verb acquisition; and distinctions between thematically based and lexically based productivity.

Acquisition of Canonical versus Noncanonical Verbs

Learning from positive evidence requires that the child parse an input sentence using existing phrase structure and inflectional rules, that he or she distinguish the various semantic arguments that a predicate takes, and that he or she know (from the nonlinguistic context) which noun phrases in the input sentence are expressing which of the verb's arguments. The use of canonical mapping requires only that the child distinguish the various semantic arguments that a predicate takes, and classify each argument in terms of its thematic role (agent, theme, and so on). Note that canonical mapping requires less knowledge (phrase structure and inflectional rules) and less processing of the input (parsing the string and observing the roles played by the NP referents) than learning from positive evidence. Therefore, the theory that canonical mapping is available as an acquisition mechanism predicts that canonical verbs, which can be acquired by the "easier" method of canonical mapping, should be learned before noncanonical verbs, which can be acquired only by the more demanding direct evidence method.

Indeed, there are dramatic differences in the age of acquisition of certain canonical and noncanonical constructions. First, the three children studied by Brown (1973) produced active sentences by the thousands, yet the number of examples of verbal passives each child uttered in the samples I examined can be counted on one's fingers. Young children are also notorious for their inability to comprehend reversible passive sentences reliably until their fifth or sixth year (Bever, 1970; de Villiers and de Villiers, 1973b; Fraser, Bellugi, and Brown, 1963; Maratsos, 1974b). Verbs that intrinsically violate the canonical mappings (e.g., *receive, please, strike as, undergo*) are virtually nonexistent in children's speech, and Slobin (1984a) notes that the Japanese equivalent of *receive*, whose recipient or goal argument takes nominative case, is acquired late by Japanese children.[5]

Experimental evidence supports the distinction between canonical and noncanonical verbs. In two experiments Marantz (1982) found that 3- and 4-year-old children had little trouble learning concocted verbs whose agent and patient arguments were expressed as subjects and objects respectively (e.g., *Bill is moaking* [= pounding with his elbow] *the table*). However, they had considerable difficulty learning identical verbs with the opposite correspondences (*the table is moaking Bill*). Note, incidentally, that the fact that learning was possible at all in the case of the noncanonical verbs shows that some form of learning from positive evidence must be available to children in addition to the use of canonical mapping.

PRODUCTIVITY IN VERB ACQUISITION

Although the evidence cited in the preceding paragraphs shows that the distinction between canonical and noncanonical lexical forms is important in acquisition, it is not sufficient for showing that children can learn verbs through the mechanism of canonical mapping. The problem is that in the cases where children were shown to acquire canonical verbs easily, the children could have heard the verbs used in grammatical sentences. Hence the children may not have created the lexical entries based on the predicates' thematic structures; they may have learned them directly from the input sentences via L1, for all we know. The differences between canonical and noncanonical verbs might reflect the operation of a positive evidence mechanism that worked more reliably or coined stronger rules when a verb was canonical, but it may have been a prerequisite for any learning that the verb be heard in a parsable sentence. What one needs in order to show that lexical entries can be created by some mechanism other than L1 (direct learning from positive evidence) are instances of the child using a verb whose lexical entry was *never* exemplified in the input.

It might be thought that the hypothesis that children only create lexical forms corresponding to verbs as they are heard in input sentences is a straw figure. After all, overgeneralization errors are legion in children's speech. However, the conservatism or learning-from-direct-evidence-only hypothesis for lexical entries is in fact a serious and motivated proposal. As mentioned, except for the instances in which the child first learns rules expressing grammatical relations in the language, direct learning from positive evidence is powerful enough to obviate the need for the other mechanisms. Second, Baker (1979) and Bresnan (1978) have pointed out that many individual verbs are ungrammatical in constructions that freely accept their near-synonyms (e.g., *Cowens gave/*donated the Jimmy Fund his sneakers; not a single Volvo was owned/*had by any of the faculty*). Direct learning would avoid making these mistakes (since they would never be exemplified in the input); more productive mechanisms would not. Given the lack of negative evidence, productive overgeneralization presents us with a nasty learnability problem. Thus Baker and Bresnan raise the possibility that lexical entries for certain classes of verbs are acquired only as they are exemplified in input sentences; this corresponds to the exclusive use of the proposed L1 procedure.

As it turns out, there are many examples in the literature of children using lexical forms that were not exemplified in the input. Prima facie, many of them could be the products either of canonical mapping, of lexical rules, or of noncanonical mapping; I will postpone that issue until the next section and simply cite the examples as clearcut evidence that learning from direct positive evidence is not the *only* mechanism available to children.

Lexical Causatives

Melissa Bowerman (1974, 1982a, b) has richly documented several systematic patterns of lexicosyntactic productivity in children. One of the most striking is a phenomenon first noted by Braine (1971a) whereby children create verbs whose subject arguments are causes or causal agents and whose objects are themes (either patients, or actors affected by the causal agent). Bowerman cites more than thirty examples produced by children between the ages of 2 and 8; some of them are reproduced in (15).

(15) (a) Mommy, can you stay this open?
     (b) Who deaded my kitty cat?
     (c) I come it closer so it won't fall.
     (d) Don't giggle me.
     (e) Will you climb me up there and hold me?
     (f) Are you gonna nice yourself?

Similar examples of the creative use of lexical causatives can be found in the speech of children learning Hebrew and Turkish (Slobin, 1984a).

Effect Complements

A related phenomenon that Bowerman (1982b, c) documents is the creation of progressive or adjectival complements for verbs that do not permit them in adult English, usually signifying an effect of the action designated by the verb; see (16).

(16) (a) Will this squeeze the blood from going through? [asked of a
          rubber band around a wrist].
     (b) Feels like you're combing me baldheaded.
     (c) It's hard not to knock them down 'cause whenever I breathe
          I breathe them down.
     (d) I pulled it unstapled.

Figure-Ground Reversals

Following Fillmore (1977), Anderson (1971), Talmy (1976), and others, Bowerman (1982c) notes that there is a certain class of verbs taking two arguments, including *load, smear, drain, empty, hit,* and *spray,* which allow either of their arguments to appear in the direct object position, the other one then appearing as an oblique object, as in (17).

(17) (a)   I loaded hay onto the truck.
     (b)   I loaded the truck with hay.

Following Fillmore, Bowerman labels the thematic role of the direct object in the (17a) sentence "Figure," and the prepositional object "Ground." I will use the standard terms "theme" and "source," "location," or "goal" for the thematic roles, and refer to this class of verbs as "figure-ground" verbs. The lexical forms for the verbs will therefore look like (18).

(18) (a)   load (SUBJ , OBJ   , OBL$_{goal}$)
                 agent theme goal
     (b)   load (SUBJ , OBL$_{instr}$, OBJ)
                 agent theme goal

The entry in (18a) is canonical; that in (18b) is noncanonical. While some verbs like *load* allow the theme to be paired with either the object of the prepositional object slot, other verbs—see (19) and (20)—allow only one syntactic configuration for the realization of their thematic roles.

(19) (a)   John poured water into the cup.
                 pour (SUBJ , OBJ   , OBL$_{goal}$)
                       agent theme goal
     (b)   *John poured the cup with water.

(20) (a)   John filled the cup with water.
                 fill (SUBJ , OBL$_{instr}$, OBJ   )
                       agent theme   goal
     (b)   *John filled water into the cup.

Bowerman (1982c) then notes that children incorrectly use verbs of one type with the grammatical relations appropriate to the other; some examples are reproduced in (21).

(21) (a)   Feel your hand to that.
           Can I fill some salt into the bear?
           I'm going to cover a screen over me.
     (b)   I poured you. [Mother: You poured me?] Yeah, with water.
           I don't want it because I spilled it of orange juice [spilled orange juice on it].

Passives

I have found a small number of reports of children using passivized verbs in their spontaneous speech that they could not have heard in parental speech. Example (22a) is from Wasow (1981); (22b) is from Bowerman (1982b); (22c) is from Slobin (1984a); (22d–h) are from Clark (1982); (22i–j) are from Roeper (personal communication).

(22) (a) I don't like being falled down on!
   (b) He's gonna die you, David. [Turns to mother.] The tiger will come and eat David and then he will be died and I won't have a brother any more.
   (c) I think it's not fulled up to the top.
   (d) Is it all needled?
   (e) How was it shoelaced?
   (f) It was bandaided.
   (g) But I need it watered and soaped [talking about a rag for washing a car].
   (h) I don't want to be dogeared today [asking for her hair not to be arranged in "dog ears"].
   (i) I don't want to get waded.
   (j) I don't want to get waved over [protesting that waves might crash over her].

In addition, Lebeaux and Pinker (1981) presented 4- and 5-year-old children with concocted verbs either exclusively in active sentences or exclusively in passive sentences. We then tested their ability to produce and comprehend the verbs both in the voice originally presented and in the voice not originally presented. Virtually all the children comprehended the verbs in the novel voice, and the majority were willing to utter them in the novel voice as well. In a replication of the Lebeaux and Pinker study with younger children, Loren Ann Frost and I also found a widespread willingness to utter verbs productively in the voice they were not presented in. Thus young children are capable of creating active or passive lexical entries for verbs even when such verb forms are not exemplified in the input. The other side of this coin is that the children did learn passivized verbs directly when we presented passive sentences with novel verbs. Hence the experiment provides some evidence for L1, direct learning from positive evidence, in addition to the evidence it provides for a productive mechanism (barring the possibility that the children created an active form from the passive stimulus sentences through canonical mapping, then instantly applied a lexical rule of passivization to it). Furthermore, children produced verbs in the taught voice more readily than in the nontaught voice, also suggesting that they used a mechanism like L1 that records the form of the verb heard in the input.

Datives

Like ungrammatical passives, ungrammatical datives are uncommon in children's spontaneous speech, but examples can be found. Roeper et al. (1981) report a personal communication from Melissa Bowerman saying that she has found such errors in the speech of her daughters, and Klein (1983) reproduces *you put me the bread and butter* and *how come you're putting me that kind of juice?* from an unreferenced paper by Bowerman. The examples in (23a) are taken from Mazurkewich and White (1984); those in (23b) are from my own examination of the transcripts of Adam's and Eve's speech (these examples are all from Eve and invoke her mistaken use of *write* as a synonym of *draw*).

(23) (a)   Mummy, open Hadwen the door.
           Pick me up all these things.
           I'll brush him his hair.

    (b)   (But) I go write you a lady now.
           I go write you something.
           I go write you train.
           I writing you something.
           You please write me lady.
           Write me another one right here.
           You please write me snowman.
           When Fraser come back he goin' to write me another snowman.

The experimental evidence is less clear. In the studies reported in Wilson, Pinker, Zaenen, and Lebeaux (1981) we were unsuccessful at getting children to produce or comprehend double-object datives for concocted verbs previously presented only in the *to*-dative form. However, the children were equally unwilling to produce or comprehend double-object sentences with concocted verbs presented in the double-object form or, for that matter, with the existing verb *give*, which we presented as a control. Hence a lack of productivity per se does not seem to be the impediment here. Mazurkewich and White (1984) had 8- and 9-year-olds judge the acceptability of double-object sentences that were either grammatical or ungrammatical in adult English by virtue of their main verbs. Almost half (47 percent) of the ungrammatical sentences such as *John reported the police the accident* were judged to be acceptable; if the judgments accurately reflected the children's grammar, this is another example of children forming double-object dative entries in the absence of direct positive evidence. (There is at least some reason to treat the children's judgments in this study as accurate reflections of their grammars: Mazurkewich and White found that certain other classes of ungrammatical dative sentences were judged acceptable far less than 47 percent of the time, belying a floor effect or a response bias for the *report*-type sentence.)

The Wilson et al. study did provide evidence for productive lexical form creation, but it was for the canonical *to*-object form, not the double-object form. Though we failed in our attempts to teach the children double-object forms even when we modeled those forms directly, children's errors in that condition did not consist of doing nothing: most of the children in fact produced and comprehended the concocted verbs as if they were *to*-dative forms, even though the input evidence (i.e., the sentences we presented) exemplified quite a different form. Thus the children did not put direct positive evidence mechanisms to work; they acquired a novel lexical form in some other way, which I will discuss in a later section.

Denominal Verbs

Clark (1982) has found 224 examples of innovative verbs that children derived from existing nouns. The examples come from children acquiring English, French, and German; some of the English examples are reproduced in (24).

(24) (a) Don't broom my mess.
     (b) I'm crackering my soup.
     (c) That truck is cementing.
     (d) When is she coming to governess us?
     (e) The buzzer is buzzering.
     (f) It's snowflaking so hard that you can't see this person.
     (g) I saw Julie match up a match.
     (h) Will you nut these? [i.e., crack them].

DISTINGUISHING AMONG THE THREE PRODUCTIVE
MECHANISMS

The developmental evidence cited above shows that children can acquire verb subcategorizations from direct positive evidence (Marantz's noncanonical verbs, Lebeaux and Pinker's passive presentation sentences, and presumably noncanonical verbs like *receive* when they are eventually learned by older children), and via more productive methods (the majority of the cases cited). The cited evidence, however, does not necessarily tell us *which* of the productive methods—canonical mapping, lexical rules, or noncanonical mapping—were in fact used. In this section I adduce evidence that uniquely points to the use of canonical mapping and to the use of noncanonical mapping. There is also some evidence uniquely pointing to the use of lexical rules, but it is weaker.

Evidence for Canonical Mapping

What is needed here are examples of canonical verbs used productively where there is no possible source for such usage in any related lexical form (otherwise, lexical rules could be the acquisition mechanism at work). One candidate is the productive use of intransitive or noncausative transitive verbs as causal transitives, the phenomenon documented by Bowerman (1982a); see (15) above. In English there are many causative-noncausative pairs (*the door opened/I opened the door; she grew some flowers/the flowers grew; Grandpa warmed up the car/the car warmed up*), and causativization is partially productive among adults. This can especially be seen in areas of expertise, for example, *I crashed the computer twice today; the Amazing Randi vanished three elephants; Eckersley intentionally walked the batter;* and *the transformation that hops an affix*, which I found myself using in Chapter 7. Thus English examples such as (15) could have been created by a lexical rule or by a canonical mapping (where causal agent = subject, and theme or causee = object). The crucial comparison must come from a language that has no verbs that alternate between intransitive and causative forms. Hebrew is such a language, because the process of causativization is accompanied by morphological changes, and unlike English there are few or no verbs that appear with the same morphological shape in causative and noncausative sentences (Tziki Walden, personal communication). Significantly, Israeli children make errors analogous to (15), using intransitive and noncausal verb forms ungrammatically as causative transitives (Walden, personal communication; Berman, reported in Slobin, 1984a). Since there is no source in the language for such usages in the form of morphologically identical causative-noncausative pairs, the child must have created them by mapping the thematic roles of the causal predicate directly onto the grammatical relations that express them. (An alternative possibility is that the children had indeed learned the part of the lexical rule that added and altered the grammatical functions, but had not yet learned the part that altered the morphological form. This seems unlikely, however, given that the morphological reflexes of causativization in Hebrew are quite salient, involving vowel changes and the addition of a syllabic prefix.)

The second example comes from the Wilson, Pinker, Zaenen, and Lebeaux studies. As mentioned, children refused to produce or comprehend any double-object dative verb, whether concocted and exemplified in the form tested, concocted and exemplified only in the *to*-object form, or nonconcocted. However, as I noted above, the children's failure to process our concocted double-object forms had a serendipitous by-product. Most children productively used the verbs presented in that condition in the *to*-object form: presented with *the lion dooped the pig the bear* accompanied by our showing a toy lion sending a toy bear on a Lazy Susan to a toy pig, the children then reliably interpreted *the giraffe dooped the horse (to) the cat* as indicating a transfer of the horse to the cat, rather than vice versa, and would describe a scenario in which a monkey was being transferred as *he's dooping the monkey to the cow*, regardless of which toy we focused their attention on. The children had never heard *doop* NP_{theme} *to* NP_{goal}, so they could not have acquired such forms from positive evidence. And they had no mastery at all of the *doop* NP_{goal} NP_{theme} form (being oblivious to our teaching scenario, as far as we could see), and so could not have acquired the *to*-dative form by applying a lexical rule (in reverse) to the double-object form. Thus they must have created the *to*-dative form by perceiving that the verb had agent, theme, and goal arguments and associating them with subject, object, and oblique grammatical relations.

In a second experiment explicitly designed to test this possibility, we introduced children to our concocted verb simply by acting out the verb meaning with the toys and saying *this is dooping* (in other words, we actually ran the *thwick* thought-experiment mentioned above). According to the line of reasoning sketched above, this should be sufficient for the children to create a *doop* NP *to* NP entry. We obtained mixed results. Most of the children did not utter *doop* NP *to* NP when describing subsequent scenarios we acted out. However, many did use the simple transitive form lacking a *to*-object (e.g., *he's dooping the pig*, where the pig was indeed the theme in the scenario). This was true even when we deliberately called the child's attention to the goal. At the very least, then, the simple transitive form must have been created by canonical mapping. (I am not quite sure why full *to*-dative forms were created in our first but not our second experiment, given that canonical mapping should have operated in both cases.)[6]

Evidence for Learned Productive Mechanisms

One of the proposed productive mechanisms, canonical mapping, might be in part innately specified. However, the other two—lexical rules and noncanonical mapping—must be in large part learned, since the particular realizations of noncanonical forms differ from language to language and many such forms are absent from particular languages altogether. This is reflected in the learning theory whereby the two productive mechanisms capable of acquiring noncanonical forms, L4 and L5, are only acquired themselves when L3 examines sets of related lexical entries each learned individually (via L1 or L2). Thus the learning mechanisms subdivide into mechanisms that can be applied from the start (canonical mapping and direct learning from positive evidence), and mechanisms that presuppose prior learning of sets of related entries (noncanonical mapping and lexical rules). If this is indeed the case, one might expect that the latter mechanisms might operate only after a stage at which the child was using versions of each of the individual forms participating in an adult lexicosyntactic alternation, but was unable to generate the noncanonical forms productively. Bowerman (1982b, c) notes that this is exactly what happens in the case of figure-ground verbs, causatives, *un*-prefixation of verbs, and effect complements. In each case, her children initially produced correct individual examples of each of the two versions related by the adult rule.[7] Only after this clearly delineated nonproductive stage did her children begin to make the productive errors described in the preceding sections. As Lebeaux (1983, in preparation) points out, this pattern is consistent with the proposal that there is a class of productive mechanisms that are acquired by the juxtaposition of related but individually acquired lexical entries. When these productive mechanisms are acquired and applied, the result is the "reorganization" phenomenon described by Bowerman and others (see Lebeaux, 1983, in preparation, for further arguments).

Evidence for Noncanonical Mapping

There are at least two cases where I have found evidence that children create unambiguously noncanonical verbs in the absence of direct positive evidence: figure-ground verbs with source or goal objects (21b) and passives (22). Since they are novel and noncanonical, they could not have been acquired via the direct or canonical mapping mechanisms. It is not clear, however, *which* of the two productive noncanonical mechanisms the child used in creating these noncanonical forms. That is, it is not clear whether the children derived the passive forms from corresponding previously acquired active versions of those verbs using lexical rules, or whether they directly mapped the verb's thematic roles onto a noncanonical set of grammatical relations, with the canonical versions of these verbs playing no role. These possibilities could be distinguished by finding examples where the child creates noncanonical verb forms for which there are no canonical counterparts in his or her lexicon. Examples (22c–h), and perhaps their French and German counterparts, would seem to be of that sort: they are clearly spontaneous creations by the child, and it seems unlikely that the child acquired all of them in their active versions beforehand. Thus it seems likely that the children created passive entries for the novel "verbs" *needle, shoelace, bandaid, soap,* and *dogear* directly, that is, by assigning the subject function to the theme or patient argument of the action and the null function ∅ to the agent argument. No doubt there are other possibilities—for example, the child might first have created a canonical active verb using canonical mapping, and then might have immediately and covertly passivized it; or the child might have compiled a single denominalization/ passivization rule that generates passivized verbs directly from nouns. However, the most parsimonious explanation is that noncanonical mapping was used.

Is There Evidence for Lexical Rules Per Se?

So far, I have cited no evidence uniquely implicating lexical rules. The sort of evidence we need here would be examples of a child using passive versions of noncanonical (e.g., *receive*) or nonthematic (e.g., abstract or idiomatic) verbs that have never been exemplified in the input to that child. Unfortunately, children use so few noncanonical or nonthematic verbs that the necessary evidence to demonstrate the operation of L4 in children is difficult to come by. However, some suggestive evidence can be found in cases where children use alternative entries related by a lexical rule in close succession at least one of which must be productive. The novel active and passive utterances in (22b) are one example; the novel double-object examples in (23b), which were uttered in the same sessions as the *for*-object datives in (25), are another.

(25) Write a lady for me.
    I writing another thing for you.

Write another eye for him.
I go write a lady for you.

Similarly, the ungrammatical double-object sentences with *put* were used by Bowerman's two children at ages at which they also used *you put the pink one to me* and *can I put it to her?*, respectively. Finally, Bowerman (1982b) cites ten examples of children using ungrammatical lexical causatives in close temporal proximity to their use of the source word in a periphrastic construction (e.g., *saying "giddi-up" doesn't make it go faster. Singing goes it faster*). Of course, these examples are no more than suggestive. The child could have created both canonical and noncanonical forms using mappings from thematic roles to grammatical functions, and may have uttered them in close succession because of his or her continuing interest in the events described coupled with a desire to focus different arguments on alternate occasions.

Somewhat better evidence can be found in a study I conducted with Loren Ann Frost in which children were taught novel verbs pertaining to reversible spatial relations, such as suspending or containing (the referents of either of the noun phrases could serve as the suspender, or as the container). The older children (5–6 years) frequently passivized the verbs even when they were taught only in the active voice. Since there were no suitable thematic roles to guide them, the children must have used a lexical rule.

Summary of Developmental Evidence for Lexical Acquisition Mechanics

I have presented evidence pertaining to four different acquisition mechanisms, partitioned into several subclasses. There was evidence that uniquely supported all four of the mechanisms. I summarize this discussion in Figure 8.18 by annotating the taxonomy in Figure 8.17 with citations of the evidence I have presented (except for the Pinker and Frost study).

Constraints on Lexicosyntactic Productivity

BAKER'S PARADOX

In recent years, the issue of how the child avoids overgeneralizing productive rules has been a focal point of discussion in the interface between learnability theory and developmental psycholinguistics (see, e.g., Baker, 1979; Bresnan, 1978; Lebeaux and Pinker, 1981; Maratsos et al., 1979; Mazurkewich and White,

Figure 8.18

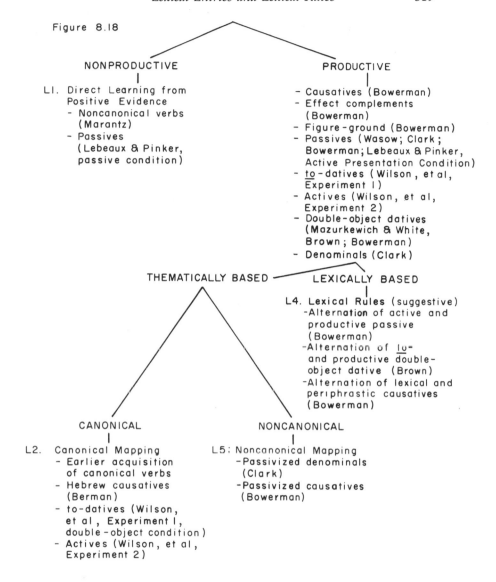

1984; Pinker, 1981b, 1982; Roeper et al., 1981; Wasow, 1981; Wilson et al. 1981). The problem was first defined by Baker (1979) in his classic paper "Syntactic Theory and the Projection Problem." Baker noted that rules traditionally thought of as transformations apply to some verbs but not others, requiring "negative exception features" to annotate the predicates that may not undergo the transformation. For example, the verb *show* undergoes dative movement but the verb *demonstrate* does not, as (26) illustrates.

(26) (a) John showed the new invention to Mary/showed Mary the new invention.
(b) John demonstrated the new invention to Mary/*demonstrated Mary the new invention.

Many other verb pairs resemble *show/demonstrate*, among them *tell/inform, give/donate,* and *send/transfer.* Furthermore, many other putative transformations have lexical exceptions, such as raising-to-subject, as in (27), and passivization, as in (28).

(27) (a) It is likely/probable that Bush will win.
(b) Bush is likely/*probable to win.

(28) (a) John has/owns three yachts.
(b) Three yachts are owned/*had by John.

One would thus have to stipulate that transformational rules with lexical exceptions cannot apply to verbs possessing a special feature, and the verbs that the transformation cannot apply to would have to possess such features (e.g., [− *dative movement*]) in their lexical entries. Baker pointed out that the problem with this account is that, given the absence of negative evidence, there is no obvious way for the child to gather evidence that certain verbs possess such features. Even if negative evidence is available on occasion, it is strikingly improbable that adults have at some point erred on, and have been corrected on, every predicate that they treat as an exception to a transformation.

Baker's solution was to discard certain transformations such as dative movement, and instead simply include two entries in the adult lexicon for each verb putatively undergoing the transformation and one entry for verbs not undergoing it, as in (29). Since each predicate would simply be entered into the lexicon when the child heard it by some procedure analogous to L1, there would be no problem of overgeneration.[8]

(29) (a) give (SUBJ , OBJ   , OBL$_{goal}$)
        agent theme goal
(b) give (SUBJ , OBJ2 , OBJ)
        agent theme goal
(c) donate (SUBJ , OBJ   , OBL$_{goal}$)
        agent theme goal

Unfortunately, the strength of this proposal is also its weakness: most of the examples of productivity in children cited in the

"Productivity in Verb Acquisition" section above are prima facie counterexamples to Baker's conservatism proposal. Nor does productivity stop with children: Wasow (1981) notes that coined verbs freely undergo operations such as dativization, so that *I will satellite you a letter* is an acceptable variant of *I will satellite a letter to you*, and so on.

We are faced, then, with an apparent paradox: children at some point must learn that certain lexicosyntactic combinations are ungrammatical; yet they receive no negative evidence, they are not in general conservative, and there is no obvious semantic criterion that differentiates the permissible from the impermissible forms (cf. *give/donate, have/own, likely/probable*). Clearly, something has to give.

One thing that might give is the supposed lack of negative evidence. Chomsky (1981) and others have conjectured that the child might somehow exploit "indirect negative evidence": if a certain form never appears in the input, he or she might assume that it is ungrammatical, without requiring overt corrections, disapproval, evidence of comprehension failure, and so on. Thus the gap in the input left by the nonoccurrence of *donate* NP_{goal} NP_{theme} and the like would signal to the child that such forms are ungrammatical, inspiring him or her to add a negative rule feature (transformational or lexical) onto the relevant verb. However, as Wexler (1981), Pinker (1981b), Bickerton (in press), and Mazurkewich and White (1984) point out, this account immediately runs up against several problems. Since language is infinite and creative, any finite sample of input is bound to lack many (indeed, an infinite number of) perfectly grammatical sentences. In order not to reject such grammatical sentences, the child would have to do one of two things. If he or she could predict from the context that a particular form would *have* to be uttered by the adult if the language would only permit it, the absence of such a form would indicate that that form was ungrammatical. Or if children were capable of calculating that if a given form was grammatical its probability of *not* occurring in an input sample of a given size was close to zero, then the absence of such a form in a sufficiently large sample would indicate that it was indeed ungrammatical. Both these proposals require that the child actively test for the occurrence of some forms (e.g., dativized *donate*) and not others (e.g., the full expansion of the English auxiliary as in *John must have been being kissed*, which is virtually nonexistent in spoken and written English speech yet instantly recognizable as grammatical).[9] Though some theory along such lines may be possible, to date I have seen no explicit proposals for how indirect negative evidence would work in practice, and hence will turn to other possible solutions to Baker's paradox.

I think that what must give in Baker's paradox is the supposed claim that the domains of productivity of the lexicosyntactic alternations are completely arbitrary, applying to some lexical items while sparing their doppelgangers. Upon closer examination, one finds that in adult English the productivity of all these processes is constrained by a combination of semantic and phonological factors. The solution to Baker's paradox that I will propose is similar to one suggested by Mazurkewich and White (1984). To get ahead of the story a bit, I will claim that (a) the child acquires productive rules whose domains of application are partially constrained; (b) productivity is a consequence of acquiring those rules; (c) successful avoidance of ungrammatical forms is a consequence of eventually acquiring appropriate constraints on those rules; (d) overgeneration is a product of initially failing to hypothesize or of misconstruing the constraints; (e) the acquisition of those few forms that disobey the constraints is accomplished by simple direct learning of those forms as they are exemplified in the input; and (f) ungrammatical forms created by an immature and overgeneral rule are expunged by mature rules and suppletive forms. Many of these processes will be effected by the mechanisms of paradigm formation and paradigm splitting originally introduced in Chapter 5. But before I propose this set of hypotheses, I will briefly examine how each of the lexicosyntactic processes is constrained.

Constraints on Lexicosyntactic Productivity

Passivization

Jackendoff (1972) has pointed out that passivization in English is largely constrained by the way that the verb's thematic roles are assigned to the subject and *by*-object. Specifically, he proposes that there is a hierarchy of thematic roles—theme; location/source/goal; agent—and a constraint that the thematic role assigned to the oblique *by*-object must be lower on this hierarchy than that assigned to the subject. Jackendoff cites two exceptions to passivization that may be subsumed under this principle. First, certain verbs are ambiguous between an agent/patient reading and a theme/location reading. For example, (30a) could mean either that John actively ran his fingers against the wire or that he happened to be in contact with it (i.e., he could be dead and his body propped up against it).

(30) (a)   John is touching the wire.
      (b)   The wire is [being] touched by John.

However, the passive version of the sentence, (30b), is not ambiguous; it could only mean that John actively touched the wire.
Jackendoff argues that the agent-theme reading requires the agent
to be associated with the *by*-object and the theme with the subject. In contrast, the theme-location reading requires the theme
to be associated with the *by*-object and the location with the
subject, violating the constraint that the *by*-object has a lower
role on the thematic hierarchy. The second example consists of
measure verbs (e.g., *twenty-five dollars is cost by Pinker's book*).
Jackendoff argues that the measure argument has the thematic
role *location*, since a measurement is conceptually a point along
an abstract scale, and since English often uses locative prepositions in measure phrases such as *Robey weighed in at 250 pounds*
or *eggs are selling at a dollar a dozen*. Passivized measure sentences
thus require that the *by*-object be assigned the theme role, which
is higher rather than lower than the location role. It is also worth
noting that several other well-known exceptions to passivization
may be subsumed under this principle, given certain reasonable
assumptions about the thematic relations involved. *Bill was resembled by John* is out if *Bill* is construed as a goal (cf. *John's
resemblance to Bill*); *Bill was escaped by John's arguments* is out if
Bill is construed as a source (cf. *John escaped from Bill*); *an explosion
in language acquisition research was witnessed by the 1960s* is out if
an explosion is construed as a goal (cf. *John was witness to an
explosion*).

Dativization

Mazurkewich and White (1984), citing earlier work by Goldsmith (1980), Oehrle (1976), and Stowell (1981), point out that
most double-object datives satisfy two constraints: the verbs must
be monosyllabic (more precisely, they must be of Anglo-Saxon
rather than Latin origin, and as a result are either monosyllabic,
or bisyllabic with stress on the first syllable), and the referent
of the indirect object must be a prospective possessor (equivalently, a goal and possessor—for *to*-datives—or a beneficiary
and possessor—for *for*-datives) of the referent of the object (this
would also include abstract possession—e.g., of ideas, messages, or stories communicated successfully). The phonological
constraint accounts for the contrast in dativizability between *give*
and *donate, transfer,* or *return*; between *tell* and *explain, report,* or
announce; between *throw* and *propel*; between *teach* and *instruct*;

between *make* and *create*; and so on.[10] The semantic constraint accounts for the contrast in dativizability between *bake, bring, buy, give, pass, send, tell, rent*, etc., on the one hand, and *cut, drive, prove, stir, wash, brush*, etc., on the other (e.g. *I baked/cut the cake for John; I baked/*cut John the cake*). It also accounts for the contrast between dativization in certain abstract versus concrete arguments: *I owe five dollars/this example to John* versus *I owe John five dollars/*this example; I made a pie/a decision for Suzanne* versus *I made Suzanne a pie/*a decision*. Mazurkewich and White thus propose that the English dative be stated so as to apply only to verbs that meet the phonological *and* semantic constraints. (There are exceptions to this constraint, but Mazurkewich and White deal with them in a way that I will briefly discuss later.)

Causativization

It has often been noted (e.g., Fodor, 1970; Talmy, 1976; Shibatani, 1976) that English lexical causatives, in contrast to periphrastic causatives, can be used only in cases of direct or immediate physical causation; see (31).

(31) (a)   John broke the window by hitting it with a bat.
     (b)   John caused the window to break by hitting it with a bat.
     (c)   *John broke the window by startling the carpenter, who was installing it.
     (d)   John caused the window to break by startling the carpenter, who was installing it.

In addition, Gergely and Bever (1982), discussing counterexamples to causativization raised by Fodor, Garrett, Walker, and Parkes (1980), point out that lexical causativization requires that the agent, manner, and goal of causation be conventional or stereotypic for the relevant action. For example, although *to paint* means "to cause to be covered with paint," one does not "paint one's brush" when one dips it in the can, nor did Michelangelo "paint the ceiling" when he caused the ceiling of the Sistine Chapel to be covered with paint. Gergely and Bever also point out that one can say *the nurse burped the baby* but not *the bananas burped the baby* even though both periphrastic forms are permissible. Gergely and Bever argue that these facts follow from *paint*'s having a stereotypic goal and manner in which a specific instrument is used and the goal is to protect or improve the appearance of the surface painted. *Burp* has a stereotypic animate agent and a stereotypic manner of patting on the back. In addition, they point out that there are no lexical causatives for verbs like *laugh* and *vomit* that lack conventional direct means of causation (e.g., **Harry laughed/vomited Bill* versus *Harry caused Bill to laugh/vomit*). Furthermore, the currently ungrammatical lexical causative **Bill bled Sam* (cf. *Bill caused Sam to bleed*) was grammatical during the historical period when causing to bleed was a standard medical practice. (Note also that specialized fields of expertise often permit lexical causatives that are not sanctioned by speakers at large: *vanish the elephant, crash the computer, walk the batter, hop the affix.*)

Figure-Ground Verbs

Anderson (1971), Talmy (1976), and Bowerman (1982c) point out that verbs that alternate between the lexical forms V NP$_1$ *into/onto/against* NP$_2$ and V NP$_2$ *of/with* NP$_1$ must involve a moving physical entity (the "theme" or "figure") and a larger location that the entity moves toward or away from (the "location" or "ground"). Hence verbs that use oblique objects to specify instruments rather than themes cannot undergo the alternation, e.g., **I ate a spoon into my cereal, *I opened my key against the door*. In addition, the *with/of* form implies that every part of the "ground" be added to or subtracted from in the way specified by the verb: if I empty garbage from the bag, there may be some garbage still left in it, but if I empty the bag of garbage, the bag is completely empty. I have noticed that this constraint seems to apply not only to the circumstances in which figure-ground alternations are possible for a given verb, as Bowerman noted, but also to the choice of which verbs can alternate at all: verbs that do not admit of the possibility of completeness of effect are less likely to undergo the alternation. Hence **he read the book of a poem* is ungrammatical even though *he read a poem out of the book* is fine, because no matter how long or hard one reads the poem, the book still contains it. Likewise *I saw Bill from the doorway* cannot be expressed as **I saw the doorway of Bill*, because the doorway, which is the source of one's gaze (see Jackendoff, 1983), is never exhausted of it.

Denominal Verbs

Clark and Clark (1979) discuss a variety of factors conditioning the acceptability of denominal verb formation. One of the most salient is that the original noun must play certain thematic roles with respect to the coined verb. Thus we have *he captained the ship* (agent), *he knotted the rope* (goal), and *he wedged the door* (instrument), and (less often) *he pieced the puzzle together* (source), and *they summered in France* (temporal location). What is ruled out altogether is the case where a verb is derived from a noun whose only connection to the verb's action or state is that it is characteristic of the noun's referent, e.g., *the bell belled*. In addition, denominal verb formation is usually blocked when there already exists a verb with the desired meaning, or when the derived verb already has another meaning (these are not semantic constraints on the rule but are related to a version of the Uniqueness Principle that I will propose later in the chapter).

ACQUIRING RESTRICTIONS ON PRODUCTIVITY

The preceding section showed that the productivity inherent in lexical rules or canonical mapping is frequently constrained by a combination of semantic and phonological factors. Given these constraints, we have a glimmering of how the productivity paradox may be resolved: children may be productive, but as soon as their productivity becomes subject to the proper constraints, they will no longer overgenerate. In this section I present a theory of how the child learns to impose these reins on his or her productive lexicosyntactic acquisition mechanisms, and examine the evidence on whether and when children do so.

One salient feature of the constraints on productivity discussed above is their heterogeneity. The constraining factors range from number of syllables to choice of thematic roles to cultural conventions of causation to completeness of effect. This is not surprising, given that the lexicon is the component of grammar that interfaces most closely with conceptual knowledge in all its intricacy. But as a result I cannot present a single theory that accounts for the acquisition of all the constraints on productivity. In particular, the constraints on English verbal passivization seem of a different kind than those on the other alternations, and so I will treat the two sets of phenomena separately. After attempting to account for the acquisition of the two sets of constraints, I turn to the final problem to be discussed in this chapter: how the child expunges the bad entries in the lexicon once he or she has succeeded in discovering the correct range of application of lexical rules.

Thematic Hierarchy Rearrangement

Recall that the principal constraint on passivization in English appears to be Jackendoff's thematic hierarchy constraint: the thematic role of the *by*-object must be higher than that of the subject on the hierarchy *agent–location/source/goal–theme*. The reader may have noticed that this constraint is formally very similar to the constraint on canonical lexical forms outlined by Lebeaux (1983, in preparation) and introduced earlier in this chapter. In each case there are two orderings, one for thematic roles and one for grammatical relations, and a constraint stating that links between the orderings must not cross in a verb's assignment of one to another. These two pairs of hierarchies are reproduced in (32a) and (32b).

(32) (a) Active: SUBJ   OBJ   OBL
                   agent theme   location/source/goal

    (b) Passive: SUBJ   OBL
                   theme   location/source/goal   agent

Note that the two thematic tiers are not reflections of one another; if they were, all canonical verbs would passivize.

I am assuming that structure (32a) is not learned by the language acquisition mechanisms (see Chapter 2). As for structure (32b), I have discovered that acquiring it is in fact quite straightforward, since the passive rule, once learned, can derive it from (32a) under a reasonable assumption. Suppose that whenever a new lexical rule is acquired it alters the canonical thematic hierarchy (32a) to produce a noncanonical thematic hierarchy in the following way: (a) all functions mentioned by the rule are paired with their canonical thematic roles; (b) rule operations that replace a function by SUBJ "promote" that function's canonical thematic role to the top of the hierarchy; (c) rule operations that replace a function by OBL "demote" that function's canonical thematic role to the bottom of the hierarchy. In the case of passivization, the new hierarchy would be created as follows. The passive rule, reproduced in (33), mentions SUBJ, OBJ, and OBL.

(33) OBJ $\mapsto$ SUBJ
    SUBJ $\mapsto$ OBL$_{agent}$

These functions are canonically paired with *agent, theme,* and *location/source/goal*, respectively. The first part of the verb "promotes" the OBJ argument to SUBJ; this would have the effect of promoting *theme* to the top of the interim hierarchy, yielding (34).

(34) theme   agent   location/source/goal

The second part of the rule "demotes" the SUBJ argument to OBL; this would have the effect of demoting *agent* to the bottom of the hierarchy, yielding (35).

(35) theme   location/source/goal   agent

The hierarchy in (35) is simply Jackendoff's thematic hierarchy, or the thematic tier of (32b). When paired with the original hierarchy of grammatical functions (OBJ is now irrelevant because it is absent from passives), it serves to define acceptable passive lexical forms via the no-crossing-links provision.[11] The grammatical function and thematic role hierarchies can now function as a more sophisticated version of the noncanonical mapping mechanism proposed earlier, serving as a sufficient condition for the creation of verb forms. When bona fide lexical rules are acquired (i.e., the child maps from active onto passive forms, without regard to thematic roles), the hierarchy can still serve as an output filter or necessary condition on the application of such rules, prohibiting the creation of passivized verbs with crossed links between thematic and grammatical relations. See Fillmore (1968), Perlmutter and Postal (1977), Perlmutter (1980), Williams (1981c), and others for independent characterizations of replacement by subject as "promotion" and replacement by oblique as "demotion." It is a question for future research whether the notion of thematic hierarchy rearrangement described above will be useful when applied to rules other than passivization.

Developmental evidence on the acquisition of passive constraints. If, as I have argued, the noncanonical thematic hierarchy governing passivization is an automatic formal concomitant of the acquisition of passivization itself, one would not expect the child to pass through a stage at which he or she passivizes productively but overgenerally. Indeed, this seems to be the case: all the examples of ungrammatical passives I cited in (22) are ungrammatical not because the child violated the thematic hierarchy condition but rather because he or she simply used a verb that does not exist in English with the intended meaning. There are no examples of errors like *twenty-five cents is cost by a game of Pac-Man*.

Interestingly, there is a certain paradoxical data pattern concerning children's *reluctance* to passivize certain verbs that may reflect the application of the thematic hierarchy condition. Maratsos, Kuczaj, Fox, and Chalkley (1979) have shown in two experiments that 4- and 5-year-old children have great difficulty comprehending passive sentences with experiential verbs such as *like, know, remember, see,* and *forget.* At the same time, they had no trouble understanding the active versions of these verbs, nor the passives of action verbs such as *kiss* and *tickle.* Though the methodology in Maratsos et al.'s first study is somewhat problematic (e.g., comprehension was assessed by asking "who did it" after each sentence, which is distinctly odd for a non-action verb and even more so when the passivized object of experience is found in the focused subject position), the effect was replicated by Maratsos et al. and by de Villiers, Phinney, and Avery (1982) using different methodologies. Furthermore, de Villiers et al. showed that the interaction does *not* manifest itself when measured by sentence verification time in older children and adults. This weakens the possibility that Maratsos's effect is an artifact of the cumulative processing difficulty of passive sentences per se and of nonaction verbs per se combining nonlinearly in their overall effects on comprehension difficulty. Maratsos et al. conclude that the child's rule of passivization applies only to agents, not to subjects in general.

In Pinker (1982), however, I pointed out that Maratsos's effect could have come about if the children were still at an unproductive stage vis à vis passive and if passivized experiential verbs are rare in parental speech (we know that verbal passives of all sorts are rare; Pinker and Hochberg, in preparation). To test Maratsos's hypothesis in a paradigm that avoids this problem, Lebeaux and I (1981) presented children with two concocted verbs appearing exclusively in active sentences and two concocted verbs appearing exclusively in passive sentences, with one verb in each pair referring to an action (nuzzling or leap-frogging), and the other referring to a perceptual relation (seeing through a binoculars-like device or hearing through an ear-trumpet-like device). Contrary to Maratsos's results and his conjecture about children's passive rule, we found our subjects perfectly willing to comprehend and produce passivized nonaction verbs, even those never heard in the passive. In another study, Loren Ann Frost and I found children able to produce and comprehend concocted verbs in novel voices whether they signified actions between toy animals or spatial relations between objects (i.e., relations roughly analogous to *suspend* and *contain*).

How are we to reconcile this discrepancy between the two sets of experiments, such that children refused to passivize nonaction verbs for Maratsos et al. but were perfectly happy to passivize them for Lebeaux and me? Here is a proposal. According to the current theory, neither the child nor the adult entertains the hypothesis that passivization is constrained by some blanket restriction like "agentive subjects only" or "action verbs only." Rather, the restriction is something similar to Jackendoff's Thematic Hierarchy Condition. If the child's passivization rule is more like a noncanonical mapping rule than like a lexical rule (and earlier I argued that there is evidence pointing to that possibility), he or she will *require* that passivized verbs *obey* the condition, rather than *preventing* passivized verbs from *disobeying* it. If so, verbs whose arguments cannot be classified as playing determinate thematic roles will not be assigned passive lexical forms. Now, the nonaction verbs used by Maratsos et al. and by de Villiers et al. were heterogeneous, including perceptual verbs like *see* and *hear* and also cognitive stative verbs such as *know, want, remember, miss, forget*, and *like*. The nonaction verbs used by Lebeaux and Pinker were strictly perceptual, having *see* and *hear* as their closest analogues. Crucially, Jackendoff (1983) notes that "perception verbs, like 'see' . . . fall under the TRH [Thematic Relations Hypothesis; viz., that the verb's arguments have determinate thematic roles]. On the other hand, there are fairly common verbs, such as 'use', 'try', 'like', 'want', and 'need', that have no obvious thematic analysis." Specifically, Jackendoff argues that *see*'s arguments play the role of the possessor/source and the goal/location of one's gaze, respectively, whereas nonsensory cognitive verbs such as *want* support no such analysis. Thus the child might create a passive form for nonaction perceptual verbs like *see*, whose arguments can be given grammatical functions via their thematic roles, while being unable to do so for the nonaction nonperceptual verbs like *want, know*, or *like* (adults could create passives for such verbs by deploying lexical rules). Thus part of the discrepancy in existing studies may be attributable to a loose definition investigators have used of what counts as a "nonaction" verb. Nonaction verbs may in fact subdivide into thematic and nonthematic verbs in a manner that is crucial to passivizability.[12]

Weakly supporting evidence for this account is the repeated discovery that the verb *follow* is particularly difficult for children to passivize, whether they are learning English, French, or German (Turner and Rommetveit, 1967; Sinclair, Sinclair, and de Marcellus, 1971). *Follow* is an unusual action verb in that it connotes a nonagentive subject. It would not be surprising if children attributed the agency in acts of following to the leader and not the follower, or if they interpreted the leader as a goal that the follower, the theme, was approaching. In either case, the reader can verify that the child's misconstrual would result in the passive form violating the Thematic Hierarchy Condition.

Are thematic relations learned? This account of passivization constraints relies heavily on the child's giving the correct thematic analysis to verbs, including semi-abstract verbs. For example, I explain the absence of childhood errors in measure verbs as a consequence of the child's correct construal of measurements as locations on a scale; I explain the passivizability of our *see*-analogue in the Lebeaux and Pinker experiment as a consequence of children's ability to construe seeing as the movement of one's gaze, and so on. Likewise, in discussing the constraints on dativization I will presuppose a correct thematic analysis on the part of the child of nonmotional verbs such as *read* and *tell*, so that *read/tell me a story* will obey the constraint that the indirect object be a prospective possessor of the theme. That is, the child must conceive of himself or herself as "possessing" knowledge of the story in order to allow the double-object dative form in this example.

Naturally this begs the question of how the child construes arguments as bearing the appropriate thematic roles. It is not a straightforward perceptual task, for no tangible object can be seen to move or assume some determinate location in the case of *see, cost, tell,* and so on. Linguists themselves must gather indirect evidence for a given thematic analysis, such as the particular preposition required by the nominalization of the verb or by some closely related verb form, the nature of the metaphors that naturally arise in that semantic field, whether the same verb takes spatial and nonspatial arguments, and so on. These sources of evidence are in many cases unavailable to the child, and even in cases where they are available, the child would have to possess some nonobvious acquisition mechanism capable of exploiting them.

An alternative and simpler account is that the thematic analyses of most of the child's verbs are an immediate consequence of his or her conceptual representation of their meaning. That is, the meaning of *tell* would actually be construed by the child as involving an abstract act of transfer conforming to a similar cognitive schema as that used for physical acts of transfer. The child would not have to learn that the indirect object argument of *tell* is like an end-state location, because he or she would already conceptualize the act that way. This is the account favored by Jackendoff (1978, 1983), who cites the widespread use of spatial terms in English and other languages to denote various entities and relations (see also H. H. Clark, 1973; Talmy, 1976, 1978).

Pertinent evidence, as usual, comes from Bowerman. If the

child has a natural tendency to conceptualize nonspatial acts in spatial terms, one would expect two sets of errors to occur: (1) the use of verbs of motion to signify changes of attributes, possession, or circumstance; (2) the use of spatial prepositions or case markers to introduce abstract goals, locations, sources, and so on in the absence of any existing verb that subcategorizes for those prepositions or case markers. As for (1), Bowerman (1982a) documents her children using spatial or motional verbs for temporal relations (36a), changes of state (36b, c), and changes of circumstance or identity (36d, e)—these do not exhaust her examples.

(36) (a)   Friday is covering Saturday and Sunday so I can't have Saturday and Sunday if I don't go through Friday.
     (b)   I putted part of the sleeve blue so I crossed it out with red [talking about a mistake in drawing].
     (c)   I'm taking these cracks bigger [while cracking a peanut shell].
     (d)   I would like him to put me into a little, little person [referring to a storybook fairy].
     (e)   I'm gonna put them having peas so they'll have some dinner that we are [referring to an arrangement of dolls].

Bowerman also documents cases of her children using incorrect spatial prepositions for temporal relations (e.g., (36a), (37a)), changes of state (36d), and causal relations (e.g., (37b, c)). In the latter example, the causal entity seems to be construed as the "source" of causation; this pattern is also documented by Maratsos and Abramovitch (1974).

(37) (a)   Can I have any reading behind the dinner?
     (b)   My dolly is scrunched from somebody . . . but not from me.
     (c)   They had to stop from a red light.

Bowerman even cites cases where a child used spatial nouns for temporal intervals: *do we have room before we go to bed for another reading*, and *today we'll be packing 'cause tomorrow there won't be enough space to pack*. Finally, Slobin (1984a) cites cases of German children incorrectly using spatial prepositions to signify possession, and Hungarian children incorrectly using the case marker for spatial goals to signify dative goals. When a language conflates spatial markers with possessional or dative markers, the two uses of the single form typically emerge simultaneously.

Thus it is possible that the child conceives of certain abstract predicate-argument relations in terms of the motional schema underlying thematic relations. To the extent that this is true, one need postulate no language-specific learning mechanism to account for the application of the thematic constraints on passivization and dativization to nonmotional verbs. The correct application will be a consequence of whatever cognitive prerequisites there are to conceptualizing the relevant semantic fields according to spatial schemata. I do not expect that this will work in all cases, since possibly some verbs are given thematic analyses on the basis of the prepositions they are found with, rather than vice versa. However, the cross-linguistic and developmental data converge to suggest that the core of the thematic relations system does not require a special acquisition mechanism dedicated to inducing it from the input.[13]

Acquisition of Other Constraints on Lexicosyntactic Productivity

The preceding section described the acquisition of the fairly elegant constraint on English passivization. The constraints on datives, causatives, figure-ground verbs, denominals, and so on, seem less well behaved, involving the postulation of heterogeneous obligatory conditions such as monosyllabicity, cultural conventionality, conditions on thematic roles, and so on. Similarly, the English nominal passive (Fiengo, 1977) and the passive in other languages (Bresnan, 1982b) are constrained in more specialized ways than the English verbal passive. Here I will propose that these conditions are acquired by a hypothesization and paradigm-splitting procedure related to the one introduced in Chapter 5.

In Pinker (1982), I noted that lexical rules often require that the affected arguments have certain thematic roles, and proposed that when the child examines parallel lexical forms in the process of coining a lexical rule, he or she imposes restrictions on the resulting lexical rule corresponding to the thematic roles found in those forms. Hence if all the verbs in the child's lexicon with alternative active and passive forms were agent-theme verbs, the child would coin a passive rule containing the proviso that the derived subject must be a theme and the derived oblique object must be an agent. (Depending on whether these thematic provisos operated as sufficient or as necessary conditions, passivization would be a noncanonical mapping rule or a bona fide but constrained lexical rule, respectively.) As the child acquired active-passive pairs for words with different thematic roles, those roles would be disjoined to the list of provisos; if at some point a complete set of roles constituted the proviso set, or if a nonthematic active-passive pair were acquired, the provisos would be expunged. The advantage of this account is that it has the child acquiring lexical rules conservatively, applying them only to domains where their application has been witnessed in the input, and obviating the need for negative evidence or other corrective mechanisms.

Unfortunately, the account suffers from two disadvantages. First, as we have seen, not *all* constraints on lexical rules pertain to thematic roles. The obvious way to modify this procedure would be to have the child hypothesize the full set of potentially grammatically relevant properties of a verb whenever a lexical rule is coined, and deleting provisos from the list as they are violated by future lexical pairs. This modification is somewhat implausible, however, because the universe of possible constraints is fairly large and the processing capacity of the child is small. A second problem is that the account predicts that children should never overapply a lexical rule, since their progression is from specific to general domains of application under the guidance of the range of forms attested in the input. Though I have claimed that passivization constraints are not violated by children, constraints on other lexical rules seem to be. Mazurkewich and White (1984) report that their 8- and 9-year-old subjects judged polysyllabic double-object datives as grammatical 47 percent of the time. They also note that even example (23a), *I'll brush him his hair*, violates the constraint on double-object datives, since the object must be a *prospective* (not current) possessor. Bowerman (1982b) notes that many of children's ungrammatical lexical causatives violate the constraint that the causation be direct (e.g., *these are nice beds . . . Enough to wish me that I had one of those beds; I want to watch you this book*). Likewise, some incorrect figure-ground usages violate the constraint that the object be completely filled, emptied, etc. (e.g., *I poured you . . .* [Mother: You poured me?] *. . . Yeah, with water*, where presumably the mother was not completely drenched by the child's pouring). Finally, Clark (1982) points out that many denominal verb errors violate the condition that the source noun be one that plays a determinate semantic role in the action (agent, manner, instrument, and so on), pertaining instead to a characteristic activity involving the noun (e.g., *the buzzer is buzzering; I'm souping* [eating soup]; *will you nut these?* [crack these nuts]).

The reader may have noted that these problems are reminiscent of those encountered by the "exhaustive hypothesization" model of inflection acquisition introduced and rejected in Chapter 5. Both models have the child hypothesizing a full set of constraints at first and gradually eliminating members of the set when they are counterexemplified. Both suffer from implausibility given the number of potentially relevant hypotheses. And both are embarrassed by examples of children overgeneralizing. I propose that the solution is the same in both cases. The child need not hypothesize *all* the potentially relevant constraints that are exemplified by a particular input item in one fell swoop; he or she simply must be capable of hypothesizing *any one* of them with nonzero probability on *some* occasion, and then not abandon a hypothesis if it is never contradicted by a subsequent input exemplar. In the case of constraints on lexicosyntactic productivity, then, whenever the child generates or strengthens a learned productive rule (either a lexical rule or noncanonical mapping) on the basis of a pair of individually acquired entries, he or she samples a potential constraint from the set of linguistically possible constraints that are satisfied by the lexical pair being examined, and adds it as an obligatory condition to the rule. If a rule ever contains a set of conditions that exhaust the possibilities in that subdomain (e.g., both values of a binary phonological feature such as monosyllabicity, or a full set of thematic roles, including "no role"), then the entire set is expunged. In this model only a single constraint need be entertained at once, and examples of overgeneration are the result of the child's not yet hypothesizing the necessary constraint.

Evidence that children's overgeneration errors are the result of not yet entertaining an appropriate hypothesis comes from Bowerman (1982b), who shows that children not only use lexical causatives to signify indirect causation, but they also use periphrastic causatives to signify direct causation, resulting in sentences that are somewhat odd-sounding to adult ears: *I maked mosquitoes dead in the park* (cf. *kill*); *would you make it* [a rollerskate] *come on my foot?* (cf. *put*); *I didn't get 'em lost* (cf. *lose*); *then I'm going to sit on him and made him broken* (cf. *break*). Thus it appears that the children at this stage are simply oblivious to the directness of causation as a constraining feature on either form of the English causative.

To make this model plausible, one would need to show first of all that the set of potential constraints is not open-ended (if it were, there is no guarantee that the child would *ever* spontaneously hypothesize a correct constraint). In other words, we need something like the (possibly hierarchically organized) finite set of grammaticizable features proposed for affixation by Slobin and Talmy and adopted in Chapter 5. Unfortunately, I know of no specific proposals for such a finite set relevant to the class of rules under consideration; one problem is that the exact membership of the class of rules is controversial, most notably in the case of passive. However, I expect that the list will not be open-ended, since the constraints that are required for the rules I have examined, while heterogeneous, do not seem to be completely arbitrary or ad hoc to individual rules. Restrictions on the thematic roles of the arguments whose grammatical functions undergo replacement seem to be a pervasive constraint on lexical rules (e.g., nominal passives in English, verbal passives in other languages, datives and denominals in English). Monosyllabicity, relevant to dativization in English, is a feature relevant to affixation in other languages, often in connection with grammatical gender; if, as seems likely, the constraint is to be stated instead as native versus non-native or Anglo-Saxon versus Latinate, then there are other lexical rules in English that respect the distinction, such as comparative formation (e.g., pretty/prettier; intelligent/ *intelligenter). Even the constraint on causativization that pertains to cultural conventionality, a seemingly remote feature for grammaticization, enters into other productive word formation processes. McCawley (1971) notes that deinstrumental verb formation requires that the instrument be a conventional or stereotypic one for the action in question; hence we can say *he nailed the pieces together* but not *he penciled the pieces together* even if a pencil was serving as a makeshift fastener.

The search problem and the splitting of lexical paradigms. Still, it is unlikely that the set of possible constraints is extremely small, or that every constraint is spontaneously hypothesizable out of thin air by the child. It would be nice to have a procedure that could draw the child's attention to a relevant constraint in cases where the constraint was low on the accessibility hierarchy for hypothesizable constraints relevant to lexical rules. Again this is not a new problem; it arose in Chapter 5 in connection with my asking what would prompt a Navajo child to attend to dimensionality as a possible agreement feature, what would prompt a Turkish child to attend to witness-versus-hearsay as a possible verb marker, and so on. The answer there was that failure to attend to such features would eventually lead to violations of the unique entry principle in inflectional paradigms. This would prompt the child to search actively for word-intrinsic features (in the case of violations discovered in general paradigms) or context-specific features (in the case of violations discovered in word-specific paradigms) that could account for the distribution of the set of affixes competing for a single cell. The same mechanism will do the job in this case under certain plausible assumptions.

I mentioned earlier that one can define a paradigm dimension corresponding to the various ways in which a verb's arguments can be mapped onto grammatical functions. The levels of that paradigm dimension could include active, passive, causative, reflexive, inchoative, middle, and so on, differing somewhat from language to language but drawn from a small universal set. (Possibly certain subsets of levels could form subdimensions that can cross with one another, such as active-passive and causative-noncausative, and, as mentioned, others might be nested under a superordinate, such as transitive-intransitive.) The child would form such a paradigm for each verb and fill each cell as an entry corresponding to it is learned from positive evidence. In addition, certain levels such as "causative" and "inchoative" would be defined as the products of certain semantic operations on the predicate, so that both lexical and periphrastic forms, and even lexical forms for morphologically unrelated verbs, would be eligible for entry into these cells if they met the semantic definitions. (The importance of this assumption will become apparent later.)

Crucially, the Unique Entry principle applies to lexical construction paradigms: no construction can be realized by more than one lexical form. Thus the child will, in certain circumstances, encounter uniqueness violations in word-specific paradigms. A prime example would be causative forms in English, where the child might at one point have constructed a paradigm roughly like the one shown in Figure 8.19. (The feature [*cause*] would be appended to causal complement-taking verbs such as *make, cause,* and *get.*) Just as in the case of uniqueness violations in word-specific inflectional paradigms, the child can resolve this violation by beginning to search for a new dimension distinguishing the two competing forms of the causative. He or she does so by focusing on context-specific features evident in future usages of one of the forms, using a procedure like I10 and I11 described in Chapter 5. Each feature would be hypothesized as a dimension nested within the causative level, and would be

Figure 8.19

open:

CONSTRUCTION

Active	Causative
(SUBJ) theme	(SUBJ, OBJ) / [cause] (SUBJ, OBJ, V-COMP) agent theme agent theme

confirmed or disconfirmed according to the familiar procedures discussed above and in Chapter 5. In particular, when the child notices on a particular occasion that the lexical causative is being used to denote an act of direct physical causation (or conversely, when he or she notices that the periphrastic form is being used to denote an act of indirect causation) and hypothesizes a dimension corresponding to it, that hypothesis will not suffer from disconfirming instances and will thus remain in the paradigm, yielding Figure 8.20. Thanks to the paradigm notation, the Unique Entry constraint, and the universally available level *Causative* (more than one realization of which triggers Unique Entry enforcement), the child is impelled to search actively for a specific set of feature hypotheses (specifically, context-specific features distinguishing lexical from periphrastic uses) that he or she might not have hypothesized spontaneously by sampling from all the properties of a single lexical form.[14]

As in Chapter 5, the distinction between context-specific features and word-intrinsic features corresponds to the distinction between uniqueness violations in word-specific and in general paradigms. Directness of causation and completeness of effect (in figure-ground verbs) are context-specific; cultural stereotypy of causation, mono- versus polysyllabicity, prospective possession, and so on, are word-intrinsic. Intermediate cases could arise when a feature is context-specific but certain predicates are intrinsically incapable of entering into one of the situation types (e.g., *I rejoiced John,* where direct physical causation of rejoicing is impossible).

Let us turn now to uniqueness violations in general paradigms. Although word-intrinsic features not spontaneously hypothesized by the child can still be learned by the resolution of uniqueness violations in general paradigms, such learning depends upon an additional assumption. Consider how the child would discover that only monosyllabic verbs allow dativization if it did not initially occur to him or her to hypothesize that as a constraint upon the double-object form. A dativizable verb like

Figure 8.20

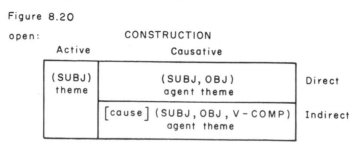

give would have the word-specific paradigm shown in part (a) of Figure 8.21, and *donate* would have the paradigm shown in part (b), both created by the learning of individual verb forms attested in the input. The general paradigms abstracted from the word-specific paradigms in Figure 8.21 would look like Figure 8.22.

Clearly, the two different sorts of verbs will yield two different sorts of general paradigms, but the difference does not, strictly speaking, result in a uniqueness violation. It is not that the exceptional verbs contribute a *different* realization of a form; they

Figure 8.21

a) give:

CONSTRUCTION

Active	Passive	Double-object
$(SUBJ, OBJ, OBL_{goal})$ agent theme goal	$(OBL_{agent}, SUBJ, OBL_{goal})$ agent theme goal	$(SUBJ, OBJ2, OBJ)$ agent theme goal

b) donate:

CONSTRUCTION

Active	Passive
$(SUBJ, OBJ, OBL_{goal})$ agent theme goal	$(OBL, SUBJ, OBL_{goal})$ agent theme goal

Figure 8.22

a)

CONSTRUCTION

Active	Passive	Double-object
$(SUBJ, OBJ, OBL_{goal})$ agent theme goal	$(OBL_{agent}, SUBJ, OBL_{goal})$ agent theme goal	$(SUBJ, OBJ2, OBJ)$ agent theme goal

b)

CONSTRUCTION

Active	Passive
$(SUBJ, OBJ, OBL_{goal})$ agent theme goal	$(OBL_{agent}, SUBJ, OBL_{goal})$ agent theme goal

contribute *no* realization of that form. For an analogue of Chapter 5's procedures I8 and I9 to work, it would have to treat "conflicts" consisting of realized and nonrealized cells in the same way as conflicts consisting of incompatible realizations, in both cases searching for features distinguishing the two sets of verbs contributing the different types of general paradigms.

Note that this is a somewhat risky procedure: many dativizable verbs will lack entries for the double-object form simply because no adult has yet had occasion to use that form in front of the child, and in such cases, the child would entertain various incorrect hypotheses stating that certain intrinsic properties of such verbs preclude their dativization in English. However, the risk is not as serious as it might first appear, for three reasons. First, it is unlikely to be a coincidence that dativizable verbs are generally of high frequency, hence likely to appear in both forms in the input. As a consequence, not appearing in a double-object form is statistically predictive of a verb's not being dativizable. Second, the creation of general paradigms with unrealized cells, and the search for word-intrinsic features differentiating the words that inspired the two types of general paradigms, presumably are frequency-sensitive in some way, and hence legitimate features are more likely to account for the overall differences between the two types of forms in the lexicon (albeit imperfectly) than spurious features. Third, all hypotheses are subject to disconfirmation by future input exemplars (i.e., when an exhaustive set of feature values for a feature are all hypothesized), so the risk is only in seducing the child to *test*, not permanently adopt, some spurious hypothesis. In any case, noting the differences between verbs with realized versus nonrealized double-object cells will direct the child to a smaller set of potential features than he or she would otherwise have to consider, even if some of the hypotheses are still spurious, and this is all that I wish for these mechanisms to accomplish.[15]

The final general paradigm, after the child has noted the phonological differences between most of the verbs that do and most of the verbs that do not have filled double-object cells, and has postulated that difference as a paradigm constraint, will look like Figure 8.23. (Of course, prospective possession by an animate goal would also at some point be a paradigm dimension, and there would be crossed dimensions differentiating the active and passive and the oblique and double-object dative forms. Both here and in the causative example the exact dimension labels shown in the figures are not exact but are simply intended to illustrate the operation of the acquisition mechanisms.) A similar

Figure 8.23

CONSTRUCTION

		Active	Passive	Double-object
SYLLABICITY	Mono	$(SUBJ, OBJ, OBL_{goal})$	$(OBL_{agent}, SUBJ, OBL_{goal})$	$(SUBJ, OBJ2, OBJ)$
	Poly	$(SUBJ, OBJ, OBL_{goal})$	$(OBL_{agent}, SUBJ, OBL_{goal})$	------------

procedure, I assume, could speed up the search for the relatively inaccessible word-intrinsic constraints on other productive lexicosyntactic alternations.

What the notion of general and specific paradigms has contributed is a mechanism whereby the child can juxtapose the appropriate sets of minimally contrasting lexical forms in order to narrow down the search for relevant constraints to just those features differentiating the contrasting forms. Universally available construction types define certain forms as easily learnable (e.g., Bresnan, 1982b, proposes that passivization is universal; hence it might be more easily learnable than other alternations), and these types define what the cells are, such that "more than one entry in a cell" is perceived as a uniqueness violation and hence triggers a feature search. In addition, the decision to search for word-intrinsic versus context-specific features can be made reliably by noting which type of paradigm gives rise to the uniqueness violation.

Developmental evidence for the unique entry principle in lexical paradigms. As always, one can consider the ability of an acquisition mechanism to account for some regularity in language—in this case, the fact that languages avoid having doubly-filled cells in lexical paradigms—as prima facie support for that mechanism. However, it would be better to have independent evidence from children's language as well. In the case of the child avoiding word-specific or general lexical paradigms with two indistinguishable instantiations of a given form, direct developmental evidence is scanty but there are some tantalizing shreds. Marantz (personal communication) tried to teach English-speaking children a concocted morphological passive rule applying to existing verbs, according to which *the wagon is pullpooming the pig* meant *the wagon is being pulled by the pig.* The children would have no part of it, which stands in stark contrast to children's willingness to generalize the existing passive rule to concocted verbs in the Lebeaux and Pinker and the Pinker and Frost studies. There are many possible explanations, but a plausible one is that children avoid the uniqueness violation that would result from entering two passives into a given verb's lexical paradigm, or two processes of passivization implicit in a general paradigm, unless the input evidence is overwhelming (at which point the child would begin his or her search for features differentiating the two forms). In a similar vein, Cromer (1975) taught children novel versions of the dative alternation with concocted case markers for the direct or indirect objects, using the familiar verbs *give* and *push*. He found that the children had a significantly harder time learning the new forms for *give*, which already has an alternative dative form, than for *push*, which lacks one. Furthermore, this discrepancy was larger (though not significantly so) for children who were found in an independent task to have acquired both English dative forms than for children who had not yet acquired them. Again there is no unique explanation, but it would not be surprising if the children had trouble with novel datives with *give* because they already had corresponding forms for it in their lexicons, which would suggest in turn that they put a premium on uniqueness.

Elimination of Incorrect Lexical Entries

If the account sketched above is correct, we have a mechanism whereby the child can eventually notice which features delineate the correct application of productive lexical rules; he or she can then coin the appropriate restrictions and will at that point cease creating ungrammatical forms. However, as in any theory in which productive processes result in the addition of entries to the lexicon, the story cannot end there. The underspecified rules will have done their damage, and the child must have some means of purging his or her lexicon of the ungrammatical forms left in their aftermath. I propose that the child accomplishes this by applying the Unique Entry principle to his or her paradigms in two slightly different ways. Both applications rely on a crucial proposal, one that I have already made in several places (e.g., Chapters 4, 5, and 6), in fact, in every instance in which I have appealed to some form of the Uniqueness principle. The proposal is that rules created by the application of a risky or productive procedure are marked as preemptable using the symbol "?". All entries created by canonical and noncanonical mapping and by lexical rules would have this annotation. Entries so annotated would then be expungeable in the two ways discussed below.

Retroactive Constraint Enforcement

Imagine a child who applied causativization to a verb before having hypothesized the constraint that the manner of causation must be direct and stereotypical. For example, the child who creates a causative version of *sing* has the paradigm shown in Figure 8.24. When the general paradigm for causativization is correctly annotated for stereotypy of causation, it will look like Figure 8.25. To eliminate the incorrect entry for *sing*, the child simply needs to verify whether causing to sing can be done in a direct and stereotypical way the next time he or she is tempted to use *sing* causatively. Assuming that the child knows enough about the world to make this judgment correctly (and this will no doubt occur at different ages for different rule constraints and different children), he or she can juxtapose the causative *sing* entry with a "nonstereotypic" cell in the general paradigm, and then let the null entry in that paradigm cell drive out the preemptable entry in the *sing* paradigm to preserve uniqueness. This need not involve any systematic perusal of the lexicon for the purpose of garbage collection; the word-specific paradigm and the general productive causative paradigm would be indexed during speech production by the word and by the causation concept, respectively, then juxtaposed just as they would be when the causative paradigm is successfully applied to incomplete paradigms. In other words, I am proposing that both in inflection and in the lexicon, whenever general productive

Figure 8.24

sing:

| | CONSTRUCTION | |
Active	Causative
(SUBJ) theme	?(SUBJ,OBJ)? cause theme

Figure 8.25

| CONSTRUCTION | | |
Active	Causative	
(SUBJ) theme	(SUBJ,OBJ) cause theme	Stereotypic
		MANNER
	– – – – –	Nonstereotypic

paradigms are applied to word-specific paradigms, they not only fill in incomplete cells that have corresponding filled cells in the general paradigm, but they also expunge preemptable entries in paradigm cells that intrinsically violate the constraints annotated to the corresponding general paradigm (see also the discussion in Chapter 5 in connection with procedure I7).[16]

Suppletion by Independent Forms

The account sketched above will work for cases in which a lexical construction is ungrammatical because it violates some general constraint. In some cases, however, a form will be ungrammatical simply because a language expresses that construction using a different, idiosyncratic form. For example, which preposition or oblique case marker a verb chooses for signaling an oblique argument can vary from verb to verb in arbitrary ways (in fact, a large percentage of the entries in style manuals such as Fowler's *Modern English Usage* consist of listings of verbs and their prepositions). We know that children make such errors (e.g., *I won't tolerate with that*—Lila Gleitman, personal communication; *he's pointing his finger to it*—Menyuk, 1969; *he took me at the circus*—Menyuk, 1969), and in such cases they cannot always count on later acquiring a general constraint to bail them out retroactively. This is exactly the situation they face when acquiring inflected strong forms (e.g., *broke*), and the solution proposed in Chapter 5 to account for their acquisition can do the job here as well. Specifically, when the child applies L1 to learn an input form, and that form belongs in a paradigm cell currently occupied by a preemptable form (i.e., one created by a productive mechanism), the child must replace the current occupant with the witnessed form. This is how the child unlearns *tolerate with* and other verbs whose correct realizations are not predictable from general principles (in fact, procedure C3(b) in Chapter 6, which acquired idiosyncratic control relations, may be a special case of this procedure). Note that the inventory of available features and feature values for lexical paradigms plays an important role in this account, since they define the cells over which alternative forms will or will not compete. For example, forms differing only in their choice of preposition, in the choice of an oblique versus a direct object, or in alternative expressions of causation compete for a single "Active" or "Transitive" or "Causative" cell, whereas passives, intransitives, causatives, raised forms, and so on, can peacefully coexist with the standard transitive form in their own cells (see Bresnan, 1982d, and Perlmutter, 1980, for further discussion).

Note that the use of suppletion to eliminate some of the childhood errors cited earlier in this chapter requires a fairly liberal criterion for which verb forms are allowed to compete over cells in a single word-specific paradigm. For examples, Clark (1982) and Clark and Clark (1979) point out that many products of the application of denominalization rules are ungrammatical for no other reason than that a semantically equivalent form already exists, regardless of the morphological relationship between the synonyms. Thus *to broom* is preempted by *to sweep, to car* by *to drive, to hospital* by *to hospitalize, to baker* by *to bake*. Similarly, lexical causativization is ruled out even in circumstances in which its constraints are satisfied if a synonymous form already exists. For example, direct physical causation of death is not expressed as *to die X* but as *to kill X*, and other examples of children's use of direct stereotypic but nonetheless incorrect lexical causatives are also ruled out for this reason (e.g., *sad/sadden, *sharp/sharpen, *straight/straighten, *come/bring, *go/take, *fall/drop, *higher/raise, *full/ fill, *hot/heat, *have/give*). Verbs whose "figure" or theme is expressed as an object seem to resist the alternation that would express the theme as oblique and the goal or "ground" as object in cases where there already exists a verb with a meaning appropriate to the derived form (especially as it concerns the "completeness" or "holism" requirement). Consider, for example, *pour/fill the glass with water, *put/cover the table with a cloth, *steal/ rob John of his money, *spill/empty the shoes of sand*.

The moral is obvious. The child should allow word-specific paradigms to cross-reference one another despite their morphological distinctness when one word is semantically appropriate to the cell defined by the composition of the intrinsic meaning of another word plus the semantic operation attached to that cell. This is a consequence of the assumption made earlier that certain lexical paradigm levels have semantic definitions. Thus we would have something like the paradigm shown in Figure 8.26(a) or perhaps 8.26(b) in the adult lexicon (as before, details concerning precise dimension names such as MANNER are irrelevant to this discussion). Any form attested in the input would drive out a form annotated by "?" (i.e., generated by productive mechanisms). Combining the principle of preemption of coined forms by attested forms with the principle of cross-referencing of morphologically unrelated lexical paradigms, we have a way for the child to expunge ungrammatical forms that are not ruled out by any semantic or phonological constraints on the productive rule. The child, upon hearing *kill* and understanding it as having direct and stereotypic causation of death

Figure 8.26

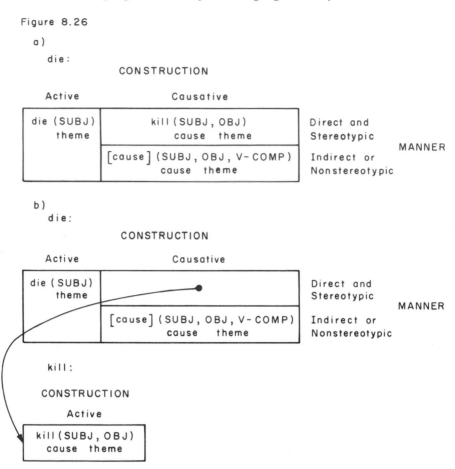

as part of its meaning, would drive out *?die?* (SUBJ, OBJ) in the "Direct and Stereotypic Causative" cell for the word *die*.[17]

In sum, I have proposed two ways in which the child can unlearn the ungrammatical lexical entries created by the over-application of underdifferentiated productive rules. In cases where the ungrammaticality is the product of the child's applying a rule before its semantic or phonological constraints are fully learned, he or she will expunge entries that are recognized as violating those constraints when the constraints have been acquired. In cases where the ungrammaticality is the product of there being an existing form corresponding to the one in question in the adult language, the child could let a newly learned form drive out its morphologically related or unrelated synonym if the latter was created by a productive rule. Of course, in both cases, the developmental course of the process would be governed in part by aspects of nongrammatical development that determine when the child can recognize the various grammatical features in the input—in particular, the acquisition of the specific vocabulary items necessary to supplete various derived forms, the decomposition or inference leading to the realization that certain verb meanings contain features like "causation" that relate them to specific paradigm cells of other verbs, the acquisition of the knowledge necessary to verify whether features like "stereotypic" apply to specific verb meanings, and the acquisition of the concepts underlying those features themselves.

This last discussion ends my examination in this book of the acquisition of specific rule systems. In many ways the treatment of the acquisition of lexical subcategorization and lexical rules is a fitting end for the book, because it approaches the type of investigation advocated in the introduction. Explicit proposals for several types of learning mechanisms were outlined such that the mechanisms were capable of acquiring a domain of grammatical rules by exploiting certain linguistic regularities. Collections of data relevant to children's abilities at a given stage and to the acquisition of new abilities, both experimental and naturalistic, were brought to bear on the evaluation of these proposals, with enough specificity that evidence uniquely implicating several of the mechanisms could be found. The twin learnability-theoretic issues of productivity beyond the input and avoidance of permanent overgeneration in the absence of negative evidence became apparent in specific ways, and tentative solutions to those problems were outlined and motivated by an examination of English grammar and of developmental evidence. There is no doubt that many of the proposals here will turn out to be incorrect for various reasons, but this chapter suggests to me that at least small amounts of progress can be made in resolving the truth or falsity of specific learning theories by appealing jointly to linguistic and developmental evidence.

9 | Conclusion

IN THIS BOOK I have presented a large collection of fairly specific hypotheses and of detailed arguments relevant to them. In this chapter I will attempt to overcome the temptation to let the entire collection of arguments stand as the conclusions reached, and the aggregate plausibility of the arguments stand as the measure of the theory's success. I will try to present some general conclusions about language acquisition distilled from the recurring issues raised in the book, and offer some programmatic recommendations for the study of language acquisition as well. But first I briefly evaluate the specific theory of language acquisition that I have proposed and argued for.

An Evaluation of the Acquisition Theory

Many books proposing comprehensive theories start out by outlining various methodological and metatheoretical desiderata, and this one is no exception. It is natural for an author to conclude such books with an evaluation of the extent to which the theory proposed satisfies the desiderata. Not surprisingly, the theories usually do, and yet often the reader is still left with a sense of dissatisfaction. This is because the desiderata often seem to have been motivated by the theory rather than vice versa, and because the desiderata are often no less controversial than the theory itself. I think it is fair to say that most of the desiderata outlined in the first chapter of this book do not suffer from these problems. They were originally proposed in a review article that antedated the development of the current research project (i.e., in Pinker, 1979). Furthermore, they are not controversial by the usual standards of debates on language acquisition. I think no one will deny that a theory of how the child succeeds at learning a language is an important goal of the study of language acquisition, and that developmental psycholinguistics has largely failed to come up even with approximations to such a theory thus far. Likewise, it should not be controversial that data about children's linguistic abilities are in principle relevant to specifying such a theory. Nor should there be much protest over the suggestion that children speak the way they do in part because they have learned some, but not all, of the grammar of whatever language their community speaks.

Thus it seems to be a nontrivial accomplishment to have shown that one can have theories that meet this particular set of desiderata. Regardless of whether the proposed theory is correct, I hope I have shown that it is possible to outline comprehensive and explicit theories of language acquisition that are motivated by linguistic universals and by the facts of language development. From this standpoint, what is most noteworthy about the present effort is not the final set of hypotheses proposed for each domain; it is, rather, the process of argumentation and theory development whereby it was possible (a) to propose a learning mechanism that was prima facie plausible, given the learnability task at hand; (b) to show ways in which details of the account were incorrect, given certain facts about development or linguistic diversity; and (c) to show how an alternative account did explain the facts. As Geoff Pullum has pointed out, it is not really fair to say that in the past linguists have ignored developmental data when making proposals about language acquisition—the linguistics literature contains numerous examples of authors pointing to developmental data that seem to support their hypotheses. What is almost entirely absent from the literature is the use of such data to *reject* or even cast doubt upon an otherwise favored proposal. It is hardly worth mentioning that the use of any data as a serious source of empirical constraints on a scientific theory requires that they be permitted to disconfirm as well as confirm a hypothesis. Thus it is a point in favor of the current approach that I was able to do this many times throughout the book.

I think, then, that a major contribution of the present theory is that, by being the first large-scale attempt at meeting the desiderata of Chapter 1, it serves as an existence proof that the desiderata can be aimed for and that the strategy advocated there is a viable one. I hope this serves as an antidote to the widespread skepticism on the part of linguists that developmental data can be informative in constructing an explicit acquisition theory, and to the widespread skepticism on the part of psychologists that linguistic theory in general, and linguistically based learning theories in particular, have a crucial role to play in accounting for the child's abilities at one stage or the transition from one stage to another.

This achievement is a modest one, to be sure. It does not in itself imply that the theory I proposed has any particular claim to the truth, since in many specific cases the *particular* developmental data examined may have been unrepresentative or tainted, the background assumptions dubious, the inferential leaps contentious, the linguistic analysis faulty, or the constraints too English-specific. I have no doubt that one or more of these problems infect many of the claims in the book. At the same time, I would like to assert that the particular theory proposed does have merit above and beyond its value in exemplifying a desired type of scientific research. The theory contains proposals concerning mechanisms that acquire many types of linguistic rules; the mechanisms are stated explicitly enough so that surprising consequences of their operation can be observed; the acquisition mechanisms are motivated by linguistic universals and by children's language development; the accounts in different domains are mutually compatible and systematically related to one another; the accounts of children's language are plausible and comprehensive and include proposals for how the child arrives at a given state and how he or she leaves it for the correct adult state; and the theory begins at the initial state of the language acquisition process and follows the process through to the acquisition of moderately sophisticated grammatical structures. All of these positive features are, it is fair to say, unusual for theories arising from language acquisition research. Finally, as we shall see in a later section of the chapter, the theory suggests some potentially important conclusions about language acquisition in general.

Despite this self-congratulation, I think the theory is unarguably deficient in many serious ways, perhaps fatally so. At this stage there is not much more that can be done other than simply to list the problems, mention the direction in which the theory would have to be changed in order to remedy the problem, and, where possible, conjecture at whether such changes would be possible within the framework of the current theory.

1. Though the theory is explicit, it is not formal, and we have no guarantee that the mechanisms taken together would converge on a set of correct rules for the domains they are addressed to. In that regard it compares unfavorably with, say, Wexler and Culicover's "Degree-2 Theory" (Wexler and Culicover, 1980; see also Pinker, 1979, 1981e). For one thing, many of the conditions

and actions in the acquisition procedures are stated in casual English and rely for their interpretation on the cooperativeness of the reader. Thus I cannot rule out the possibility that buried within the structures and actions of a learning mechanism there lie acquisition problems more severe than the ones the mechanism is proposed to solve. Likewise, I do not know whether the procedures are precisely enough defined to give rise to a unique and correct set of rules for every input sequence a child is likely to face. There is always the possibility that the various procedures, though working well in isolation, could go haywire when operating simultaneously on inputs that exemplify rule interactions (bleeding one another's triggering conditions, creating spurious rules that would then cause other procedures to proliferate the damage throughout the grammar, entering into infinite loops, and so on).

It might be thought that computer simulation of the theory would be the remedy for this problem, and indeed the formal rigor that such a project would encourage could only help (see Pinker, 1979). However, it is also easy to overestimate the benefits that simulation would bring. A model is not a theory. Any model must have an overlay of interpretation designating which aspects of the model are theory-relevant, which aspects are theory-irrelevant or theory-neutral, and which real-world entities and processes the theory-relevant aspects are meant to correspond to (see Kosslyn, 1980; and Pinker and Kosslyn, 1983, for discussion and examples). This body of interpretation can be as fraught with vagueness, incoherence, or inconsistency as a theory that is not formalized to begin with. In addition, it is quite easy to devise simulations that, through the use of "wishful mnemonics" (McDermott, 1981), actually accomplish far less than one might think if one simply looked at their top-level descriptions (see Pinker, 1979, for some examples from simulations of language acquisition). In other words, formal rigor is not something that automatically comes with simulation-based theories; it is a criterion that must be applied to simulation-based and nonsimulation-based theories alike. (It is comforting nonetheless to note that Walsh, 1981, devised a computer simulation of the acquisition procedures for phrase structure, control, lexical entries, and lexical rules as spelled out in Pinker, 1982, and found few areas of inconsistency or vagueness standing in his way.)

For the time being I believe that the most fruitful way of addressing the problem of formal rigor is simply to state the acquisition procedures with ever-increasing precision and explicitness and to examine borderline and interactive inputs on a case-by-case basis. This is the strategy exemplified in most of the discussion in this book, where the acquisition mechanisms proposed in Pinker (1982) were found to be incomplete or wanting on various formal grounds and more precise and explicit versions substituted in their place (the discussion of the acquisition of passive phrase structure in Chapter 3, of inflectional paradigms in Chapter 5, of auxiliary co-occurrence restrictions in Chapter 7, and of lexical rules in Chapter 8 are prime examples). The theory is not as explicit as it should be, but I think progress of just the right sort is being made.

2. The acquisition mechanisms are too specific to Indo-European languages and to English in particular. I have attempted to address this problem by outlining brief proposals for how certain rules that differentiate languages according to various typologies might be learned, such as SVO versus SOV versus VSO, ergative versus accusative, configurational versus non-configurational, free versus fixed word order, synthetic versus analytic, fusional versus agglutinating, subject-prominent versus topic-prominent, and PRO-drop versus no PRO-drop. In addition, English itself is sufficiently eclectic that acquisition procedures addressed to it alone are likely to be capable of acquiring a large subset of the mechanisms that languages may avail themselves of. However neither of these mitigating conditions can mask the real problems that exist. The discussions of the acquisition of languages radically departing from English has at times been perfunctory, and many technical problems and contingencies among rule systems within a typology were not even considered. There are also far more significant facts about the development of non-English-like languages than I was able to examine (see Slobin, 1984a), and no doubt still more that have not yet been documented. A particularly fundamental problem for future development of the theory is how to state the semantic correlates of grammatical categories and relations in a way that does full justice to linguistic diversity, and that enables the child to acquire the languages that counterexemplify the universals that the use of these semantic correlates presupposes.

3. I think it is fair to say that the theory can account for many developmental phenomena in a non–ad hoc way, since the mechanisms were always motivated by the necessity of solving the learning problem facing the child in that domain as well as by the developmental data themselves. Furthermore, in all instances I endeavored to address the mechanisms to sets of related developmental phenomena rather than to single phenomena. However, the predictive power of the theory when applied to

these phenomena is no better than moderate. There are few instances in which I can say that the theory rigidly predicted that some nonobvious developmental pattern should occur and indeed it turned out that the facts were exactly so. More often, the theory was extended in some (I argue) nonarbitrary way to account for a known phenomenon and the resulting explanation was justified by appeal to learning considerations and to data concerning related acquisition phenomena. Whether the theory can be justified by large-scale predictive success is unknown at present, and will only be resolved by a program of systematic experimentation that I have just begun.

Dan Slobin has put the issue to me as follows. Imagine that one is given a full grammar for a hitherto unexamined language, plus the parental side of the dialogue from transcripts of parent-child conversation. Could one then use the theory to predict the developmental course of acquisition, such as the order of acquisition of different rules or the typical errors made? In fact, I would make Slobin's challenge even harder and ask if the theory could do that and also show how the developmental sequence produced by the theory's procedures acting unsupervised on the parental speech culminated in a roughly correct grammar for the adult language. It is brutally clear to me that the acquisition theory is not developed to the point at which it could do very well at the Slobin test or my extended version of it. We may not have the right to expect that *any* theory will pass the extended Slobin test in our lifetimes, but the test is a sobering reminder of how far we all have to go.[1]

4. I have argued throughout that a theory of language acquisition should not only account for the fact that existing languages are learnable, but also for the generalizations holding of existing and possible human languages. And in fact I attempted to motivate each of the learning procedures by appealing to the relevant linguistic universals. However, there is no doubt that in my attempt to build an explicit theory of the computations the child performs in acquiring rules, I often proposed mechanisms that are in fact too powerful. That is, they may be able to acquire not only existing and possible rules but also rules that no language would ever contain. This excessive power betrays areas of inelegance in the learning mechanisms, areas where the mechanism was stipulated to take the child from A to B without incorporating some deeper principle as to why B was the only possible destination. For example, the first version of the acquisition procedures for complementation and control in Chapter 6 could acquire arbitrary control relations, making it mysterious

why objects are virtually always the controllers. Though that procedure was amended so as to conform to the prevailing pattern, it still is capable of learning more patterns of complementizers and finiteness in complements than children ever face. Likewise I would not be surprised if the mechanisms could acquire nonexistent lexical rules, inflectional patterns, or auxiliaries far too easily. The sorts of constraints and deductive systems proposed by Chomsky (1981) and Bresnan (Bresnan and Kaplan, 1982; Bresnan, 1982c) probably could be used to increase the elegance and decrease the power of the learning mechanisms in a number of instances.

This problem may afflict learning theories of this sort for some time to come. Indeed I think that there is a proper partial division of labor between theoretical linguists, who attempt to find the most elegant characterization possible of the set of human languages, and learning theorists, who attempt to characterize the computations that allow the child to select the correct language given conditions of input, memory, time, and so on. The two problems may be too complex for us to expect an optimal simultaneous solution to both at present. For now, theories of each type may have to put a premium on optimizing the solution to one of the problems while making reasonable simplifying assumptions about the other, and ultimately a maximally comprehensive theory could emerge when theories of each sort are brought together.

5. Many of the acquisition procedures are rigidly sequential: the child looks for *a* in the input, constructs a rule as a consequence, and is then in a position to predict that phenomena *b*, *c*, and *d* are true or likely to be true in the language (e.g., in the acquisition of the grammatical categories, grammatical relations, oblique phrase structure, and the auxiliary feature, to name just a few). Typically this has been proposed in cases where some symbol X participates cross-linguistically in a family resemblance structure involving phenomena *a–d*, and phenomenon *a* is a privileged member of the family on account of its having telltale perceptual correlates (usually, semantic or pragmatic ones). Although sequential acquisition procedures of this sort simplify the process of exposition, of verifying that the theory operates correctly, and of predicting and accounting for developmental phenomena, they also have problems.

First, sometimes the symbol X in a language may lack the perceptually accessible phenomenon *a* but still have *b*, *c*, and *d* associated with it, and detection of one member of the remaining subset could still be used to predict the rest. That could happen if *b*, *c*, or *d*, though lacking direct semantic correlates itself, could be learned through its involvement with some other rule that is itself recognizable in the input. An example of this situation may be found in the discussion of raising-to-object verbs in Chapter 6, where homonymity with simple transitive verbs, accusative case marking of the complement subject, passivizability of the complement subject, and identical surface structure with object-equi verbs all predict one another in the target grammar. It became clear that it was very difficult to justify any hypothesis that the child looked out for only one privileged member of the set and used its presence to infer the other three. Likewise, in the case of the passive *by*-phrase structure in English, similarities in the lexical heads, internal structures, and external distributions of locative and case-marking prepositional phrases could each be used to predict the other two, and it was unclear which served as premise and which served as conclusion in the child's inferences.

A second problem arises in connection with those relatively rare languages where the perceptually transparent phenomenon *a* in fact does not correlate with phenomena *b–d*, for example, languages where patients rather than agents have the abstract privileges of occurrence usually associated with subjects. Presumably the child at some point can learn some sufficiently large set of other properties diagnostic of subjecthood (using some learning mechanism yet to be specified) such as controllability in infinitival complements or alternation with certain oblique functions in passivization, and can use them to predict the others, semantic evidence to the contrary notwithstanding.

Similar problems might arise if the child, because of various misconstruals or unfortunate patterns of parental speech, makes an error and hypothesizes a rule with the wrong symbol. Many incorrect predictions about the rest of the grammar would then follow, resulting in wasted hypothesization at best and permanent damage at worst. It would seem desirable to allow the child to override an early incorrect rule if that rule makes predictions about other phenomena in its universal family resemblance structure that fail to jibe with subsequent learning.

Finally, we know that there are often considerable individual differences in language development (see, e.g., Bloom, Lightbown, and Hood, 1975; Braine, 1976); nonetheless all children in a linguistic community end up with pretty much the same language as adults. Sequential inferential mechanisms such as the ones I have proposed could have difficulty explaining such progressions if the order of acquisition is something other than from the critical, most perceptually transparent member of the correlated set to the remaining members.

The fundamental fact facing us is that languages contain sets of mutually predictive phenomena, some of them abstract and others unlearnable from positive evidence—a "rich deductive structure," as Chomsky (1981) has characterized it. To solve the problem of how the infant breaks into these networks of cross-referenced phenomena, I proposed that one or more privileged members of each set served as the perceptually transparent entry point, and that the others could be deduced subsequent to the identification of the privileged member. An alternative possibility that would avoid the problems described above is that the inferential relations are multidirectional. Haphazard sets of individual members of a family could be tentatively and fallibly identified through heterogeneous methods, and many local parts of the grammar could strengthen one another by small amounts when they are mutually compatible (e.g., the various individual phenomena associated with subjecthood). Thus if strong evidence for several members of a family is found in the input, the remaining members would automatically be generable; if only moderate evidence is found, the remaining members would need some positive evidence to be acquired but less evidence than they would need if no members of the family had been previously discovered. The innate "knowledge" of grammar would consist in large part of which families of syntactic, semantic, and phonological phenomena stood in mutually reinforcing relationships to one another (equivalently, which families of phenomena cross-referenced the same grammatical symbols). The elegant structure of the adult grammar would then arise from the many local processes of mutual reinforcement or inhibition, emerging as the most stable overall state. This distributed control architecture is reminiscent of "cooperative," "relaxation," and "constraint satisfaction" techniques in the study of early visual processes (e.g., Marr and Poggio, 1976). Incidentally, such models are not necessarily any less nativist than the sort I have been entertaining; in fact they might have to posit even more internal structure to ensure that the correct stable state is reached despite the possible indirectness of the learning path.

The main problem with this alternative proposal is that at present no one has the faintest idea of how to get such a model to work properly in the case of language acquisition. (In fact, it can be hard to show whether particular models of this sort work properly in vision.) Until someone is able to trace out explicitly how such a model can progress from the initial state of language acquisition to a state where some concrete set of reasonably complex rules are mastered, "cooperative" or "constraint satisfaction" models of language acquisition will remain mere conjecture. In the meantime, I think that the more tractable sequential models like the one proposed in this book are more conducive to progress in understanding language acquisition. But as George Miller has put it, the human being was not created for the benefit of the psychologist, and we must entertain the possibility that some less tractable theory is nonetheless the correct one.

6. Quantitative aspects of learning, such as gradients of rule strengthening, salience of different input properties, hierarchies of accessible features, degrees of inhibitory interaction (e.g., in uniqueness violations), priorities of competing acquisition mechanisms, and the like, have remained in the background in most of the discussions in the book. I have put them in the background because injudicious appeals to quantitative parameters in the absence of relevant data could gut the theory of whatever predictive power it may have. It would always be too easy to account for some developmental sequence in ad hoc ways by positing that one acquisition mechanism has higher priority than another, that one input property is more salient than another, and so on. However, in some cases I was unable to avoid such accounts (e.g., in Chapters 5 and 7), and ultimately no comprehensive and predictive account of language development and language acquisition can avoid making quantitative commitments altogether. After all, it may turn out to be *true* that one rule is learned more reliably than another only because of the steepness of the relevant rule strengthening function or the perceptual salience of its input triggers. (This concern is especially relevant if language acquisition turns out to be a process of distributed local strengthenings and weakenings, as suggested above.) One problem is that we currently lack both robust quantitative data on language development and explicit quantitative models from which reliable parameter estimates could be derived. This is likely to remain true for some time to come. For now there is little choice but to appeal to quantitative parameters sparingly, and only in cases where cross-linguistic data such as those analyzed by Slobin (1984a) can motivate such parameters.

Let me simply summarize, without comment, two remaining problems. The theory is fairly data-driven, and at present cannot account in any simple way for the creation of novel grammars under the conditions of radically degenerate linguistic input documented by Bickerton (1981). And there are several important classes of rules for which I have made few or no detailed proposals. For example, anaphora, coordination, and trace binding immediately come to mind. It remains to be seen whether the list of problems outlined in this chapter will turn out to be fatal to the theory. Some may simply be eliminated via incremental changes of the sort that led from the theory proposed in Pinker (1982) to the present theory; some may be problems for any theory we can currently imagine, given the state of the art. It is clear that the resolution of these problems in general will require theories with a degree of precision, explicitness, and detail that the current theory has strived for but has achieved only in small part. But I think it is also clear that it is only by constructing explicit theories and examining their shortcomings that we will be able to attain an ultimately satisfying theory of language acquisition.

Some Conclusions about Language Development

1. Children acquire language by exploiting rich formal and substantive constraints on the types of rules that languages may have. This is not a pure discovery since it was a principle that motivated the development of the theory to begin with, but now that I have constructed specific accounts of rule acquisition in several domains it seems as inescapable a conclusion as ever. In areas as diverse as the acquisition of word order, phrase structure geometry, inflectional paradigm dimensions, agreement rules, control, auxiliary co-occurrence restrictions, inversion, and lexical forms, I was able to show how the child might acquire the relevant rule systems in psychologically plausible ways only by proposing that he or she entertained a small subset of the hypotheses consistent with the data, often entertaining them only in certain orders or in response to narrow triggering conditions. Less restrictive mechanisms in all these cases would have led to slower learning, often implausibly slow, to errors that children in fact never make, or to incorrect adult grammars.

The skeptical reader may conjecture that learning is possible without such constraints, since only their sufficiency, not their necessity, has been argued for, or that the constraints may be special cases of more general cognitive principles. Indeed, either of these may be true. However, I think there has been far too much handwaving on the part of such skeptics. It will always be possible to say of any theory that perhaps there are alternatives that can do the job just as well. We are currently blessed with detailed characterizations of adult grammars, with increasing knowledge about developmental progressions, and with a growing stock of possible acquisition algorithms and heuristics.

It is now incumbent on skeptics of nativist learning theories to propose explicit theories that do full justice to the process whereby complex systems of linguistic rules are acquired.

2. An important component, indeed a necessary component, of the child's use of linguistic universals is his or her recognition of when and how they are applicable to specific inputs, and correlations between syntactic symbols and semantic symbols (and possibly phonological and pragmatic symbols) in basic structures play a crucial role in this recognition process. Again this is not a discovery, strictly speaking, since it was a guiding principle in constructing the theory. However, the principle turned out to be so indispensable in so many domains, including domains that were encountered only as the theory was developed (e.g., the auxiliary system), that I think its plausibility can be said to have been increased as a result of the efforts reported herein.

3. Children do not invariably solve the learnability problem posed by the absence of negative evidence by first hypothesizing the most restrictive rule system sanctioned by universal grammar, then hypothesizing increasingly less restrictive systems as positive input evidence warrants. This monotonicity principle is an attractive one but it does not appear tenable as an explanation of language acquisition in the general case in light of the many cases of children's overgeneration (some examples: intermittent use of closed-class morphemes in early speech, underdifferentiation of inflection, overregularization, failure to use obligatory complementizers for certain verbs, errors with exceptional control verbs, failing to invert when one should and inverting when one should not, overapplying productive lexical rules). This is not to say that children invariably overgenerate either, since we have seen many examples where children remain within the bounds of adult grammar or even undergenerate (some examples: correct word order and phrase coherence in fixed order configurational languages, word order conservatism in free word order languages, absence of agreement rules for NPs lacking grammatical relations, absence of inversion of main verbs or uninvertible auxiliaries, absence of overinflection of auxiliaries, absence of co-occurrence errors involving two or more auxiliaries, absence of passives violating thematic restrictions, failure to passivize nonthematic verbs).

If the proposals in this book are correct, then rather than conforming to some general principle of conservatism, children avoid permanent overgeneration by three sorts of mechanisms. The first consists of mechanisms that are indeed conservative (examples: default assumption of fixed word order, default assumption of configurationality, conservative learning of auxiliary inflection and privileges of occurrence). The second consists of probabilistic hypothesization of feature constraints. The child does not entertain all hypotheses consistent with an input at first, but samples randomly from a set of weighted hypotheses conforming to the input and to universal principles. Before the child hypothesizes a given correct equation, his or her grammar could generate more sentences than it generates after the equation is hypothesized. The child cannot help but continue to coin feature hypotheses whose effect is to reduce the set of generable sentences, and he or she does so even if, strictly speaking, a current grammar can account for all the inputs heard prior to a given point (some examples: differentiation of case and agreement inflections into formal subclasses, inversion constraints, constraints on lexicosyntactic productivity). Finally, the child can exploit the various versions of Wexler's Uniqueness principle proposed in the preceding chapters that allow him or her to expunge self-generated forms when he or she hears forms heard in the input that compete with it for the same "cell" or function (some examples: unlearning of miscategorized words, of copulaless predication and prepositionless locative phrases, of null complementizers, of overregularized inflected forms, of unmarked control for exceptional verbs, of suppleted causatives and other derived lexical forms).

Strictly speaking, cases in which the Uniqueness principle is invoked are not counterexamples to the conjecture that children hypothesize the less inclusive of two languages first. The conservatism strategy is really only required when one hypothesis language properly includes another—if two hypothesis languages incompletely intersect, the child can always decide between them using only positive evidence by awaiting the appearance of the sentences that are in one language but not the other. What the Uniqueness principle does is ensure that languages are generally not in proper inclusive relationships. When the child hears an irregular form and consequently drives out its productively generated counterpart, he or she is tacitly assuming that there exists a language that contains the irregular form and lacks the regular form, and a language that contains the regular form and lacks the irregular form, but no language that contains both. Thus the decision can be made using positive evidence. To the extent that children solve the negative evidence problem by relying on the Uniqueness principle, then, their success is not the consequence of choosing the less inclusive of two hypotheses first, but of entertaining hypotheses neither of which properly includes the other. (In the rare cases of uniqueness violations, the child uses positive evidence—the appearance of both forms in the input—to advance to the more inclusive language. This grudging acceptance of uniqueness violations is, of course, a genuine example of conservatism.)

4. I am willing to conjecture that versions of the Uniqueness principle will play an increasingly important role in explaining children's recovery from errors. If this is true in the ways I have suggested, it would have some nonobvious implications. First, children would distinguish in their grammar between forms attested in the input and forms created by some general rule or principle (using something like the "?" symbol or its complement). This is necessary so that the child can determine whether to resolve uniqueness violations by driving out a form (e.g., suppletion of overregularized forms), by creating a new paradigm dimension (e.g., for purely formal or relatively inaccessible distinctions), or by keeping both forms as free variants (e.g., for pairs like *dived/dove*). The second implication is that the child may have an antecedently defined set of possible domains over which uniqueness holds. For example, it would hold in inflectional paradigms, but perhaps not in monomorphemic lexical semantics or in alternative phrase structure expansions, given the possibility of synonymity or stylistic variation. This conclusion must remain tentative, however, since it has been argued (by Dwight Bolinger, 1975, for example) that there is really no such thing as synonymity or free variation, that "when we say two things that are different we mean two different things by them." If that is the case, perhaps rather than there being a set of uniqueness domains, there is a general Uniqueness principle defined over meaning that operates pervasively throughout the grammar. It is not clear to me which of these alternatives is true. What *is* clear to me is that the resolution of the issue of whether and when synonymity is possible has profound implications for language acquisition, since it will shape our conception of precisely how uniqueness principles are exploited by the child to avoid or recover from overgeneration.

5. The child uses something like a paradigm or matrix representation in the acquisition of sets of related lexical or inflectional forms. In various sections of the book I have used matrix operations to account for segmentation, eliminating incorrect feature hypotheses, discovering zero morphemes, differentiating fusional from agglutinating morphology, postulating relatively inaccessible semantic, phonological, and formal distinctions,

suppleting incorrect forms, learning the extent of cross-classi-fication versus nesting of features, and coordinating verbs and auxiliaries with sentence modalities. Another way of putting it is that many aspects of grammar can only be learned in a plau-sible manner through systematic comparisons among minimally contrasting forms along a number of dimensions, or through the explicit labeling of as-yet-unlearned forms defined by con-junctions of feature values, and the paradigm notation makes such operations easy to do.

6. We should regard two popular assumptions with suspicion: that during the course of language development there are qual-itative, maturationally induced changes in the child's language acquisition mechanisms, and that the child's grammar consists of rules that are formally different from those in adult grammar. The former assumption is not uncommon among linguists; the latter is implicit in large parts of the psycholinguistics literature and explicit in many psycholinguistics textbooks. There may indeed be qualitative changes in grammars or grammar acqui-sition mechanisms, but as far as I can see, the data on language development provide little support for either hypothesis. In sev-eral places in the book I was able to argue that seemingly bizarre or unadultlike linguistic behavior could easily be the product of incomplete (rather than fundamentally incorrect) rules, that de-velopmental sequences could be explained by intrinsic depend-encies or by feeding relations among acquisition procedures, and that other deficits could result from nonlinguistic limitations such as in processing capacity or conceptual richness.

To be sure, I was motivated by the parsimony considerations of Chapter 1 and hence strove for developmental continuity in my accounts. In contrast, other theorists may have been moti-vated to find qualitative changes so as to isolate recalcitrant developmental data from debates over linguistic or learning the-ories, or to justify the autonomous study of children's linguistic behavior. Motives aside, the ease with which I was able to de-scribe developmental progressions without ad hoc appeals to exogenous qualitative changes in the child's computational mechanisms should at least give pause to proponents of quali-tative change.[2]

7. If the theory is correct, then I have placed a considerable burden on theorists of conceptual and communicative devel-opment, saddling them with an inventory of cognitive abilities far richer than many current cognitive theories allow for. I have assumed that the language induction mechanisms exploit in-dependently existing cognitive abilities to represent mentally

many conceptual type-distinctions and to recognize tokens of each type from the perceptual and conversational context of an utterance. Examples include objects, actions, attributes, manners, agents, causes, patients, instruments, goals, locations, sources, subjects of predication, predicate-argument relations, restrictive modification, nonrestrictive modification, propositional arguments, coreference, binding of variables by quantifiers, declaration, interrogation, negation, exclamation, emphasis, durativity, relative times of events, speech acts, and reference points, person, number, humanness, animacy, evidential nature, definiteness, possession, modal concepts, topic, focus, presuppositionality, types of causation, stereotypy of manner, completeness of effect, and certainly many others. Although several mechanisms within the theory draw the child's attention to these distinctions during the language learning process, the mechanisms operate in a way that presupposes that the child is independently capable of perceiving and representing the distinctions. The theory is, of course, mute as to whether these cognitive distinctions are themselves innate or learned, as long as the child is capable of making them.

In general, I do not see this implication as a weakness of the theory, despite many psychologists' distaste for rich typologies of mental content (especially in children). Whether or not children exploit correlations between syntax and semantics in the syntax learning process in the ways I have proposed, at some point or other they must be capable of representing the relevant semantic distinctions so that they can learn how their language encodes those distinctions in general and so that they can communicate those distinctions in particular instances as mature language users. See Chomsky (1975), Fodor (1975, 1981), and Jackendoff (1978, 1983) for further arguments about the possible richness of representational types.

Some Programmatic Implications for the Study of Language Acquisition

1. Our understanding of linguistic universals and the constraints on grammar that give rise to them will be the rate-limiting step in our understanding of how the child is so successful as a language learner. This is certainly not an original conclusion given Chomsky's arguments, but the discussions in this book point to some of the areas in which increased knowledge of universals would be especially helpful to the learning theorist. In particular, we have seen how substantive universals (i.e., the inventory of categories, relations, features, and rule

formats that languages can draw from), and the correlations among semantic and formal phenomena that define them, might play a crucial role in explaining the initial stage in which the child bootstraps his or her way into the first set of grammatical rules. Thus the type of universals proposed by Keenan concerning subjects, by Grimshaw concerning subcategorization, by Jackendoff concerning phrase structure geometry, by Slobin, Talmy, and Bybee concerning grammaticizable notions, and by Steele and her collaborators concerning auxiliaries, turned out to be extremely important constraints in the acquisition theories I have proposed. More discoveries along those lines are a prerequisite to further progress in language acquisiion.

2. The information-processing component of a language acquisition theory need not consist of trivial hypothesis-projection and hypothesis-confirmation operations. Though it is sometimes convenient to think of acquisition processes in this way in order to focus on the question of how linguistic constraints ensure that language acquisition can be successful at all, we also need to explain how the child acquires rules in reasonable amounts of time using psychologically plausible cognitive mechanisms. Doing so might call for specific algorithms designed to optimize the application of linguistic constraints in concrete instances. For example, I have proposed learning operations that build trees, collapse rules, untangle crossing tree branches, strip inflections from stems by examining paradigm cells in particular combinations, split paradigms by crossing or nesting dimensions, examine minimally contrasting sets of cells in lexical or inflectional paradigms, directly read information off trees and functional structures, exploit top-down parsing operations, and so on. And my deployment of such operations merely scratches the surface: Walsh (1981) points out, for example, that the process of juxtaposing two phrase structure rules for the purpose of collapsing corresponding symbols in the two rules requires algorithms of considerably greater complexity than my fairly abstract description of the process would suggest. I suspect that there is a rich collection of information processes that has been barely explored thus far and that will play an important role in explaining the rapidity of acquisition.

3. It may be premature to use language acquisition as a battleground in the debates between competing linguistic theories. Such debates played an extremely minor role throughout this book for several reasons. First, conventional sorts of empirical evidence such as judgments of well-formedness can be brought to bear on such debates in far more direct and specific ways

than can developmental data and learnability arguments. Second, there is a large collection of basic acquisition issues concerning how the child seeks out particular sorts of input evidence to learn particular aspects of language, and how these issues should be resolved is in many cases independent of the differences among contemporary generative theories of syntax. For example, in virtually any theory one must account for how the child acquires noun and verb categorizations and subcategorizations, phrase structure rules, inflectional paradigms, and so on, and similar problems arise regardless of the notation used for these rules. There is much work to be done on these important acquisition problems, and no reason why such work must invariably be channeled into the debate about rival linguistic theories when the issues hold such intrinsic interest of their own. But most important, there are several layers of theory that lie between a generative grammar and accounts of children's language—most notably, acquisition theory and parsing theory—and until such layers are specified for all the linguistic theories under scrutiny, any attempt to decide among linguistic theories by appealing to children's language is bound to be ad hoc and unconvincing. The logical problem of language acquisition, and the factors that give rise to developmental data, are simply too complex to license simple arguments based on direct applications of competence theories to developmental problems.

This is not to say that developmental data and learnability problems are irrelevant to deciding among linguistic theories; quite the contrary. No linguistic theory can be correct unless it is compatible with some viable theory of acquisition, and the choice between linguistic theories should ultimately be based not on the theories of adult competence themselves but on conjunctions of theories of adult competence and their corresponding theories of acquisition (and, for that matter, parsing). The sorts of learnability and developmental issues discussed in this book will play a crucial role in determining what sorts of acquisition theories are viable.

I should add that I think that the work reported here does offer some indirect support for Bresnan and Kaplan's theory of Lexical Functional Grammar. In no case did the LFG formalisms stand in the way of constructing an adequate account of the acquisition of some aspect of grammar; in almost all cases the formalisms lent themselves naturally to the construction of adequate accounts; and in some cases the theory formalized just the sorts of distinctions that a plausible account required (e.g., in Chapters 6 and 7). Furthermore, many of the universal con-

straints of LFG were incorporated directly into acquisition procedures in ways that helped to solve some learnability problem
or account for some developmental pattern (e.g., in Chapters 3,
5, 6, and 8). LFG is now accompanied by accounts of acquisition
as well as parsing and production (see Ford, Bresnan, and Kaplan, 1982; Ford, 1982) and so there can be no general worries
about its degree of compatibility with processing or acquisition
considerations. It seems to me that it thus has an advantage over
other theories in terms of comprehensiveness, and a corresponding burden of proof has been placed on the other theories. This
is a modest type of support, to be sure, but at this stage it is the
most that can reasonably be expected from an acquisition theory.
I think an important implication of the research reported herein
is that the use of acquisition arguments in linguistic debates,
like any other debate concerning language acquisition, requires
explicit, comprehensive, and empirically motivated theories of
the acquisition process, rather than offhand proposals about
isolated phenomena.

4. Whenever a developmental psycholinguist discovers some
pattern of error in children's speech, he or she raises the problem
of how the child recovers from such error. This problem has
been almost completely neglected within developmental psycholinguistics, and recognizing it might dampen some of the
glee with which children's errors are typically reported in the
literature and in introductory textbooks. Nonetheless, the problems are nontrivial and must be faced unflinchingly. In the previous section I summarized the sorts of error recovery mechanisms
that I think provide the key, but no doubt there is a large class
of possible hypotheses that has not even begun to be explored.

5. We need more experimentation on children's learning abilities. Despite the importance of spontaneous speech data and
of data from comprehension experiments, at best these data
pertain to the child's linguistic abilities at particular stages, and
not to the induction process that maps from the child's abilities
and the input at one stage to the child's abilities at the next
stage. In the discussions of learning mechanisms in this book,
often the most informative studies were those that attempted to
teach the child something and observed what he or she in fact
learned (e.g., studies by Lebeaux, Pinker, Wilson, Zaenen, Macnamara, Gelman, Taylor, Marantz, Cromer, MacWhinney, Karmiloff-Smith, Berko, and Brown). Ironically, experiments of this
sort played an important role in the early history of developmental psycholinguistics (e.g., Brown, 1957; Berko, 1958), but
they have dwindled to a tiny fraction of contemporary work.

One important methodological roadblock standing in the way of further use of such paradigms is that the teaching techniques that have been employed have been successful at getting the child to acquire new open-class morphemes, but fairly disappointing at getting him or her to acquire new closed-class morphemes (though the Cromer, 1975, study is an informative exception). Another roadblock is that we have few techniques that induce the child to utter his or her version of a particular grammatical construction on cue, or to judge the well-formedness of sample sentences. However, progress is being made at removing all these roadblocks. We need more studies, and new methodologies, that present the child with linguistic inputs that are tailored specifically so as to enable us to distinguish between acquisition hypotheses,and that assess the grammatical conclusions that the child draws from such inputs. Together with advances in the precision and explicitness of language acquisition theories, advances in our ability to observe the process and consequences of language acquisition are prerequisites to meeting the goals described in the first chapter.

Notes

1. Introduction

1. George Miller (1979) has proposed September 11, 1956, as the birthday of cognitive science.

2. I use the term "learnability" loosely in this book to refer to the scientific problem of accounting for the child's ability to learn languages on the basis of the input available to him or her. This is distinct from the branch of recursion theory sometimes called "learnability theory" or "formal learning theory" (e.g., Gold, 1967; Osherson, Stob, and Weinstein, in press; Osherson and Weinstein, in press; see also Pinker, 1979, and Wexler and Culicover, 1980), which concerns theorems delineating when learning is possible in principle. I adopt this terminology because the term "learning theory" has taken on connotations in psychology that would be misleading in this context (McDermott, 1981; Wexler, 1981).

3. This paper first appeared in a slightly different form in July 1980 as a technical report, #6 in MIT's Center for Cognitive Science Occasional Paper Series.

2. The Acquisition Theory: Assumptions and Postulates

1. Interestingly, having the phrase structure rules generate all types of phrases directly does not increase the number of rules in the phrase structure component much. Emonds (1976) made the significant discovery that many transformations create surface structures that must be independently generable by phrase structure rules. This is an important motivation for doing away with such transformations altogether (see Grimshaw, 1979a).

2. Here and elsewhere I simply annotate the name of a grammatical function to the constituent it labels, rather than use the full functional equation like $\uparrow \text{SUBJ} = \downarrow$ which states explicitly that the constituent is the subject of the functional structure corresponding to the node immediately dominating the constituent. Grimshaw (1982a) points out that the full functional equation is usually redundant within LFG and

that the name of the function usually specifies all the necessary information; accordingly I will delete the redundant equations and metavariables in the interests of notational simplicity unless the full information they contain is needed. See Kaplan and Bresnan (1982) for a full explanation of the symbols used in functional equations.

3. The symbol OBL_{by} refers to the oblique object of the preposition *by*. Hereafter, I will follow Bresnan (1982c) and will refer to the function of the *by*-phrase as OBL_{agent}, signifying that the argument is expressed as a prepositional phrase containing the agentive preposition or case marker, which happens to be *by* in English (note that it does not constrain the argument to be agentive). This allows one to state a language-independent inventory of oblique grammatical functions.

4. Note that this argument does not claim that the original linguistic theory must not be altered as a result of developmental or learnability considerations, only that the entire theory not be created from scratch for the purposes of the acquisition theory. In fact, in a number of places in the book I alter various aspects of LFG to make it more compatible with acquisition considerations.

5. Some examples of phenomena that Bresnan argues show the superiority of LFG accounts are: (a) the interaction of passivization with lexical rules of word formation, indicating that passive is a lexical rule (Bresnan, 1978, 1982b); (b) the independence of syntactic subcategorization and semantic selection of arguments by their verbs, which supports the use of different notations for them (Grimshaw, 1979b; Bresnan, 1982d); (c) the structure-preserving property of many syntactic alternations such as passive, dative, and raising, which suggests that such alternations are effected by rules that do not manipulate constituent structure (Grimshaw, 1979a); (d) the failure of transitive verbs with subject control of complement subjects to passivize ("Visser's generalization"—Bresnan, 1982c), supporting a theory of control based on grammatical functions; (e) the fact that in Romance languages sentence completeness is better predicted by the set of grammatical functions found in a sentence than by the structural properties of the sentence (Grimshaw, 1982a, b), supporting a theory where verbs subcategorize for grammatical functions. Furthermore, Bresnan argues that LFG provides universal characterizations, in terms of grammatical functions, of processes such as passivization, government, and control, whereas other theories eschewing grammatical functions would have to give separate accounts for these phenomena in configurational and nonconfigurational languages. See the contributions to Bresnan (1982a) for further arguments of this sort. Naturally, all these claims are controversial.

6. Jo-Ann Miller and Jacques Mehler have pointed out to me that this proposal could not possibly work if it has the child storing acoustic templates and matching them against strings, because words have very different acoustic realizations depending on whether they appear in sentence-medial, sentence-final, or isolated positions. My conjecture could be salvaged if the child was capable of assigning position-inde-

pendent phonetic or phonemic representations to words and sentences without having to learn syntax first, since in that case he or she could successfully match a template extracted from an isolated word against an occurrence of that word within a full sentence. Mehler has also pointed out to me that the child might fix certain phonological parameters of the language on the basis of simple inputs, such as being stress-timed versus syllable-timed, and use this parameter setting to constrain the search for word boundaries using only within-sentence information.

7. Chomsky (1981) entertains the possibility of a different type of negative evidence, namely, the "indirect negative evidence" that the child could exploit if he or she takes the absence of a certain form in the input as evidence that it is ungrammatical. I will examine this suggestion in Chapter 8.

8. It is noteworthy in this regard that John Anderson (1974, 1975, 1976) and Kenneth Wexler (Wexler and Culicover, 1980), starting from very different theoretical perspectives, both claimed to be forced to a nativist stance as a result of attempting to construct precise language acquisition theories.

9. I assume here, and throughout this discussion, that all the alternative theories under consideration not only acquire language successfully but do so in accord with the empirical facts about child language development.

10. Note that if such a procedure took the form of the procedures depicted in Figure 2.8(a) or (b), the rest of the acquisition theory would survive intact sans the innateness claim. The acquisition theory itself would be falsified by a task-general acquisition theory that made it superfluous (e.g., as in Figure 2.8(c)), a simpler or more general language-specific acquisition procedure, or one that explained children's language better.

11. The argument in these pages presupposes the combination of functionalism, cognitivism, and computationalism that dominates modern cognitive science (e.g., Newell and Simon, 1961; Fodor, 1968; Pylyshyn, 1980, in press; Haugeland, 1981). However, it is possible that cognitive processes are instead best explained by synergistic or emergent field effects, resonances, holographic effects, and so on, stemming from particular biochemical or electrical properties of neural tissue when engaged in particular tasks (see the papers in Haugeland, 1981, for discussion). If so, the status of this innateness argument, which assumes that the nature of cognitive processes can be deduced from properties of a fixed computational architecture, is unclear. In any case, I have not seen even the outline of such an argument as it would apply to language acquisition.

12. I beg the thorny question as to the proper definition of the various semantic terms I appeal to such as "agent," "physical object," and the like. All that is required for this account is that (a) there exists a definition of these notions as they enter into the perceptual and cognitive world of the child, regardless of whether such a definition is inadequate for these notions as adults understand them, and (b) the child is equipped

with recognition procedures for the referents of these notions. (More specifically, the referents picked out by the child's recognition procedures should constitute a subset of those picked out by the adult definition of the relevant semantic notion. Thus the theory is compatible with Huttenlocher et al.'s findings (1983) that infants may restrict their use of subjects to themselves when they are agents of self-initiated actions, rather than to agents in general.)

13. I discuss a more sophisticated set of semantic conditions for grammatical functions in Chapter 8.

14. Li and Thompson (1976) point out that in virtually every language in which the function TOPIC plays a prominent role, there exist "double subject" sentences containing distinct subject and topic constituents. Thus the child could use the presence of a topic that does not have any of the correlates of subjecthood as evidence that the target language defines a distinct topic constituent. This strategy would prevent him or her from being confused by non-topic-prominent languages, in which the discourse topic might be identifiable from context but it does not receive any special encoding within the grammar.

15. I assume that the child eventually chooses either the pair nominative/accusative or the pair ergative/absolutive, by noticing whether the case marker for the intransitive actor is identical to the marker for the transitive agent (in which case nominative/accusative will be chosen) or to the marker for the transitive patient (in which case ergative/absolutive will be chosen). An alternative would be to have only two possible cases: ergative, for subjects of transitives, and accusative, for objects of transitives; subjects of intransitives would be assigned accusative or ergative case depending on whether their markers were phonologically identical to one or another.

16. One might wonder why the existence of a correlated set of linguistic phenomena justifies positing a single symbol that enters into each phenomenon. Why not instead simply list each entity (word or phrase) that enters into each of the phenomena, and let the pattern of correlation itself symbolize the regularities, rather than a symbol which has no meaning other than its behavior in the set of correlated phenomena to begin with (e.g., as in Maratsos and Chalkley, 1981)? The answer is that there is a principle of computational efficiency that Marr and Nishihara (1978) call the Principle of Explicit Naming: when a particular data structure must be referred to often, or by a wide range of processes, that data structure should be given an explicit label. As it applies to grammatical symbols, this principle affords a gain in efficiency in the following way. If there were no symbol for "subject," for example, then the phenomena in (a)–(l) would have to be listed separately for each predicate that has a subject argument. If there are m subject phenomena and n predicates, the grammar would need mn rules. On the other hand, if the grammar were allowed to state that the n individual predicates took SUBJ arguments, and that the m phenomena pertained to SUBJs, it would need only $m + n$ rules. Thus we have a reduction from multiplicative to additive complexity.

17. The following fact has been pointed out to me as a possible counterexample to these generalizations. Verbs in American Indian languages such as Navajo and Cherokee contain a great deal of information about the objects serving as their arguments. For example, a verb might encode whether the object is long, flat, or solid and whether it is rigid or flexible. Perhaps, then, the child would mistakenly categorize such verbs as nouns under the semantic bootstrapping hypothesis. In fact, this is unlikely. These phenomena are not significantly different in a formal sense from English number agreement; they do not constitute cases of a verb being a *name* for an object. The verb retains the same stem and refers to the same action regardless of the nature of its arguments; the markers for object properties take on different forms and appear in different positions within the word depending on which semantic roles their referents are playing with respect to the verb; and the markers are not used with particular basic level objects but with any object in a much more inclusive class defined by the relevant set of features. These are properties that any viable theory of name learning would have to be sensitive to. For a theory of how the child learns the relevant verb inflections in these languages once he or she has correctly classified the stem as a verb, see Chapter 5.

18. The semantic bootstrapping hypothesis is not logically tied to any single formulation of substantive universals (for example, see Marantz, 1982, for a universal theory of grammatical relations different from Keenan's). The hypothesis would have to be fleshed out in a different way, but not abandoned, should it turn out that logical subjecthood, for instance, is a better semantic inductive basis for grammatical subjecthood than is agenthood. If it should turn out that there are no independent grammatical consequences of something being a subject at all, then the semantic bootstrapping hypothesis would be irrelevant to the acquisition of subjects, though it could be relevant to the identification of other universal symbols, such as those for syntactic categories. The semantic bootstrapping hypothesis would be made totally dispensable if there were *no* substantive universals, or no substantive universals with reliable semantic inductive bases, or if all substantive universals had perceptual inductive bases other than semantic ones (e.g., serial position, phonological properties).

19. There is a computational tradeoff between the dimensionality of the correlation matrix and the necessity of checking that different cells contain the same set of items. The higher the dimensionality, the more likely it is that a correlation will manifest itself simply as a unique cell within a dimension that is filled, rather than as a collection of cells scattered throughout the matrix filled with the same set of words.

20. The conclusions I am drawing in this paragraph are controversial. For example, Michael Maratsos has pointed out that there are few reported instances of children using words in semantically appropriate but syntactically incorrect ways, and far fewer than one would expect if the child was inferring words' categorizations on the basis of their semantic properties (Maratsos and Chalkley, 1981; Maratsos, in press).

For example, *noisy* and *angry* could be construed as actions if they were heard in the presence of a person making noise or behaving angrily, yet there are no reported examples of *he is noisying, Mommy is angrying,* and so on. Though Maratsos has called attention to a very important phenomenon, I do not think it is evidence against semantic bootstrapping. For one thing, in almost all of Maratsos's examples, it is not clear whether the child construes the words in ways that would lead him or her to make errors. For example, there is a semantic distinction between making noise on a given occasion and being in the state or having the attribute or disposition of noisiness. If one shouts three times in rapid succession, one has made noise three times, but one has not been noisy three times. Only if children's perceptual and representational apparatus was too impoverished to record the difference would one expect the child to construe being noisy as performing noise-making actions, which would be a prerequisite to errors such as *noisying*. In Japanese, there is a syntactic distinction between true adjectives and nominal adjectives that may not have as salient a semantic distinction as that between English adjectives and verbs, and, as mentioned, Japanese children do overgeneralize the markers for true adjectives to nominal adjectives (Slobin, 1984a).

Another problem with Maratsos's prediction of category errors is that they involve existing words that the child hears in sentences in the input. If the child has rules for adjective placement based on semantically transparent cases (e.g., when the adjective denotes a physical attribute), then upon hearing a word in an adjectival syntactic context, he or she can categorize it properly using distributional methods (in fact, as we shall see in Chapters 3, 4, and 8, the distributional mechanisms must be allowed to override the semantic ones). A better sort of evidence would consist of data from experimental situations in which infants would be exposed to words with orthogonal combinations of semantic referents and syntactic contexts, including no context.

21. We argued that children had in fact learned a passive lexical entry from the exposure to the passive verb in that condition, rather than a semantically induced active entry converted into a passive entry by a productive rule, because the child was more likely to produce the passive of the verb in production tests than the active, the opposite of what happens when children are exposed to novel verbs in the active voice. See Chapter 8 for further details.

3. Phrase Structure Rules

1. The procedure as stated attaches the subject NP as a daughter of S simply by virtue of its having the SUBJ label. It is possible that this attachment is a consequence of some specific logical property holding of subjects, such as being an argument of the entire verb phrase rather than of the verb alone (e.g., see Marantz, 1982; Williams, 1981c; but also Bresnan, 1982c). If so, the attachment properties of subjects might not have to be stipulated in a separate subprocedure, but might be a

consequence of the operation of part (b) of procedure P4, which exploits X-bar theory to attach arguments as sisters of their predicates.

2. Two comments about the attachment of determiners are necessary here. First, one might wonder how the child knows that each instance of *the* modifies the noun following it rather than the other definite noun in the sentence. One possible solution would arise if the child had previously encountered an input sentence with different determiners in the subject and object NPs, or a determiner in one NP but not the other. In that case there would have been no possibility of confusion, and the child would have posited a rule introducing determiners as immediate constituents of N"s. Since existing rules are always applied first in processing input sentences, that rule would provide a sufficient analysis of the two NPs in this example. If no such sentence had been encountered earlier, the child would still be spared from making an error, since procedure P4 always tries to attach constituents to the smallest possible phrase within the X-bar constraints, attaching them to more inclusive constituents in response to imminent branch-crossing only as a last resort. Attaching the first determiner to the object noun would cross branches; hence the alternative analysis, with determiners attached to the NPs dominating the adjacent nouns, would be preferred.

A second problem is that it is not clear that the "specifier = daughter of *X"* " rule is truly universal, nor that there is an adequate universal definition of specifiers (which, in this case, would have to include determiners as specifiers). If not, how would the child learn that in English, *det* is attached as a daughter of N"? One possibility is that the child could accomplish this when he or she encounters phrases like *the dog in the park* and realizes that the scope of the definiteness operator *the* includes the entire NP *dog in the park* and not just the noun *dog*.

3. This analysis holds that the oblique PP is an exocentric construction with NP as its head and P as a minor category contributing only a PCASE (prepositional case) feature. See Bresnan (1982c) for arguments for this analysis.

4. The equation $\uparrow \text{OBL}_{\text{agent}} = \downarrow$, which I list for simplicity, will unjustifiably restrict this rule to the preposition *by*. A rule that would generate any oblique PP, giving it the particular $\text{OBL}_{\text{PCASE}}$ function appropriate for the preposition it includes, would be $\uparrow (\downarrow \text{PCASE}) = \downarrow$. The feature $\downarrow \text{PCASE}$ is contributed by the particular lexical entry for the case-marking preposition, such as *goal* for *to*, *source* for *from*, *instrument* for *with*, and so on. (See Kaplan and Bresnan, 1982, and Bresnan, 1982b, c, for details. I discuss the placement of the P" as a daughter of V" rather than V' later.)

5. By "mutatis mutandis" I mean that when the procedures described in 10(i–iii) recognize a configurational similarity between the adjunct and oblique PPs and then set up a new parallel phrase structure rule or lexical entry for the oblique PP, those procedures also automatically make the necessary changes in the functional equations annotating the new rule or entry. This can be done because, according to LFG, the

equations for NPs that are oblique arguments are completely predictable from the fact that they are arguments of that sort.

6. I am indebted to Tom Wasow for pointing this out to me.

7. As in prior examples, there is a fair amount of superfluous non-branching structure in the rules acquired, so the tree is not truly "flat" as in (i), but nonbranching, as in (ii). This has no undesirable effects in terms of weak generative capacity. In the next chapter, I discuss a variant of the learning procedure that does not acquire unnecessary nonbranching structure.

8. Tavakolian (1981) claims to find evidence that American children in fact posit *less* branching structure than adult English mandates. However, since all her data are from comprehension experiments, it is possible that the data simply reflect capacity limitations in the processes that build phrase structure during sentence comprehension.

9. As is well known, the ability to use these symbols does not change the weak generative power of a context-free grammar.

10. Japanese itself is not really a free-constituent order language, of course, since there is a strongly preferred SOV order and since alternative positions of subject and object are correlated with particular pragmatic functions (topic and focus). The discussion in the text should be interpreted as applying to a hypothetical verb-final language with true NP constituent order freedom.

4. Phrase Structure Rules: Developmental Considerations

1. Brown's "Stages I–V" denote roughly evenly spaced intervals in children's early language development as indexed by mean length of utterance (MLU). The five stages correspond in English-speaking children to mean utterance lengths of 1.75, 2.25, 2.75, 3.5, and 4.0 morphemes.

2. Apparent exceptions are phrases like *Mommy in*, reported in Braine (1976). However, the contexts of these utterances suggest that the utterances are being used as intransitive prepositions akin to the adult *get in!* or *the doctor is in*, or prolocatives similar to *here, there*, or *downstairs*.

3. An intriguing possibility is that the criteria for orphanhood are related to the criteria for exocentrism (i.e., a constituent headed by another major constituent with a different category label, where the latter constituent is not labeled with a grammatical function and contributes the main predicate of the phrase). Bresnan (1982c) argues, for example, that NP is the head of oblique PP, and a possible LFG analysis of the English copula would be to annotate *be* with $\uparrow = \downarrow$, and have the predicate complement serve as the head of the clause (though see

Jackendoff, 1983, for arguments that *be* is represented as a full predicate in semantic representations). In that case, when the child preempted an old rule with a new one, he or she would make the new rule exocentric. (Unfortunately, this hypothesis would not be applicable to PP spatial complements, which are both endocentric and potential orphans.)

4. In the extensive survey of children's auxiliary errors reported in Chapter 7, the only instance even remotely resembling this type of error was *where's going to be the shopping center*, reported by Menyuk (1969). Thus it appears that in general children do not make the sort of error that one would expect if they learned rules with only maximal categories.

5. It is not clear that a rule generating submaximal APs within the NP (e.g., N″ → A N′, N′ → A N, N″ → A′ N′, or N′ → A′ N) will be adequate either. One can say:

(i) the very angry man

with *very angry*, a maximal constituent, serving as a prenominal adjective phrase. One solution would be to posit the rules A″ → A′ P″ and A′ → Adv A, which would account for the grammaticality of (i) and the ungrammaticality of (9). Unfortunately, X-bar theory rules this out because it has arguments attached at a higher level than modifiers.

6. One might ask whether the orphan designation for submaximal phrases is necessary since the existence of two constituent structure analyses with identical meanings could serve as evidence for the child that something has gone awry in the grammar. This is an intriguing possibility, but I will tentatively not adopt it for two reasons. First, the child would still have to know which of the two rules generating the ambiguity should be preempted by the other, which is exactly what the orphan designation indicates. Second, there appears to be at least one case in LFG where a spurious ambiguity is unavoidable, and one would not want the child to eliminate either rule generating it. The example concerns sentences with predicates such as *rely on*, whose prepositional object can be passivized (*John can be relied on*) and whose prepositional phrases can also serve as unified constituents (e.g., *on whom did you rely?*). Bresnan (1982b) proposes that such predicates have two lexical entries, one where the preposition is incorporated into the verb and which subcategorizes for a direct object (i.e., *rely-on* (SUBJ, OBJ)), and one where the verb is distinct from the preposition and which subcategorizes for an oblique object (i.e., *rely* (SUBJ, OBL$_{on}$)). The former entry would participate in passivization, the latter in clefts and questions that treat the PP as a unit. However, simple sentences such as *Mary relied on John* would then be spuriously ambiguous: [$_V$ *relied on*] [$_{NP}$ *John*] versus [$_V$ *relied*] [$_{PP}$ *on John*]. If this is the correct solution for the distribution of verbs like *rely on*, then the child cannot be equipped with an acquisition procedure that rejects any rule generating a spurious ambiguity.

7. Note that in the last example, common in children's speech, if the child categorized *catch* as a noun, it is not because it denoted a person,

place, or thing. Possibly the child was exercising the third X-bar schema, which allows any category symbol to be rewritten as a verb (Jackendoff, 1977). This could be triggered either distributionally, when the child hears sentences like *do you want a spanking?*, or semantically, when the child has the need to refer to and quantify an entire action. Alternatively, perhaps, the semantic correlate of *noun* proposed in the bootstrapping hypothesis is incorrect or only partially correct, and a logical concept like "quantifiable argument," rather than or in addition to a semantic correlate like "person, place, or thing," is what the child uses as evidence for nounhood.

8. Later in development, apparently miscategorized words become evident again (Clark, 1982; Bowerman, 1982b), but these are probably better analyzed as being the product of an overproductive lexical rule rather than of semantic bootstrapping. See Chapter 8 for further discussion.

9. It is possible that I have misstated the collapsing procedures in P6 so that, given a set of English phrase structure rules, the procedures collapse rules into ones that generate orders that are not grammatical in adult English. In that case, the child would indeed utter ungrammatical orders, contrary to the predictions I am deriving. However, such a case should be viewed as a defect in the statement of the learning mechanisms for phrase structure rules rather than as a true prediction of theories of that sort. A correctly formulated theory in the spirit of the one I am considering here would not make illicit generalizations about English constituent order and hence would predict that children's grammars should always respect the constituent orders of the target language.

10. Of course, strict subcategorization will rule out many of the $w \times s$ possibilities and thus would reduce the total somewhat.

11. Here and in the chapters to follow I present a number of tabulations of data from Brown's subjects Adam, Eve, and Sarah (see Brown, 1973, for a description of the longitudinal study in which their speech was recorded). The primary source for these tabulations is a set of exhaustive listings of a child's utterances in each sample, categorized in a number of ways, including by length and by various sequences of part-of-speech categories. These lists were compiled by Brown and his students and colleagues in the 1960s for Adam (first twenty-three samples, through Stage IV) and for Eve (first sixteen samples, through Stage IV). The lists do not include much in the way of contextual information, but they do indicate whether an utterance was an imitation of a preceding adult utterance and whether it was semantically anomalous given its context. In some cases I was able to check the utterances in the lists against original transcriptions or against Brown's grammars (see below) to verify an analysis; in other cases I was unable to do so. When the analysis of an utterance was indicated to be an imitation, uncertainly transcribed, or semantically anomalous, or when its analysis seemed ambiguous, I did not include it in any of the tabulations. However, because of these limitations and because

some of the tabulations were done by a single rater (myself), the conclusions I draw from such tabulations should be regarded as only suggestive.

In addition, some of the analyses were based on Brown's detailed grammars for the speech of his three subjects at each of five stages. These are the grammars that Brown (1973) referred to as the "15 weighty manuscripts which no more than half-a-dozen people in the world have the *knowledge*, the *patience*, and the *interest* to read; nay, not so many as half a dozen." It is a pleasure to note publicly my disagreement with Brown over the potential interest of those richly insightful works, and to express my gratitude to him for making the grammars and the coded lists of utterances available to me.

12. Some of these words were in combinations that appeared to be semantically anomalous. In all, only five words appeared in both subject and object positions in combinations where the semantic interpretation was unambiguous.

13. Readers familiar with other studies of children's early word combinations (e.g., Braine, 1976) may be surprised at the linguistic sophistication of Brown's subjects. As Braine points out, all three of Brown's subjects were older or more advanced than the ones treated in Braine (1976), where only the very earliest word combinations were examined. Data from children at the level of Adam, Eve, and Sarah, in late Stage I and beyond, are appropriate for the arguments considered in this section both because of the sheer number of sentences and because of the presence of longer sentences.

14. Some of these heuristics were suggested by John Anderson (1974, 1975, 1977) in the context of an interesting computer model of language acquisition whose first implementation learned phrase structure rules without drawing categories from an antecedently specified set. Many of the problems I point out with these procedures are discussed in more detail in Pinker (1979). Interestingly, Anderson, too, was eventually forced to posit an innate noun phrase schema in order to solve some problems of the sort discussed below.

15. The principal exception to this claim would occur if a child heard a word violating canonical syntax-semantics correspondences inside a phrase type that had never been successfully analyzed before (if it had been previously analyzed, the distributional procedures would impose the correct classification on the unknown word). In that case, the child would misanalyze both the category of the word and the category of the phrase it headed. As I mentioned earlier in this chapter, it is safe to assume that this conjunction of events is rare.

16. Gvozdev (reported in Slobin, 1973) reports that his son Zhenya first applied the Russian accusative marker to patients of actions but not to objects of verbs such as *draw* or *read*. Since Zhenya marked objects by using characteristic word orders, this would appear to be a counterexample to the claim that different sorts of rules in the child's grammar all use grammatical relations. Slobin (1984a) describes a similar phenomenon in the use of ergative case markers by children learning Kaluli.

However, in LFG grammatical relations are expressed separately in phrase structure rules and in case annotations to verbs' lexical entries such as OBJ's CASE = *acc*. Thus, the use of a grammatical relation in word order does not imply that it must also be used in case marking— the relevant phrase structure rules could be learned before the relevant case equations. If the child uses patienthood as evidence for accusative case (as he or she does for the OBJ relation), the first verbs containing accusative case equations would be those that took patients as objects. Thus the accusative marker would first appear with action verbs even if the grammar contained the purely syntactic equation OBJ's CASE = *acc*. The data are not inconsistent with the children's promiscuous agreement rule in English, since unlike the case-marking rule in Russian, the number agreement rule in English does not have separate mentions of a grammatical relation and a case. Thus unlike Zhenya, children learning agreement in English could not find themselves in a state at which they had a semantically unrestricted grammatical relation (in this case, subject) but a semantically restricted corresponding case (in this case, nominative). There is no way for them to respect word order for a given verb regardless of the semantics of the subject, but to apply number agreement only to subjects of that verb possessing a certain semantic property. And indeed this does not happen.

Another possible counterexample to the claim being discussed is the finding that children at first passivize only action verbs (Maratsos et al., 1978). I discuss this case in detail in Chapter 8.

17. Braine also presents arguments against the syntactic categories N and V as components of the Stage I child's grammar, but these arguments take different forms from the ones he used in discussing grammatical relations. First, he notes that what are NPs for adults are not always used as such by children—for example, in uttering *big tobacco* the child was not referring to the tobacco can that happened to be big, he was predicating of the tobacco can *that* it was big. Thus *big tobacco* might be an S with predicate-subject order. However, this argument assumes without independent justification that when children express a subject-predicate relation, they do so only within the S constituent. Children could possess an NP constituent and incorrectly use it to predicate something of the head noun; for that matter, it is not even clear that predication within NPs *is* incorrect. Adults can utter bare NPs in discourse (*a ship! a ship!*) and they can make predications within the NP (*that is a big tree*). *Big tobacco* thus could simply be a reduction of *that's a big tobacco can*. Braine's second argument that children lack nouns is that all the supposed nouns in children's speech serve as arguments of predicates (e.g., children do not use idiom chunks or pleonastic elements like dummy *it* or *there*), so the symbol *argument* is truer to the facts than *noun*. As in some other arguments reviewed in this chapter, this could simply mean that children have not yet learned constructions with nonargument nouns. Braine's third argument is that children violate putative part of speech boundaries when the semantics warrant it, as in *Mommy eye* (Mommy is drawing an eye) or *more catch*. But this

claim requires some dubious assumptions. In the former case, Braine is claiming that *eye* refers to an action, presumably because it appears after an agent word and because the child rarely used any agent-object schema and frequently used an agent-action schema. However, this argument borders on circularity: the child is said to lack nouns, because she can use *eye* to denote an action, and is said to use *eye* to refer to an action, because it appears in a slot that is defined as being specific to actions, not nouns. It seems just as plausible or more plausible that the utterance is a fragment of a subject-verb-object sequence with an unexpressed verb (see Bloom, 1970, and the next section in this chapter). The latter example, *more catch*, can simply be analyzed as a miscategorized word, not as evidence that no words are ever categorized. N. 7 of this chapter and the corresponding text show how such mistakes can be learned and unlearned. Thus none of the arguments *against* the hypothesis that children possess syntactic categories (as opposed to arguments that there is no evidence that they do) is compelling.

18. Braine (1976) claims that the expansion of one term of a two-term relation in a limited-scope formula falls out of two facts: that each term denotes a semantically defined referent, and that the cognitive abilities of the child allow him to conceive of such referents as themselves being decomposable into two or more concepts. However, this account would not guarantee that the within-phrase *order* of a constituent in a hierarchically organized sentence would be the same as the order of that phrase in isolation or across a range of matrix patterns. To ensure that to happen without requiring each construction to be learned separately, one must have a symbol for the ordering of the within-phrase elements and allow the symbol to be substitutable in a variety of patterns. Furthermore, when the formulae list items in terms of their relation to the predicate, as opposed to their intrinsic semantic properties (e.g., action + object-acted-upon, or *have* + possessed object), there is no invariant concept that the child could use to generalize a within-item order from one formula to another.

19. For verb-object and verb-locative sequences, Braine proposes that the child simply chooses a word denoting a salient feature of an event and inserts it directly into a node representing a semantic constituent of a limited-scope formula. Thus, in *Mommy eye* (= *Mommy is drawing an eye*) Kendall would simply use the salient term *eye*, which is part of the action witnessed, as the action term in an *actor* + *action* formula without mentally representing the predicate *draw* in linguistic structure. I do not doubt that random insertion of a salient item into a word string is possible—it is not in the nature of 1- and 2-year-olds to let an observation or demand go unexpressed on the technicality that the main verb has not yet been learned or was not retrievable. However, in invoking formulae using thematic terms in the first place, which Braine must do to have an action slot for *eye* to fit into, the proposal falls prey to the criticisms raised in the last section, and also depends on the dubious assumptions discussed in n. 17. Furthermore, it cannot eco-

nomically account for cases in which the child utters not only *ab* and *ac* but also *abc*, nor cases in which the child utters *ab*, *ac*, and *bc* where no two members of *a*, *b*, and *c* form a semantic or syntactic constituent.

5. Inflection

1. By including TOPIC and FOCUS as hypothesizable features, the child would automatically hypothesize equations for verb affixes that were sensitive to various properties of elements serving those functions. For example, equations such as TOPIC = OBJ or perhaps TOPIC's CASE = *acc* must be hypothesizable in order to learn Philippine languages that signal grammatical functions by inflecting the verb in a manner specific to the grammatical role played by the topic. Equations mentioning TOPIC properties would repeatedly be confirmed in topic-prominent languages, whereas those mentioning SUBJECT properties would soon be contradicted and hence expunged. The converse would happen, of course, when subject-prominent languages were being acquired. See Li (1976) and Li and Thompson (1976) for discussion of this typological difference.

Note also that the child could infer that subjects can be unexpressed in "PRO-drop" languages on the assumption that the feature PRO is available to symbolize predicates that are constrained by inflections but not expressed overtly in the surface phrase structure. Thus the child could add the equation SUBJ's PRED = PRO to a verb inflection if an inflected verb that was previously found to agree with subject features is also found in an input matrix sentence that lacks an expressed subject. Such an inflection would then allow future verbs to appear sans subject without violating Kaplan and Bresnan's completeness requirement. If there is no verb inflection, there is no entity specific to the subject that can be appended with the PRED = PRO equation, in accord with the fact that PRO-drop languages tend to have rich systems of agreement affixation (Chomsky, 1981).

Needless to say, this discussion barely scratches the surface of the acquisition problem for topic-prominent and PRO-drop languages, but it suggests that some of the mechanisms necessary for characterizing such languages could fall under the purview of the acquisition procedures discussed in this chapter.

2. Brown used as an index of complexity the presence of various affix-placing transformations in the derivation of a sentence containing the affixes of interest. Such a metric cannot be transplanted to LFG since it lacks transformations. However, if we use as a crude measure of complexity the sheer numbers of equations in the lexical entries of the fourteen morphemes, we find that that measure is significantly correlated with the mean acquisition order for Brown's three subjects: Spearman's rho = .72, one-tailed $p < .05$.

3. Throughout this chapter, and also in Chapters 7 and 8, I will cite many developmental data reported in Slobin (1984a). This is the concluding chapter to a volume (Slobin, 1984b) containing reviews of the developmental course of acquisition in a variety of languages; in that

chapter Slobin attempts to summarize and explain the recurring patterns documented in the preceding reviews. Since at the time of this writing I had access to Slobin's summary but not to the chapters themselves, I will cite Slobin, but the data themselves were reported or reviewed by the following contributors to that volume: Eve Clark (Spanish, French, Italian), Anne Mills (German), Ruth Berman (Hebrew), Brian MacWhinney (Hungarian), Patricia Clancy (Japanese), Bambi Schieffelin (Kaluli), Magdalena Smoczynska (Polish), Ayhan Aksu and Dan Slobin (Turkish), and Dan Slobin (Russian). I am extremely grateful to Professor Slobin for making drafts of his chapter, and the extensive notes that went into writing it, available to me.

4. If, as suggested, the child expunges contradicted equations "permanently," he or she must store a record of the expunged equations so that they will not be hypothesized again. Thus the first model's demands on short-term memory have been converted into demands on long-term memory in the second model, which is more realistic. Even this long-term record is not strictly necessary; the child could severely reduce the strength of a contradicted equation rather than expunge it permanently. In that case the child would be hypothesizing incorrect equations all his life but none would attain any measure of strength.

5. The two-dimensionality of the printed page makes the nesting of certain dimensions and collapsing of adjacent cells easy to represent visually. If one were to represent paradigms in an n-dimensional medium, nesting would correspond to the relative "permeability" or eliminability of cell walls separating the levels of a dimension when it is crossed with various other dimensions.

6. In this modified version, entire inflected words are given hypothesized equations. How is the child to recognize that a word is likely to be inflected, so that he or she will not waste effort in hypothesizing equations for every word in a potentially inflectable category? One possibility is that the child exploits phonetic cues that a word has been affixed, such as having a final syllable whose vowel is in harmony with that of the stem, or rhymes with the stem, or is a reduplication of a stem syllable, or whose voicing is the same as the final stem segment, and so on. See Slobin (1984a) and MacWhinney (1978) for versions of this hypothesis and for evidence that children learn affixes more quickly when they display these phonological properties.

7. It is an open question whether the I-acquisition procedures should be modified so as to account for the relative strengths of morphemes in the competition over cell occupation. Possibly other factors are at work. If an inflected form already exists in the lexicon, for example, the child can analyze it (albeit incorrectly) and is less likely to add something to his or her linguistic knowledge when it appears in the input because of the parse-first feature of the procedures. Zero-inflected words are unlikely to be recognized as inflected items (see n. 6), and so would be less likely to trigger procedure I1. And since languages forbid neither homonymity within paradigms nor zero morphemes (un-

like synonymity of inflections, which the Unique Entry principle forbids universally), it seems best not to amend the acquisition procedures themselves so as to avoid homonymity or zero marking in an attempt to predict which affix will be driven out. The acquisition procedures, by conforming to the Unique Entry principle, simply predict that imperialism or the initial choice of a single morpheme to encode a feature will occur.

8. In fact, Jane Grimshaw has pointed out to me that French-speaking adults generally cannot guess the gender of rare words beginning with vowels, presumably because vowel-initial nouns are preceded by the ambiguous consonant *l'* rather than *le* or *la*.

9. It has often been noted that masculine and feminine genders are not given arbitrary phonological correlates, but that masculine nouns tend to be shorter, to end in open syllables, and, in general, to contain less phonetic material than feminine nouns (e.g., Cooper and Ross, 1975). This suggests that grammatical gender might in some sense have a quasi-semantic correlate after all, but one that is deeper than the biological sex of human referents (what could be deeper than that, you are probably asking). Cooper and Ross (see also Tanz, 1971; Brown, Black, and Horowitz, 1955; Pinker and Birdsong, 1979) point out that the sorts of phonological properties that distinguish masculine and feminine genders also correlate cross-linguistically with other bipolar features, such as spatial and temporal proximity to the speaker in deictic words and serial position in frozen conjoined phrases. In each of these cases the phonological properties associated with masculine gender are paired with the more basic or unmarked feature value. Thus masculine and feminine gender might be correlated not with the concept of male versus female sex, but with the concept of the unmarked versus marked, zero versus positive, or basic versus nonbasic poles of a continuum or feature. The correlation of this concept with pronouns for males and females would then be merely a sexist epiphenomenon.

10. One might wonder why it is necessary to have a procedure that eliminates incorrect dimensions at all. After all, a dimension that defines a morpheme as encoding all possible values of an irrelevant feature should be harmless, at worst occupying some extra memory space. The answer is that a morpheme that encodes all values of a feature still requires that the feature be defined, that is, that it have *some* value. This would lead to trouble if the child hypothesized some feature for an affix and the affix could be used in the target language even if the feature had no value at all (e.g., the case feature for a topic affix in a topic-prominent language; a tense feature with the values *present, past,* etc., for an affix that was indifferent to whether the clause was finite or infinitival). Procedure I3 can eliminate a feature entirely, allowing the affix to be used regardless of how and even whether the feature is defined, using degeneracy of a dimension as evidence. Note that this predicts that no affix can simply encode the fact that a feature is defined without encoding which value of that feature is specified; the procedures I have proposed would be unable to learn such an affix. (Thus

a complementizer specific to finite complements, for example, must have access to an explicit feature *finite*, rather than being defined as the disjunction of all possible tenses.) An alternative and less constrained model could allow the child to hypothesize the feature value *undefined* and thus perhaps could do without procedure I3 altogether.

11. In cases where the child only hypothesizes a single form in a paradigm cell, there are certain potential patterns of syncretism that could fool this procedure. For example, if a language encoded case and gender by paradigm (i), and if the child had not yet hypothesized the gender dimension, and if the child happened to choose the morphemes in cells 1, 2, 3, and 8 to exemplify each of the four cases and only those morphemes, then the paradigm would look like (ii) and procedure I3 would incorrectly eliminate the case dimension. Several factors mitigate against this possibility. First, the child must have made each of four unfortunate choices, an improbable conjunction especially for larger

i.

CASE

		Nom	Acc	Dat	Abl
GENDER	M	a (1)	a (2)	a (3)	b (4)
	F	c (5)	d (6)	e (7)	a (8)

ii.

CASE

Nom	Acc	Dat	Abl
a	a	a	a

paradigms than this. Second, I have shown how the child is biased against entering homonymous morphemes within a paradigm when the Unique Entry principle compels a choice to be made, so the fatal conjunction of choices is even less likely. Third, languages tend to make more distinctions in a given feature when it is combined with one of the more basic, easy, or salient levels of a second feature. For example, there are more distinctions of gender and case in the singular number than the plural number; there are more such distinctions in the third person than in the more difficult first person (Greenberg, 1963). Thus the child would probably be predisposed to choose the row of cells whose morphemes happen to be most likely to differ from one another. Finally, according to Williams's (1981b) generalizations about syncretism, patterns like that in (i), where a single morpheme appears in disjoint rows and columns, should be "unnatural" and rare. For all these reasons procedure I3 seems viable as it stands.

12. Bybee (in press; see also Greenberg, 1963) points out that more "accessible" notions (those more prevalent in languages, and, by hy-

pothesis, more likely to be hypothesized by the child) tend also to be affixed closer to the stem. Assuming that the order of consideration of dimensions for I5 and I6 is the same as for I1, the child would then be building his word structure template from the stem outward, without ever having to reanalyze the template in order to insert an *affix* symbol between the stem and an existing *affix* symbol.

Note also that the I-procedures could treat free closed-class morphemes as if they were bound morphemes (e.g., *thedog*, with *the* analyzed as a definiteness-marking prefix). I6 could then be modified so as to categorize an affix as a free morpheme if another free morpheme (e.g., an open-class word as in *the big dog*) was heard to intervene between the supposed "affix" and the stem.

13. The resulting general paradigms for the two sorts of languages differ in size in the same way as the respective short-term computations differ in complexity. However, since these are long-term memory structures, where space is not at a premium (Anderson and Bower, 1973; Crowder, 1976), it is unlikely that this size difference is itself responsible for the difference between the two language types in acquisition speed, historical stability, and so on. In fact, as Michael Maratsos has pointed out (Maratsos and Chalkley, 1981; Maratsos, in press), the fact that nightmarish fusional paradigms in Indo-European languages are re-learned generation after generation (albeit more slowly for a given child than in Turkish) is itself testimony to the absence of long-term storage limitations for human grammatical representations.

14. This account predicts that differences between the acquisition rates for fusional and agglutinating languages should only emerge when the child begins to strip affixes from stems and applies the affixes productively; no differences are predicted for the initial formation of word-specific paradigms. However, this prediction only applies to the agglutinating/fusional distinction itself; other factors that tend to be confounded with agglutinating morphology (e.g., a lack of idiosyncratic stem-governed exceptions, and the fact that affixes constitute distinctly articulated syllables) could muddy certain tests of the prediction in practice.

15. It has been noted that the preemption of an overregularized form by the correct irregular is not instantaneous, but both forms may coexist for a period (Cazden, 1968; Brown, 1973; Kuczaj, 1977). As with any discovery of gradualness in language development, this can be accommodated by a simple strength parameterization of the relevant acquisition procedure. In this case, the preemption would consist not of all-or-none replacement, but of reciprocal changes in strength between the preempted and preempting entries (e.g., their strengths could sum to a constant and an equal distribution of strength across multiple entries within a cell could be an unstable state of the paradigm).

16. Another possible explanation of this correlation would attribute it not to the frequency of the stem per se, but to the fact that for an infrequent word the probability that a child will witness the word *in*

each of the cells of its word-specific paradigm is low. The paradigm will thus be incomplete and subject to filling-in by a general paradigm, with little chance of an irregular version of each paradigm entry coming along in the input to preempt the overregularized entries.

17. The child should also have some way of distinguishing between uniqueness violations that are the result of failing to hypothesize a dimension and uniqueness violations that are the result of not hypothesizing enough levels in an existing dimension. For example, a child might encounter a uniqueness violation because he or she had hypothesized only a singular and a plural number in a language like Arabic that also has a dual number, or a single dative/allative "hypercase" in languages that distinguish the two, or a single possessive marker in a language that makes a distinction between alienable and inalienable possession. The evidence that the child would need to distinguish between such predicaments and those arising from his or her lacking a dimension altogether is this: if there are parallel uniqueness violations in each level of a dimension, some other dimension is missing, whereas if there is a single uniqueness violation in one level of a dimension, that level should be split into two levels within that dimension. Procedures I10 and I11 could easily be modified so as to be sensitive to this difference and to act accordingly. Note, incidentally, that for the child to be able to exploit this source of evidence, he or she must be able not only to recognize when a uniqueness violation is occurring for a given cell, but must be able to look for other uniqueness violations in neighboring cells. This may be another reason to allow cells to contain nonunique entries of high strength pending the decision of how to alter the paradigm, as proposed in connection with the original discussion of the Unique Entry principle above and in connection with procedure I3.

6. Complementation and Control

1. The actual feature set used for the English tense and participle system is immaterial here. I will assume for convenience that the symbol MORPH (for "morphology") is a feature that can have the values *inf*, *fin*, *progpart*, *perfpart*, *passivepart*, and so on, as suggested by Gazdar, Pullum, and Sag (1982). (In English, of course, the features *perfpart* and *passivepart* would constitute a single feature; see Lieber, 1981.) Note also that these equations will be appended to the lexical entries of individual complementizers as well; for example, the entry for *to* will contain the equation MORPH = *inf*, whereas *that* will be appended with MORPH = *fin*.

2. This procedure could be modified to attach only the level of projection exemplified in the input, rather than the maximal projection (see Chapter 4), if it turned out that for some category X the corresponding X-COMP could not be expanded as a full X^{max}.

3. This procedure should perhaps be modified to examine the finiteness of sentential but not VP complements in the input, automat-

ically assigning the equation V-COMP's MORPH = *inf* to the latter, in light of the fact that subjectless VP complements are always tenseless (Chomsky, 1977, 1981).

4. In LFG, the copula *be* is a raising verb, but I do not count missing copula sentences here since there is little evidence that children producing them have mastered the copula (see Chapter 4). I also did not count *see running* from Kendall, which may be a gerund, or examples like *want* + N or *see* + N which involve lexical entries taking objects, not complements. Braine also notes that David said *want Daddy fix it*, which may be a raising-to-object construction (see the section "The Acquisition of Raising-to-Object Constructions" below); however, Braine cautions that the immediately preceding utterance was *want, Daddy* with *Daddy* as a vocative, and hence that *Daddy* might serve as an interjected vocative in *want Daddy fix it* as well.

5. Braine reports the two examples *want fix it* and *want come on* from David's corpus where the intended agent was not David himself. However, since David's utterances were generally only two words in length, with many obligatory constituents missing, it is plausible that *you* or *Daddy* was intended to appear in the object position of those utterances but never made it into the output string for the reasons discussed in Chapter 4. In samples of the speech of children who are uttering sentences of four words or longer, I have found no reports of control errors.

6. Dan Slobin (personal communication) has called to my attention the fact that such errors have been reported in the acquisition of Polish. Why they should occur in Polish and not in English is obscure to me.

7. Actually, procedure C4 would either have to create two lexical entries, each with one of the complementizer constraints, or a single entry with disjoined constraints, rather than a single entry with both constraints. This is because an entry with both constraints could never be used in a sentence without violating Kaplan and Bresnan's (1982) Consistency requirement.

8. Tom Wasow has pointed out to me that all English verbs taking tensed sentential complements allow the complementizer *that* regardless of whether they permit non-null complementizers as well, a fact the model does not account for. To account for this generalization, one could have the child hypothesize a lexical redundancy rule (see Chapter 8) such that any non-null complementizer that was acquired for one lexical entry (or perhaps some minimum number of entries *n*) would automatically be appended to all other lexical entries with the same complement structure. However, any such annotation would have to be preemptable by evidence for a null complementizer, since otherwise verbs forbidding complementizers (e.g., *make*) could never be acquired. However, the reader might notice that this is the opposite of the preemption principle that non-null complementizers preempt null complementizers. To resolve the paradox, one could have the complementizer redundancy rules hypothesized only for sentential complements, not VP complements, but this would be ad hoc and of dubious cross-linguistic generality. A better alternative would be to distinguish

among (i) overt complementizers hypothesized from an input sentence containing the verb in question; (ii) overt complementizers created by a lexical rule; (iii) null complementizers hypothesized at a stage at which some overt complementizers had been acquired; and (iv) null complementizers hypothesized at a stage before any overt complementizers had been acquired. Then (i) and (iii) would preempt (ii) and (iv) but never each other. This solution invokes the Uniqueness principle in ways similar to what is done in Chapters 4, 5, and 8.

9. Another possibility, suggested by Tom Roeper (personal communication), is that the child isolates the complementizer *to* by first learning the "purposive" *to* in adjuncts like *I drove home* [*in order*] *to get my books*. Because that *to* does have a meaning ("for the purpose of"), it might be easier to isolate and learn than the meaningless complementizer. In support of this hypothesis is Tavakolian's finding (1978) that 3-year-olds correctly interpret the subject of *to* adjuncts 83 percent of the time in sentences such as *the lion jumps over the pig to stand on the fence.* Unfortunately, the possibility of a "bird in the hand" bias mentioned earlier makes it hard to interpret this result as strong evidence for mastery of purposive *to* adjuncts. Moreover, Helen Goodluck (personal communication) has pointed out to me that all of Tavakolian's stimuli contained prepositional objects rather than direct objects. Since children avoid coreference between prepositional objects and missing subjects in adjuncts (Goodluck and Tavakolian, 1982), their excellent performance in the 1978 experiment cannot be uniquely attributed to their mastery of purposive *to* adjuncts. Finally, Bloom et al. (in press) report only 12 instances of purposive *to* as compared to 3,800 instances of *to* as a complementizer in their corpora from four children. Thus it seems unlikely that prior acquisition of purposive *to* is a prerequisite for the acquisition of the complementizer *to*.

10. This latter prediction is only necessary if one wishes to avoid having the child ever misanalyze raising-to-object verbs as verbs taking infinitival sentential complements. If such early mistakes could be eliminated later when the correct forms are acquired, perhaps by a version of the Uniqueness principle that I will propose toward the end of this chapter, this prediction could be relaxed.

11. There is a second parsing bias that will also favor the analysis of a postverbal NP as an object rather than as the subject of a sentential complement. Adults have a bias to attach incoming constituents to the current partial phrase structure tree with as few intervening nodes as possible (the "Minimal Attachment" bias described by Kimball, 1973, and Frazier and Fodor, 1978). This would favor the analysis of the post-*want* NP as an immediate constituent of the VP over it being a daughter of an S-node which is itself a daughter of VP.

12. There are other forms of control, called "anaphoric control" by Bresnan (1982c), which do not obey the constraints on the matrix controller that apply to functional control. Thus a procedure similar to C3 might serve as a plausible acquisition mechanism for those forms of control even if it fails here.

13. Robert May has suggested to me that instead of the child having to access semantic information to learn the anomalous nature of *promise*, he or she could note that *promise* has an intransitive counterpart, *I promised to leave*, with, of course, subject control. No object-equi verb with object control has such a counterpart (e.g., **I told to leave, *I ordered to leave, *I saw to leave*). Furthermore, the other well-known example of an object-equi verb with subject control, *ask* as in *the boy asked his teacher to be allowed to leave*, also has an intransitive alternative version, *the boy asked to leave*. May's hypothesis was that the child could exploit this generalization and hence learn marked control relations without ever requiring semantic information. I do not adopt May's interesting suggestion here for two reasons. First, the strategy would not help the child acquire the marked subject-control verbs *strike* and *impress* as in *John struck/impressed me as silly*). In the same vein, the strategy would lead to errors in a theory like LFG in which object-equi and raising-to-object verbs are treated by the same principles of control. It would notice that *expect* has the intransitive entry in *I expected to leave*, and would then falsely conclude that the transitive version *I expected John to leave* dictated subject control, like *promise*. It could make similar mistakes for the equi form of *get* roughly synonymous with *managed to*, such as *I finally got to leave* and *I finally got the guests to leave*.

14. As with any other theory positing one-trial learning, some amount of gradualness in the learning curves may be introduced by other cognitive processes operating between the all-or-none representation and the overt responses by which it is measured.

15. Given that only some children erred on *promise* in Chomsky's experiment, and given that many adults find *promise* NP *to* VP ungrammatical, one might wonder whether just those children grow up into just those adults. If so, no theory of how children unlearn a bad entry for *promise* is necessary; these children may be predisposed never to acquire a marked control verb, neither as children nor as adults. Only a longitudinal study could establish whether or not this is the case, and all I can offer in this regard is the following anecdote. As an undergraduate, I took a psycholinguistics course one of whose assignments was to carry out a version of Chomsky's experiment. The 8-year-old subject, who made the same errors as Chomsky's subjects, was my brother Robert. When I recently showed him *promise* sentences, Robert, at that time 15, judged them as a bit odd-sounding but as undoubtedly having subject control. This would seem to suggest that the childhood errors are outgrown.

16. One might argue that *ask* does not really violate the principle, because the two versions have different meanings: to order politely versus to request permission. However, this difference in meaning appears to be a simple semantic consequence of the difference between subject and object control as it relates to the single meaning "requesting politely that it be the case that." Furthermore, the difference between the two shades of meaning corresponds exactly to the difference between the correct and incorrect forms of *promise*: with object control, it

would mean "guarantee the opportunity for," and with subject control, it means "commit one's own future behavior." Yet despite this meaning difference, the subject-control form of *promise* drives out the object-control form. I conclude that there is no intrinsic difference in meaning between the two versions of *ask* that would account for the coexistence of both forms.

17. It has been suggested to me that the prevalence of object-control verbs may be a consequence of social factors, presumably that when an individual A initiates some relation between him and another individual B apropos of some action or state relevant to one of them, it will be the action or state of B that would be relevant. I do not see how this could explain the distribution of control relations, because (a) often relationships with B initiated by A concern A's state, but still they cannot be expressed by a control relation between matrix subject and missing complement subject (e.g., *John told Mary that he was leaving/#to leave; John perceived that he was beginning to hate Mary/#perceived Mary to begin to hate her*, etc.; (b) even if the supposed social regularities were generally true, it would remain an open question whether every child had induced those regularities in the period of time before he or she started using unmarked object-equi verbs with no control errors, or whether during the evolutionary history of language, those regularities became reflected in the child's language acquisition mechanisms (see Chomsky and Lasnik, 1977, for discussion).

7. Auxiliaries

1. I adopt Figure 7.2(a) as the phrase structure rule generating inverted sentences, rather than Kaplan and Bresnan's rules i(a–b) for three reasons.

i. (a) $S \rightarrow (V_{AUX = {}_c +})$ $\quad NP_{SUBJ}$ $\quad VP_{\uparrow TENSE}$
   (b) $VP \rightarrow (V)$ $\quad (NP_{OBJ})$ $\quad (VP'_{V\text{-}COMP})$

First, the optional verb in i(b) violates the X-bar constraint that phrasal heads must be obligatory. Second, i(a–b) generates an extra level of nonbranching phrase structure for every inverted sentence: [$_S$ can John [$_{VP}$ [$_{VP'}$ $_{V\text{-}COMP}$[$_{VP}$ swim]]]], as compared to the present analysis [$_S$ can John [$_{VP'}$ $_{V\text{-}COMP}$ [$_{VP}$ swim]]]. Third, I have had trouble devising a plausible account as to how i(b) would be learned.

2. Presumably, the defectiveness of these paradigms is not completely arbitrary but is a consequence of the semantic ill-formedness of certain compositions of the individual meanings of sets of auxiliaries (e.g., *(progressive (perfect (predicate))).

3. In the literature on auxiliaries the word "modality" is used ambiguously for the set of semantic notions including necessity, possibility, permission, obligation, advisability, and epistemic status (i.e., the meanings of modal verbs), and for the syntactic realizations of various types of illocutionary force, such as affirmation, emphasis, negation,

questioning, and exclamation. I will use the term "modality" to refer to the former, and "sentence modality" to refer to the latter.

4. It is crucial that these levels correspond to *syntactic* features that may be used to express sentence modalities, rather than *semantic* features for sentence modalities themselves (e.g., QUESTION, NEGATION). That is because the interaction of sentence modalities and choice of auxiliaries depends only on the syntactic construction expressing the sentence modality. For example, *better*, which may not appear in inverted yes-no questions, also is prohibited in inverted constructions that are not questions, such as negative polarity and exclamative constructions (*only then should/*better you go, should/*better he go!*), while being permissible in interrogatives lacking inversion (*who better not cry?, you better not what?*). Likewise, main verbs may not be negated by following them with *not* (**John ate not the artichoke*), though they may be negated in other ways (*no one ate an artichoke*). Possibly these syntactic features actually do express some well-defined meaning or range of meanings (e.g., Steele, 1981, discusses the possibility that inversion encodes degree of epistemic certainty); here I will simply assume that phrase structure rules and possibly other rules (e.g., prosodic rules) introduce a set of syntactic features, including *inv(ersion)*, *neg(ation)*, *emph(atic)*, and *neut(ral)*, that enters into processes of semantic interpretation in indirect ways.

5. Modal *need* is marginally acceptable to me in negated emphatic sentences (*?No, I NEEDN'T buy a smoke detector!*). If so, the sentence modality paradigms would have to be complicated in one of several ways (e.g., by crossing a NEG = +/− dimension with each of the other three levels of the sentence modality dimension).

6. Crucial to this account is the assumption that the *inv*, *neg*, and *emph* features apply to infinitival complements when they are complements to *do* but not when they are complements to modals (equivalently, the features are defined for a predicate when that predicate is itself questioned, negated, or emphasized, but not when it is an argument of some other modal predicate that is being questioned, negated, or emphasized). This assumption is necessary to block **does he be going?* and **does he have gone?* while still allowing *could he be going?* and *could he have gone?*. To effect this, sentence modality features defined in matrix clauses must be available to the complement verb when the matrix verb is *do* but not when it is a modal. Intuitively this should follow from the fact that *do*, being meaningless, has no corresponding semantic predicate, and so should in some sense be "transparent" to sentence modality features from the point of view of its complement verb. I have thought of several versions of a Lexical Functional Grammar for English auxiliaries that would have this property, none of them optimal; rather than spell these alternatives out I will simply leave this as a problem for future research.

7. Since complementizers tend to be sensitive to sentence modality and to other features that auxiliaries are sensitive to (Pullum and Wil-

son, 1977), one might propose in addition that the child uses these dimensions in paradigms for complementizers.

8. It is to the credit of Erreich, Valian, and Winzemer (1980) that they recognize these problems and propose a possible solution. They suggest that when the child hears sentences such as *do you like it?*, he or she misinterprets the verb as tensed, since the second-person present forms of regular English verbs happen to be identical to their infinitival forms. Thus the child might mistakenly construe such sentences as evidence for multiple marking of tense in questions, inspiring a tense-copying transformation. This is an interesting proposal, but I do not think it is viable. If the child has acquired a rich enough paradigm to recognize a base verb as the second-person present form, he or she can also recognize that such a form in the input is nondiagnostic of finiteness (since it would also be listed in the infinitive cell of the paradigm). It seems doubtful that the child would be equipped wih a procedure that made distributional decisions based on information that it knows to be ambiguous with respect to that very decision (see Chapter 3). Furthermore, it predicts that the child would obliterate all distinctions between finite and infinitival forms, leading to errors such as *to walked* that in fact are extremely rare.

As for eliminating the incorrect rule, Erreich et al. note that input sentences such as *did you like it?* cannot be generated by the copying rule, and suggest that when two rules have the same domain of application and generate intersecting sets of sentences, attested sentences generated by one rule and not the other cause the latter to be abandoned. (I assume this is their intent; they also mention processes driven by the accumulation of evidence that is "contradictory to the aux-copying rule," but that would appear to be negative evidence, so I consider the more complex formulation summarized above.) Assuming that there is some reasonable procedure whereby the child would determine whether the entire sets of sentences generated by two rules intersect (which is not obvious), this proposal faces the problem that it would seem to eliminate, mistakenly, many pairs of rules contributing to legitimate ambiguities (e.g., *visiting professors can be boring*) whenever the child heard a sentence uniquely generated by one of the rules.

9. Maratsos and Kuczaj did not check to see whether the preponderance of irregular verbs in overtensed constructions is simply a consequence of the preponderance of strong verbs in children's speech in general. However, some simple analyses I have performed suggest that it is not. In a sample of over five hundred of Adam's utterances containing a modal and a verb, the verb was irregular in 52 percent of the utterance tokens that were not routines. In the samples that Maratsos and Kuczaj (1978) report, in contrast, 100 percent of the overtensed questions and approximately 70 percent of the overtensed declaratives contained irregular verbs. Thus the preponderance of irregular overtensed verbs indeed is in need of explanation. Incidentally, I have found counterexamples to the pattern Maratsos and Kuczaj observed whereby

all overtensed questions contained irregular verbs: Adam said *does it opens?* twice, and Eve said *did you turned it?* once; in addition, Menyuk (1967) reports *where does the wheel goes*, which is regular in the present tense. This is just as well, since neither Maratsos and Kuczaj nor anyone else had been able to explain the purported pattern.

10. For example, I first learned of the phenomenon of overtensing when Kenji Hakuta caught me making such an error in my own speech.

11. Once again, one might worry that the preponderance of overtensing in sentences with *do* is an uninteresting consequence of a greater base frequency for *do* than for modals in children's speech. And once again, I have performed simple analyses that belie this possibility. Tokens of *do* appear in 59 percent of Adam's utterances with *do* or modals in the samples examined, 30 percent of Eve's, and 51 percent of Sarah's. In contrast, there are over fifty reported tokens of overtensed sentences with *do* in the sources cited earlier in the chapter, but only four reported tokens of overtensed sentences with modals: *can you broke those?* and *they wouldn't haved a house* from Kuczaj (1976), *can you broke it?* from Maratsos and Kuczaj (1978), and *you will gone away* from Eve's eighteenth sample (though it is a past participle, not a simple past-tense form, that is used here). Two additional examples with *be* can be found: *what are you did?* from Kuczaj (1976), and *they are fell down on Paul's feet*, from Adam's twentieth sample.

12. One possible exception: Adam once said *d'you want me . . . should be careful?*. This is highly dubious as a counterexample, however: it is transcribed as containing a hesitation; it begins with *d'you want me*, which was a routine Adam used in hundreds of sentences; and Brown (n.d.) notes that the other portion of it was imitated from a preceding adult utterance. One other exception: among the hundreds of imitations and syntactic transformations of stimulus sentences recorded by Major, there is a single instance of *are you going to might play* uttered by a 5-year-old in an attempt to form a question from *you might play*.

13. Interestingly, of the fifty-eight questions uttered by Major's subjects that contained two modals (e.g., *will you might play?*), forty-one (71 percent) began with *will* or *would*. These two modals are similar to *do* in not having a clear-cut predicate of which the main proposition is an argument. For adults, *will* serves to contribute a future-tense feature to the sentence; in the language of children and of adults talking to them, *will* and *would* are used in interrogatives mainly as indirect requests with insistent and polite illocutionary force, respectively (e.g., *will you put your toys away?; would you put your toys away?*). Thus it seems that an inverted auxiliary may be used with a modal in the matrix verb position when the auxiliary does not express a predicate taking as an argument the proposition expressed by the matrix sentence.

14. I am departing from my own canons in failing to provide an explicit account of how the child eventually does acquire the PRED entry for *do*, which is semantically predicateless even for adults. One possibility is that the child borrows the PRED entry from the nonauxiliary pro-verb *do* (e.g., *I am doing something*), giving it the approximate

meaning "to enter into or be engaged in some unspecified activity or relation." This account has the advantage that it is consistent with the fact that when the auxiliary *do* entered the English language, it was adapted from the pro-verb *do* (Steele, 1981). Unfortunately, the account has the disadvantage that it would require a complication of the constraint proposed earlier against auxiliaries borrowing information from their nonauxiliary homonyms. Other hypotheses come to mind (e.g., the child comes to generalize that all verbs must have a PRED entry regardless of their semantics; the child eventually notices the fact that *do* co-occurs only with infinitival verbs and posits a V-COMP and a PRED entry so as to express this fact), but lacking independent arguments for any of these accounts, I will not discuss them further.

15. There are some near misses in the literature. First, Major (1974) reports *had've talked*, *would've have talked* (one instance each), and *must've not've hurried* (two instances), but, as I have done throughout the chapter, I will refrain from interpreting contracted auxiliaries owing to uncertainties about the child's segmentation of these forms. Second, in her fourth sample Eve said *he (goed to) make another one. He (went) to make another one*, which her mother interpreted, with Eve's assent, as *he was going to make another one. Be going to* is semantically similar to English modals, but the *go* component is not a modal syntactically (**are going you to eat?*, **going you to eat?*, **I am going not to eat*, and so on); furthermore, the transcription of *goed to* was labeled as uncertain. Hence I do not consider this to be an example of an inflected modal.

16. Possible exceptions: (1) Baker (1981) reports his daughter saying emphatically *it might DO rain*. (2) Many contracted auxiliaries co occur with other auxiliaries, e.g., from Menyuk (1969), *he'll might get in jail*; these seem best interpreted as segmentation errors, given the examples provided by Kuczaj (1976), Brown (1973), and MacWhinney (1982). (3) There are several examples in the literature of auxiliaries repeated in inverted and medial positions:

(a) How can he can look? (Menyuk, 1969)
(b) What shall we shall have? (Bellugi, 1971)
(c) Is this is the powder? (Menyuk, 1969)
(d) Whose is that is? (Hurford, 1974)
(e) Why did Peter did sleep here? (Fletcher, 1979)
(f) Do she don't need that one? (Adam, Sample 32)

Since the auxiliaries are always the same in both positions (i.e., there are no spontaneous productions such as *how can he will go?*), and since there are no reports of repeated auxiliaries in declaratives, the examples are best interpreted as speech errors in which two verb positions are redundantly expanded, with a phrase structure analysis such as that in Figure 7.11(b). See Prideaux (1976) and Goodluck and Solan (1979) for similar analyses.

17. By now the reader may be exasperated by this series of developmental generalizations followed by citations of counterexamples and

disclaimers about their relevance. I feel that this is the only way to proceed in an area in which a large part of the data base consists of singular events (i.e., a particular child utters a particular word combination at a particular moment). Not to look for counterexamples in a serious way would be disingenuous, but to reject any hypothesis that met up with a counterexample would be to guarantee that there will be no theories. I have opted to summarize the overall pattern of the data in the most judicious and nontendentious way possible, noting the counterexamples as well so that skeptics may draw their own conclusions.

18. It is unclear why *go* is the only nonauxiliary verb ever inverted. Erreich, Valian, and Winzemer (1980) note that *go* is inverted in constructions like *there goes Bill;* one might add that *be going to* + *V* expresses future tense and thus is semantically similar to certain auxiliaries; also, that there is something obscure about *go* that allows certain adults to invert it in the jocular expression *how goes it?* (but not *how feel you?*, *how do you?*, and so on). In any case these errors are so rare that the issue may be academic.

19. One wrinkle in this argument is that Kaplan and Bresnan propose that the preposed *wh*-phrase position be assigned a grammatical function of its own, Q-FOCUS, which would have the unfortunate effect of blocking the access of the inversion constraint to the verb position, just as in echo and double questions. However, the Q-FOCUS function is formally different from the subcategorizable SUBJ and OBJ functions (see Bresnan, 1982c), and there is good reason to believe that the feature propagation mechanism could be made to respect this distinction in one of several ways. For example, constraining equations could be allowed to pass through nonsubcategorizable functions; the Q-FOCUS function could be eliminated; a new function could be assigned to the S within S′ and the inversion constraint could refer directly to the inversion feature within the constituent annotated by that "function," and so on. There are few grounds for arguing for one of these accounts over the others; it suffices at this point simply to note that Q-FOCUS differs formally from SUBJ, OBJ, etc., which is all that the account of inversion constraints requires.

20. This is why the constraint must be stated in terms of forbidding noninversion rather than requiring inversion. If inversion were required, the sentences in (17) would be ruled out regardless of the scope of application of the constraint. I am grateful to Ronald Kaplan for pointing this out to me. I stress that these considerations are necessary simply to make the account formally consistent. The substantive points I am making are largely independent of the precise statement of the constraint.

21. Traces would be learned for object and oblique *wh*-questions (e.g., *who did John see?*, *what did John crawl under?*) and for embedded subject questions (e.g., *who did John think left?*), since in those cases it is easy to see that an obligatory constituent is missing. When rules for traces *are* eventually learned from these sentences, the spurious ambiguity of

having both structures in Figure 7.14(a) and (b) for subject *wh*-questions such as (17d) is ruled out by the inversion constraint imposed by the *wh*-word, which is free to apply in Figure 7.14(b) because no grammatical function is assigned to the *wh*-phrase. Figure 7.14(b) may also be ruled out by Kaplan and Bresnan's (1982) version of the Subjacency Condition if NP_{SUBJ} is a bounding node, as certain extractability phenomena in English suggest. If so, that would also rule out *who did t go?* which would otherwise be generable. I thank Ronald Kaplan for pointing this out.

22. A non-neglible minority of these children did insert extraneous auxiliaries in *how come* questions, however, and for these children Kuczaj and Brannick's overgeneralization account may be appropriate.

8. Lexical Entries and Lexical Rules

1. In the standard theory of transformational grammar and its successors, an item's subcategorization frame is specified in terms of the positions of various syntactic categories in deep structure, rather than in terms of a set of grammatical functions. Grimshaw (1982b) presents evidence that verbs in fact subcategorize for grammatical functions, not categories, but most of what I will say in the rest of this chapter does not hinge on which theory is correct.

2. As I have done throughout, I will use Bresnan's notational convention whereby different prepositional objects are differentiated by thematic subscripts on the OBL function. Hence OBL_{goal} = *to*-object; OBL_{source} = *from*-object; OBL_{agent} = *by*-object; OBL_{loc} = *in*-object or *on*-object; and so on. This terminology does not imply that only arguments playing the various thematic roles may be expressed by the corresponding oblique objects (for example, not all *by*-phrases are agentive); it is just a universal notation for differentiating oblique objects according to the canonical thematic roles they express.

More terminology: the thematic relation "theme" refers to the entity that is moved in an act of motion (or symbolically moved in changes of state or circumstance or transfers of possession), or to an entity of which something is predicated (see Gruber, 1967; Jackendoff, 1972, 1983). (The semantic role "patient" is identical to "theme" whenever there is an explicit or implicit agent.) Analogously, the roles "source" and "goal" refer to origin and destination of motion, to the initial and final states of a change of state or circumstance, or to the former owner and the recipient in a transfer of possession.

3. Presumably there would also be suborderings within the sets of oblique functions and thematic relations, so that different thematic roles such as instrument, location, source, goal, comitative, and so on, could be associated with their appropriate case markers or prepositions, and so that certain thematic relations would be "promoted" to subject (e.g., instrument) before others (see, e.g., Fillmore, 1968).

4. There are also "true ergative" languages in which the canonical mappings appear to be violated in basic sentences. However, this phenomenon interacts in complex ways with pronominalization and other

factors that are beyond the scope of this book. I simply note here that "true ergative" languages (which are not to be confused with "morphological ergative" languages) are fairly rare, and that the acquisition theory at present cannot easily account for their acquisition. One possibility suggested in Pinker (1982; n. 7) is that the child can use other perceptually available evidence for subjecthood in the family resemblance structure in Chapter 2 (e.g., occurring serially before objects in basic sentences, lacking overt case marking, being unexpressed and controlled in complements) to override the thematic evidence. This problem is raised again in Chapter 9.

5. It is occasionally proposed that the double-object form of the dative is a marked form relative to the *to-* or *for*-dative form. Unfortunately the developmental evidence is far from straightforward. Brown (1973) reports that datives of either form are fairly rare in Stage I speech, but cites several examples of double-object forms used by the children. Bloom, Lightbown, and Hood (1975) report similar data. In later stages, I have found that Eve produced a few dozen examples of datives approximately evenly divided between the *for-* and the double-object forms. Adam, too, produced both types of datives. The majority of the double-object datives these children uttered expressed the goal or beneficiary as a pronoun (e.g., *gimme, show me, I made you some pictures*), raising the suspicion that the indirect object is cliticized onto the verb. This was not invariably true for many of the children, however, since they also occasionally used full nouns as indirect objects in double-object constructions (e.g., *give doggie paper*, from Adam's Stage I speech); it is also worth noting that the vast majority of the prepositional objects in the *to-* and *for*-datives were also personal pronouns. Comprehension studies on older children show a much clearer asymmetry: double-object datives are far harder to comprehend than *to-* or *for*-datives (Fraser, Bellugi, and Brown, 1963; Cook, 1976; Osgood and Zehler, 1981; Cromer, 1975; Fischer, 1974; Roeper, Bing, Lapointe, and Tavakolian, 1981; Wilson, Pinker, Zaenen, and Lebeaux, 1981). However, here the results must be interpreted with caution, since the observed difficulty of double-object datives in these experiments interacts strongly with the animacy of the indirect and direct objects, and since a number of parsing and task-specific strategies could lead to double-object forms being difficult to parse regardless of the ease of initially learning their lexical forms. For example, Frazier and Fodor (1978) point out that strings of adjacent uninflected NPs are difficult to parse in general. Thus I will leave the question of the relative basicness of *to/for* and double-object forms open for now.

6. I am currently exploring two possibilities. First, perhaps it is a prerequisite for the acquisition of a lexical entry with source/goal/location arguments that all of its arguments must be witnessed in some sentence, even if the thematic roles the child assigns to them are not drawn from that sentence. Second, perhaps oblique arguments are more likely to be acquired when they have recently been "primed" by other sen-

tences—in our first, but not our second experiment, NP *to* NP sentences were presented in other experimental conditions.

7. In the case of figure-ground verbs, Bowerman's claim must be qualified somewhat: all of the cited examples of the supposed *fill*-type forms (i.e., goal = object; theme = oblique) in the initial unproductive period lacked an expressed theme/figure argument (e.g., *touch my pussycat, cover me up*). Interestingly, this pattern is predictable from the canonical mapping between thematic and grammatical structure: if a goal or location is expressed as an object and there is an expressed agent, then the theme cannot be expressed at all without crossing links.

8. As Pinker (1982) and Wasow (1981) have pointed out, strictly speaking Baker's argument confounds two issues: productive versus nonproductive mechanisms, and lexical versus transformational mechanisms. To see that they are independent, we need only consider that lexical rules can be productive, and that transformations can be nonproductive if they stipulate positive features in their conditions (e.g., imagine that the Dative Movement transformation has the condition "V must be [+DM]" and that the [+DM] feature is appended to verbs only when they are exemplified in double-object phrases in the input). In defense of Baker, it might be added that positive rule features are considered an undesirable mechanism within the Standard Theory of transformational grammar, since they undermine the assumption that transformations are structure-dependent (Bresnan, 1977), and that uncontroversial lexical rules (e.g., *un-* prefixation, *-en* suffixation) are typically only partially productive. Thus the lexical/unproductive conflation does have some theoretical motivation. In any case, I will say no more about the debate between transformational and lexical treatments of the alternations under consideration here. Arguments for a lexical treatment of passivization and dative alternation can be found elsewhere (e.g., Bresnan, 1978, 1982b; Oehrle, 1976), and acceptance of Baker's learnability-theoretic argument for a lexical treatment of dativization must await a satisfactory resolution of the learnability problems to be examined in the rest of this chapter, as well as more precise explication of the relevant metatheoretical issues such as structure-dependence.

9. This example was suggested by Kenneth Wexler.

10. There are a number of exceptions to this generalization. Some, like *offer*, may turn out to obey the generalization if it is stated using more subtle phonological features relevant to syllable structure than the simple "monosyllabic" versus "polysyllabic." Others may not and the child may simply have to learn them directly from the input as they are exemplified. See n. 15 for some problems this process might cause, however.

11. To generalize the constraint to the case of truncated passives, the null symbol "∅" used in the agent slot of the lexical entries for such passives would have to have a position in the grammatical function hierarchy equal to or lower than that of OBL.

12. One raincloud for this account is the fact that in Maratsos et al.'s

first experiment, passivized *see* was in fact no easier than other passivized nonaction verbs. (Passivized *see* and *hear* were comprehended in a pilot study mentioned in Maratsos, 1978, but not in the full experiment reported in Maratsos et al., 1979.) Possibly this is a consequence of their subjects' not having inferred the proper thematic analysis of *see*—our subjects had more contextual cues to the meaning of our *see*-analogues, and also seemed to be linguistically more advanced than those of Maratsos et al. Other hypotheses spring to mind but are unmotivatable without further experimentation.

13. Which is not to say that the system is not language-specific. There are many other linguistic parallels between abstract and concrete domains (e.g., locutions about debate being similar to those about war, locutions about love being similar to those about diseases or journeys; see Lakoff and Johnson, 1980). Unlike thematic relations, these parallels do not enter into any specifically grammatical phenomena; they just enter into the choice of open-class lexical items. Furthermore, the thematic relation *theme*, though deducible from semantic roles, does not correspond to any cognitive "natural kind." Its defining characteristics seem to be a disjunction of moved object or entity, subject of an attribution, and whatever is left over after the other arguments have been assigned their own thematic roles. Thus while specific thematic analyses of abstract verbs need not be learned from the input in all cases, the system of thematic analysis itself might still be an innate part of the language acquisition faculty.

14. It is possible that such a procedure could lead the child to hypothesize a paradigm dimension differentiating the discourse-relevant aspects of alternative forms—for example, goal-focus versus theme-focus for the *to*-object and double-object forms of the dative, respectively (see Oehrle, 1976; Erteschik-Shir, 1979), or for alternative forms of figure-ground verbs. Presumably the child would need such features as indexes to the various verb forms in order to select the form in speech production that is appropriate to his or her communicative intentions. Furthermore, it is at least conceivable that the child could use such a paradigm dimension to learn exceptions to lexical rules in circumstances where the exceptional verb is used and the child can predict from the context which argument the speaker wishes to focus. If the context demands that the theme be focused, for example, and the speaker uses the *to*-dative form, the child could enter that form into the theme-focus cell of that verb's paradigm. Since both the theme-focus and goal-focus cells are filled with the *to*-dative form, the child has in effect learned that that verb does not undergo dativization. This conjecture was originally formulated in Pinker (1981b); the notion of a paradigm with discourse-relevant cells helps make that conjecture more precise.

15. It will also be necessary to appeal to statistical considerations to solve a related problem raised by Mazurkewich and White's proposal concerning exceptions to their constraint that double-object forms must be monosyllabic with a prospective possessor as derived object. They suggest that the child can simply learn such forms one by one as they

are witnessed in the input. Unfortunately, once such forms are learned in this way they would nullify or at best pollute the generalization itself. The only way one can salvage their proposal is to say that when some minimum number of lexical entries exemplifies a constraint, the child should not discard that constraint when he or she encounters a small number of exceptions to it.

Another potential impurity that might contaminate the search for correct features is the presence of entries in word-specific paradigms that the child mistakenly generated using overgeneral productive mechanisms. Later in the chapter I will argue that the child must annotate such entries with the preemptability symbol "?" in order to recover from such lexical overgeneration. Since this annotation is independently necessary, one can exploit it in solving the present problem. All that one needs to do is make the paradigm-splitting mechanism ignore productively generated forms when searching for features that differentiate filled and unfilled cells in lexical paradigms.

16. It is also possible to characterize this process in a way that does not require every constraint to be stated as a binary feature. When a constraint is hypothesized, it could be annotated to the relevant cell in a paradigm as a constraint equation of the form FEATURE $=_c$ *value*, and the mechanism that coordinates general and specific paradigms could expunge preemptable entries if the verb failed to bear that feature or bore a contradictory feature.

17. An intriguing yet somewhat half-baked proposal is that suppletion by unrelated forms is a process that can operate even in cases where the semantic concomitants of a rule are less obvious, such as passivization. I have noticed, for what it is worth, that many unpassivizable verbs have high-frequency counterparts that express the same semantic predicates as those verbs, and whose subjects correspond semantically and pragmatically to what would be the subjects of the passivized verbs: *I don't follow/*am escaped by John's arguments; a revolution in Russia occurred in/*was seen by the year 1917; Bill resembles/*is resembled by John*; also *beer is contained in/*by the green bottle* and *the United States is comprised of/*by fifty states* (in the nonstandard dialect in which one can also say *fifty states comprise the United States*).

9. Conclusion

1. Slobin, who is a braver man than I am, plans to apply his test to his "operating principles" for language acquisition (Slobin, 1984a) using previously unavailable data on the acquisition of a South African language.

2. None of this bears on the issue of whether the *onset* and *rate* of acquisition (rather than the nature of the mechanisms used or of the rules acquired) are affected by maturational changes. See Gleitman (1981, 1983) for interesting discussion of the former possibility.

References

Akmajian, A., Steele, S., and Wasow, T. 1979. The category AUX in universal grammar. *Linguistic Inquiry* 10: 1–64.

Aller, W. K., Aller, S. K., and Saad, L. M. 1977. The acquisition of Ask, Tell, Promise, and Show structures by Arabic children. Paper presented at the 6th Annual University of Wisconsin-Milwaukee Linguistics Symposium, Milwaukee, March.

Anderson, J. R. 1974. Language acquisition in computer and child. Human Performance Center Technical Report No. 55, University of Michigan, Ann Arbor.

———— 1975. Computer simulation of a language acquisition system: a first report. In R. L. Solso, ed., *Information processing and cognition: the Loyola Symposium*. Hillsdale, N.J.: Erlbaum Associates.

———— 1976. *Language, memory, and thought*. Hillsdale, N.J.: Erlbaum Associates.

———— 1977. Induction of augmented transition networks. *Cognitive Science* 1: 125–157.

———— 1978. Arguments concerning representations for mental imagery. *Psychological Review* 85: 249–277.

———— 1983. *The architecture of cognition*. Cambridge, Mass.: Harvard University Press.

Anderson, J. R., and Bower, G. H. 1973. *Human associative memory*. Washington: Winston.

Anderson, S. 1971. On the role of deep structure in semantic interpretation. *Foundations of Language* 6: 197–219.

Andrews, A. D. 1982. The representation of case in modern Icelandic. In J. Bresnan, ed., *The mental representation of grammatical relations*. Cambridge, Mass.: MIT Press.

Aronoff, M. 1976. *Word formation in generative grammar*. Cambridge, Mass.: MIT Press.

Atkinson, M. 1982. *Explanations in the study of child language development*. Cambridge: Cambridge University Press.

Baker, C. L. 1979. Syntactic theory and the projection problem. *Linguistic Inquiry* 10: 533–581.

—— 1981. Learnability and the English auxiliary system. In C. L. Baker and J. J. McCarthy, eds., *The logical problem of language acquisition*. Cambridge, Mass.: MIT Press.

Baker, C. L., and McCarthy, J. J., eds. 1981. *The logical problem of language acquisition*. Cambridge, Mass.: MIT Press.

Bates, E. 1976. *Language and context: studies in the acquisition of pragmatics*. New York: Academic Press.

Bellugi, U. 1965. The development of interrogative structures in children's speech. In K. Riegel, ed., *The development of language functions*, pp. 103–138. University of Michigan Language Development Program, Ann Arbor, Report No. 8.

—— 1967. The acquisition of the system of negation in children's speech. Ph.D. dissertation, Harvard University.

—— 1971. Simplification in children's language. In R. Huxley and E. Ingram, eds., *Language acquisition: models and methods*. New York: Academic Press.

Berko, J. 1958. The child's learning of English morphology. *Word* 14: 150–177.

Berwick, R. C. 1981. Computational complexity and Lexical Functional Grammar. In *Proceedings of the 19th Annual Meeting of the Association for Computational Linguistics*, Stanford, pp. 7–12.

Berwick, R. C., and Weinberg, A. S. 1983. The role of grammars in models of language use. *Cognition* 13: 1–62.

Bever, T. G. 1970. The cognitive basis for linguistic structures. In J. R. Hayes, ed., *Cognition and the development of language*. New York: Wiley.

Bever, T. G., Mehler, J. R., and Valian, V. 1973. Linguistic capacity of very young children. In T. G. Bever and W. Weksel, eds., *The acquisition of structure*. New York: Holt, Rinehart and Winston.

Bickerton, D. 1981. *The roots of language*. Ann Arbor: Karoma.

—— In press. The language bioprogram hypothesis. *Behavioral and Brain Sciences*.

Bloom, L. 1970. *Language development: form and function in emerging grammars*. Cambridge, Mass.: MIT Press.

Bloom, L., Lahey, M., Hood, L., Lifter, K., and Fiess, K. 1980. Complex sentences: Acquisition of syntactic connectives and the semantic relations they encode. *Journal of Child Language* 7: 235–261.

Bloom, L., Lifter, K., and Hafitz, J. 1980. Semantics of verbs and the development of verb inflections in child language. *Language* 56: 386–412.

Bloom, L., Lightbown, P., and Hood, L. 1975. Structure and variation in child language. *Monographs of the Society for Research in Child Development* 40.

Bloom, L., Tackeff, J., and Lahey, M. In press. Learning *to* in complement constructions. *Journal of Child Language*.

Bolinger, D. 1975. Meaning and form—some fallacies of asemantic grammar. In E. F. K. Koerner, J. Odmark, and J. H. Shaw, eds., *Current issues in linguistic theory*, vol. 1: *The transformational-generative paradigm and modern linguistic theory*. Amsterdam Studies in the Theory and History of Linguistic Science, series 4. Amsterdam: J. Benjamin.

Bowerman, M. 1973. *Early syntactic development: a cross-linguistic study with special reference to Finnish*. Cambridge: Cambridge University Press.

—— 1974. Learning the structure of causative verbs: a study in the relationship of cognitive, semantic and syntactic development. In E. Clark, ed., *Papers and reports on child language development*, No. 8, pp. 142–178. Stanford University Committee on Linguistics.

—— 1976. Semantic factors in the acquisition of rules for word use and sentence construction. In D. M. Morehead and A. E. Morehead, eds., *Normal and deficient child language*. Baltimore: University Park Press.

—— 1982a. Children's mental representation of events: some clues to structures and categories from recurrent speech errors. Stanford Psychology Department Colloquium, March 29, 1982.

—— 1982b. Starting to talk worse: clues to language acquisition from children's late errors. In S. Strauss, ed., *U-shaped behavioral growth*. New York: Academic Press.

—— 1982c. Reorganizational processes in lexical and syntactic development. In E. Wanner and L. R. Gleitman, eds., *Language acquisition: the state of the art*. Cambridge: Cambridge University Press.

Braine, M. D. S. 1963. On learning the grammatical order of words. *Psychological Review* 70: 323–348.

—— 1971a. On two types of models of the internalization of grammars. In D. I. Slobin, ed., *The ontogenesis of grammar: a theoretical symposium*. New York: Academic Press.

—— 1971b. The acquisition of language in infant and child. In C. E. Reed, ed., *The learning of language*. New York: Appleton-Century-Crofts.

—— 1976. Children's first word combinations. *Monographs of the Society for Research in Child Development* 41.

Brame, M. K. 1978. *Base-generated syntax*. Seattle: Noit Amrofer.

Bresnan, J. 1977. Transformations and categories in syntax. In R. E. Butts and J. Hintikka, eds., *Basic problems in methodology and linguistics*. Dordrecht, Netherlands: Reidel.

—— 1978. A realistic transformational grammar. In M. Halle, J. Bresnan, and G. Miller, eds., *Linguistic theory and psychological reality*. Cambridge, Mass.: MIT Press.

—— 1981. An approach to universal grammar and the mental representation of language. *Cognition* 10: 39–52.

—— ed. 1982a. *The mental representation of grammatical relations*. Cambridge, Mass.: MIT Press.

—— 1982b. The passive in lexical theory. In J. Bresnan, ed., *The mental representation of grammatical relations*. Cambridge, Mass.: MIT Press.

—— 1982c. Control and complementation. In J. Bresnan, ed., *The mental representation of grammatical relations*. Cambridge, Mass.: MIT Press.

—— 1982d. Polyadicity. In J. Bresnan, ed., *The mental representation of grammatical relations*. Cambridge, Mass.: MIT Press.

Bresnan, J., and Grimshaw, J. 1978. The syntax of free relatives in English. *Linguistic Inquiry* 9: 331–391.

Bresnan, J., and Kaplan, R. M. 1982. Grammars as mental representations of language. In J. Bresnan, ed., *The mental representation of grammatical relations*. Cambridge, Mass.: MIT Press.

Bresnan, J., Kaplan, R. M., Peters, S., and Zaenen, A. 1982. Cross-serial dependencies in Dutch. *Linguistic Inquiry* 13: 613–635.

Broadbent, E. 1958. *Perception and communication*. New York: Pergamon Press.

Brown, R. N.d. Grammars for the speech of Adam, Eve and Sarah. Unpublished manuscript, Harvard University.

—— 1957. Linguistic determinism and the part of speech. *Journal of Abnormal and Social Psychology* 55: 1–5.

—— 1958. *Words and things: an introduction to language*. New York: Free Press.

—— 1968. The development of *wh* questions in child speech. *Journal of Verbal Learning and Verbal Behavior* 7: 279–290.

—— 1973. *A first language: the early stages*. Cambridge, Mass.: Harvard University Press.

—— 1977. Word from the language acquisition front. Invited address at the meeting of the Eastern Psychological Association, Boston, April.

Brown, R., Black, A. H., and Horowitz, A. E. 1955. Phonetic symbolism in natural languages. *Journal of Abnormal and Social Psychology* 50: 388–393.

Brown, R., Fraser, C., and Bellugi, U. Explorations in grammar evaluation. In U. Bellugi and R. Brown, eds., The acquisition of language. *Monographs of the Society for Research in Child Development* 29.

Brown, R., and Hanlon, C. 1970. Derivational complexity and order of acquisition in child speech. In J. R. Hayes, ed., *Cognition and the development of language*. New York: Wiley.

Bruner, J. S. 1975. From communication to language—a psychological perspective. *Cognition* 3: 255–287.

Bybee, J. H. In press, a. *Morphology and morphophonemics*.

—— In press, b. Diagrammatic iconicity in stem-inflection relations. In J. Haiman, ed., *Iconicity in grammar* (tentative title).

Caplan, D., ed. 1979. *Biological studies of mental processes*. Cambridge, Mass.: MIT Press.

Carey, S. In press. Are children fundamentally different kinds of thinkers and learners than adults? In S. Chipman, J. Segal, and R. Glaser, eds., *Thinking and learning skills*, vol 2. Hillsdale, N.J.: Erlbaum Associates.

Cazden, C. B. 1968. The acquisition of noun and verb inflections. *Child Development* 39: 433–448.

Chomsky, C. 1969. *Acquisition of syntax in children from 5 to 10*. Cambridge, Mass.: MIT Press.

Chomsky, N. 1957. *Syntactic structures*. The Hague: Mouton.

—— 1959. A review of B. F. Skinner's "Verbal behavior." *Language* 3: 26–58.

—— 1965. *Aspects of the theory of syntax*. Cambridge, Mass.: MIT Press.

—— 1970. Remarks on nominalization. In R. Jacobs and P. Rosenbaum, ed., *Readings in English transformational grammar*. Waltham, Mass.: Ginn.

—— 1975. *Reflections on language*. New York: Random House.

—— 1980. *Rules and representations*. New York: Columbia University Press.

—— 1981. *Lectures on government and binding*. Dordrecht, Netherlands: Foris Publications.

Chomsky, N., and Lasnik, H. 1977. Filters and control. *Linguistic Inquiry* 8: 425–504.

Clark, E. V. 1973. What's in a word? On the child's acquisition of semantics in his first language. In T. Moore, ed., *Cognitive development and the acquisition of language*. New York: Academic Press.

—— 1982. The young word maker: a case study of innovation in the child's lexicon. In E. Wanner and L. R. Gleitman, eds., *Language acquisition: the state of the art*. Cambridge: Cambridge University Press.

Clark, E. V., and Clark, H. H. 1979. When nouns surface as verbs. *Language* 55: 767–811.

Clark, H. H. 1973. Space, time, semantics, and the child. In T. Moore, ed., *Cognitive development and the acquisition of language*. New York: Academic Press.

Clark, H. H., and Haviland, S. E. 1977. Comprehension and the given-new contract. In R. O. Freedle, ed., *Discourse production and comprehension*. Norwood, N.J.: Ablex Publishing.

Clark, R. 1971. Performing without competence. *Journal of Child Language* 1: 1–10

Cole, R. A., and Jakimik, J. 1980. A model of speech perception. In R. A. Cole, ed., *Perception and production of fluent speech*. Hillsdale, N.J.: Erlbaum Associates.

Cook, V. J. 1976. A note on indirect objects. *Journal of Child Language* 3: 435–437.

Cooper, W. E., and Paccia-Cooper, J. 1980. *Syntax and speech*. Cambridge, Mass.: Harvard University Press.

Cooper, W. E., and Ross, J. R. 1975. World order. In R. E. Grossman, L. J. San, and T. J. Vance, eds., *Papers from the Parasession on Functionalism*. Chicago: Chicago Linguistic Society.

Cromer, R. F. 1975. An experimental investigation of a putative linguistic universal: marking and the indirect object. *Journal of Experimental Child Psychology* 20: 73–80.

Crowder, R. G. 1976. *Principles of learning and memory*. Hillsdale, N.J.: Erlbaum Associates.

Curtiss, S., Yamada, J., and Fromkin, V. 1979. How independent is language? On the question of formal parallels between grammar and action. *UCLA Working Papers in Cognitive Linguistics* 1: 131–157.

Dale, P. S. 1976. *Language development: structure and function*. New York: Holt, Rinehart and Winston.

Dennet, D. C. 1978. *Brainstorms: philosophical essays on mind and psychology*. Montgomery, Vt.: Bradford Books.

de Villiers, J. G. 1981. The process of rule learning in child speech: a new look. In K. Nelson, ed., *Children's language*, vol. 2. New York: Gardner Press.

de Villiers, J. G., and de Villiers, P. A. 1973a. A cross-sectional study of the acquisition of grammatical morphemes. *Journal of Psycholinguistic Research* 2: 267–278.

—— 1973b. Development of the use of word order in comprehension. *Journal of Psycholinguistic Research* 2: 331–341.

—— 1974. Competence and performance in child language: are children really competent to judge? *Journal of Child Language* 1: 11–22.

—— 1977. Semantics and syntax in the first two years: the output of form and function and the form and function of the input. In F. D. Minifie and L. L. Lloyd, eds., *Communicative and cognitive abilities: early behavioral assessment*. Baltimore, Md.: University Park Press.

—— 1978. *Language acquisition*. Cambridge, Mass.: Harvard University Press.

de Villiers, J. G., Phinney, M., and Avery, A. 1982. Understanding passives with non-action verbs. Paper presented at the 8th Annual Boston University Conference on Language Development, Boston, October.

Eimas, P., Siqueland, E. R., Jusczyk, P., and Vigorito, J. 1971. Speech perception in infants. *Science* 171: 303–306.

Emonds, J. 1976. *A transformational approach to English syntax: root, structure-preserving, and local transformations*. New York: Academic Press.

Erreich, A. 1980. "Why you won't play with me?": non-inversion errors in Wh-questions. Paper presented at the 5th Annual Boston University Conference on Language Development, Boston, October.

Erreich, A., Valian, V., and Winzemer, J. 1980. Aspects of a theory of language acquisition. *Journal of Child Language* 2: 157–179.

Erteschik-Shir, N. 1979. Discourse constraints on dative movement. In T. Givon, ed., *Syntax and semantics*, vol. 12: *Discourse and syntax*. New York: Academic Press.

Ervin, S. 1964. Imitation and structural change in children's language. In E. Lenneberg, ed., *New directions in the study of language*. Cambridge, Mass.: MIT Press.

Falk, E. N. 1980a. Word order and rules of syntax. Bachelor's thesis, Brandeis University.

—— 1980b. The English auxiliary system: a lexical-functional analysis. Unpublished manuscript, MIT.

Fay, D. 1978. Transformations as mental operations: a reply to Kuczaj. *Journal of Child Language* 5: 143–150.

—— 1980. Performing transformations. In R. A. Cole, ed., *Perception and production of fluent speech*. Hillsdale, N.J.: Erlbaum Associates.

Ferguson, C. A., and Slobin, D. I., eds., 1973. *Studies of child language development*. New York: Holt, Rinehart and Winston.

Fiengo, R. 1977. On trace theory. *Linguistic Inquiry* 8: 35–61.

Fillmore, C. J. 1968. The case for case. In E. Bach and R. J. Harms, eds., *Universals in linguistic theory*. New York: Holt, Rinehart and Winston.

―――― 1977. The case for case reopened. In P. Cole and J. Saddock, eds., *Syntax and semantics*, vol. 8: *Grammatical relations*. New York: Academic Press.

Finke, R. A. 1980. Levels of equivalence in imagery and perception. *Psychological Review* 87: 113–132.

Fischer, S. 1971. The acquisition of verb-particle and dative constructions. Ph.D. dissertation, MIT.

Fletcher, P. 1979. The development of the verb phrase. In P. Fletcher and M. Garman, eds., *Language acquisition*. Cambridge: Cambridge University Press.

Fodor, J. A. 1966. How to learn to talk: some simple ways. In F. Smith and G. Miller, eds., *The genesis of language*. Cambridge, Mass.: MIT Press.

―――― 1968. *Psychological explanation*. New York: Random House.

―――― 1970. Three reasons for not deriving "kill" from "cause to die." *Linguistic Inquiry* 1: 429–438.

―――― 1975. *The language of thought*. New York: T. Y. Crowell.

―――― 1981. The present status of the innateness controversy. In J. A. Fodor, *Representations*. Cambridge, Mass.: Bradford Books/MIT Press.

Fodor, J. A., Bever, T. G., and Garrett, M. F. 1974. *The psychology of language: an introduction to psycholinguistics and generative grammar*. New York: McGraw-Hill.

Fodor, J. A., Garrett, M. F., Walker, E. C., and Parkes, C. H. 1980. Against definitions. *Cognition* 8: 263–267.

Ford, M. 1982. Sentence planning units: implications for the speaker's representation of meaningful relations underlying sentences. In J. Bresnan, ed., *The mental representation of grammatical relations*. Cambridge, Mass.: MIT Press.

Ford, M. 1983. A method for obtaining measures of local parsing complexity throughout sentences. *Journal of Verbal Learning and Verbal Behavior* 22: 203–218.

Ford, M., Bresnan, J., and Kaplan, R. M. 1982. A competence-based theory of syntactic closure. In J. Bresnan, ed., *The mental representation of grammatical relations*. Cambridge, Mass.: MIT Press.

Fraser, C., Bellugi, U., and Brown, R. 1963. Control of grammar in imitation, comprehension, and production. *Journal of Verbal Learning and Verbal Behavior* 2: 121–135.

Frazier, L., and Fodor, J. D. 1978. The sausage machine: a new two-stage parsing model. *Cognition* 6: 291–325.

Fromkin, V. A. 1980. *Errors in linguistic performance: slips of the tongue, ear, pen, and hand*. New York: Academic Press.

Garrett, M. F. 1980. The limits of accommodation: arguments for independent processing levels in sentence production. In V. A. Fromkin, ed., *Errors in linguistic performance: slips of the tongue, ear, pen, and hand*. New York: Academic Press.

Gazdar, G. 1981. Unbounded dependencies and coordinate structure. *Linguistic Inquiry* 12: 155–184.

———— 1982. Phrase structure grammar. In P. Jacobson and G. K. Pullum, eds., *The nature of syntactic representation*. Dordrecht, Netherlands: Reidel.

Gazdar, G., Pullum, G. K., and Sag, I. A. 1982. Auxiliaries and related phenomena in a restrictive theory of grammar. *Language* 58: 591–638.

Gelman, S., and Taylor, M. 1983. Semantic vs. syntactic clues: the proper-common distinction in 2-year-olds. Paper presented at the Boston University Conference on Language Development, Boston, October.

Gentner, D. 1982. Why nouns are learned before verbs: linguistic relativity vs. natural partitioning. In S. A. Kuczaj II, ed., *Language development*, vol 2: *Language, thought, and culture*. Hillsdale, N.J.: Erlbaum Associates.

Gergely, G., and Bever, T. G. 1982. The mental representation of causative words. Unpublished manuscript, Columbia University.

Gleason, H. A. 1961. *An introduction to descriptive linguistics*, rev. ed. New York: Holt, Rinehart and Winston.

Gleitman, L. R. 1981. Maturational determinants of language growth. *Cognition* 10: 103–114.

———— 1983. Biological dispositions to learn language. Unpublished manuscript, University of Pennsylvania.

Gleitman, L. R., and Wanner, E. 1982a. Language acquisition: the state of the state of the art. In E. Wanner and L. R. Gleitman, eds., *Language acquisition: the state of the art*. New York: Cambridge University Press.

———— 1982b. Richly specified input to language learning. Unpublished manuscript, University of Pennsylvania.

Gold, E. M. 1967. Language identification in the limit. *Information and Control* 16: 447–474.

Goldsmith, J. 1980. Meaning and mechanism in grammar. In S. Kuno, ed., *Harvard Studies in Syntax and Semantics*, 3.

Goodluck, H., and Roeper, T. 1978. The acquisition of perception verb complements. In H. Goodluck and L. Solan, eds., *Papers in the structure and development of child language*. University of. Massachusetts Occasional Papers in Linguistics, 4. Graduate Linguistics Students Association, University of Massachusetts, Amherst.

Goodluck, H., and Solan, L. 1979. A reevaluation of the basic operations hypothesis. *Cognition* 2: 85–91.

Gordon, P. 1982. The acquisition of syntactic categories: the case of the count/mass distinction. Ph.D. dissertation, MIT.

Green, G. M. 1974. *Semantic and syntactic regularity*. Bloomington: Indiana University Press.

Greenberg, J. H. 1963. Some universals of grammar with particular reference to the order of meaningful elements. In J. H. Greenberg, ed., *Universals of language*. Cambridge, Mass.: MIT Press.

Grimshaw, J. 1977. English Wh constructions and the theory of grammar. Ph.D. dissertation, University of Massachusetts, Amherst.

—— 1979a. The structure-preserving constraint: a review of "A transformational approach to English syntax" by J. E. Emonds. *Linguistic Analysis* 5: 313–343.

—— 1979b. Complement selection and the lexicon. *Linguistic Inquiry* 10: 279–326.

—— 1981. Form, function, and the language acquisition device. In C. L. Baker and J. J. McCarthy, eds., *The logical problem of language acquisition*. Cambridge, Mass.: MIT Press.

—— 1982a. On the lexical representation of Romance reflexive clitics. In J. Bresnan, ed., *The mental representation of grammatical relations*. Cambridge, Mass.: MIT Press.

—— 1982b. Subcategorization and grammatical relations. In A. Zaenen, ed., *Subjects and other subjects: proceedings of the Harvard Conference on the Representation of Grammatical Relations*. Bloomington, Ind.: Indiana University Linguistics Club.

Gruber, J. 1965. Studies in lexical relations. Doctoral dissertation, MIT. Bloomington, Ind.: Indiana University Linguistics Club.

Hakuta, K. 1982. Interaction between particles and word order in the comprehension and production of simple sentences in Japanese children. *Developmental Psychology* 18: 62–76.

Hale, K. 1981. On the position of Walbiri in a typology of the base. Bloomington, Ind.: Indiana University Linguistics Club.

Halle, M. 1973. Prologomena to a theory of word formation. *Linguistic Inquiry* 4: 3–16.

Halliday, M. A. 1975. Learning how to mean. In E. H. Lenneberg and E. Lenneberg, eds., *Foundations of language development: a multidisciplinary approach*, vol. 1. New York: Academic Press.

Halvorsen, P.-K. 1983. An interpretation procedure for functional structures. *Linguistic Inquiry* 14: 567–615.

Haugeland, J., ed. 1981. *Mind design: philosophy, psychology, artificial intelligence*. Montgomery, Vt.: Bradford Books.

Higginbotham, J. 1983. Linguistic relations. Unpublished manuscript, MIT.

Hoff-Ginsberg, E., and Shatz, M. 1982. Linguistic input and the child's acquisition of language. *Psychological Bulletin* 92: 3–26.

Hornstein, N. 1977a. S and X' convention. *Linguistic Analysis* 3: 137–176.

—— 1977b. Towards a theory of tense. *Linguistic Inquiry* 8: 521–557.

Hurford, J. R. 1975. A child and the English question formation rule. *Journal of Child Language* 1: 299–301.

Huttenlocher, J., Smiley, P., and Charney, R. 1983. Emergence of action categories in the child: evidence from verb meanings. *Psychological Review* 90: 72–93.

Huxley, R. 1970. The development of the correct use of subject personal pronouns in two children. In G. B. Flores d'Arcais and W. J. M. Levelt, eds., *Advances in psycholinguistics*. Amsterdam: North-Holland.

Jackendoff, R. S. 1972. *Semantic interpretation in generative grammar*. Cambridge, Mass.: MIT Press.

——— 1975. Morphological and semantic regularities in the lexicon. *Language* 51: 639–671.

——— 1977. *X-bar syntax: a study of phrase structure*. Cambridge, Mass.: MIT Press.

——— 1978. Grammar as evidence for conceptual structure. In M. Halle, J. Bresnan, and G. A. Miller, eds., *Linguistic theory and psychological reality*. Cambridge, Mass.: MIT Press.

——— 1983. *Semantics and cognition*. Cambridge, Mass.: MIT Press.

Jesperson, O. 1964. *Language: its nature, development and origin*, 12th printing. London: Allen and Unwin.

Kaplan, R. M. 1974. Transient processing load in relative clauses. Ph.D. dissertation, Harvard University.

——— 1975. On process models for sentence comprehension. In D. Norman and D. Rumelhart, eds., *Explorations in cognition*. San Francisco: Freeman.

Kaplan, R. M., and Bresnan, J. 1982. Lexical-functional grammar: a formal system for grammatical representation. In J. Bresnan, ed., *The mental representation of grammatical relations*. Cambridge, Mass.: MIT Press.

Karmiloff-Smith, A. 1979. *A functional approach to child language: a study of determiners and reference*. Cambridge: Cambridge University Press.

Katz, B., Baker, G., and Macnamara, J. 1974. What's in a name? On the child's acquisition of proper and common nouns. *Child Development* 45: 269–273.

Keenan, E. O. 1976. Towards a universal definition of "subject." In C. Li, ed., *Subject and topic*. New York: Academic Press.

Keenan, E. O., and Comrie, B. 1977. Noun phrase accessibility and universal grammar. *Linguistic Inquiry* 8: 63–99.

Keil, F. C. 1981. Constraints on knowledge and cognitive development. *Psychological Review* 88: 197–227.

Kessel, F. S. 1970. The role of syntax in children's comprehension from ages six to twelve. *Monographs of the Society for Research in Child Development* 35.

Kimball, J. 1973. Seven principles of surface structure parsing in natural language. *Cognition* 2: 15–47.

Klavans, J. 1982. Configuration in non-configurational languages. In *Proceedings of the West Coast Conference on Formal Linguistics*. Bloomington: Indiana University Linguistics Club.

Klein, S. M. 1983. Overgeneralization and the developing grammar. Paper presented at the Boston University Conference on Language Development, Boston, October.

Kosslyn, S. M. 1978. Imagery and cognitive development: A teleological approach. In R. S. Siegler, ed., *Children's thinking: what develops?* Hillsdale, N.J.: Erlbaum Associates.

—— 1980. *Image and mind*. Cambridge, Mass.: Harvard University Press.

Kosslyn, S. M., Pinker, S., Smith, G. E., and Shwartz, S. P. 1979. On the demystification of mental imagery. *Behavioral and Brain Sciences* 2: 535–548.

Kramer, P. E., Koff, E., and Luria, Z. 1972. The development of competence in an exceptional structure in older children and young adults. *Child Development* 43: 121–130.

Kuczaj, S. A., II. 1976. Arguments against Hurford's auxiliary copying rule. *Journal of Child Language* 3: 423–427.

—— 1977. The acquisition of regular and irregular past tense forms. *Journal of Verbal Learning and Verbal Behavior* 16: 589–600.

—— 1978. Why do children fail to overgeneralize the progressive inflection? *Journal of Child Language* 5: 167–171.

—— 1981. More on children's initial failure to relate specific acquisitions. *Journal of Child Language* 8: 485–487.

Kuczaj, S. A., II, and Brannick, N. 1979. Children's use of the *wh* question modal auxiliary placement rule. *Journal of Experimental Child Psychology* 28: 43–67.

Kuczaj, S. A., II, and Maratsos, M. 1975. What children *can* say before they *will*. *Merril-Palmer Quarterly* 21: 89–111.

Kuczaj, S. A., II, and Maratsos, M. 1979. The initial verbs of yes-no questions: a different kind of general grammatical category. Presented at the symposium "The Child's Formulation of Grammatical Categories and Rules," Biennial Meeting of the Society for Research in Child Development, San Francisco, March.

Labov, W., and Labov, T. 1978. Learning the syntax of questions. In R. Campbell and P. Smith, eds., *Recent advances in the psychology of language: formal and experimental approaches*. New York: Plenum.

Lakoff, G., and Johnson, M. 1980. *Metaphors we live by*. Chicago: University of Chicago Press.

Langley, P. 1982. Language acquisition through error recovery. *Cognition and Brain Theory* 3: 211–255.

Lapointe, S. 1980. A theory of grammatical agreement. Ph.D. dissertation, University of Massachusetts, Amherst. Graduate Linguistics Students Association, University of Massachusetts, Amherst.

—— 1981a. A lexical analysis of the English auxiliary verb system. In T. Hoekstra, H. v.d. Hulst, and M. Moortgat, eds., *Lexical grammar*. Dordrecht, Netherlands: Foris Publications.

—— 1981b. Free order phrase structure rules. In W. Chao and D. Wheeler, eds., *University of Massachusetts Occasional Papers in Linguistics*, 6. Graduate Linguistics Students Association, University of Massachusetts, Amherst.

—— 1981c. The representation of inflectional morphology within the lexicon. In V. Burke and J. Pustejovsky, eds., *Proceedings of the XIth Meeting of the North East Linguistic Society*. Graduate Linguistics Students Association, University of Massachusetts, Amherst.

Lasnik, H. 1981. Learnability, restrictiveness, and the evaluation metric. In C. L. Baker and J. J. McCarthy, eds., *The logical problem of language acquisition*. Cambridge, Mass.: MIT Press.

Lebeaux, D. 1982. The acquisition of affixation. Unpublished manuscript, Department of Linguistics, University of Massachusetts, Amherst.

—— 1983. The acquisition of lexical entries and lexical rules. Unpublished manuscript, Department of Linguistics, University of Massachusetts, Amherst.

—— In preparation. Three problems for the child. Unpublished manuscript, Department of Linguistics, University of Massachusetts, Amherst.

Lebeaux, D., and Pinker, S. 1981. The acquisition of the passive. Paper presented at the Boston University Conference on Language Development, Boston, October.

Legum, S. 1975. Strategies in the acquisition of relative clauses. Southwest Regional Laboratory Technical Note TN–2–75–10, Los Alamitos, Cal.

Lenneberg, E. H. 1967. *Biological foundations of language*. New York: Wiley.

Li, C., ed. 1976. *Subject and topic*. New York: Academic Press.

Li, C., and Thompson, S. A. 1976. Subject and topic: a new typology of language. In C. Li, ed., *Subject and topic*. New York: Academic Press.

Lieber, R. 1981. On the organization of the lexicon. Ph.D. dissertation, MIT.

Limber, J. 1973. The genesis of complex sentences. In T. Moore, *Cognitive development and the acquisition of language*. New York: Academic Press.

Lindsay, P. H., and Norman, D. A. 1972. *Human information processing: an introduction to psychology*. New York: Academic Press.

Lust, B. 1981. Constraints on anaphora in child language: a prediction for a universal. In S. L. Tavakolian, ed., *Language acquisition and linguistic theory*. Cambridge, Mass.: MIT Press.

McCawley, J. D. 1971. Prelinguistic syntax. In R. J. O'Brien, ed., *Linguistics: developments of the sixties—viewpoints for the seventies*. 22nd Annual Georgetown University Round Table on Languages and Linguistics. Washington, D. C.: Georgetown University Press.

McDermott, D. 1981. Artificial intelligence meets natural stupidity. In J. Haugeland, ed., *Mind design: philosophy, psychology, artificial intelligence*. Montgomery, Vt.: Bradford Books.

Macnamara, J. 1972. Cognitive basis of language learning in infants. *Psychological Review* 79: 1–13.

—— 1976. Stomachs assimilate and accommodate, don't they? *Canadian Psychological Review* 17: 167–173.

—— 1982. *Names for things: a study of child language*. Cambridge, Mass.: Bradford Books/MIT Press.

McNeill, D. 1966. Developmental psycholinguistics. In F. Smith and G. Miller, eds., *The genesis of language*. Cambridge, Mass.: MIT Press.

MacWhinney, B. 1978. Processing a first language: the acquisition of morphophonology. *Monographs of the Society for Research in Child Development* 43.

—— 1982. Basic processes in syntactic acquisition. In S. A. Kuczaj II, ed., *Language development*, vol. 1: *Syntax and semantics*. Hillsdale, N.J.: Erlbaum Associates.

Major, D. 1974. *The acquisition of modal auxiliaries in the language of children*. The Hague: Mouton.

Marantz, A. 1981. On the nature of grammatical relations. Ph.D. dissertation, MIT.

—— 1982. On the acquisition of grammatical relations. *Linguistische Berichte: Linguistik als Kognitive Wissenschaft* 80/82: 32–69.

Maratsos, M. P. 1974a. How preschool children understand missing complement subjects. *Child Development* 45: 700–706.

—— 1974b. Children who get worse at understanding the passive: a replication of Bever. *Journal of Psycholinguistic Research* 3: 65–74.

—— 1978. New models in linguistics and language acquisition. In M. Halle, J. Bresnan, and G. Miller, eds., *Linguistic theory and psychological reality*. Cambridge, Mass.: MIT Press.

—— In press. Some current issues in the study of the acquisition of grammar. In P. Mussen, ed., *Carmichael's manual of child psychology*, 4th ed.

Maratsos, M. P., and Abramovitch, R. 1975. How children understand full, truncated and anomalous passives. *Journal of Verbal Learning and Verbal Behavior* 14: 145–157.

Maratsos, M. P., and Chalkley, M. 1981. The internal language of children's syntax: the ontogenesis and representation of syntactic categories. In K. Nelson, ed., *Children's language*, vol. 2. New York: Gardner Press.

Maratsos, M. P., and Kuczaj, S. A., II. 1978. Against the transformationalist account: a simpler analysis of auxiliary overmarkings. *Journal of Child Language* 5: 337–345.

Maratsos, M. P., Kuczaj, S. A., II, Fox, D. E., and Chalkley, M. 1979. Some empirical studies in the acquisition of transformational relations: passives, negatives, and the past tense. In W. A. Collins, ed., *Minnesota Symposium on Child Psychology*, vol. 12. Hillsdale, N.J.: Erlbaum Associates.

Marr, D., and Nishihara, H. K. 1978. Representation and recognition of the spatial organization of three-dimensional shapes. *Proceedings of the Royal Society of London* 200: 269–294.

Marr, D., and Poggio, T. 1976. Cooperative computation of stereo disparity. *Science* 194: 283–287.

Mayer, J. W., Erreich, A., and Valian, V. 1978. Transformations, basic operations, and language acquisition. *Cognition* 6: 1–13.

Mazurkewich, I., and White, L. 1984. The acquisition of the dative alternation: Unlearning overgeneralizations. *Cognition* 16.

Menyuk, P. 1969. *Sentences children use.* Cambridge, Mass.: MIT Press.

Miller, G. A. 1979. A very personal history. MIT Center for Cognitive Science Occasional Paper #1.

—— 1981. Comments on the symposium papers. Presented at the symposium "The Development of Language and of Language Researchers: Whatever Happened to Linguistic Theory?"; F. Kessel and R. Brown, chair. Biennial Meeting of the Society for Research in Child Development, Boston, April.

Miller, G. A., Galanter, E., and Pribram, K. H. 1960. *Plans and the structure of behavior.* New York: Holt, Rinehart and Winston.

Mohanan, K. P. 1982. Grammatical relations and clause structure in Malayalam. In J. Bresnan, ed., *The mental representation of grammatical relations.* Cambridge, Mass.: MIT Press.

Morgan, J., and Newport, E. L. 1981. The role of constituent structure in the induction of an artificial language. *Journal of Verbal Learning and Verbal Behavior* 20: 67–85.

Mulford, R., and Morgan, J. L. 1983. The role of "local cues" in assigning gender to new nouns in Icelandic. Paper presented at the Boston University Conference on Language Development, Boston, October.

Nash, D. 1980. Topics in Walbiri grammar. Ph.D. dissertation, MIT.

Neidle, C. 1982. Case agreement in Russian. In J. Bresnan, ed., *The mental representation of grammatical relations.* Cambridge, Mass.: MIT Press.

Nelson, K. 1973. Structure and strategy in learning to talk. *Monographs of the Society for Research in Child Development* 38.

Newell, A., and Simon, H. 1961. Computer simulation of human thinking. *Science* 134: 2011–17.

—— 1972. *Human problem solving.* Englewood Cliffs, N.J.: Prentice-Hall.

Newport, E. L., Gleitman, L. R., and Gleitman, H. 1977. Mother, I'd rather do it myself: some effects and non-effects of maternal speech style. In C. E. Snow and C. A. Ferguson, eds., *Talking to children: language input and acquisition.* Cambridge: Cambridge Unversity Press.

Oehrle, R. 1976. The grammatical status of the English dative alternation. Ph.D. dissertation, MIT.

Olivier, D. 1968. Stochastic grammars and language acquisition mechanisms. Ph.D. dissertation, Harvard University.

Osgood, C. E., and Zehler, A. M. 1981. Acquisition of bitransitive sentences: pre-linguistic determinants of language acquisition. *Journal of Child Language* 8: 367–384.

Osherson, D. N., Stob, M., and Weinstein, S. 1982. Learning strategies. *Information and Control* 53: 32–51.

—— In press. *Introduction to formal learning theory.* Cambridge, Mass.: Bradford Books/MIT Press.

Osherson, D. N., and Wasow, T. 1976. Task-specificity and species-specificity in the study of language: a methodological note. *Cognition* 4: 203–214.

Osherson, D. N., and Weinstein, S. In press. Formal learning theory. In M. Gazzaniga and G. Miller, eds., *Handbook of cognitive neuropsychology*. New York: Plenum.

Palmer, S. 1978. Fundamental aspects of cognitive representation. In E. Rosch and B. B. Lloyd, eds., *Cognition and categorization*. Hillsdale, N.J.: Erlbaum Associates.

Park, T.-Z. 1970a. The acquisition of German syntax. Unpublished paper, Psychological Institute, University of Bern, Switzerland.

Park, T.-Z. 1970b. Language acquisition in a Korean child. Unpublished paper, Psychological Institute, University of Bern, Switzerland.

Perlmutter, D. 1980. Relational grammar. In E. Moravcsik and J. Wirth, eds., *Syntax and semantics*, vol. 13: Current approaches to syntax. New York: Academic Press.

Perlmutter, D., and Postal, P. 1977. Toward a universal characterization of passivization. In *Proceedings of the Third Annual Meeting of the Berkeley Linguistics Society*, Berkeley, CA.

Peters, A. M. 1983. *The units of language acquisition*. Cambridge: Cambridge University Press.

Piatelli-Palmarini, M., ed. 1980. *Language and learning: the debate between Jean Piaget and Noam Chomsky*. Cambridge, Mass.: Harvard University Press.

Pinker, S. 1979. Formal models of language learning. *Cognition* 1: 217–283.

——— 1981a. What spatial representation and language acquisition don't have in common. *Cognition* 10: 243–248.

——— 1981b. Comments on the paper by Wexler. In C. L. Baker and J. J. McCarthy, eds., *The logical problem of language acquisition*. Cambridge, Mass.: MIT Press.

——— 1981c. On the acquisition of grammatical morphemes. *Journal of Child Language* 8: 477–484.

——— 1981d. Crucial properties of the learnability proof for lexical functional grammar. Paper presented at the symposium "Workshop on Nontransformational Syntax," Stanford University, June.

——— 1981e. What is a language, that a child may learn it, and a child, that he may learn a language? (Review of K. Wexler and P. Culicover, "Formal principles of language acquisition.") *Journal of Mathematical Psychology* 23: 90–97.

——— 1982. A theory of the acquisition of lexical interpretive grammars. In J. Bresnan, ed., *The mental representation of grammatical relations*. Cambridge, Mass.: MIT Press.

——— In press, a. Language learnability and children's language: a multidisciplinary approach. In K. Nelson, ed., *Children's language*, vol. 5. Hillsdale, N.J.: Erlbaum Associates.

——— In press, b. Markedness and language development. In R. Matthews, R. May, and W. Demopoulos, eds., *Language and learnability*. Dordrecht, Netherlands: Reidel.

Pinker, S., and Birdsong, D. 1979. Speaker's sensitivity to rules of frozen word order. *Journal of Verbal Learning and Verbal Behavior* 18: 497–508.

Pinker, S., and Hochberg, J. In preparation. Syntactic and semantic properties of parental speech to children.

Pinker, S., and Kosslyn, S. M. 1983. Theories of mental imagery. In A. Sheikh, ed., *Imagery: current theory, research and application.* New York: Wiley.

Pinker, S., and Lebeaux, D. 1981. A learnability-theoretic approach to children's language. Unpublished manuscript.

Pinker, S., Stromswold, K., and Hochberg, J. In preparation. Children's number agreement: syntactic, semantic, or lexical?

Prideaux, G. 1976. A functional analysis of English question acquisition: a response to Hurford. *Journal of Child Language* 3: 417–422.

Pullum, G. K. 1982. Free word order and phrase structure rules. In J. Pustejovsky and P. Sells, eds., *Proceedings of the Twelfth Annual Meeting of the North East Linguistic Society.* Graduate Linguistics Students Association, University of Massachusetts, Amherst.

Pullum, G. K., and Wilson, D. 1977. Autonomous syntax and the analysis of auxiliaries. *Language* 53: 741–788.

Putnam, H. 1960. Minds and machines. In S. Hook, ed., *Dimensions of mind: a symposium.* New York: New York University Press.

Pylyshyn, Z. W. 1980. Computation and cognition: issues in the foundations of cognitive science. *Behavioral and Brain Sciences* 3: 111–132.

——— In press. *Foundations of cognitive science.* Cambridge, Mass.: Bradford Books/MIT Press.

Roeper, T. 1973. Connecting children's language and linguistic theory. In T. Moore, ed., *Cognitive development and the acquisition of language.* New York: Academic Press.

——— 1981. In pursuit of a deductive model of language acquisition. In C. L. Baker and J. J. McCarthy, eds., *The logical problem of language acquisition.* Cambridge, Mass.: MIT Press.

——— 1982. Comments on M. Bowerman's "On evaluating competing linguistic models with language acquisition data: implications of developmental errors with causative verbs." *Quaderni di Semantica* 3: 75–85.

Roeper, T., Bing, J., Lapointe, S., and Tavakolian, S. L. 1981. A lexical approach to language acquisition. In S. L. Tavakolian, ed., *Language acquisition and linguistic theory.* Cambridge, Mass.: MIT Press.

Ross, J. R. 1967. Constraints on variables in syntax. Ph.D. dissertation, MIT.

Rudnicky, A. I. 1980. Structure and familiarity in the organization of speech perception. Ph.D. dissertation, Carnegie-Mellon University.

Schlesinger, I. M. 1971. Production of utterances and language acquisition. In D. I. Slobin, ed., *The ontogenesis of grammar.* New York: Academic Press.

——— 1977. The role of cognitive development and linguistic input in language development. *Journal of Child Language* 4: 153–169.

Selfridge, M. G. R. 1980. A process model of language acquisition. Research Report #172, Department of Computer Science, Yale University.

Sherman, J. C. 1983. The acquisition of control in complement sentences: The role of structural and lexical factors. Ph.D. dissertation, Cornell University.

Shibatani, M. 1976. The grammar of causative constructions: a conspectus. In M. Shibatani, ed., *Syntax and semantics*, vol. 6: *The grammar of causative constructions*. New York: Academic Press.

Shipley, E. F., Smith, C. S., and Gleitman, L. R. 1969. A study in the acquisition of language: free responses to commands. *Language* 45: 322–342.

Simpson, J. 1982. Control and predication in Warlpiri. Ph.D. dissertation, MIT.

Sinclair, A., Sinclair, H., and de Marcellus, O. 1971. Young children's comprehension and production of passive sentences. *Archives de Psychologie* 41: 1–22.

Slobin, D. I. 1966. The acquisition of Russian as a native language. In F. Smith and G. A. Miller, eds., *The genesis of language: a psycholinguistic approach*. Cambridge, Mass.: MIT Press.

———— 1973. Cognitive prerequisities for the development of grammar. In C. Ferguson and D. I. Slobin, eds., *Studies of child language development*. New York: Holt, Rinehart and Winston.

———— 1977. Language change in childhood and in history. In J. Macnamara, ed., *Language learning and thought*. New York: Academic Press.

———— 1979. The role of language in language acquisition. Invited address at the Fiftieth Annual Meeting of the Eastern Psychological Association. Philadelphia, April.

———— 1982. Universal and particular in the acquisition of language. In E. Wanner and L. R. Gleitman, eds., *Language acquisition: the state of the art*. Cambridge: Cambridge University Press.

———— 1984a. Crosslinguistic evidence for the language-making capacity. In D. I. Slobin, ed., *The crosslinguistic study of language acquisition*. Hillsdale, N.J.: Erlbaum Associates.

———— ed. 1984b. *The crosslinguistic study of language acquisition*. Hillsdale, N.J.: Erlbaum Associates.

Snow, C. E. 1977. Mothers' speech research: from input to interaction. In C. E. Snow and C. A. Ferguson, eds., *Talking to children: language input and acquisition*. Cambridge: Cambridge University Press.

Snow, C. E., and Ferguson, C. A., eds. 1977. *Talking to children: language input and acquisition*. Cambridge: Cambridge University Press.

Steele, S. (with Akmajian, A., Demers, R., Jelinek, E., Kitagawa, C., Oehrle, R., and Wasow, T.) 1981. *An encyclopedia of AUX: a study of cross-linguistic equivalence*. Cambridge, Mass.: MIT Press.

Stemberger, J. P. 1982. The lexicon in a model of language production. Ph.D. dissertation, University of California, San Diego.

Stowell, T. 1981. Origins of phrase structure. Ph.D. dissertation, MIT.

Stromswold, K. 1983. The nature of categories in children's early language. Bachelor's thesis, Harvard University.

Talmy, L. 1975. Semantics and syntax of motion. In J. Kimball, ed., *Syntax and semantics*, vol. 4. New York: Academic Press.

—— 1976. Semantic causative types. In M. Shibatani, ed., *Syntax and semantics*, vol. 6: *The grammar of causative constructions*. New York: Academic Press.

—— 1978. The relation of grammar to cognition—a synopsis. In D. Waltz, ed., *Proceedings of TINLAP-2* (Theoretical Issues in Natural Language Processing). Urbana: University of Illinois.

Tanz, C. 1971. Sound symbolism in words relating to proximity and distance. *Language and Speech* 14: 266–276.

—— 1974. Cognitive principles underlying children's errors in pronominal case-marking. *Journal of Child Language* 1: 271–276.

Tavakolian, S. L. 1978. The conjoined-clause analysis of relative clauses and other structures. In H. Goodluck and L. Solan, eds., *Papers in the structure and development of child language*. University of Massachusetts Occasional Papers in Linguistics 4. Graduate Linguistics Students Association, University of Massachusetts, Amherst.

—— 1981. The conjoined-clause analysis of relative clauses. In S. L. Tavakolian, ed., *Language acquisition and linguistic theory*. Cambridge, Mass.: MIT Press.

Townsend, J. T. 1974. Issues and models concerning the processing of a finite number of inputs. In B. H. Kantrowitz, ed., *Human information processing: tutorials in performance and cognition*. Hillsdale, N.J.: Erlbaum Associates.

Tucker, G. R., Lambert, W. E., Rigault, A., and Segalowitz, N. 1968. A psychological investigation of French speakers' skill with grammatical gender. *Journal of Verbal Learning and Verbal Behavior* 7: 312–316.

Tulving, E. 1972. Episodic and semantic memory. In E. Tulving and W. Donaldson, eds., *Organization of memory*. New York: Academic Press.

Turner, E. A., and Rommetveit, R. 1967. Experimental manipulation of the production of active and passive voice in children. *Language and Speech* 10: 169–180.

Twadell, W. F. 1963. *The English verb auxiliaries*. Providence, R.I.: Brown University Press.

Tyack, D., and Ingram, D. 1977. Children's production and comprehension of questions. *Journal of Child Language* 4: 211–228.

Walker, E. C. T., ed. 1978. *Explorations in the biology of language*. Montgomery, Vt.: Bradford Books.

Walsh, R. W. 1981. A computer model for the acquisition of lexical interpretive grammar. Bachelor's thesis, Harvard University.

Wanner, E., and Maratsos, M. 1978. An ATN approach to comprehension. In M. Halle, J. Bresnan, and G. A. Miller, eds., *Linguistic theory and psychological reality*. Cambridge, Mass.: MIT Press.

Wasow, T. 1977. Transformations and the lexicon. In P. W. Culicover, T. Wasow, and A. Akmajian, eds., *Formal syntax*. New York: Academic Press.

—— 1981. Comments on the paper by Baker. In C. L. Baker and J. J. McCarthy, eds., *The logical problem of language acquisition*. Cambridge, Mass.: MIT Press.

Wells, G. 1979. Learning and using the auxiliary verb in English. In V. Lee, ed., *Language development*. New York: Wiley.

Wexler, K. 1979. Untitled presentation at the Workshop on Learnability, Laguna Beach, California, June 4–8.

—— 1981. Some issues in the theory of learnability. In C. L. Baker and J. J. McCarthy, eds., *The logical problem of language acquisition*. Cambridge, Mass.: MIT Press.

Wexler, K., and Culicover, P. 1980. *Formal principles of language acquisition*. Cambridge, Mass.: MIT Press.

Williams, E. 1981a. Language acquisition, markedness and phrase structure. In S. L. Tavakolian, ed., *Language acquisition and linguistic theory*. Cambridge, Mass.: MIT Press.

—— 1981b. On the notions "lexically related" and "head of a word." *Linguistic Inquiry* 12: 245–274.

—— 1981c. Argument structure and morphology. *Linguistic Review* 1: 81–114.

Wilson, R., Pinker, S., Zaenen, A., and Lebeaux, D. 1981. Productivity and the dative alternation. Paper presented at the Sixth Annual Boston University Conference on Language Development, Boston, October.

Wolff, J. 1977. The discovery of segments in natural language. *British Journal of Psychology* 68: 97–106.

Yngve, V. 1960. A model and an hypothesis for language structure. *Proceedings of the American Philosophical Society* 104: 444–466.

Index